Fighting from Home

STUDIES IN CANADIAN MILITARY HISTORY

The Canadian War Museum, Canada's national museum of military history, has a three-fold mandate: to remember, to preserve, and to educate. It does so through an interlocking and mutually supporting combination of exhibitions, public programs, and electronic outreach. Military history, military historical scholarship, and the ways in which Canadians see and understand themselves have always been closely intertwined. Studies in Canadian Military History builds on a record of success in forging those links by regular and innovative contributions based on the best modern scholarship. Published by UBC Press in association with the Museum, the series especially encourages the work of new generations of scholars and the investigation of important gaps in the existing historiography, pursuits not always well served by traditional sources of academic support. The results produced feed immediately into future exhibitions, programs, and outreach efforts by the Canadian War Museum. It is a modest goal that they feed into a deeper understanding of our nation's common past as well.

Fighting from Home
The Second World War in Verdun, Quebec

Serge Marc Durflinger

UBCPress · Vancouver · Toronto

15 14 13 12 11 10 09 08 07 06   5 4 3 2 1

Printed in Canada on ancient-forest-free paper (100% post-consumer recycled) that is processed chlorine- and acid-free, with vegetable-based inks.

Library and Archives Canada Cataloguing in Publication

Durflinger, Serge Marc, 1961-
    Fighting from home : the Second World War in Verdun, Quebec / Serge Marc Durflinger.

(Studies in Canadian military history, ISSN 1449-6251)
Includes bibliographical references and index.
ISBN-13: 978-0-7748-1260-3
ISBN-10: 0-7748-1260-5

    1. World War, 1939-1945 – Québec (Province) – Verdun. 2. Verdun (Quebec) – History – 20th century. I. Title. II. Series.

FC582.D87 2006   971.4'28   C2005-9069

Canadä

UBC Press gratefully acknowledges the financial support for our publishing program of the Government of Canada through the Book Publishing Industry Development Program (BPIDP), and of the Canada Council for the Arts, and the British Columbia Arts Council.

This book has been published with the help of a grant from the Canadian Federation for the Humanities and Social Sciences, through the Aid to Scholarly Publications Programme, using funds provided by the Social Sciences and Humanities Research Council of Canada.

Publication of this book has been financially supported by the Canadian War Museum.

The author and publisher acknowledge the financial assistance of the Research and Publications Committee of the Faculty of Arts, University of Ottawa.

Printed and bound in Canada by Friesens
Set in Minion and Helvetica Condensed by Artegraphica Design Co. Ltd.
Copyeditor: Sarah Wight
Proofreader: Tara Tovell
Cartographer: Eric Leinberger
Indexer: Noeline Bridge

UBC Press
The University of British Columbia
2029 West Mall
Vancouver, BC V6T 1Z2
604-822-5959 / Fax: 604-822-6083
www.ubcpress.ca

For Janine and Maxime et à la mémoire de ma mère, Béatrice Ste-Marie

The present war is everyone's war and every citizen is expected to do his share in bringing it to a successful conclusion.

– Edward Wilson, mayor of Verdun, 1940

I suppose you all heard over the air we were in France on the morning of the 19th. It is a morning I will never forget. I seen my buddies killed one after the other on all sides of me. We did what we went to do and that is the mane thing, and I can tell you all the men were tickled when they new where we were going, you never saw a happier bunch of men in all your life. There were quite a few boys from Verdun like myself and I am proude that some Verdun boys were in it.

– Lance-Cpl J. Flood, RCASC, attached 10th
Field Ambulance, RCAMC, 20 August 1942,
in the aftermath of the Dieppe raid

Contents

Maps, Tables, and Illustrations

George Beurling speaking at his homecoming ceremony at the Verdun Auditorium, 10 November 1942. *Library and Archives Canada, PA-176977*

Flight Lieutenant George Beurling meets highly decorated Alf Hamer, a sixty-nine-year-old British-born veteran of three previous wars. *Verdun Borough Archives*

Display donated by Imperial Tobacco for the Mayor's Cigarette Fund in the lobby of the Fifth Avenue Theatre, May 1941. *Verdun Borough Archives*

A "tag" worn by Verdunites having contributed to the Mayor's Cigarette Fund during special fund-raising campaigns. *Author's collection*

A typical coupon for the extremely popular Mayor's Cigarette Fund as published in the *Guardian*. *Verdun Borough Archives*

Lt-Cdr William Woods, Royal Canadian Naval Reserve, commanding officer of the antisubmarine frigate HMCS *Dunver*. *Verdun Borough Archives*

The Verdun Salvage Committee collection and sorting depot on the waterfront behind the Verdun General Hospital, 16 June 1943. *Verdun Borough Archives*

HMCS *Dunver* off the coast of Nova Scotia, 1943. *Department of National Defence*

Poster for fundraising dance organized by the Women's Volunteer Reserve Corps in honour of the crew of HMCS *Dunver*. *Guardian* (Verdun), 17 September 1943

Harvard training aircraft installed next to Verdun's impressive First World War cenotaph in the city's east end. *Verdun Borough Archives*

Advertisement for Victory Bonds. *Guardian* (Verdun), 30 May 1941

Miss R.B. Joan Adams, in the uniform of commandant, Women's Volunteer Reserve Corps, Verdun Branch, March 1941. *Courtesy Joan Adams*

Women from Verdun's Red Cross chapter preparing material for dispatch overseas, 2 October 1943. *Verdun Borough Archives*

Children selling candy apples and other sweets at the corner of Rielle and Verdun avenues, 20 September 1941, to aid the Queen's Canadian Fund. *Verdun Borough Archives*

A typical wartime display in the lobby of a Verdun business, 2 February 1942. *Verdun Borough Archives*

Grave marker from Brettville-sur-Laize Canadian War Cemetery, showing the final resting place of fallen Verdunite Gordon Hutton. *Author's collection.*

Preface

Verdun is an unusual and fascinating place. Someone should set a novel there – and I'm not suggesting this just because I was born and raised in Verdun. But sometimes truth is more interesting than fiction. To really understand the local culture and grasp the nuances of daily life in that city, you almost have to be a Verdunite. To get a measure of Verdun in the early 1940s, the following imaginative exercise might help: take about 70,000 working-class people of almost exclusively British or French ethnic origin, confine them in a rectangular area of about six square kilometres, oblige them to live on top of each other in nearly identical two- and three-storey tenement flats where everyone knows everyone else's business, nearly surround the whole by a river and an aqueduct, and deprive the residents of a rail connection, an intercity bus depot, any hotels, nearly all forms of industry, or any licensed establishments. At this point you have created a rough uniformity of experience and an unmistakable sense of geographic distinctiveness. Finally, overlay the greatest military conflict the world has ever seen and observe what kind of responses and intracommunity dynamics develop. This is what this book is about.

In 1990 or so I purchased a splendid book from a remainder table in a well-known bookstore chain. Len Burrow and Émile Beaudoin's *Unlucky Lady: The Life and Death of HMCS* Athabaskan describes the operational history and eventual sinking in 1944 of one of the Royal Canadian Navy's most powerful fighting ships, the Tribal-class destroyer *Athabaskan*. At the end of the book the authors listed the names and hometowns of the ship's crew who had survived and those who had perished. To my surprise, there were five or six Verdunites. Growing up in Verdun in the 1960s and 1970s, I knew that there were many First and Second World War veterans residing in the community. I lived for eleven years on the street named for one of Canada's most famous wartime figures: George F. Beurling, the legendary fighter pilot, who was from Verdun. But it was in reading the names of a handful of Verdunites who had died in Canada's war that I was suddenly seized with the desire to learn more about my hometown's wartime history. What kind of place was Verdun in the 1940s, and who were the Verdunites? How many residents enlisted? How many became casualties? How did the community participate in the war effort, and how did it respond to the consequent loss of life? Did the war change Verdun? Within a year, I had quit my job as a technical editor with a defence contractor and enrolled in the doctoral program in history at McGill University.

While researching these questions for the doctoral thesis on which this book is based, and in finalizing the present manuscript, I learned much about my home-town during the war. But I realized early on that I was also learning a great deal about myself, my past, and that of my family. Historical investigation enabled me to place my own formative years firmly within a broader chronological and geo-graphical context. Many of the names, places, events, and issues of the 1940s that I encountered in my explorations persisted into the 1970s and beyond. An unexpected benefit of seeking to explain Verdun to others in a scholarly historical work has been the enhanced meaning of the streets, buildings, public spaces, institutions, and people of my community. For me, no walk down Wellington Street, the city's main thoroughfare, can be separated from the ghosts that are everywhere now plainly visible to me. They tell an important and inspired story in which the community's Second World War experiences figure prominently.

Notwithstanding the sad losses and lasting bereavement that struck the city, the years of the Second World War were, in many respects, Verdun's halcyon days. Perhaps they were also Canada's. Verdunites faced the challenges of war while seizing its opportunities. This book is their story.

THE AVAILABILITY OF SOURCES has influenced the scope and shape of this study. Most of the archival sources are of Verdun origin, most were in English, and most were generated by or maintained at city hall. The municipal archives are a rich repository of meticulously kept records of local wartime organizations as well as of much important material related to the local war effort. This collection yielded the essential correspondence, memoranda, reports, minutes of meetings held by various wartime bodies, and other material on which the core of this study is based. The records of such local institutions as schools, churches, and community orga-nizations, however, were a different matter: few remain. The municipal council minutes were very helpful but, as is the case with most such material, sparse. Vari-ous record groups at Library and Archives Canada, especially those of the Depart-ments of National Defence (RG 24), Munitions and Supply (RG 28), and National War Services (RG 44) were valuable for specific topics. These complement local sources and help place wartime Verdun in its national context.

Verdun's two wartime weekly newspapers provide a bonanza of detailed local information, full of flavour for the era, and rife with political opinion and social commentary. They were especially useful in helping connect the dots and fill in some gaps in the official records. The fervently patriotic, conservative, and even dour *Guardian,* available in bound copies at the Verdun Cultural Centre, served Verdun's English-speaking community and reflected many "old country" views. Ever a civic booster, it also regularly paid homage to Verdun's working-class char-acter. Virtually everything to do with the war in Verdun was reported in the *Guard-ian:* a multitude of fundraising activities, enlistments and casualties, air-raid precaution news, war-related economic and social conditions, municipal involvement in the war effort, local community groups' responses, and religious views. In fact, the *Guardian* helped galvanize Verdunites' domestic war effort. A close reading of every edition between January 1939 and mid-1946 yielded valuable results. In February 1942, the *Guardian* claimed a circulation of 18,200.

The bilingual (though mainly French) *Messenger/Le Messager* had a circulation of 15,000 during the war and also served readers in neighbouring districts of Montreal, such as Ville Émard and Point St Charles. This weekly was demonstrably less robust in its reporting on local war activities than was its competitor. Nevertheless, it regularly detailed events of local wartime significance, published details on enlistees, and diligently reported casualties. Unlike the *Guardian*, the *Messenger* proudly cited French-speaking Verdunites' war service, in and out of uniform. Unfortunately, a postwar fire destroyed extant copies prior to January 1943, and this has left some important gaps in the record of Verdun's war from the French Canadian perspective.

Both of these weeklies provided a comprehensive chronicle of events and acted as superb sources from which to glean the texture of local social culture. The vagaries of community public opinion and the specific details of many events are often to be found only in local newspapers. In addition, the Montreal press, especially the *Montreal Daily Star* and *La Presse*, offered details concerning wartime Verdun. These sources at times also added a metropolitan context for events taking place in Verdun.

Perhaps two dozen Verdunites were interviewed for this study, though not all their voices are heard in the narrative that follows. Curiously, despite Verdun's astounding enlistment record during the war, tracking down local veterans was not always easy in the 1990s and later. Not only had natural attrition taken its toll, but during the politically turbulent and economically distressed 1970s and 1980s, large numbers of aging Verdunites had moved to other communities. Oral history is also frequently easier to obtain than to use effectively. Here, it helps reflect Verdun's wartime mood. Some Verdunites' recollections led to other intriguing leads and, in general, provided helpful background information, cleared up misunderstandings, and nuanced some information obtained elsewhere.

Acknowledgments

This study suggests that Verdun was a closely knit and proud community during the Second World War and that these characteristics help explain the city's experiences at that turbulent time. More than half a century later Verdunites remain proud of their wartime history, and many have contributed to this work. The following people facilitated and encouraged my research for the doctoral dissertation on which this book is based: Patrice Byloos, archivist, Borough of Verdun, Lois-Ann Clouthier, chief librarian, Borough of Verdun, and Benoit Arcand, Salle Canadiana, Verdun Cultural Centre. Patrice was of enormous help in tracking down photos for this publication. The men and women of the Verdun Branch (No. 4) of the Royal Canadian Legion were also unfailingly helpful and enthusiastic. Many other Verdunites working on behalf of community or parish organizations also welcomed my inquiries for information.

Dozens of men and women took the time to meet with me or wrote or telephoned me in response to solicitations for research assistance. The late Miss R.B. Joan Adams of Williamsburg, Ontario, was exceedingly generous with her time and shared her valuable collection of press clippings and correspondence relating to wartime Verdun. I am indebted to Gordon Galbraith of Brockville, Ontario, for introducing me to Miss Adams, as well as for other valuable assistance. Charles Elliott of Verdun put me in contact with many people who offered their memories and memorabilia. Mary Peate of Williston, Vermont, was always encouraging and helpful. Stewart Carson of Verdun made available his remarkable scrapbook of Verdunites at war. Paul Moreau of Lasalle, Quebec, provided many useful documents and photographs. William Weintraub of Westmount, Quebec, lent me his photographs and memories. Many other people were also kind enough to help.

I would especially like to acknowledge the assistance provided by Canada's veterans of the Second World War. Over a dozen former crew members of HMCS *Dunver* responded in writing to my inquiries about wartime life aboard "Verdun's Own Frigate." Other former crewmen were good enough to telephone me. I would like to express special thanks to the late Walter Finlay of Terrebonne, Quebec. The late Joseph Way of Mascouche, Quebec, a naval veteran and "dyed-in-the-wool" Verdunite, was helpful in many ways and took a great personal interest in this project. Some local veterans and members of the community agreed to be interviewed for this study, and some of their recollections appear throughout the narrative. I thank them all.

Professor Carman Miller of McGill University supervised the original dissertation and helped sharpen its focus. From 1998 to 2003 I worked as an historian at the Canadian War Museum in Ottawa and had the privilege of working with some of Canada's finest military historians. I remain immensely grateful for the friendship and professional counsel of Jack Granatstein, Roger Sarty, Dean Oliver, Laura Brandon, Cameron Pulsifer, Tim Cook, Peter MacLeod, Martin Auger, and my other colleagues at the museum. Few academics have had the luxury of working with such a stellar group of specialized scholars in a non-university environment. I never worked harder than during the years of Jack Granatstein's tenure as head of the museum (1998-2000). But these were among the most exhilarating moments of my career thus far, and I thank him specially for this. For their advice and help in various ways I would also like to thank Professor Terry Copp, of the Laurier Centre for Military Strategic and Disarmament Studies, Wilfrid Laurier University, Professor Desmond Morton of McGill University, Professor Marc Milner of the University of New Brunswick, Professor Jeffrey Keshen, my colleague at the University of Ottawa, and Dr Serge Bernier, Director, Directorate of History and Heritage, Department of National Defence. John Parry, one of Canada's finest editors of historical texts, edited the original thesis and improved the manuscript immeasurably. It is a pleasure to acknowledge the outstanding support and professionalism of all at UBC Press who expertly guided me through the publication cycle: Emily Andrew, Camilla Blakeley, and Sarah Wight, a skilled copy editor. Eric Leinberger produced some fine maps. I would like to thank Dr Dean Oliver, Director, Historical Research and Exhibit Development, Canadian War Museum, for agreeing to support this publication as part of UBC Press's excellent Studies in Canadian Military History series.

On a personal level, all members of my family supported my decision to pursue a higher education and, subsequently, to focus on the community in which they have lived for some eighty years. My mother, the late Béatrice Ste-Marie, provided unflagging encouragement throughout this project and has helped me to achieve its realization. My uncle, the late Arthur Ste-Marie, may have been responsible for igniting within me the flame of interest in our community's past.

My wife, Janine Stingel, a brilliant historian of Canada, has been the source of wisdom, helpful criticism, and good advice. I am grateful for her understanding, caring, and love; they have made all seem so much brighter. Finally, I wish to acknowledge our wonderful son, Maxime, not quite two years old at the time of publication. He's helped give meaning to all that I do.

Abbreviations

ARP	air-raid precautions
CCA	Canadian Corps Association
CCF	Co-operative Commonwealth Federation
CDC	Civilian Defence Committee
CECV	Commission des Écoles Catholiques de Verdun
CPC	Civilian Protection Committee
CWA	Child Welfare Association
CWAC	Canadian Women's Army Corps
DIL	Defence Industries Limited
DMS	Department of Munitions and Supply
DND	Department of National Defence
DNWS	Department of National War Services
ESA	Emergency Shelter Administration
HMCS	His Majesty's Canadian Ship
HMS	His Majesty's Ship
IODE	Imperial Order Daughters of the Empire
MCF	Mayor's Cigarette Fund for Verdun Soldiers Overseas
MD 4	Military District 4
MSWL	Montreal Soldiers' Wives' League
NHA	National Housing Act
NOIC	Naval-Officer-in-Charge
NPAM	Non-Permanent Active Militia
NRMA	National Resources Mobilization Act
NSHQ	Naval Service Headquarters
RAF	Royal Air Force
RCA	Royal Canadian Artillery
RCAF	Royal Canadian Air Force
RCAF-WD	Royal Canadian Air Force – Women's Division
RCAMC	Royal Canadian Army Medical Corps
RCASC	Royal Canadian Army Service Corps
RCE	Royal Canadian Engineers
RCN	Royal Canadian Navy
RCNR	Royal Canadian Naval Reserve

RCNVR	Royal Canadian Naval Volunteer Reserve
UN	Union Nationale
VCSC	Verdun Catholic School Commission
VE Day	Victory-in-Europe Day
VHS	Verdun High School
VJ Day	Victory-over-Japan Day
VSC	Verdun Salvage Committee
VWSC	Verdun War Savings Committee
WPTB	Wartime Prices and Trade Board
WRCNS	Women's Royal Canadian Naval Service
WVRC	Women's Volunteer Reserve Corps
YMCA	Young Men's Christian Association

Fighting from Home

Introduction: Studying War at the Local Level

In *Victory 1945: Canadians from War to Peace*, published in 1995, Canada's two leading military historians, Desmond Morton and J.L. Granatstein, wrote, "There is as yet no good published study of life in wartime Canada." Since then, Jeffrey Keshen has produced a wide-ranging overview of Canada's home-front war with particular emphasis on the conflict's moral and societal consequences. Magda Fahrni has made a detailed study of families in late-war and postwar Montreal.[1] But the field remains extremely fertile for historians. Even Keshen's fine study was just the start of what is hoped to be an abundance of publishing on Canada's domestic war experience. The present work contributes to this developing field by closely examining wartime conditions in a single Canadian community, one that, to a large extent, can serve as a microcosm of the wider national experience. Verdun, Quebec, is an urban, working-class, mixed-language community adjacent to Montreal.[2] This book reveals how Verdun and Verdunites were affected by Canada's participation in the Second World War and assesses the city's military, civilian, and industrial contributions to the national war effort.

Verdun offers an ideal setting for exploring the consequences of the war at the municipal, institutional, neighbourhood, and individual levels. According to the 1941 Dominion census, Verdun had more than 67,000 residents, making it the third-largest city in Quebec and the thirteenth-largest in Canada. The city's labour force consisted mainly of industrial and clerical workers, most of whom worked in Montreal. Verdun's population was 58 percent English speaking and 42 percent French speaking, and only 4 percent of Verdunites were of neither French nor British ancestry. Nearly one-third of Verdun's English speakers were born in the British Isles, most having immigrated to Canada in the 1920s, many as children. The male heads of families tended to be skilled or semiskilled workers, frequently with trade union backgrounds, which gave the city a nucleus of British working-class political culture and social identity. Even Verdun's wartime mayor, Edward Wilson, was British born. Verdun's high-profile British presence defined the city and made it something of an anomaly in Quebec. It also made Verdun uncommonly patriotic in the defence of British, and therefore Canadian, interests. Verdun boasted the highest voluntary enlistment rate in Canada for a municipality of its size: no less than 6,400 and probably some 7,000 Verdunites served in the Second World War.

Verdun's population, geography, ethnicity, language, religion, economy, class structure, and sense of tradition gave it a unique wartime character. Verdunites of both language groups exhibited an exceptional sense of community identification and civic pride. The city's wartime mood and its social dynamics shaped and were affected by this powerful feeling of local identity. Still, some of the particularities of wartime life in the city, such as salvage collections or Red Cross work, followed national trends. Closely studying these commonalities helps provide insight into the wider Canadian home-front experience.

This work therefore adopts a community approach to the examination of Canada's Second World War experience. This new interpretive model for both wartime social history and community studies complements existing national studies.[3] Policies affecting such diverse wartime subjects as compulsory military service, the role of the state, and electoral politics have been examined by historians in national terms.[4] But just as local history is sometimes criticized for lacking a broader context, so national studies may neglect local conditions and communities. How, for example, did Verdunites, their social organizations, and their municipal administration react to the National Resources Mobilization Act of 1940, to the perceived need to institute air-raid precaution measures, or to the 1942 conscription plebiscite? This volume offers a grassroots analysis of wartime Canada, interpreting the effects of national events and policies at a local level. It addresses the meaning of the war for individual Canadians in one community while offering interpretations that have some national applicability. Many important aspects of the war on the home front receive detailed treatment here, such as the organization and operation of local patriotic groups, the conduct of Victory Loan campaigns, and the implementation of civil protection arrangements.[5]

Many Canadian municipal biographies are poor analytical tools. In 1979 Gilbert A. Stelter and Alan Artibise, two of Canada's most prolific urban historians, noted that urban histories have traditionally been either "antiquarian venture[s] with genealogical overtones or historical boosterism."[6] Detailing the minutiae of local existence without interpreting its significance through a broader context results in fragmentary history. In the words of another urban historian, perhaps the most useful micro approach is "to work from the general to the particular and back to the general again."[7] Municipal history ought to link national processes to the people. This work is about people, located in one place, reacting in a variety of ways to the exigencies of their Second World War experiences. It is about the sort of place that Verdun was in the years 1939 to 1945 and about the sort of place that Canada was.

In portraying Verdun's war, this work must respond to certain basic questions. How and to what degree did Verdunites participate in war-related activities on the home front? Which Verdunites enlisted and why did the city boast so high an enlistment rate? How did the war effort affect family life, social relations, and political behaviour? To what extent did the municipal government cooperate with federal authorities in the prosecution of the war? Were Verdun's social cleavages overcome during the war, the result of a shared "national experience,"[8] or were existing divisions shelved for the duration? Or did social conflict manifest itself more sharply in wartime Verdun?

Divisions existed in Verdun between French- and English-speaking residents, although a prevailing sense of local identity and the need for social accommodation helped shape the common and generally united responses of many Verdunites to the war. They cooperated, even when they might have disagreed. The lack of overt and significant linguistic disharmony on war-related issues challenges somewhat the accepted historical orthodoxy on French Canada's muted participation in the war. While much more work needs to be done on the subject of Quebec and the Second World War, Verdun's story offers insights into the organized and individual responses of an urban, working-class segment of the French-speaking population. Many in this group seemed to participate in the war effort from a sense of local identity. In turn, mass participation across ethnic and linguistic lines in, for example, fundraising ventures in support of Verdunites on active service became a defining part of the city's wartime identity. The actions of residents overseas were also directly relevant to the community's self-perceptions. One Verdun native, fighter pilot George F. Beurling, achieved international prominence in 1942 for his exploits in the skies over Malta. His fame thrilled his hometown and helped focus Verdunites' sense of their community's significant military contributions. Thus this study explains Verdunites' energetic collective response to the war in terms of ethnicity, demography, class structure, and sense of community pride, which was itself intensified by citizens' identification with Verdun's impressive war record.

This work is an example of the "new" military history practised in Canada within the last generation. More traditional operational histories are being supplemented by social, economic, administrative, and political histories. Social-military and operational-military history each require some understanding of the other. The battle front helps define the home front, and vice-versa.[9] Accordingly, the present study situates domestic social-military history within a broader wartime context.

Few existing Canadian studies focus specifically on Second World War municipal experiences. Jay White's fine 1994 doctoral dissertation examines Halifax's wartime infrastructural and physical development, but only obliquely the Haligonians themselves. White realized that Halifax was the logical place to start, especially for his kind of specialized research. Yet some parts of his study, such as those pertaining to housing and labour, have broader national implications.[10] Since Halifax was on the naval front lines during the war, however, it is not a fully effective model for other Canadian cities. The present work proposes to satisfy some of the broader requirements of such a study and to serve as an example for comparisons with other Canadian urban centres. Most Canadian municipal histories or community studies devote little space to the years of the Second World War. Similarly, only a few Canadian military or social-military histories focus on the efforts of individual communities during the war. I hope that this book, by attempting to fill this vacuum partially, can suggest ways in which such research can illuminate individual and collective community responses to war.

1
Forging a Community

Verdun entered the Second World War as a municipality with a distinct character whose working-class inhabitants shared a strong community identity. The city's nineteenth-century isolation, its impressive record during the First World War, and the common experiences of its residents during the Depression cemented its self-perception as a unique place, of which Verdunites were proud. These characteristics facilitated Verdun's strong and united wartime social and military responses. This chapter sketches the development of the city up to the outbreak of war in September 1939.

Isolation: Early History to 1914

Verdun is located along the shore of the St Lawrence River on the southwestern side of the Island of Montreal, a few kilometres northeast of the Lachine Rapids and only several kilometres above the site of Montreal's original settlement. In 1671, Major Zacharie Dupuis, acting commander of the garrison at Montreal and a well-known colonist, received a notable fief of 320 acres along this shoreline, which he named "Verdun" in honour of Saverdun, his birthplace in southwestern France. His fief included much of the territory of present-day Verdun.[1] Despite some sporadic settlement in the seventeenth and eighteenth centuries, the Verdun that Dupuis knew grew very little until the nineteenth century.

As the land was low-lying, marshy, and easily flooded in spring, the area was slow to develop. In 1825 there were probably no more than fifty families occupying this riverside location.[2] The completion of the Lachine Canal that year effectively cut off the southwestern bulge of the Island of Montreal. This area later became, from west to east, Lasalle, Verdun (which does not touch the canal), and the Montreal neighbourhoods of Ville Émard, Côte St Paul, and Point St Charles. On 1 January 1875 the village of La Rivière St Pierre came into being, named for a stream running through its territory. The approximately 200 inhabitants changed its name to Verdun the next year, and the town subsequently adopted 1876 as the year of its founding.[3]

In the mid-nineteenth century, Montreal's increasing water requirements had prompted the digging of an aqueduct stretching from the St Lawrence at the western extremity of what became Lasalle and ending near what became the northwestern limits of Verdun, not far from the Lachine Canal. Completed in 1856, this aqueduct forms the northwestern boundary of Verdun, roughly parallel to the St

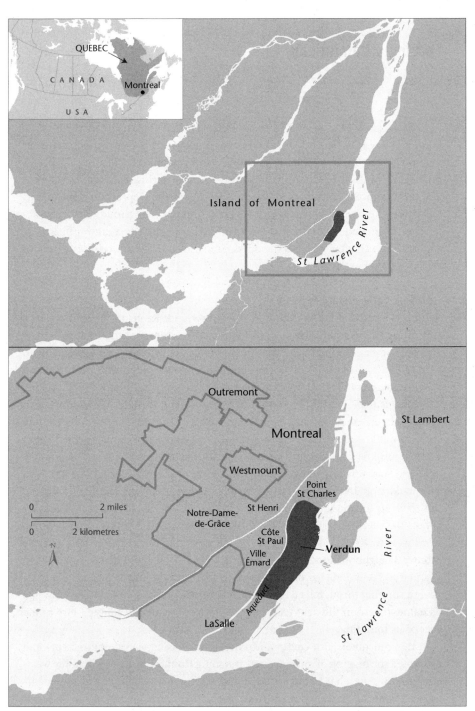

MAP I   Verdun in its surroundings

Lawrence, which forms its southeastern limit. Ville Émard and Côte St Paul developed on the north side of the aqueduct as non-contiguous neighbours of Verdun. The "tailrace," a water runoff ditch almost ten metres wide, extended in a straight line from the aqueduct's waterworks station in northeastern Verdun directly to the St Lawrence River, 1½ kilometres away. Consequently, at its incorporation in 1876, Verdun was hemmed in by water along most of its periphery. Fields, farms, and woods stretched to the west. Alongside the tailrace, railway tracks and steep embankments created an additional physical boundary with Point St Charles.

Despite Verdun's proximity to Montreal, a lasting sense of remoteness and detachment developed. Verdun grew southwestwards as a residential and farming community. In 1901 the population had increased to 1,898. By that time Montreal's expansionist civic politicians and some members of its business community were regularly calling for Verdun's annexation. Other small neighbouring municipalities were also targets, and many succumbed to financial pressures. But annexation had little appeal in Verdun so long as the village provided services and kept its municipal debt manageable.[4]

To maintain its much-valued tranquillity, Verdun's municipal council, as a matter of policy since the founding of the village, refused to grant permits for the building of licensed establishments, hotels, or any industrial concerns, including tanneries, distilleries, slaughterhouses, or any other installations potentially causing foul odours, noise, and other nuisances.[5] Many of Verdun's small farms (often owned by successful Montreal entrepreneurs) were eventually broken down into smaller lots, a trend fuelled by local realty speculation at the turn of the century. The individual lots, especially in eastern and east-central Verdun, were then sold for housing construction to accommodate developers as well as the thousands of potential tenants streaming into the Montreal area as a result of increasing urbanization and immigration.[6]

Verdun became a town in 1907 and grew rapidly, attaining 6,000 inhabitants that year. Early twentieth-century residential construction transformed Verdun from a rural outpost into a community of wage-earning families. Most of the new dwellings were modest two- and three-storey buildings, each with four to six rented flats. They went up in the east end, radiating out from the intersection of Wellington Street and Church Avenue – the city's commercial centre. Shops and banks were also part of the construction boom, usually occupying the ground floor of residential buildings. Symbolic of Verdun's growing stature, a new city hall, also housing the police and fire departments, was built in 1908 on Church Avenue above Wellington Street. In 1911 the Dominion census showed 11,629 residents. While the ethnic balance was closely split between French and English speakers, in the next few years the English-speaking proportion increased as hundreds of British immigrant families sought cheap accommodation. In 1912 Verdun was incorporated as a city.[7]

Verdun had no railway station, no canal access, nor, before the 1920s, much public transit. The main egress routes were along Wellington Street into Point St Charles and across a bridge spanning the aqueduct at Church Avenue, which led to Côte St Paul. Public transit linking Verdun with Montreal was augmented in 1926 by bus service along Verdun Avenue to Montreal's Atwater Avenue, across the bridge spanning the Lachine Canal there, and up Atwater to Ste Catherine Street. This route took a mere nineteen minutes at rush hour.[8] Lasalle Boulevard, which wound its way along the riverbank, linked southwestern Verdun to Lasalle. Landing from the river provided the only other significant access to the municipality.[9] But the river also posed problems. Even before 1900 civic officials had recognized that development and expansion depended on the prevention of annual spring flooding. In 1895, work on the first riverside dyke began. It proved a burden for the small municipality, which struggled for thirty years to overcome the rising waters and to finance the project.

In a 1933 study of Verdun and Point St Charles, Mary Davidson noted each community's sense of isolation: "both areas remained impregnated with small-town attitudes until the post[-1918] period of development. This past tradition of isolation still persists."[10] Davidson's work also emphasizes the deep-rooted sense of local pride in Verdun, which spurred community spirit and helped foster neighbourhood contacts and local institutions; self-sufficiency also helped Verdun to prosper.

The First World War: A Proud Record

The years 1914-19 were pivotal for Verdun. The city experienced spectacular growth, among the highest in Canada, attaining perhaps 21,000 inhabitants by the end of 1918 and over 24,000 a year later.[11] Perhaps the onset of war had even greater meaning for Verdunites than for many other Canadians, since so many residents were recent British immigrants.[12] Verdunites recorded startlingly high enlistment rates. Most postwar press estimates put the number of Verdunites in uniform during the First World War at between 3,000 and 4,000 – up to 20 percent of the entire population.[13] In 1940 the Verdun branch of the Canadian Legion estimated that 2,500 Verdunites served overseas during the First World War while "a conservative estimate" of 500 others remained on duty in Canada.[14] This seems a more measured assessment.

Patriotism could also prove profitable. In February 1916, the British Munitions Company, a "national factory" (forerunner to the Crown corporations of the Second World War), asked Verdun for permission to erect a munitions plant to produce time fuses loaded with powder and fitted to 18-pounder artillery shells.[15] Anxious to participate in the war effort and to attract investment, the city allowed the company – Verdun's first significant industry – to build on a large vacant lot on the city limits bordering Point St Charles.[16] It obliged British Munitions to employ, as much as possible given the requirements for specialized workers, "Verdun labour in preference to outside labour."[17] A later press account estimated that some 4,000 people, most of them women and many of them locals, had worked at the plant up to November 1918.[18] Verdun thus reaped its share of the nationwide industrial boom.

Although it brought employment to Verdun, the war also imposed a social burden. In April 1919, Mayor J.A.A. Leclair recalled the stresses of the war. He told city council that Verdun "has had to struggle against difficult financial, moral and social situations created through the state of war."[19] In addition to the bereavement caused by hundreds of local casualties, the war led to hardship for many of their dependants.

Meanwhile, the burning wartime issue of conscription had elicited little debate in Verdun city council. The mayor and eight aldermen, including five English speakers from April 1917 on, did not oppose the idea, and no documentary evidence exists that the French-speaking members disapproved. In January 1917 the council unanimously sanctioned federal identity cards for national service registration and vowed to ensure that Verdun residents completed and returned them to the proper authorities.[20] Notwithstanding its national prominence, conscription never reappeared in council minutes. Yet when two federal ministers, Charles Doherty and C.C. Ballantyne, spoke at city hall in defence of the Military Service Act, they were shouted down with cries of "Vive Laurier!" The ministers left the building under police protection, while fighting broke out in the gathering crowd.[21] Conscription divided Verdunites, like the country itself, along linguistic and political lines.

Two postwar events solidified the memory of the city's First World War patriotism and helped shape responses in the period 1939-45. First, the Prince of Wales visited Verdun on 30 October 1919 during his Canadian tour. He allowed city hall to fly his personal standard in recognition of Verdun's having had the highest per capita enlistment rate of any city in the British Empire. This feat, and the prince's visit, generated considerable local pride and was often remarked upon in the interwar period, for example in local newspaper articles, political speeches, correspondence from city hall, and at the local branch of the Great War Veterans' Association, later the Canadian Legion. English speakers usually explained the high participation by invoking the city's desire to serve the Empire. A high percentage of enlistees were, in fact, British born.

Second, on 5 October 1924 the city unveiled its First World War cenotaph in a small but prominent park located at the intersection of Lasalle Boulevard and Wellington Street, near the northeastern city limits. Entitled simply "Vimy," the monument was cast in bronze by the well-known Montreal sculptor Coeur de Lion McCarthy, who also cast the famous First World War memorial statue for Montreal's Windsor Station, copies of which can be found in Vancouver's and

Toronto's main train stations.[22] The unveiling was an important event. The former commander of the Canadian Corps, Gen Sir Arthur Currie, principal of McGill University, delivered the inaugural address. Every unit in the Montreal area's Military District 4 was represented at the ceremony, which attracted an estimated 25,000 onlookers, including thousands of veterans and relatives of the fallen.[23] Mrs Jane Leavitt, Verdun's most celebrated Silver Cross mother, also called "the Mother of Verdun," unveiled the memorial. She had immigrated with her family from London to Verdun in 1913, when the youngest of her nine children was fourteen. Of her five sons on active service, her three eldest had been killed, and another wounded.[24]

Verdunites had set a standard of military service apparently unequalled in the Empire. In the interwar period and during the Second World War, this fact helped foster a strong sense of civic patriotism. Verdun's British character persisted, and the city's large veteran community spent twenty years perpetuating the ideals of loyalty, civic pride, and service. Despite the hardship that it engendered, the First World War also encouraged population growth and industrial expansion without especially exacerbating linguistic tension. It had helped build the community.

The Years of Growth

Soon after Verdun welcomed home its demobilized soldiers in 1919, the city became a virtual boom town, Montreal's major bedroom community. New dwellings – mostly low-rent rows of triplexes, and later duplexes – went up, and the city built schools, parks, playgrounds, streets, sewers, and other infrastructure as development moved steadily southwest. Large swaths of open land succumbed to new neighbourhoods. Canadian immigration policy in the 1920s kept out most immigrants but the British, and many newcomers found a ready and welcome support network in Verdun.

Densely populated central Verdun consisted of long, unvarying narrow avenues of triplexes interrupted by perpendicular laneways parallel to main arteries. Little sunlight filtered into these dwellings, which had windows only in the front and back. These structures, like most in the older neighbourhoods, had winding external wooden staircases with metal railings of the type for which the Montreal area is well known. At the back, corrugated tin sheds with interior wooden staircases stored wood, coal, and personal belongings. These sheds – great fire hazards – overlooked narrow lanes and the next avenue's back sheds. There were no yards, though families in ground-floor flats might have a patch of land off the laneway suitable for small gardens or for simple recreation. The back lanes themselves became communal backyards.

These dense housing conditions fostered a sense of common identity and shared experience. People came to know each other well and neighbourhood friendship networks became a staple of Verdun life. The four to six rooms in each flat were usually small, and the single sunlit ventilation shaft for all six flats in a triplex allowed little privacy, especially since it adjoined each flat's bathroom. Davidson described this shared vent as "as good a conductor of family quarrels as are the flimsy walls which separate the flats."[25]

Yet Verdun's public spaces could be spectacular, and the city's natural riverside beauty defined the community and instilled it with pride. In 1926 the city constructed a wide, handsome, four-kilometre-long wooden promenade, known as the boardwalk, on top of the riverfront dyke. A linked series of stone pillars, many with lampposts, lined the walkway along its river side. Civic boosters insisted that Verdun was ideal for raising children, and many young working-class couples settled in the city. Verdunites themselves believed that its low rents, beautiful riverside location, and proximity to downtown Montreal attracted large numbers of new residents.[26]

Following completion of the boardwalk, Verdun's population grew even more quickly. In the period 1921-31, it increased by an astonishing 143 percent to 60,745. Verdun became the third-largest city in the province and Canada's fastest-growing city.[27] With a surface area of a mere 2.5 square miles (approximately 6.5 square kilometres), it was easily the most densely populated city in Canada, with an alarmingly high 24,298 inhabitants per square mile.[28] Suburbanization was a nationwide phenomenon, and the Montreal-area cities of Westmount, Outremont, and St Lambert also doubled their (considerably smaller) populations in this decade. Montreal's growth rate was less impressive, and Verdun was the only significant working-class community in the Montreal area to grow between the wars.[29]

Pulling Together during the Depression

The effects of the Great Depression of 1929-39 in Canada have been well documented.[30] Unemployment rose steadily from 1930 on, peaking nationally at 32 percent of the non-agricultural labour force in the winter of 1933 and remaining high for the rest of the decade.[31] Canada's least skilled workers in industry, construction, and manufacturing were usually the first to lose their jobs or become chronically underemployed and remained so for the longest periods. The metropolitan region of Montreal was one of the worst-affected urban areas of the country. In February 1934, 240,000 residents of Montreal proper, or 28 percent of its population, were dependent on municipal relief. Many of the families had had working hours or wages, or both, slashed, or lacked the means of subsistence, and yet remained ineligible for direct relief.[32]

As most Verdun families derived their principal income from wage work in nearby factories and transportation industries, or from clerical work in downtown Montreal, this unprecedented economic crisis devastated the city. Verdun in the early 1930s suffered unemployment on a par with other large Canadian urban centres and a jobless rate approximating the national average of 20-25 percent.

(Verdun's rate was consistently lower than Montreal's.) While Verdun had granted some aid to desperate cases since late 1929, especially during winter, in January 1932 it set up the municipally operated and financed Verdun Unemployment Relief Commission to handle the increasing number of applications. This was "the first independent unemployment relief commission in the Province, if not in the Dominion."[33] In 1933 just under 30 percent of Verdunites depended on municipal assistance. This figure dropped to stabilize in the next several years at about 19 percent until 1937, when it declined further.[34] But conditions remained harsh. By 1938, 40 percent of unemployed Verdunites were unskilled and therefore probably experiencing the most difficulty finding and keeping jobs.[35]

The city's generous response to residents' plight reinforced a strong sense of community and exemplified the ethos of mutual aid. In May 1933, after putting "considerable pressure" on the budget-conscious provincial government of Liberal premier Louis-Alexandre Taschereau to permit municipalities to offer shelter assistance, the city began paying part of the rents of the unemployed.[36] It also distributed oil lamps to residents who had lost their electricity because of unpaid bills. Subsequently, the city provided allowances for the payment of electricity bills and even for moving costs (out of Verdun), as well as for the purchase of extra milk, stoves, furniture, mattresses, and clothing.[37] These measures made Hervé Ferland, the populist mayor from 1933 to 1939, a favourite of the poor. The city was proud of its relief organization and of the careful financing of payments. In 1941 Verdun's general manager and chief financial administrator, Joseph R. French, announced that since 1936 traditional sources of revenue such as property taxes and licence fees had paid for the entire relief effort.[38] Few Canadian cities could boast as much.

While the unemployment rate had dropped noticeably by 1937, Verdun's thinner relief rolls were attributable to the city's "hiring" of relief recipients for public works projects. Its program was one of Quebec's most extensive and became the benchmark for other municipalities.[39] As early as 1930 the city sought tangible results from its relief expenditures. In return for providing building materials, supervision, and specialized labour, the city obtained the services of unemployed, able-bodied Verdunites. Their willingness to work was a prerequisite for the continuation of their payments; as work relief, these payments were 20 percent higher than basic direct relief. In this way, the city completed, at minimal cost, large capital projects such as the Verdun Auditorium (completed in November 1939) and the Natatorium swimming pool complex (1940), undertook road work, improved the sewer system, and provided municipal services such as snow removal and landscaping. When the Verdun Unemployment Relief Commission wound up in July 1941 (after nine years of operation but just a few months after the provincial government stopped subsidizing municipal direct relief) only 130 Verdun heads of families were receiving payments, in a city of 67,000.[40]

Statistically, the Depression does not appear to have hurt Verdun as much as its working-class population might suggest. If Verdunites with memories of the era are unlikely to describe their experiences as miserable, it may be because the many people affected seem to have been reasonably well cared for by a farsighted municipal administration.[41] But the widely shared experience of hard times in closely knit Verdun also solidified intracommunity ties and helped shape the city's common responses during the trying years to follow.

Britain on the St Lawrence

One of the principal concerns of this book is to examine some of the war's effects on Verdun's social structure and the extent to which Verdun's contribution to the war effort reflected its social composition. Consequently, a brief sketch of the people of Verdun is in order. English speakers of all ethnicities made up nearly 60 percent of Verdun's population. But any discussion of Verdun society in the period 1939-45 must recognize the British-origin character of the city, which is evident in Table 1.1.[42] As much as class, family circumstance, or individual motivation, its significant British population explains the city's remarkable record of military

Table 1.1

Ethnic origin of Verdunites, 1931 and 1941

	1931		1941	
Origin	Number	%	Number	%
English	20,342	33.49	21,530	31.97
Scottish	8,631	14.21	8,263	12.27
Irish	5,665	9.33	5,966	8.86
Other British	331	0.54	303	0.45
Subtotal	*34,969*	*57.57*	*36,062*	*53.55*
French	23,277	38.32	28,242	41.93
German	464	0.76	376	0.56
Scandinavian	356	0.59	320	0.48
Hebrew	344	0.57	471	0.69
Italian	204	0.34	295	0.44
Other European	821	1.35	1,241	1.84
Asian	62	0.10	88	0.13
Other/not stated	248	0.40	254	0.38
Total	60,745	100.0	67,349	100.0

Source: 1931 Census, vol. 2, 374-5; 1941 Census, vol. 2, 382-3.

enlistments during the Second World War. Verdun was home to the densest per capita concentration of British-born residents in the Montreal area and was a bastion of "old country" values and allegiances. Most of the families from Britain (including a small number from the Irish Free State) contained semiskilled workers and originated from such cities as London, Liverpool, Manchester, Glasgow, Edinburgh, and Belfast.[43]

About one-quarter of the almost 30,000 interwar British immigrants to Montreal had settled in Verdun.[44] The 1931 census indicates that 14,570 (24 percent) of Verdun's 60,745 inhabitants were born in the British Isles, and perhaps two-thirds of them had emigrated following the First World War. The English made up 55.7 percent of the British total, the Scots 34.5 percent, the Irish 8.3 percent, and the Welsh 1.2 percent.[45] The 1941 census did not reveal a significant shift in the ethnic mix of Verdun's British Isles-born residents, but the British-born population of the city had dropped to 16.7 percent (12,309 of 67,349 residents) – a decline of 30 percent in a decade.[46] This number included the wartime mayor, Edward Wilson, and the city clerk, Arthur Burgess. With so many of its residents born in the British Isles, Verdun was very much an anomaly in wartime Quebec; indeed, no other city in the province boasted as high a percentage of British-born citizens, and few Canadian cities could match these proportions.[47] Nevertheless, sharply curtailed immigration during the Depression meant that Verdunites were increasingly Canadian born.

Chain migration led many Britons to Verdun, where they found a comfortable atmosphere and a support network of cultural, social, fraternal, and political organizations, as well as local branches, or their equivalents, of familiar institutions such as churches or sporting associations. Verdun hosted more of these organizations than any other community in the Montreal area.[48] It was common to hear English spoken with "broad" old-country accents and to see shops displaying British-style food, furnishings, and clothing. (There was a profusion of fish-and-chips shops, for example.) Davidson and Reynolds noted that the homes of British immigrants often contained British literature, photos of the royal family or British country scenes, and souvenirs of British events and occurrences, such as royal jubilees, sporting events, or military service. In 1932, half of all British-immigrant families in Verdun received British newspapers.[49]

When war came in September 1939, Verdun's British character allowed many English speakers a personal, widespread, and immediate identification with the cause of Britain. Many among the British born, notably Wilson and Burgess, assumed leadership of Verdun's war effort. In 1939 "patriotism" in Verdun meant lending support to Britain. Subsequently, as the war widened and grew in intensity, Verdunites mobilized on behalf of Canada, and the community lent its support primarily to local causes, demonstrating an attachment to local identity.

Class and Community

While Verdun was culturally mixed, a strong common bond of place and community claimed residents' loyalties. Hervé Ferland, the Depression-era mayor, described the local ambience as "une mentalité toute spéciale," proudly different from other Montreal-area communities.[50] This positive self-perception encouraged a shared citywide response during the war and led to local initiatives in support of the war effort and especially in aid of Verdunites on active service.

A clear link existed between Verdunites' sense of community and local culture and their sense of class. Working-class consciousness constituted a badge of identification worn by many inhabitants, especially those of long residency. For example, many Verdunites had jobs at the Canadian National Railways shops in Point St Charles and felt a bond between themselves that did not extend to co-workers from other parts of Montreal.[51]

Verdunites as a whole were among the top wage earners of the Montreal-area working class. Independent-minded Verdunites retained an internalized belief that they enjoyed a higher standard of living than many other Montreal neighbourhoods. This standard of living was defined by more than just skill level and family income. Verdun was far newer and cleaner and contained fewer of the obvious social ills that afflicted Montreal's poorer industrial neighbourhoods, such as nearby Point St Charles and St Henri.[52] This was not how most Montrealers (except those in southwestern working-class neighbourhoods) saw Verdun, and Verdunites themselves were aware that their city did not attract an upwardly mobile, managerial, or professional middle class. Whatever boasts the city could offer therefore seemed that much more impressive. Verdun had the lowest proportion of slum dwellings in the entire country, 7 percent, even though it was the runaway leader in terms of rented dwellings (90.3 percent) and population density.[53] Verdunites were aware that their city was different, special even, and certainly knew this better than other Montrealers.

External perceptions helped determine Verdun's class status, and working-class distinctiveness was what many non-Verdunites noted about the city. For example, in one week in 1941, the *Gazette* reminded readers that Verdun was "practically devoid of wealthy citizens," while the *Montreal Daily Star* noted, "there are very few wealthy people in Verdun."[54] Aileen Ross, in her 1941 study of Montreal's social elites as seen through the membership and activities of the Junior League (English-speaking debutantes) and the Ligue de la jeunesse feminine (similar, though less exclusive), observed, "it could never happen that an English-speaking girl could join the Junior League were she living in Verdun."[55]

Intraclass differences in Verdun defied an outsider's monolithic view, however. This local stratification had a residential and linguistic basis, dividing the more affluent English-speaking west end from the mostly French-speaking east end.

Even though most landlords and shop owners were French speaking, class remained defined as much by language as by income. The oldest and shabbiest parts were considered overwhelmingly French speaking, while the newer, less congested areas were felt to be the preserve of the city's English-speaking population. Davidson wrote of British immigrants: "The more poorly situated family is forced to live in the older, cheaper residential section of Verdun, mingling with the French ... As the family progresses in economic and social status, it moves ... [and] becomes separated from the French."[56] She implies that it was not quality of life, as determined by immediate physical surroundings, but rather proximity to sizable elements of the French-speaking population that defined the social position of the British immigrant family. Perception did not always reflect reality. Although most west-enders were indeed English speaking, many English speakers lived in the east end. Conversely, French speakers could be found in some numbers in Crawford Park, Verdun's most westerly and most prosperous section.[57]

As the notion of a Montreal "metropolitan community" began to form in the 1900s and 1910s, the concept of a satellite locale like Verdun existing independently from the nearby metropolis grew increasingly invalid. The advent of motorized vehicles, the extension of public transit systems, and other factors such as the availability of radios and telephones in the home led to a more wide-ranging view of community. An overarching sense emerged that separate districts belonged to larger, linked urban collectives, which in turn belonged to wider national or international networks. Natural boundaries, either municipal or neighbourhood, became less meaningful socially.[58]

Nevertheless, in 1948 the political sociologist Leo Zakuta defined a "natural area" as "a specialized and differentiated part of the community in its selection of population types, in its performance of particular functions in the community and in its separation from other areas by distinguishable barriers" such as rivers, canals, railway tracks, or large parcels of vacant or wooded land. Ethnicity, housing, occupation, and income were all relevant to his definition. The boundaries of a natural area were clear and physically defined. According to Zakuta, "local self-consciousness" and a shared sense of history were also major defining factors. These factors united members of the community and formed a barrier to outside influence. Verdun possessed these physical, social, and psychological boundaries. Zakuta labelled Verdun one of the strongest natural areas in the Montreal area.[59]

Verdunites were proud of their city. In a strikingly self-assured tone, the *Guardian* spoke for many when it stated: "No city or town is more imbued with the true spirit of 'community.' Verdun ... does not take any particular interest in what occurs in its immediate vicinity. It is 'Verdun' and 'Verdun' exclusively."[60] While this newspaper clearly relished its role as a community leader and booster, this affirmation nevertheless denotes a commonly held local self-perception. A French-language letter in the bilingual *Messenger* showed that this civic pride crossed linguistic barriers. In response to a Montrealer who had described Verdun as "un petit village," the anonymous, irate writer rebutted: "you've never set foot in Verdun, which explains why you think we live in a small village."[61]

Verdun on the Eve of War

In May and June 1939, King George VI and Queen Elizabeth toured Canada. The entire country appeared to be seized by imperial sentiment. Public figures and ordinary Canadians, groups and associations, corporations and communities vied for royal attention.[62] The British city of Verdun was no exception. When the schedule for the royal visit was announced in January 1939, Verdunites were disappointed. Their Majesties' visit to Montreal would be very brief, and no time could be spared for Verdun. On 18 May the king and queen arrived in Montreal, an event that the *Guardian* reported with a large red banner headline. Verdun organized its own parade and fireworks display that evening, and the city's streets were festooned with bunting and flags in their honour. As the *Guardian* put it, the "cup of fealty was found to be overbrimming."[63] This assertion would soon be put to the test.

As the summer of 1939 wore on, the drift to war appeared unmistakable; Canadians had seen this before. Despite the recent royal visit, there was no rush to embrace the sacrifices occasionally demanded by imperial loyalty. On the twenty-fifth anniversary of Britain's declaration of war on 4 August 1914, the *Guardian* reminded readers that some 4,000 men from Verdun had seen service during the First World War but expressed the hope that another war might yet be averted.[64]

As a whole, Canada entered the Second World War of its own accord but did so with resignation. The citizens who recalled the terrible bloodletting of the earlier conflict did not repeat the near-euphoria that had greeted the call to arms in 1914. In its last prewar edition, 1 September 1939, the *Guardian* made few references to the upcoming conflict. It requested local employers to cooperate with the authorities in protecting vital installations and informed citizens that social group and community activities would be cancelled in the event of war. Notwithstanding the muted enthusiasm, Verdunites had already begun enlisting.

Verdun's English-speaking youths, too, had noticed the approach of war. The spring 1939 *Annual* of Verdun High School, a Protestant institution, reflected interest in the European situation. Apprehensive essays focused on aerial bombing, and one was entitled "Could War Destroy Modern Civilization?" In an article on "Leadership," one student wrote, "Men like *Der Fuehrer* and *Il Duce* show us how much leadership is needed, but it is not the kind of leadership essential to the well-being of a nation." There was also a moving essay on the futility and tragedy of war.[65] Despite the war scare produced by the Czechoslovakian crisis during the autumn of their graduating year, only one student professed his desire to join the military – Britain's Royal Air Force, not the Royal Canadian Air Force.[66] The eighty-six students of the class of 1940 began their final year of high school just as war erupted in the autumn of 1939. Perhaps surprisingly, just one of the forty young men in the class stated his intention to enlist. Archibald Boyce Cameron aspired to be an air force commander. Instead Flight-Sergeant Cameron was killed in action in 1944.[67]

2
Once More into the Breach

In 1939 Verdun had no armoury and no regiment to carry its name into battle, just local branches of several veterans' organizations, an impressive First World War memorial, and two large German cannons – war trophies the Dominion government presented to the city in 1919. Yet whenever the opportunity arose, Verdunites displayed interest in military matters and fervently supported patriotic and veterans' causes. The city frequently hosted parades, banquets, and sporting events sponsored by Montreal-area regiments. The annual Ypres Day Parade, organized by the city, the local branch of the Canadian Legion, and military authorities, commemorated Canada's role in the historic 1915 battle. Held the Sunday nearest 22 April, the parade provided a local display of military ceremony and tradition.

Moreover, many Verdunites were members of the Non-Permanent Active Militia (NPAM) and belonged to various Montreal units, including the Royal Highland Regiment of Canada (the Black Watch), the Royal Montreal Regiment, the 17th Duke of York's Royal Canadian Hussars, the Victoria Rifles of Canada, and Le Régiment de Maisonneuve. In late August and early September, many Montreal-area NPAM units were mobilized, some to protect vital installations such as canals, rail bridges, and power plants. Many of the men engaged in these duties were Verdunites. "In one [unnamed] regiment alone, a large one," boasted the *Guardian*, "more than half the members are Verdun residents."[1]

When Britain and France went to war with Germany on 3 September, two days after Germany's invasion of Poland, Canadians knew that they, too, would soon be at war. Verdunites immediately responded like Canadians everywhere, with determination and by enlisting. Less than one week after Canada's formal entry into the war on 10 September, the city of Verdun and the local press were already claiming the highest enlistment rate in Canada for a city of Verdun's size. This unconfirmed perception remained strong in Verdun throughout the war. Press accounts in Verdun and Montreal routinely repeated the boast, and Verdunites spent the next six years living up to the claim.[2] In the period 1939-45 more than 6,300 Verdunites (people who resided in Verdun at the time of their enlistment), including more than 150 women, served in the armed forces overseas. Every branch of every service contained Verdunites. Hundreds of others were on general service in Canada, served in home defence units authorized by the 1940 National Resources Mobilization

Act (NRMA), or served as volunteer members of the reserve army in Canada. Verdun's contribution was impressive nationally, and especially in a Quebec context.[3] This chapter considers why so many residents of Verdun joined the armed forces, the services they chose, and the effects of age, language, class, neighbourhood, and gender on enlistment.

Why So Many?

Why did Verdunites enlist in such large numbers? Ethnicity was obviously a factor, as was a sense of local identity and community spirit; there was also a conscious desire to match the city's proud and commonly known First World War enlistment record. Joseph Way, who served in the navy, believed that most Verdunites joined because of civic pride and duty, and that adventure-seeking and even patriotism were secondary motivations. Verdunites just enlisted, as they were expected to. For Way, it remained that simple.[4]

Numerous English-speaking Verdun families had four, five, and, taking into account the service of parents, even six members on active service. For example, the Hill family of Woodland Avenue sent five sons to the war, serving in the army, air force, and navy. All survived.[5] Many of these families lived in heavily populated Ward 3, in the heart of the city, which, as is shown below, provided an astonishing number of recruits. About ten French-speaking families also had four or more members in uniform, sometimes a mix of volunteers and conscripts. For example, the Tremblay family from First Avenue had five sons on active service.[6] In 1942 one Verdun woman, not atypical, noted that two brothers, four cousins, an uncle, and two brothers-in-law were on active service in the army, while her husband and another brother-in-law were in the Royal Canadian Air Force. Nine of these eleven men were Verdunites and four were overseas at that time, a fifth having already returned. "We are quite proud of this, of course," she wrote.[7] One student at Verdun High School during the war has recalled: "My Dad served with the Black Watch during the First World War ... My brother served with the same regiment in World War II ... I don't think there was a girl in my class who didn't have a brother, father or some relative or boyfriend in the service ... Many of them were from families like our own, that had a tradition of fighting for their country. It also became the norm, and if one didn't go, I'm sure there was a sort of stigma attached."[8] But private or public enlistment pressure generally does not appear to have taken on the characteristics of shaming or cajoling, as occurred in Canada during the First World War. Another Verdunite, Gordon Galbraith, was unable for medical reasons to enter the armed services. He does not recall ever being questioned about his not being in uniform.[9]

Among English speakers in Verdun, perhaps more so than in most Canadian communities, military service was a widespread family tradition to be emulated. Given the very large veteran population in the city, many young men's fathers had served in the First World War, and enlisting was considered the proper thing to do. Deeper political reasons apparently did not much influence most young men. They simply joined up and did not often provide any detailed rationale for their decision.[10] First World War veterans, some with interwar experience in the NPAM, also rejoined the colours, especially early in the war. One Verdunite, J.A Powers, wounded in the First World War, told the Canadian Press upon arriving in Britain that he hoped to "find the fellow that hit me last time." Sgt J. Emo, serving in the Black Watch, wrote to city hall: "As a resident of Verdun for the last fourteen years I am proud to say that the people of our city is still TOPS in sending over more boys than any other city its size. I was a resident of Verdun [in] the last war and overseas with the 42 Batt[alion] and there is a lot of Verdun boys in our Batt[alion]."[11]

Many among Verdun's unemployed men enlisted. On 14 September 1939, the *Montreal Daily Star*, quoting a press release from Verdun city hall, noted that "just as in the last war, Verdun can boast ... the highest percentage of men enrolled in the army, at least among the unemployed." Of Verdun's 1,300 people on relief, 153 had enrolled by that date, including 150 married men. (The city did not grant relief to single men under forty.) But unemployment alone could not explain these responses to the call to arms. The Dominion government's General Advisory Committee on Demobilization and Rehabilitation determined that 85 percent of a sample base of 347,900 Canadians on active service as of 30 June 1942 "left gainful employment to enlist." Only about 10 percent were categorized as unemployed, and many had never yet held jobs.[12] While suggesting that "unemployment was a form of conscription," military historians W.A.B. Douglas and Brereton Greenhous note that more than half the men of the 1st Canadian Infantry Division, which proceeded overseas in December 1939, came from the ranks of the Permanent Force or the NPAM.[13] Yet the erroneous view has persisted that the men of this first contingent enlisted primarily to escape the dole.

In her study of unemployment in Verdun during the Depression, Suzanne Clavette reinforces the notion that joblessness declined drastically in 1941 owing to enlistment. R.B. Joan Adams, a Verdun social activist and head of the wartime Women's Volunteer Reserve Corps, also attributed the city's high enlistment rate to unemployment and local financial hardship. In her opinion, patriotism and ethnic ties to Britain were secondary factors.[14] These views are only partially correct. Joseph Way has insisted that most of the many Verdunites he knew who enlisted, including himself, quit jobs to enter military service.[15] The *Guardian* often noted residents' enlistments and briefly elaborated on their employment backgrounds, thus indicating that many were gainfully employed at the time of enlistment. Unemployment played some role in the early enlistment of Verdunites, but men continued to sign up in large numbers after unemployment in Canada had virtually disappeared. As with all Canadian volunteers, their reasons for enlistment were varied and complex, defying strict categorization.

Some Verdunites' enlistments put the city's military contribution into more concrete terms. Douglas Whyte had been an air cadet with Verdun High School's No. 69 Squadron. When he enlisted in the RCAF in 1943, Whyte lived in Ward 3 and was employed by Canadian National Railways. One of his parents was born in Scotland and the other was Canadian-born of Scottish parents. They had always encouraged military life, although his mother was "a little uptight" about his enlistment. One of Whyte's principal reasons for joining up was that it was considered the "thing to do," and he "couldn't wait" to get into the RCAF – which his cadet training facilitated. An additional incentive to join the RCAF was that his forty-year-old father had joined the air force in 1941 as a service policeman.[16] His father's enlistment had come as "a complete surprise" to his family, although his wife supported his decision. Once overseas, Whyte actually served with his father for a time in Britain and even outranked him. But he spent most of the war with a Royal Air Force Coastal Command squadron.[17]

Sydney Ashford had always been interested in naval matters, and in 1938, aged thirteen, he joined the sea cadets. In 1939 he was a drummer in the sea cadet band that welcomed the king and queen to Montreal's Windsor Station. Even at an early age he noted that "the military spirit was ingrained in me," partly because his family was patriotic. He lived in Ward 2, and both his parents were Catholics born in the British Isles. He enlisted in 1942, eventually finding his way into the Royal Canadian Corps of Signals and serving in Britain and Europe. For Ashford, active service was more important than being in any particular branch of the military. Like Whyte, one of his reasons for enlisting was simply that it was the thing to do. He recalled many seventeen- and eighteen-year-old Verdunites volunteering.[18]

Joseph Way attempted to join the Royal Canadian Naval Volunteer Reserve (RCNVR) unit in Montreal in 1938, but no recruits were then being accepted. On 4 September 1939, however, before Canada's declaration of war, he enlisted in the RCNVR. Patriotism was not a significant factor in his decision. Both his parents were Canadian born. He lived in Ward 2 and was among the first of all his friends to enlist; most eventually joined the army. He served aboard seven warships during the war and met fellow Verdunites on all of them.[19] This was hardly surprising given the large number of Verdunites on active service, especially in the navy.

In Which They Served

The historiography of Canada's Second World War experience does not include any in-depth analyses of who, exactly, were the men and women who enlisted from a particular locale or sectoral background. Such a study, limited in this case to Verdun, allows for a social-military profile of a distinct group of Canadians on active service. The enlistment statistics tabulated here come from thousands of file cards that made up the mailing list of the Mayor's Cigarette Fund for Verdun Soldiers Overseas (MCF).[20] The information recorded on these cards normally included an enlistee's name, rank, serial number, and last home address before enlistment. The fund's files sometimes contained additional information, such as the name of next-of-kin, whether the individual was killed or taken prisoner, and whether shipments of cigarettes were to be discontinued because of discharge or return to Canada. Although the files did not list actual military mailing addresses, coded serial numbers reveal which services, and often which regiments and units, the enlistees joined.

The 6,316 names listed are of men and women who served overseas at some point between the inauguration of the MCF in December 1940 and the summer of 1945. These Verdunites form the basis of the social-military analysis offered below. Not all Verdunites serving overseas were listed, since the fund depended on enlistees' relatives or friends for the necessary information. Verdunites who had served overseas but were discharged or returned to Canada before December 1940, or who served only in Canada, were not included. The figure of 6,316 Verdunites on active service overseas therefore is the minimum for which a cohesive body of evidence exists.[21] Although no accurate Verdun honour roll was ever compiled, the final tally of Verdunites who served anywhere, at any time, during the war probably exceeds 7,000.[22] Given that more than one in eleven Canadians was in uniform during the war, if we use the 1941 census figure of 67,349 for Verdun's wartime population, then Verdun's equivalent proportion would be approximately 6,311 people.[23] This figure was easily exceeded.

At the end of 1945, Verdun's population was estimated to be 74,000 (including those in military service), of whom no less than 42 percent, and by this time probably as many as 44 percent, were French speakers. Most of the increase was due to large numbers of mainly French-language families moving into Verdun during the war. Many of these new families' members were employed in military or related industries. The age, gender, and occupation of many of the new arrivals meant that they would not have significantly increased the size of Verdun's pool of available military manpower.

Table 2.1 shows Verdunites serving overseas by language and service; Table 2.2 shows the percentage of overseas Verdunites by service and language; and Table 2.3, the service distribution by language.[24] These statistics tell the basic story of Verdunites' overseas war service and, indeed, war service in general. Two-thirds served in branches of the Canadian Active Service Force, later renamed the Canadian Army (Active), approximating the national average, while the navy and air force divided the remainder among themselves, with naval service being slightly more popular. Verdun was overrepresented in the navy, with 17 percent of the city's uniformed total being sailors, compared to 10 percent nationally. Verdun's 1,055 men and women in the navy represented slightly over 1 percent of Canadian naval personnel, while the city's population, according to the 1941 census, represented only 0.58 percent of the nation's population.[25] The nearly 16 percent of

Table 2.1

Verdunites overseas by service and language, 1940-45

	Army	NRMA	CWAC	Navy	WRCNS	Merchant marine	RCAF	RCAF-WD	RAF	Misc.	Total
English	3,247	23	69	896	35	17	775	40	7	17	5,126
French	646	247	6	123	1	0	162	3	1	1	1,190
Total	3,893	270	75	1,019	36	17	937	43	8	18	6,316

Source: File cards of Mayor's Cigarette Fund, box A-536, Verdun Borough Archives.

Table 2.2

Verdunites overseas, percentage by service and language, 1940-45

	Army[a]	%	Navy[b]	%	RCAF[c]	%	Total[d]	%
English	3,339	78.78	948	88.43	822	83.19	5,109	81.12
French	899	21.21	124	11.56	166	16.80	1,189	18.88
Total	4,238	67.29	1,072	17.02	988	15.68	6,298	100.0

a Includes NRMA and CWAC.
b Includes WRCNS and merchant marine.
c Includes RCAF-WD and RAF.
d Does not include seventeen English speakers and one French speaker listed as miscellaneous.
Source: File cards of Mayor's Cigarette Fund, box A-536, Verdun Borough Archives.

Table 2.3

Verdunites overseas, service distribution by language, 1940-45 (%)

	Army[a]	Navy[b]	RCAF[c]	Total[d]
English	65.36	18.55	16.09	100.0
French	75.61	10.43	13.96	100.0

a Includes NRMA and CWAC.
b Includes WRCNS and merchant marine.
c Includes RCAF-WD and RAF.
d Does not include seventeen English speakers and one French speaker listed as miscellaneous.
Source: File cards of Mayor's Cigarette Fund, box A-536, Verdun Borough Archives.

active service Verdunites who were in the Royal Canadian Air Force (RCAF) was well below the 24 percent of uniformed Canadians who belonged to that service. A few Verdunites also served in the fighting forces of Britain, including the Royal Marines. Most Verdunites on British service were members of the Royal Air Force, and several were already serving when war broke out. A handful of Verdunites also found their way into the American military, while others plied the seas as merchant seamen. French speakers in Verdun were more likely to join the army and least likely to join the Royal Canadian Navy (RCN). This was in keeping with national trends, which reflected French speakers' lack of interest in the particularly unilingual navy and air force.

Men who had been conscripted for home defence under the NRMA constituted 4.27 percent of Verdunites overseas. By the beginning of 1943 the government had extended the geographical limits of NRMA service to include the entire Western Hemisphere, though in practice this normally meant service in Newfoundland, Alaska, and the West Indies. In November 1944 Ottawa authorized the dispatch of up to 16,000 NRMA troops overseas beyond the Western Hemisphere. Nearly 13,000 proceeded to the United Kingdom in early 1945 and 2,463 actually served with front-line units.[26] Of the 270 Verdun NRMA men who subsequently volunteered for general service, served as garrison troops outside of Canada, or, later in the war, were sent overseas, 91.5 percent were French speakers. Of all English speakers known to have proceeded overseas, 99.6 percent were volunteers, as opposed to 80 percent of French speakers. Verdun conscripts served in home defence establishments across North America, from the 6th Canadian Infantry Division in British Columbia to the coastal defence units of the Royal Canadian Artillery (RCA) in Nova Scotia and Newfoundland.

One French-speaking Verdun soldier, Driver René Bisson, Royal Canadian Ordnance Corps, was conscripted in July 1943 at the age of nineteen. After his initial training he "went active" and proceeded overseas to join a reinforcement unit. It is probable that most of Verdun's known conscripts were voluntarily on active service overseas, following the same route as Driver Bisson.[27] A slightly greater proportion of French-speaking Verdunites served overseas than was the case generally for French Canadians conscripted and on general service. Overall, 18.9 percent of Verdunites overseas were French Canadians, roughly equivalent to the proportion of French speakers among armed forces personnel serving both at home and overseas.[28] Examined another way, 4.2 percent of all French-speaking Verdunites were in uniform, compared to roughly the same proportion of French-speaking Canadians. Of English-speaking Verdunites, 13.1 percent were in uniform, compared to about 10.6 percent of English-speaking Canadians generally.[29]

In the army, Verdunites were well represented in the combat arms – infantry, artillery, armour, and engineers – as well as in the medical corps, ordnance corps, service corps, and signal corps. Smaller corps such as dental, forestry, postal, and provost also attracted Verdunites. In short, they were found in all branches and in many individual units of the army, including some raised outside the Montreal area. Verdunites served everywhere Canadian (or British) arms were deployed overseas, including the Middle East and the Far East. In 1945 Sgt L. Taylor, Royal Canadian Army Medical Corps, wrote from Holland: "One is constantly bumping into Verdun boys over here. They are everywhere, they are in the front lines, building roads, manning artillery, driving tanks, flying overhead and bringing the vital supplies in by boat."[30]

The evidence supports Taylor's observations. Many wartime publications or newspaper articles describing the activities of Canadian service people overseas named or quoted Verdunites. (Individuals' hometowns were customarily identified if their names were mentioned, especially in captions to photographs.) Verdunites are ubiquitous in the profusely illustrated *Canada's Weekly*, published in Britain for Canadian military personnel overseas. They also appear in virtually every casualty and many honours lists appearing in its pages. Verdunites appear also in more obscure publications such as *First Steps to Tokyo: The Royal Canadian Air Force in the Aleutians*, postwar fiction such as Hugh Garner's powerful naval novel, *Storm Below*, and in postwar regimental or ships' histories.[31] Nearly 1 percent of overseas Canadians were Verdunites (more than 6,300 of about 700,000).

Verdun's substantial military-age population proved attractive to units mobilized from the cities of Montreal and Westmount, which recruited in Verdun to fill out their complements. The Royal Montreal Regiment, headquartered in Westmount, established a temporary recruiting centre at Wellington Street and Church Avenue, Verdun's busiest intersection. This unit was especially popular with Verdunites; nearly 100 served in the regiment when its 800 men sailed for Britain in December 1939. The 5th (Westmount) Field Battery, RCA, also recruited a large number of Verdunites among its authorized strength of 280 men.[32] Given the class and educational differences between Verdun and well-to-do Westmount, it was hardly surprising that workplace patterns repeated themselves in military service: large numbers of English-speaking private soldiers and non-commissioned officers from Verdun were led by officers from Westmount or the adjoining Montreal district of Notre-Dame-de-Grâce. The many Verdun members of the Black Watch, too, were commanded by men from Montreal's wealthiest and most influential English-speaking families.[33] The 17th Duke of York's Royal Canadian Hussars, from Montreal, attracted as many Verdunites as did the Royal Montreal Regiment and the Black Watch. The Canadian Grenadier Guards of Montreal was also a popular regiment with Verdunites. Early in the war Verdun's French speakers did not enlist in the numbers they later would, but the Royal 22e Régiment and the Régiment de Maisonneuve attracted some Verdun recruits.

At the outset of war, several other artillery and infantry regiments, including the Royal Canadian Regiment, which had a detachment in St Jean, southeast of Montreal, sent their mobile recruiting stations to Verdun.[34] One indication of Verdunites' initial rush to enlist is the profusion of residents found in some of the earliest Montreal-area units to mobilize and be attached to the 1st and 2nd Canadian Infantry Divisions, both authorized in 1939. In addition to the infantry regiments noted above, the 7th Medium Battery, RCA, the 4th Field Company, Royal Canadian Engineers, and the 9th Field Ambulance, Royal Canadian Army Medical Corps, possessed large Verdun components for the remainder of the war.[35]

One service to which relatively few Verdunites gained entry early in the war was the air force. Not only did it take time for this service to expand, but educational requirements, as well as the need for applicants to produce various official documents and reference letters, were at first so stringently applied that interested Verdunites were commonly turned away. Not coincidentally, the high-income and generally well-educated Westmount population supported its own RCAF reserve fighter squadron, No. 115 (City of Westmount). Verdun members of the Canadian Legion recall relatively few RCAF veterans joining their branch.[36] Greater numbers of Verdunites joined the air force from 1942 onwards, after a relaxation of the educational entry requirements during a period of expansion. While lack of education was rarely an impediment for the non-commissioned ranks of the navy, it is difficult to explain fully Verdunites' preference for naval service. Perhaps Verdun's riverside location and the existence of several boating clubs encouraged the choice. Or the reputation of the Royal Navy may have been strongly imbued among Verdun's British-born and their offspring. Whatever the case, Verdunites served aboard virtually every warship in the RCN and at all shore establishments in Canada, Newfoundland, and overseas.

Age, Language, and Religion

Among the many factors that influenced the decision to enlist, age and family obligations were especially important. So too were broader cultural factors such as ethnicity, language, and faith. According to the 1941 census, Verdun had 33,243 male residents. Table 2.4 shows their age and ethnic distribution; their ethnic distribution within age groups; and their age distribution within ethnic groups. In 1941, 58 percent of Verdun residents were English speaking, and 42 percent French speaking.

Of 12,221 Verdun males aged fifteen to thirty-four in 1941, approximately 6,144 (50.3 percent) are known to have served overseas, and others served in Canada. Of 6,565 English speakers in that age group, 4,948 (75.4 percent) were overseas; the comparable number for French speakers is 1,178 overseas of 5,156 available (22.8 percent). If we take into account those who were medically unfit, engaged in specialized industrial labour, or for other reasons unable to enlist, we see that the proportion of available English speakers enlisted is nearly as high as possible. Verdun's exceptionally strong British demographic character is the basis for this remarkable response. The data further indicate that while a disproportionate number of French speakers were under fifteen in 1941, a disproportionate number of English speakers were over forty-five. Therefore, the language groups were roughly balanced in the relative proportions of youths and men aged fifteen to thirty-four. For French speakers, 37.3 percent of males were of this age group, while for English speakers (including non-British ethnicities) the figure was 36.8 percent.[37] Because enlistees also came from the population older than thirty-four, and because fifteen- and sixteen-year-olds in 1941 reached the age for military service before the war ended, the figures indicate that English-speaking Verdunites enlisted in a proportion approximately 3.3 times greater than the proportion of French speakers.

If wartime enlistments had matched the overall linguistic balance among males aged fifteen to thirty-four in Verdun in 1941, then 42 percent of Verdunites in uniform would have been French speaking (the percentage of French speakers in Verdun's population). As indicated above, the actual figure was 18.9 percent. Given the large number of French speakers under fourteen, it is likely that family considerations inhibited a larger proportion of eligible French speakers from enlisting than was the case for English speakers, who on average married later and had fewer children. The 1941 census indicates that an average family of British ancestry in Verdun contained about 3.6 persons, whereas French Canadian families averaged 4.2. The French Canadian average was 2.64 children per family versus the British ethnics' average of 1.95. Although there were fewer French Canadian families than British-ethnic families overall, 1,145 French Canadian families had four or more children under twenty-four years of age still living at home, compared to 781 such families of British origin. Of the 14,461 families resident in Verdun, slightly more than one in five French-language households but slightly fewer than one in ten English-language households contained four or more children. One French-speaking couple had between thirteen and fifteen children living with them.[38]

Table 2.4

Age and ethnic distribution of Verdun males, 1941

	British			French			Other			Total all ethnicities
	Number	Age group as % of ethnic group	Ethnic group as % of age group	Number	Age group as % of ethnic group	Ethnic group as % of age group	Number	Age group as % of ethnic group	Ethnic group as % of age group	
0-14	4,260	23.9	48.5	4,152	30.0	47.3	369	23.1	4.2	8,781
15-19	1,560	8.8	51.3	1,363	9.9	44.8	118	7.4	3.9	3,041
20-24	1,533	8.6	52.9	1,249	9.1	43.1	117	7.4	4.0	2,899
25-34	3,472	19.4	55.3	2,544	18.4	40.5	265	16.5	4.2	6,281[a]
35-44	2,791	15.7	55.1	1,965	14.2	38.8	306	19.1	6.1	5,062[b]
45+	4,207	23.6	58.6	2,548	18.4	35.5	424	26.5	5.9	7,179
All ages	17,823	100.0	53.6	13,821	100.0	41.6	1,599	100.0	4.8	33,243

a Consisting of 3,191 aged 25-29 and 3,090 aged 30-34. No breakdown according to ethnicity was provided for these age groups in the 1941 Census.
b Of whom 2,778 aged 35-39.
Source: 1941 Census, vol. 2, 256-7, and vol. 3, 198.

English-speaking enlistment was especially heavy in the first two years of the war, whereas few French-speaking Verdunites were on active service overseas even as late as December 1941, according to the Mayor's Cigarette Fund's nominal roll.[39] In December 1940 and December 1941, the *Guardian* published honour rolls of Verdunites on active service, to "again ... show the World the Loyalty Verdun is noted for."[40] The newspaper had solicited names from servicemen's relatives and friends; readers were mainly English speaking, and so few French names appeared. But as the MCF was publicized in French in the *Messenger* as well as elsewhere in the city, and as, by 1941, compilation of the *Guardian*'s honour roll benefited from the files of the MCF (then one year in operation), the absence of French names indicates that relatively few French-speaking Verdunites enlisted early in the war.

Of 1,790 names on the *Guardian*'s 1941 list, only 111 (6.2 percent) appeared to be French speakers.[41] It was not until 1942 that French-speaking Quebecers enlisted in greater numbers. By the end of the war, the percentage of French speakers from Verdun overseas had tripled. Continued Axis successes well into 1942 (and the perceived threat to Canadian territory that some of these signalled), US entry into the war, and the mobilization for overseas service of some French-speaking regiments were all contributing factors.[42] With a strong war economy and easy employment opportunities, enlisting clearly was not the only option available for Canadians willing to aid the war effort.

In January 1941, 2,000 Verdunites were in uniform; by the end of 1941, over 2,900. According to the municipal census, in December 1943, 4,942 Verdunites were on active service in Canada or overseas, distributed among the services in proportions similar to the final ratios noted in Table 2.3.[43] Nearly four out of five Verdunites who entered military service during the war did so by 1943.

Surviving church honour rolls further illustrate the remarkable enlistment rate of Verdun's English-speaking population. In November 1939, Verdun's only English Catholic parish, St Willibrord's, numbered 2,292 families, of which only 450 lived in Ward 4, west of Desmarchais Boulevard. (Heavily populated Ward 4 was overwhelmingly English speaking and Protestant.) By April 1944, the number of English Catholic families in Verdun had climbed to 2,700 – approximately 10,000 people.[44] The enlistment statistics of St Willibrord Parish are impressive; by 1943 it was believed to be the Canadian Catholic leader in voluntary enlistments. About 12 percent of parishioners enlisted, a proportion comparable to the congregations of Protestant churches.[45] With less than 15 percent of the city's population, this parish supplied 26 percent of Verdun's naval enlistments, for example.[46] Verdun's Irish Catholics joined up in ratios comparable to Protestants. Their strong commitment suggests that they responded more to a sense of national spirit, community identity, or other personal motivations than to the call of Irish history.

The Protestant churches' honour rolls, too, reveal high enlistment rates. The congregation of Chalmers United Church averaged 907 members in the years

1939-45, and nearly 200 of these were in uniform at some point during the war.[47] This is an extremely high proportion of able-bodied, military-age males. St Clement's, on Wellington Street, was by far the largest Anglican parish in Quebec. At the beginning of 1939 it boasted 1,432 families totalling 4,564 people. By early 1945 the figure had risen to an estimated 1,500 families made up of 5,000 people.[48] St Clement's yielded 640 enlistees, about 13 percent of its total numbers. From a parish of about 3,350 people, 418 members (more than 12 percent) of Ward 4's Anglican parish of St John the Divine enlisted.[49] Verdun's five French-language parishes offered no comparable records of military service. In September 1944, Notre-Dame-de-la-Garde Parish, stretching from Osborne Avenue in Ward 4 to the western city limits, counted 607 families totalling approximately 2,400 people. The parish claimed only 24 men on active service, even though at least 111 French speakers from Ward 4 served overseas.[50]

Disincentives for French Speakers

There were significant impediments to recruitment for French-speaking Canadians, especially those who were unilingual. Few had emotional ties to France, while nearly none had any to Britain. So at war's outbreak, a lesser sense of military urgency prevailed in the French-speaking community than in the English.[51] But greater problems existed in attracting French-speaking Canadians to wartime military service. Virtually English-only military institutions presented enormous challenges, even to the willing. More than half of French-speaking Canadians who voluntarily joined the army during the war served in largely English-speaking regiments and units. Many of these enlistees were functionally bilingual. But many army units or corps professing a need for English-language technical skills, such as the engineers and the armoured corps, were reluctant to accept unilingual or nearly unilingual French-speaking recruits. For a French speaker, joining the army usually meant one of the four French-language infantry regiments or the single artillery regiment made up almost exclusively of French speakers. A few other minor units and detachments were also mainly French speaking. Language training was not at first available in the armed forces and does not seem to have been encouraged much when it became available. French speakers were normally expected to learn English as they learned their trades. On some military bases, speaking French was expressly forbidden.[52] Public knowledge of this situation discouraged recruitment among French speakers.

As for the other services, the RCN had no French-language units and no interest in creating any; until 1943 unilingual French speakers were rejected for naval service almost out of hand, and those who were enrolled thereafter had virtually no chance of advancement beyond menial positions such as shipboard stewards or shore-based support personnel requiring minimal training.[53] The English-language educational and technical qualifications required early in the war by the RCAF disallowed entry for most French speakers (and many English speakers as well).[54] For example, in January 1940 the RCAF sought unskilled men for "general duties" such as mess help and batmen (officers' servants). French speakers about thirty years old with a working knowledge of English seemed ideal, according to one RCAF newspaper advertisement. The thought of joining a uniformed class structure based on ethnicity had little appeal in French Canada, and the RCAF did not open a full-time recruiting centre in Montreal until the summer of 1941.[55]

For the French speaker, the linguistic reasons for not joining fuelled the social pressure to remain a civilian. The novels of Gabrielle Roy and Roger Lemelin, set in wartime Montreal and Quebec City, respectively, clearly demonstrate the degree to which social barriers inhibited enlistment even among French speakers seemingly inclined to join.[56] In Verdun, too, French speakers seemed disadvantaged by the enlistment process. In April 1941, the reserve units of the 3rd Canadian Infantry Division's Royal Canadian Army Service Corps detachment opened a recruiting depot on Wellington Street under an English-only sign, reinforcing the army's image as an English-only institution.[57] Even in 1942 half the recruiting officers in the Montreal area's Military District 4 were unilingual English speakers.[58]

According to the 1941 census, only 329 of Verdun's French-speaking military-age males aged fifteen to thirty-four reported themselves as unilingual.[59] While not all who declared an ability to speak English could do so with fluency, their self-perception suggests that language was not an insurmountable barrier to enlistment. Nevertheless, French speakers often could not train or work in their own language. Lingering resentment over the military's language policies may have discouraged French-speaking Verdunites from enlisting, although this is difficult to determine. On the other hand, one French-speaking Verdunite on naval service during the war, Léopold Lefort, has recalled that he was motivated to enlist at eighteen out of patriotism and that two of his French-speaking friends did so for the same reasons.[60] Volunteering, or not, was not only about language.

Factoring in Class

Establishing Verdunites' places of residence at the time of enlistment adds a class dimension to their active service. Even though Verdun was broadly working-class, intraclass dynamics existed within the city, based usually on neighbourhood. Moreover, a rough correlation existed between language and neighbourhood. Among the English-speaking community, class (in Verdun terms) to some extent dictated propensity for military service. The city's better-off neighbourhood supplied far less than its share of volunteers.

Table 2.5 shows the populations of Verdun's electoral wards for 1941-43 and a 1943 estimate of the linguistic balance in each ward. All wards cut across the city from the St Lawrence in the southeast to the City of Montreal aqueduct in the northwest (see Map 2). In July 1943 Ward 1 ran from the northeastern limits of

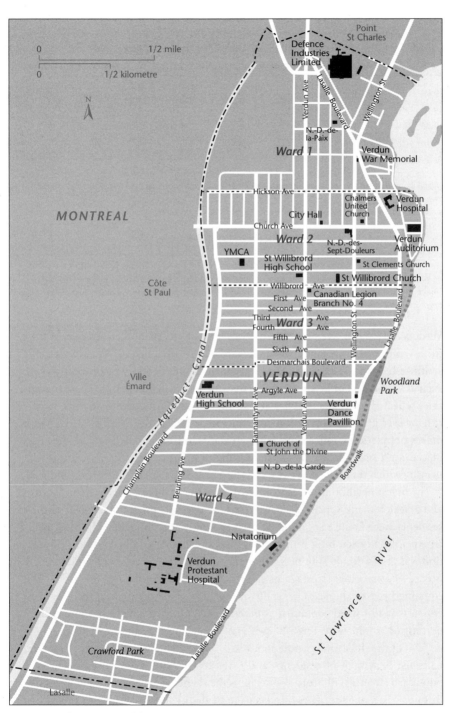

0 ——————— 1/2 mile

0 ——————— 1/2 kilometre

N

Point
St Charles

Defence
Industries
Limited

Verdun Ave

Lasalle Boulevard

Wellington St

N.-D.-de-
la-Paix

Ward 1

Verdun
War Memorial

MONTREAL

Hickson Ave

Chalmers
United
Church

Verdun
Hospital

City Hall

Church Ave

Ward 2

N.-D.-des-
Sept-Douleurs

Verdun
Auditorium

YMCA

St Willibrord
High School

St Clements Church

Côte
St Paul

Willibrord Ave

St Willibrord Church

First Ave

Canadian Legion
Branch No. 4

Second Ave

Third
Ave

Ward 3

Fourth
Ave

Wellington St

Lasalle Boulevard

Fifth Ave

Sixth Ave

Desmarchais Boulevard

Aqueduct Canal

Ville
Émard

VERDUN

Argyle Ave

Woodland
Park

Verdun
High School

Bannantyne Ave

Verdun Ave

Verdun
Dance
Pavillion

Church of
St John the Divine

Champlain Boulevard

N.-D.-de-la-Garde

Boardwalk

Beurling Ave

Ward 4

Natatorium

River

Verdun
Protestant
Hospital

St Lawrence

Crawford Park

Lasalle Boulevard

Lasalle

MAP 2   Verdun streets and locations

Table 2.5

Population distribution of Verdun by electoral ward and by language (estimated)

	Ward 1	Ward 2	Ward 3	Ward 4	Total[a]
1941	7,748	15,743	7,533	34,988	66,012
1942	7,814	15,751	7,528	36,533	67,626
1943[b]	8,297	16,920	8,106	40,248	73,571
% English[c]	35	35	45	75	55
% French	65	65	55	25	45

Note: Figures for each year are as of 31 December. These are the only years for which ward breakdowns are available.

a   Municipal census figures differ slightly from federal census figures. Percentages are author's estimates for 1943.

b   These figures take into account the ward redistribution of July 1943.

c   Estimated in the *Guardian*, 2 April 1943, based on names of those registered to vote in that month's municipal election. Ward 2 was probably more than 65 percent French speaking, while Ward 3 was more evenly split than indicated. The 25 percent estimate for French speakers in Ward 4 also seems too high.

Source: Derived from published municipal census results. *Guardian*, 15 May 1942, 15 January 1943, 2 April 1943, 16 July 1943, and 17 February 1944.

Verdun to Hickson Avenue; Ward 2 from Hickson to Willibrord Avenue; Ward 3 from Willibrord to Desmarchais Boulevard; and Ward 4 from Desmarchais to the southwestern limits of the city. Each ward included residents living on main streets, such as Wellington or Verdun Avenue, that cut across all four wards. These boundaries reflect changes instituted that year in a largely unsuccessful attempt to correct the ever-growing population imbalance in densely settled Ward 4.[61] This change makes population comparisons between wards in the years before and after 1943 inaccurate. Consequently, the most meaningful statistics, used here, are those from 1943, by which time the majority of Verdunites to have served had already enlisted.

The oldest neighbourhoods in Verdun, with the shabbiest flats, were in Wards 1 and 2, which many Verdunites considered the poorest; at least two-thirds of their residents were French speaking. Ward 3 was only slightly better off. Most of its tenements had been built immediately after the First World War, and its population was about evenly split between French and English speakers. Despite the existence of some older streets in its eastern extremities, Ward 4 was the newest and contained mostly duplexes generally occupied by the city's highest income earners. In 1943 this ward contained 55 percent of Verdun's population, more than 75 percent of whom were English speakers. Wards 1 and 2 combined made up 34 percent of the city's total population. Ward 3 was by far the smallest in population, with just 11 percent of residents, and consisted of only seven extremely densely populated streets: Willibrord Avenue plus the six numbered avenues, First Avenue through Sixth Avenue. These streets were made up almost entirely of unyielding rows of three-storey, six-family tenement houses.

The home addresses of enlistees provided on the file cards kept by the Mayor's Cigarette Fund help determine enlistees' home wards. In 94 percent of cases the file cards noted a home address. Table 2.6 shows the distribution of Verdunites overseas by service, language, and place of residence. The enlistment statistics from Ward 3 are astounding. No less than 38 percent of the Verdun enlistees whose addresses are known originated from this small ward – more than three and a half times the proportion of this ward's population in the city as a whole. Since Ward 3 had only 8,106 residents as of 31 December 1943, the 2,237 men and women on active service from Ward 3 constituted 27.6 percent of the ward's entire population.[62] Even more imbalanced is the linguistic makeup of Ward 3's service population: English speakers accounted for 86 percent of the total. If the *Guardian*'s April 1943 estimate is accurate – that Ward 3 residents were at least 45 percent English speaking – then the English-speaking enlistment rate from this working-class ward was an astonishing 53 percent of the *entire* English-speaking population, including women, children, and the aged (approximately 3,648 people). This virtually impossible situation suggests that the ward was about 50 percent English speaking (if not more), which would reduce the possible enlistment rate to a maximum of 46 percent, still exceedingly high. The municipal census data are also likely to have underrepresented Ward 3's actual population, further reducing the estimated enlistment rate. The 1,875 English-speaking men listed in the files of the MCF represent very nearly 100 percent of those medically fit and of military age living in the ward.

Ward 3's seven streets, plus those portions of Lasalle Boulevard, Wellington Street, Verdun Avenue, and Bannantyne Avenue that cut across the ward, must surely represent one of the densest concentration of enlistees for a neighbourhood of its size anywhere in Canada. French speakers also enlisted in greater numbers from this ward than from any other ward in the city. Class, neighbourhood identity and pride, community spirit, shared experience, and living conditions all contributed to this extraordinary phenomenon. (Ward 3, called "the Avenues," was known by everyone in Verdun for its unique atmosphere.) According to data compiled from the MCF file cards, Third Avenue held the distinction of having the greatest proportion of residents on active service of any street in the city.

Figures for the other wards pale in comparison, especially those of Ward 4, whose 1,780 men and women overseas represented only 4.4 percent of the ward's reported 40,248 residents, and 30 percent of overseas enlistees for whom an address is known. The 1,033 enlistees from Ward 2 amount to only 6.1 percent of its 16,920 residents (17 percent of enlistees), while the 909 from Ward 1 translate into a proportional 11 percent of locals (15 percent of enlistees). For English-speaking enlistees only, approximately 19.6 percent of the total English-speaking population from Ward 1, 11.3 percent from Ward 2, and a mere 5.5 percent from Ward 4 was in uniform.

The apparently low enlistment rate from Ward 4 is difficult to explain. That newer ward conceivably housed more financially established Verdun families, possibly making the median age higher in Ward 4 than in the other wards. The higher income and educational backgrounds suggest more white-collar or skilled workers, perhaps a less forthcoming pool of potential recruits. Still, Ward 4 not surprisingly was the leader by a wide margin in RCAF enlistments, both in absolute numbers and as a proportion of overall enlistments by ward. Of all men and women from Verdun in the air force for whom a home address is known, 43 percent originated from Ward 4. Of all English-speaking Verdunites in that service, 49 percent were from Ward 4. A disproportionately high number of Ward 4 residents in the RCAF lived in the tiny Crawford Park neighbourhood, near the southwestern city limits. This was the newest, most English-speaking, and highest-average-income neighbourhood in Verdun.

The statistics indicate that poorer Verdunites enlisted in greater proportion than those somewhat better off, and that the latter were more likely to join the air force than either of the other services. Among NRMA men, 77 percent of French speakers and 64 percent of English speakers lived in the poorest neighbourhoods, indicating that compulsion, like voluntarism, had some links to class background and neighbourhood, notwithstanding language. Verdun's military service record therefore reflected its internal social stratification.

Of French speakers in the armed forces for whom addresses are known, fully 62.5 percent lived in Wards 1 and 2 (702 of 1,123). Even though an estimated two-thirds of the population in these two wards was French speaking, English-speaking service people from these two wards outnumbered French speakers nearly two to one.

The preponderance of Ward 3 men in the army and navy, and a correspondingly low ratio of men in the air force, indicate a generally lower educational level among men of this ward than among men of Ward 4. Unemployment in 1939 was almost certainly higher in Ward 3 than in Ward 4, which might have induced at least some enlistment. By 1941, however, wartime industrial expansion had provided thousands of jobs in Montreal, Verdun, and nearby municipalities. In 1941 the average annual income of a family head in Verdun was $1,331, whereas in Montreal it was $1,267. For Verdun this translated into nearly $26 a week in a city where the average monthly rent was $21, second-lowest to Hull in Canada for cities over 30,000 inhabitants.[63] On average, even though Ward 3 was not economically advantaged by Verdun standards, most families were reasonably financially secure by 1942. In any event, limited family finances alone could not explain the residents' inclination to enlist in such massive numbers. If it were this simple, then Wards 1 and 2 should have been equally affected. Language, ethnicity, and stronger identification with the cause of Britain and the Allies among English speakers were also definite factors.

Recruitment from Ward 3 was high partly because of the kind of neighbourhood it was. One Ward 3 veteran's recollections exemplify the social environment and

Table 2.6

Verdunites overseas by service, language, and place of residence, 1943 ward divisions

	Army	NRMA	CWAC	Navy	WRCNS	RCAF	RCAF-WD	Misc.[a]	Total
Ward 1 (E)	381	7	11	95	7	62	3	3	569
Ward 1 (F)	184	86	2	19	–	48	1	–	340
Subtotal	*565*	*93*	*13*	*114*	*7*	*110*	*4*	*3*	*909*
Ward 2 (E)	453	7	9	111	3	83	2	3	671
Ward 2 (F)	192	98	2	28	1	40	1	–	362
Subtotal	*645*	*105*	*11*	*139*	*4*	*123*	*3*	*3*	*1,033*
Ward 3 (E)	1,259	3	28	358	11	236	13	19	1,927
Ward 3 (F)	171	46	2	47	–	43	–	1	310
Subtotal	*1,430*	*49*	*30*	*405*	*11*	*279*	*13*	*20*	*2,237*
Ward 4 (E)	931	5	17	298	13	369	21	15	1,669
Ward 4 (F)	60	9	–	20	–	21	1	–	111
Subtotal	*991*	*14*	*17*	*318*	*13*	*390*	*22*	*15*	*1,780*
Unknown (E)	223	1	4	34	1	25	1	1	290
Unknown (F)	39	8	–	9	–	10	–	1	67
Subtotal	*262*	*9*	*4*	*43*	*1*	*35*	*1*	*2*	*357*
Total	3,893	270	75	1,019	36	937	43	43	6,316

a Includes 17 merchant seamen, the total for whom is far too low in the MCF mailing list. St Willibrord Parish alone reported 21 merchant seamen in service during the war. In 1948, there were still 30 merchant seamen from Verdun in that occupation who had seen service during the war. Their average age was twenty-three in 1948, and seven to nine were French speakers. RG 46, vol. 1282, "Survey of Seamen's Registry 1948 – War Service," Library and Archives Canada.

Source: File cards of Mayor's Cigarette Fund, box A-536, Verdun Borough Archives; Guardian (Verdun), 16 July 1943.

motivations of many young Verdun recruits. Douglas Whyte, who joined the RCAF in 1943 at the age of eighteen, lived with his family on First Avenue. Whyte was a member of a close-knit group of twelve English-speaking friends ("a gang"), nine of whom were Protestants, while three belonged to St Willibrord Parish. They were all from Ward 3 and played organized sports together – a form of neighbourhood social arrangement common to thousands of Verdun youths. According to Whyte, most of the teenagers in this gang had some military experience through membership in various cadet corps. Eleven members of the group enlisted.[64] Whyte felt most Verdunites were extremely conscious of the war, if only because most had at least one family member on active service or with military experience. In the 1930s Whyte's father had been a member of the Victoria Rifles of Canada, and he sometimes accompanied him to training sessions at the regimental armoury.[65] Whyte's socialization before and during the war reinforced his strong local spirit and community culture. These social patterns and military traditions furthered the enlistment process in Verdun, especially in congested, closely knit Ward 3.

Only 5.5 percent of Verdunites on active service overseas were officers. In the army this was roughly the percentage of officers found in an infantry division of more than 18,000 men, but was lower than the overall percentage of officers in the army generally.[66] The same is probably true of Verdunites' service in the navy and certainly true of the air force. Verdun servicemen's generally low educational levels explain the small proportion of officers among them. For example, in the Royal Canadian Naval Volunteer Reserve, so popular with Verdunites, completion of senior matriculation (which followed grade 12) was the minimum requirement for officers. The 1941 census shows that considerably more residents of Westmount than of Verdun, both as proportions of their respective populations and absolutely, completed high school and obtained higher education. Westmount had a very high ratio of officers.[67]

According to the MCF data, half of Verdun's officers were in the RCAF, the service that contained the highest percentage of officers, while 53 percent of all officers originated from Ward 4. Ward 3 provided 25 percent of Verdun's officers, as well as 38 percent of all overseas Verdunites. Only 3.8 percent of enlistees from Wards 1, 2, and 3 were officers, while for Ward 4 the figure was 10.4 percent. Twenty-two percent of all officers were French speaking, as were 35 percent of army officers. These figures are far higher than those for French-speaking enlistees in general. Yet Verdun produced only a single French-speaking naval officer.[68] Jean-Yves Gravel, who has studied French-speaking enlistment in Canada during the war, cites a wartime Department of National Defence report noting that French-speaking officers were young, bilingual, and well educated.[69] This was probably true of Verdun's French-speaking officers, one of whom even served with the Toronto Scottish Regiment.

Recruiting Women and the Reserve Army

Not all recruiting efforts were runaway successes. Verdun's women enlisted in small numbers. A total of 154 Verdun women are known to have enlisted, of whom only ten were French speaking. Overall, these 154 women represented less than 2.5 percent of Verdunites on active service overseas. But since relatively few Canadian women went overseas (perhaps no more than 9,000 of the 50,000, including nurses, on active service), it is not surprising that the files of the Mayor's Cigarette Fund list so few.[70] Others were undoubtedly on active service in Canada. Women were active in a variety of other ways, however, especially through paramilitary participation in the Women's Volunteer Reserve Corps (described in Chapter 4).

The Canadian Women's Army Corps opened a recruitment centre in Verdun city hall in October 1942. Results were disappointing and three weeks later it closed. The recruiting officer for Military District 4 explained to Verdun's mayor, Edward Wilson, that "the population in your City, due to war activities, has by now been well drained."[71] Despite this, the CWAC opened another recruiting centre on Wellington Street in August 1943. To mark the opening, the *Guardian* published a full-page advertisement sponsored by local politicians, as well as by French- and English-speaking merchants. "Verdun's Bugle Call to Women," read the headline. Prospective recruits were told that the CWAC allowed women the opportunity to "Serve Shoulder to Shoulder with Your Fighting Men."[72]

In 1943 the head of the Verdun Women's Volunteer Reserve Corps, Joan Adams, who operated a local women's business school, joined the CWAC; at least seven other members of the WVRC had preceded her into this service. Despite Adams's desire to go overseas, she was shunted to Ste Anne de Bellevue to instruct recruits in secretarial and clerical work. This posting continued a well-established pattern of women's social and civilian employment roles being replicated in uniform. Adams was so displeased at being forced to assume her civilian vocation while on active service that she resigned in 1944. Moreover, uniformed women were sometimes smeared as sexual thrill seekers and likely carriers of venereal disease. Only 7 percent of Canadians felt that a woman's most effective wartime contribution would be to enlist.[73] This did not encourage recruiting.

In addition to the active army and the NRMA army, Canada also organized a reserve army (formerly the NPAM) made up of male volunteers under eighteen or between forty and fifty. It also included men who, for medical reasons or because they provided services deemed essential to the war effort, were unable to join the active army. Many Verdunites served in the reserve army in units such as the Victoria Rifles of Canada and the Régiment de Joliette, or in reserve units of other branches of the army.

When the 3rd Canadian Infantry Division's reserve Royal Canadian Army Service Corps unit established a recruitment centre on Wellington Street in April

1941, in anticipation of relocating its units to the Verdun Auditorium (see Chapter 3), it focused its recruitment on "skilled tradesmen." Many among the city's working class were experienced drivers, mechanics, fitters, welders, painters, and metalsmiths – all occupations available in the reserve RCASC.[74] Part-time soldiering, however, had only a limited appeal with Verdunites, whose response was insufficient to bring the locally based unit up to full strength. Similarly, in September 1941 a reported 500 men of the 2nd Battalion (Reserve), Canadian Grenadier Guards marched through Verdun in aid of a recruitment effort. But the display yielded just sixty-four recruits, some "so young that they could only be employed as buglers." This disappointingly small number translated into the sum of $10 per recruit in advertising expenses.[75]

Despite the city's already outstanding enlistment record, more seemed to be expected of Verdun. In 1942 the reserve army launched a major drive for 10,000 recruits from the Montreal area, and it considered Verdun's densely populated neighbourhoods fertile ground. Mayor Wilson strongly supported the aims of the reserve army and officially involved the city in the campaign. Recruitment booths were set up across the city, including in all public buildings. Reserve army promotional material stressed that members would not be posted overseas. Although several hundred Verdunites served in the wartime reserve army, the results of this particular recruitment drive were dismal, not only in Verdun but across the Island of Montreal.[76]

In June 1943, the CWAC, the Black Watch, and the Veterans' Guard of Canada set up a large summer recruitment tent in riverside Woodland Park.[77] A Black Watch parade in Verdun on 22 June included motorized units displaying machine guns and antitank guns. Wilson then spoke to a crowd at Woodland Park, encouraging enlistment. Next, Alderman Gérard Tétrault, an active member of the Société Saint-Jean-Baptiste and no political ally of Wilson's, addressed the gathering in French and urged enlistment. Tétrault's was an odd plea given that French Canadians joining the Black Watch would have had to work in English. Still, the *Guardian* reminded readers that the Black Watch "has had specially close associations with Verdun both in this and the last war," and the regiment's recruiting officers appealed to young Verdunites to follow in their fathers' First World War footsteps. Col Paul P. Hutchison, hoping to attract recruits for the Black Watch reserve battalion, told the crowd that "Verdun has never let the Black Watch down ... we are certain [it] will again answer our call." But Verdunites already had; only thirty-five reserve army recruits were found on this occasion.[78]

Some Hometown Heroes

Every major Canadian ground engagement, naval action, or bombing mission included Verdunites. After the war, Arthur Burgess wrote that "the Montreal daily newspapers bore eloquent testimony, with an almost embarrassing frequency, to the exploits of Verdun's sons on land, air and sea, in promotions and honours and, unfortunately, in casualties."[79] On 1 March 1945, the Verdun *Guardian* stated without much exaggeration that "there are few homes in Verdun [without] at least one of its members in the Allied fighting forces or [which have] not already been bereaved through the loss of a dear one in this war." Many British-born residents had relatives on British service as well as Canadian. Sgt L.G. Taylor of the Royal Canadian Army Medical Corps (RCAMC) wrote from Holland in 1945, "It would be a good thing if we had an infantry Battalion, a squadron and a destroyer named after Verdun and composed of Verdunites. The percentage of Verdun men is, as we all know, quite heavy in Montreal units and we do know, to our sorrow, that many a family has suffered the loss of a loved one in Verdun."[80]

A number of Verdunites on active service became well known in their hometown and neighbouring districts; a handful gained national prominence, and one became an international celebrity. Local military heroes had a significant impact on community spirit. They came to embody the wartime service and sacrifice for which the city had become renowned. Their widely publicized achievements stimulated local interest in the war and spurred the city's war effort.

One of the first Verdun heroes was Able Seaman Mike Scullion, a well-known amateur boxer from the east end. While serving aboard the destroyer HMCS *Assiniboine* in August 1942, Scullion earned a Mentioned-in-Dispatches, a minor decoration, for his key role in disabling the German submarine *U-210* during a dramatic engagement in the North Atlantic. Press accounts noted that while the destroyer's captain, Lt-Cdr John Stubbs, "was manoeuvring for an opportunity to ram, an able seaman, Michael Scullion, of Verdun, Quebec, found his opportunity. He saw the submarine looming up and got her on the sights of his 4.7-inch gun. The shell went into the U-boat's bows."[81] Canadian newspapers also published photos of Rear-Admiral L.W. Murray in Halifax congratulating Scullion for his deeds. In October 1942 Scullion returned to Verdun on leave and spoke to students at his former school, St Willibrord High, where, according to the *Guardian*, he "received thunderous applause" and "his words were followed with undivided attention."[82] Scullion had shown the country, and Verdunites themselves, what a Verdunite could do.

Another local hero became perhaps Canada's best-known military figure of the war: Pilot Officer George F. Beurling. The outlines of his remarkable service career as a Spitfire fighter pilot are documented already.[83] What has gone unreported is the effect of his career on his hometown's morale and the sense of pride that his fame instilled among all Verdunites. Beurling was born in 1921 in east-end Verdun, where he grew up. He had always been interested in aviation and learned to fly when he was fourteen. At the outbreak of war he attempted to enlist in the RCAF but, despite his impressive flying record, he failed to meet the minimum educational requirements. Somewhat discouraged, in 1940 he joined the RAF with the lowly rank of aircraftsman.

Beurling soon proved himself a natural fighter pilot. In the spring of 1942, as a sergeant-pilot, he registered his first two confirmed "kills" during fighter sweeps over the French coast. That June he was transferred to Malta. In two weeks in July 1942, Beurling downed an astonishing sixteen enemy aircraft, including two in ten seconds. Before he was shot down and wounded on 14 October 1942, Beurling had destroyed twenty-seven aircraft over Malta, probably destroyed nine others, and damaged three more. Allied fortunes in the Mediterranean and North Africa had ebbed dangerously during the summer of 1942, and Beurling's exploits constituted an outstanding success story that received international press attention. He was dubbed "The Knight of Malta," promoted to pilot officer, and decorated with the Distinguished Service Order, the Distinguished Flying Cross, and the Distinguished Flying Medal and Bar.[84] Beurling, only twenty, was celebrated as Canada's greatest war hero. Canadian war correspondent Lionel Shapiro described him in November 1942 as "the 'hottest' individual in the war so far as London is concerned. And, it goes without saying, as far as Verdun, Quebec, is concerned." The *Montreal Daily Star* dubbed Beurling the "Verdun Ace" and "Verdun's hero."[85]

Closer to home, in the late summer and autumn of 1942 the *Guardian* published gushing news items about Beurling. Not surprisingly the local press allotted impressive front-page coverage to "Verdun's pride" and its "most famous son," sometimes featuring admiring commentary from Beurling's family, acquaintances, or local public officials. In late October 1942, the government released information from the Air Ministry in London that the wounded Beurling would soon return to Canada (at Ottawa's request). Excitement gripped Verdun. Douglas Whyte recalled that people "could not carry on a conversation [at] that time unless it was about the fact that Beurling ... Verdun's hero was coming home."[86]

Beurling's fame was used extensively in Verdun to promote the war and war-related home-front activities. When the Verdun Civilian Protection Committee planned a demonstration of its air-raid precaution and rescue skills in November 1942, its slogan was "We won't let Beurling down on the Home Front." Advertisements in the *Guardian* for the demonstration appeared beneath large photos of Beurling, with the accompanying text: "The Hero of Malta is doing more than his bit overseas! Shall we be ready on the Homefront to protect our homes – his home?"[87] Several major Montreal department stores, such as Eaton's and Henry Morgan and Co., used Beurling's name or likeness in their newspaper advertisements.[88]

On 9 November Beurling and his family were warmly greeted in Ottawa by the prime minister, William Lyon Mackenzie King. Photos of the meeting appeared in many Canadian newspapers the next day.[89] On the evening of 10 November, Beurling arrived in Verdun in a motorcade that wound its way through crowd-lined streets from Montreal's Windsor Hotel, where he had given a news conference and where thousands of well-wishers had congregated throughout the day. The city of Verdun, the RCAF (of which Beurling was not yet a member), and the National War Finance Committee cooperated to honour Beurling in a lavish and nationally publicized ceremony at the Verdun Auditorium attended by over 6,000 enthusiastic people of all backgrounds.[90] High-ranking military dignitaries from the RCAF, RAF, and Military District 4 were in attendance, as were Verdun's political and social elite.

The auditorium was decorated with flags and bunting, and an immense portrait of Beurling was suspended from the ceiling. A large and elaborate stage accommodated the dignitaries, including members of Beurling's family. Amid phalanxes of honour guards drawn from all three services stood a throne-like dais where Beurling sat. Mayor Wilson formally welcomed him home and expressed the city's pride in his achievements. Further speeches were made and demonstrations of precision drill were performed in his honour. CBC radio broadcast the entire spectacle live, coast to coast.[91] Among the Verdun air cadets performing drill that evening was seventeen-year-old Douglas Whyte, who recalled that "the whole building shook" when Beurling entered the auditorium.[92]

When the weary Beurling's time to speak came, he appeared nervous in front of the wildly cheering crowd. He laconically told his fellow Verdunites, "This is no place for me ... I'm a fighter pilot." With this, Beurling "brought the house down."[93] The *Guardian*, which issued a special "extra edition," proclaimed that "never in the history of this city has any man or woman, no matter what might have been their achievement, received such an ovation." Indeed, Beurling's brief four-minute speech was interrupted nine times by the frenzied crowd. On behalf of the city, Wilson presented Verdun's hero with a portrait of himself. Two weeks later the city named an undeveloped street in its western extremity Beurling Avenue.[94]

The whole country was watching, and the fighter ace's homecoming was thoroughly covered in the Montreal press. The *Star* devoted two-thirds of a page to his welcome in Verdun. The "delirious" crowd was described as the greatest in Canadian history ever assembled to welcome home a single war hero.[95] *La Presse* commented approvingly on the reception provided Beurling and noted the "terrific spirit of the City of Verdun, which has always contributed ... a large number of personnel to our armed forces." Air Commodore Albert de Niverville, noting Verdun's outstanding enlistment record in both world wars, stated "that there could be no more appropriate locale than Verdun to host him."[96]

Like Scullion before him, Beurling returned to his former school, Verdun High School, to discuss his war experiences with the students. "He had his youthful audience either in roars of laughter or gasping with horror," reported the *Guardian* in April 1943. (Beurling had to wait several months to recover from his wounded foot.) Beurling was treated like a matinee idol by the teenagers, who mobbed him, seeking autographs and the chance for a quick word. The *Gazette* noted that the boys in attendance "watched him with hero worship pouring out of their eyes." One boy present, John Buck, remembered that he and his classmates "idolized" Beurling and that they were "spellbound" when he spoke to them. A girl in the class recalled that there was at least some apprehension connected with Beurling's visit, for it signalled that the "winds of war had blown through our classroom." As Beurling was only several years older than the students, some may have reflected that his harrowing experiences might some day become their own.[97]

Canadian servicemen overseas also derived pride and encouragement from Beurling's military achievements – none more so than Verdunites. Driver George J. Weeks, RCASC, wrote the Mayor's Cigarette Fund from Britain in 1943 that "we Verdun boys over here will carry the Glory of Verdun in our minds, when the time comes, the same as Beurling did at Malta. That's the same spirit we all have." Lance-Bombardier J.F. Cruick, RCA, wrote approvingly that Beurling "certainly has put the home town in the news lately," and all Verdunites could be grateful for that.[98]

The *Guardian* proclaimed Beurling's spectacular homecoming the "outstanding feature" of the year 1942 in Verdun.[99] As the epitome of Verdunites' impressive enlistment and fighting record, and as a symbol of the community's war effort, Beurling's triumphant return proved to be the public relations highlight of Verdun's war.

The Ties That Bind

The letters sent to the Mayor's Cigarette Fund by overseas Verdunites demonstrate that the men perceived the war as as much Verdun's struggle as Canada's. Civic pride induced some to enlist, and it is certain that being in uniform increased a sense of pride and belonging among Verdunites. Pte J. Flood, RCAMC, wrote from England in 1941, "we are over here to help smash Hitler and all he stands for ... I am proud that Verdun has shown the world that her menfolk have the fighting blood in their veins."[100] Another soldier, Sgt R.M. Thomas, wrote: "where I am situated there are quite a few boys from Verdun (needless to say I believe that Verdun's percentage of enlistments will be on top as in the last affair) and every one of them is feeling the same way as I am, that it is wonderful to have come from a City and to be trying to do *our bit* for a City and Country that shows the spirit the way VERDUN is doing."[101] Thomas's first loyalties as expressed in this letter were to his hometown.

Verdunites frequently served together or met each other while overseas, particularly in Britain, and often expressed pleasure at that fact. Sgt J. Dunster wrote, "There are a lot of Verdun boys in my unit ... They make the 16th Field Company, [Royal Canadian Engineers], a unit to be really proud of and a man proud to belong to Verdun." Sgt L.G. Taylor stated, "I meet Verdunites over here nearly every day. We compose a good percent[age] of our unit [9th Field Ambulance,

RCAMC], and ... other units are the same." Sgt C. Adams of the 17th Duke of York's Royal Canadian Hussars wrote from Britain in 1942, "anywhere a fellow goes over here he bumps into a Verdunite."[102]

Driver Kenneth Slade, RCASC, who enlisted in the reserve army in June 1940 and went active in September, put hometown links in perspective. Perhaps owing to the large number of Verdunites to be found in Britain, Slade felt "it wasn't [that] tight. Nobody was going to fight for the other guy just because he came from Verdun. But you were always proud to meet someone from Verdun. I think you could borrow money from someone from Verdun ... if you didn't have a nickel to your name." The regimental system itself develops unit cohesion partly by deemphasizing previous roots and backgrounds and by rallying men around a new common bond, that of the regimental family. For many, loyalty began and ended within the regimental or other unit structure. Joseph Way noted that even though he could recall Verdunites serving aboard most of the ships on which he served, he felt no exaggerated sense of kinship with them. Aboard ship, loyalty was applied first and foremost to the men's trade groups and messdecks. On the other hand, Way also served aboard *Assiniboine* at the time of the action for which his good friend Mike Scullion had been honoured, and he was very proud of his fellow Verdunite's deeds that day.[103]

But the views of Slade and Way are exceptional; most serving Verdunites found kinship and local loyalty meaningful. The evidence in the files of the Mayor's Cigarette Fund is simply overwhelming. Sapper F. Gibbons, RCE, wrote that "coming from Verdun is quite a bond between the boys over here and no matter where you go and what arm of the Services you meet, the chances are that you will find somebody from Verdun." Trooper E. Elder, 14th Canadian Armoured Regiment (The Calgary Regiment), wrote from Italy in 1944: "There is a large number of Verdunites in this battle zone. I often run into a bunch here and there and the main subject of conversation is Verdun ... how we all wish we were there now."[104] Sapper H.H. White commented in 1942, "it is over two years since I left good old Verdun, but I have my Verdun friends here with me so we get along pretty well." Many Verdunites expressed community kinship in letters to the MCF when they thanked the fund on behalf of *all* Verdunites overseas. In 1941 Cpl W.A. Horsely of No. 1 Fighter Squadron (later 401 Squadron), RCAF, wrote a warm note of appreciation on behalf of all Verdunites in his squadron, insisting that they "all ... feel the same way even if they don't write."[105] It is clear from these letters that, despite the acquisition of service or unit identities and loyalties, the Verdunites' sense of community continued to exert a powerful grip on them overseas.[106]

Mail, gifts, and news from home were also very important to these men. Many loved getting Verdun newspapers, especially the *Guardian,* and reading news of familiar places, institutions, and people, even if the news was several weeks old. No overseas Verdunite could fail to notice the coverage that those on active service received in the ever-patriotic *Guardian*. Leading Stoker E.J. Pyndus, serving aboard the corvette HMCS *Cobourg*, wrote to the MCF from St John's, Newfoundland, "My mother often sends me Guardians ... it's a wonderful paper with all the home news in it. It's quite monotonous at times at sea and it's sure enjoyable to pick up a Guardian and read all about the news at home."[107]

Verdun's main English-language newspaper could be found wherever there were Verdunites, which was throughout the British Isles at this time. To his pleasant surprise, Lt-Cdr William Woods, commanding officer of Verdun's namesake warship, HMCS *Dunver* (see Chapter 3), and a Verdunite, saw copies of the *Guardian* in Salvation Army canteens in London, Liverpool, and Londonderry.[108] In 1943 Gunner R.H. Smith, 7th Medium Regiment, RCA, wrote: "our battery is made up 50 percent of Verdunites, the other 50 percent from Montreal. On our wall in the stores is a double page of the 'Guardian' with the honor roll of Verdun boys serving overseas." Smith also fought homesickness: "I have been away from Verdun for three years and a half, and I guess there have been quite a few improvements since I left ... I think that all the fellows from Verdun would appreciate a folder of pictures showing us what our city looks like now."[109]

Many other letters refer to an urgent desire to return home to family, friends, and familiar surroundings. Few had a better claim to long for Verdun than Signalman B.C. Palmquist, who wrote in 1942:

> I can say with all sincerety [sic] that the day I walk along Wellington Street again will be the happiest day I have ever experienced. No one by any stretch of the imagination can picture what it is like to be away from a wife and six adorable children, until they have experienced it. Naturally we have our moments of home-sickness and feel really upset, then we ask ourselves is it all worth it[?] Of course we snap out of it and know deep in our hearts that we have to finish the biggest job of all our careers. I am sure that the results will be well worth the misery and heart aches we have had to suffer.[110]

Cpl W.A. Kitching claimed, "Wellington Street would look like paradise to a lot of the Verdun boys."[111]

In 1941 Pte Fred Wray, RCASC, had a conversation with King George VI while the king was on an inspection tour of Canadian units in Britain. The *Guardian* quoted Wray as writing in a letter home that the king "asked me where I came from and I told him Verdun, and he said 'Oh yes, that is the city I wanted to see on my visit, but was unable to.' He asked me ... how I liked it over here. I told him it was alright but that I liked Verdun better."[112] Pte L. Brunet, a stretcher bearer with the Fusiliers Mont-Royal, yearned for home and his wife and child. Still, he was fervently proud of Verdun and hoped that "before leaving Europe we will erect a cross in memory of Verdun soldiers." He signed his 1941 letter, "Un soldat de Verdun."[113]

Coming as they did from a compact city with a strong sense of local culture, and reinforced by the knowledge that their hometown apparently led the nation in enlistments, Verdunites on active service overseas felt a fraternal tie and enjoyed a common bond. The body of evidence that Verdunites have bequeathed in their letters home expresses the attitudes and concerns of Canada's Second World War generation. The men longed for their homes, and Verdun came to symbolize everything that was good and proper in life. Many letters sent from Britain showed the writers to be anxious, restless, and bored. Their moods changed once they saw action in Europe, but even then, they recognized a difficult and burdensome job to do, made endurable by vicarious contact with home, either through fellow towns-people or the hometown newspapers.

By the end of the war, the participation level of Verdun's men of military service age was very high, and near its maximum for English speakers. The backgrounds of enlisted Verdunites crossed linguistic, religious, class, age, and gender lines. Still, in keeping with the composition of the city's population, most Verdunites serving overseas were English-speaking. More than one-third lived in Ward 3, which contained only 11 percent of the city's residents. The highest-income neighbourhoods produced the lowest proportion of enlistments, though the highest proportion of officers. The enlistment rate for Verdun's French-speaking population was no less than the overall French-speaking proportion of the armed forces. Most French speakers who enlisted did so from 1942, while most English speakers in uniform had joined by 1943.

If "national sacrifice is the sum of individual sacrifice," as Lt-Gen E.L.M. Burns wrote after the war,[114] then Verdun's contribution in terms of manpower, especially from its English-speaking population, was of national significance. With five times its 1914 population, Verdun was far more important to the Canadian war effort during the Second World War than it had been in the earlier conflict. Verdunites' local identity, nurtured at home and sustained under more difficult conditions overseas, provided a thread to which many could cling. The resulting boost to morale assisted them on the long road to victory.

3
City Hall Goes to War

Verdun's patriotic municipal government played a leading role in organizing the local war effort. The city's elected and non-elected officials cooperated closely with military and federal and provincial civil authorities in almost every way possible. Municipally organized fundraising ventures, especially the extremely popular Mayor's Cigarette Fund, allowed Verdunites to support directly their friends and kin overseas. The city "adopted" a ship named in its honour, HMCS *Dunver*, and played a leading role in providing comforts to crewmen serving aboard, encouraging Verdunites to do the same. And Verdun helped its citizens organize an elaborate air-raid precaution and civil protection network, as municipal officials took seriously the threat of hostile action in their bailiwick – including that from the few local enemy aliens. Occasionally, city hall was also able to use the war to improve its own finances, as when the Verdun Auditorium was leased to the Department of National Defence. In taking so robust a patriotic stance, Mayor Edward Wilson had in mind the best interests of the nation *and* Verdun (and perhaps his own political fortunes). City hall took the war seriously, and Verdun's war-conscious residents could not help but notice; many followed the example that had been set personally by the mayor.

Unity at the Top
Verdun's British character was reflected in its civic leadership. On 3 April 1939, Edward Wilson, a fifty-seven-year-old alderman, defeated the colourful incumbent mayor, Hervé Ferland. Born into a working-class family in Burnley, Lancashire, in 1882, Wilson was of mixed Anglo-Scottish parentage. He and his wife, Elizabeth, had immigrated to Canada in 1910, settling first in Montreal and finally in Verdun in 1917. Before being elected mayor, Wilson had represented Ward 4 as alderman from 1931 to 1933 and again from 1935 to 1939. Throughout this period and during the war, he owned and managed a wholesale egg and poultry business that he operated from Montreal's Bonsecours Market. Wilson, who always wore a trademark bow-tie in public, spoke passable French and was an avid gardener, lawn bowler, and reader of English literature. Ever concerned with civil liberties and the conditions of the working class, he became a member of the socialist Co-operative Commonwealth Federation (CCF). He was a Mason, belonged to the Anglican church, and lived in a modest detached house on Woodland Avenue in the west-central part of the city.[1]

Edward Wilson was a busy mayor. During the war he directed or participated in numerous patriotic and war-related organizations and fundraising campaigns, large and small. He held executive positions in the Civilian Protection Committee, the Mayor's Cigarette Fund, the Salvation Army, the Verdun branch of the Red Cross, and the Verdun Salvage Committee, among others. He also chaired the Verdun Protestant Board of School Trustees, represented Verdun on the Montreal Metropolitan Commission, and was a director of the Quebec Union of Municipalities.[2] The popular Wilson served as mayor until he retired in 1960, at age seventy-eight.

Another Briton, Arthur Burgess, was the indefatigable city clerk from 1929 to 1962. He was born in Walsall, near Birmingham, England, in 1889. He arrived in Montreal in 1910 and found employment with the Canadian Pacific Railway. He settled in Verdun in 1911. In 1922, he married a Verdun woman originally from Yorkshire. They lived on one of Verdun's more fashionable streets, Beatty Avenue, in the west end. Burgess was an outstanding cricketer, founder of the Verdun 500 Swimming and Social Club, and a "recognized authority" on the city's history.[3]

Balancing the powerful influence of Verdun's British-born at city hall was Joseph Rienzo French, a bilingual French Canadian bachelor who became Verdun's city manager in 1933. He was born in 1898 in Valleyfield, southwest of Montreal. City manager systems of civic government were new to Canada in 1933, and Verdun was one of the first municipalities in the country to adopt this structure. French, Verdun's top non-elected official, was responsible for overall administration and acted as chief financial officer. City council decided policy, while French, and the department heads whom he oversaw, executed it. He remained city manager for nearly three decades.[4]

In addition to Wilson, Burgess, and French, such ranking municipal officials as the police director, the city engineer, and the head of public works became heavily involved in war charities and patriotic causes. Their solidly entrenched positions, combined with the essential unity of their views, shaped Verdun's responses to the war. With little fuss, they made possible the success of Wilson's ultrapatriotic agenda. Top-ranking city employees led or attended committee meetings of various wartime groups, organized municipal resources in aid of patriotic causes, and often simply added the prestige of their presence to special war-related events. Although their efforts were not always officially those of the city, most of their war-related activities implied municipal sanction.

The local administration's enthusiasm for the war effort matched that of many Verdunites. No serious disagreements took place in council over the principle of cooperation with Ottawa on military matters or over the city's material and financial contributions to the war. The authorities were able to commit the resources of Verdun – the majority of whose landholding ratepayers were French speaking and Catholic – without evoking significant protest.[5] Backed by rock-solid support from the city's English-speaking electorate, Wilson's views normally dominated council and, in general, reflected those of both of Verdun's linguistic communities. Political opposition to measures supporting the war, as occurred in some Quebec municipalities, would have been difficult in Verdun; there is no evidence of explicit antiwar sentiment on city council.

Verdun's official involvement in the home-front war had many facets. Few assemblies of patriotic-minded citizens or fundraising ventures took place without some form of cooperation from the city. City hall opened its facilities to many local groups involved in war work. Meeting rooms, parks, and playgrounds were available free of charge. It also provided administrative, material, or financial support to many activities. Sometimes aid simply consisted of granting permits to groups wishing to assemble or canvass on behalf of a war charity. The administration's commitment was present in virtually all of Verdun's patriotic undertakings.

Municipal Politics, 1939-45

Every two years Verdunites voted for a mayor and eight aldermen, two from each ward. As discussed in Chapter 2, more than half of all Verdunites and most of the city's English speakers lived in west-end Ward 4. Therefore six aldermen represented the three small eastern wards, while two represented most of the population. The landlords in each ward directly elected four of the aldermen, and these aldermen made up the city council's executive committee, which voted all municipal spending. Elections took place the first Monday in April in 1939, 1941, 1943, and 1945. Voting was almost entirely a male right, as only women owning businesses in Verdun and married female property owners voted in municipal elections.[6]

Edward Wilson and the populist mayor Hervé Ferland had developed an antagonistic and bitter relationship during the Depression, and the 1939 election divided the electorate mainly along linguistic lines. Of the 517 Verdunites who signed Wilson's nomination papers, only 22 had French surnames.[7] In a pre-election advertisement in the *Guardian*, Wilson assured French-speaking voters that he would be "everybody's mayor without distinction of class, race or religion."[8] He aimed his bilingual message at the large French Canadian minority in Verdun as well as at Verdun's landlords, most of whom were French speaking and whose control of the city's executive committee Wilson had opposed from its inception in 1933. Wilson's promise suggests social divisions in the community that voters might have remembered at election time.

In uniting most of the English-speaking electorate, however, Wilson stood a good chance of winning. He won by a close margin, but the *Guardian* believed he had polled reasonably well among French-speaking voters, which "proved that the population at large favoured a change."[9] Of the eight aldermen elected along with Wilson, the two representing west-end Ward 4 were English speaking, while the six elected from Wards 1, 2, and 3 were French speaking. (Four of these were Wilson allies who had long wanted to unseat Ferland, a mayor with a reputation for extravagance and a questionable use of his municipal office.) This pattern repeated itself with only minor variations in 1941, 1943, and 1945. Most of the aldermen elected throughout this period, save one or two French speakers per council, sided with Wilson on most issues, even while sitting on the executive committee. Wilson and the French-speaking aldermen, especially some of the landowners, had been united in their dislike for Ferland and his generous spending on public relief efforts during the Depression. This solidarity continued after Wilson's election to the mayoralty and greatly eased his ability to engage the city in wartime activities. As a whole, Verdun's wartime city council, despite its linguistic imbalance, generally represented the views of Verdun's war-minded English-speaking majority.

Although the candidates' attitudes towards the war may have influenced some voters, Verdun's municipal contests were fought on local issues. For example, in 1941, despite the city's increasing war effort, a full-page Wilson campaign advertisement in the *Guardian* noted only two points: the candidate's irreproachable honesty and his success in driving out slot machines from the backrooms of certain local establishments.[10]

One ongoing divisive issue was the existence of the executive committee, made up of French-speaking proprietors, which controlled the city's budget. Wilson was outraged that the non-executive committee aldermen could not authorize the purchase of "a lead pencil" and so were no more than the landlords' "waterboys."[11] Throughout the war he campaigned for the committee's abolition. He felt it to be a "prostitution of justice" and fundamentally undemocratic. The English-speaking community perceived the committee's election by landlords as reducing most Verdunites "to serfdom," as one opponent of the executive committee phrased it.[12] Over 90 percent of Verdunites were tenants. But the arguments against the committee continued to be based on language as much as on class or principle. One person identified in the *Guardian* only as "a proprietor of Ward 4" claimed that the municipal structure eliminated "the inherent rights of the British subjects of Verdun." This letter writer did not believe that the interests of English speakers could be adequately served by French speakers on city council. "The net result of this remarkable electoral system," he noted with some exaggeration, "is that the minority rule the majority."[13] Another writer reminded all English-speaking men that it was imperative to vote for Wilson.[14] Even if these letters were attempts to mobilize electoral support for Wilson, the issue in them was language representation, not wards or population distribution. This issue divided the French Canadian landlords from the English-speaking working class. Sensing the potential for linguistic animosity, Wilson consistently attempted to make the matter solely one of class, given that the system also disadvantaged French-speaking tenants.

On polling day 1941 Wilson owed his narrow win over Ferland to English-speaking electors, especially from Wards 3 and 4.[15] Class was also an issue, because lower-income French-speaking residents of Wards 1 and 2 considered Ferland, the combative Depression-era mayor, as one of their own. One woman in Ward 2 remembered him as "the poor people's mayor" and claimed that he was "a god in the older sections of Verdun. Everyone there liked Ferland."[16] One factor that worked against Wilson was that hundreds of Verdun men, the vast majority of them English speakers from Wards 3 and 4, were away on active service and could not vote. One soldier, unaware of the election outcome, wrote the mayor from overseas that he was "keeping his fingers crossed as I realize that a greater number of the voting power of Ward 4 must be on Active Service."[17]

Most aldermen elected in 1941 were Wilson followers, four of them resided in Ward 4, and all of them, like Wilson, were proprietors and merchants. Few disputes based on language marred council deliberations, although ethnicity at least influenced some political outlooks. Council sessions scrupulously avoided the divisive 1942 conscription debate. In fact, no resolutions were passed in the period 1939-45 that criticized Canada's conduct of the war, unlike what occurred in many other communities across the province.

In no wartime election did English speakers bother to stand for office in Wards 1 and 2, and only one of two Ward 4 candidates was English speaking until 1945, when both were English speaking. It was inevitable that French speakers would dominate city council. Not surprisingly, ward redistribution was hotly debated and, in July 1943, council agreed to extend ward boundaries a few streets westward, significantly increasing the number of English speakers in Ward 3 without decreasing the proportion of English speakers in Ward 4.[18] Although this change only slightly affected the ward populations, it facilitated the election of an English speaker in Ward 3 – probably an acceptable compromise to both language groups.

The linguistic imbalance in council, particularly on the executive committee, made the English-speaking community keen to have one of its own win the mayoralty, which had veto power over council resolutions. Wilson used this veto infrequently, however, largely because of council's cooperative attitude and his fear of splitting the community along language lines. Most of Wilson's support continued to come from English speakers. In 1943 one of his campaign advertisements listed 212 residents who supported him; only 12 had French names.[19]

In 1943 Wilson stood again on his record of fiscal responsibility, balanced budgets, no new loans, and no tax increases. This demonstrated administrative success appealed strongly to Verdunites of both language groups, especially proprietors. With little risk of alienating French-language voters, Wilson also trumpeted his heavy personal involvement in patriotic causes: "I feel I can say without fear of contradiction that since the outbreak of war I have striven conscientiously to provide ... leadership and to encourage the people of our City to give their maximum support in every way possible both to our armed forces and to our government. Needless to say, I shall continue to do so ... Verdun has justly gained the reputation of being one of the most patriotic communities in the Dominion. With your help, I want to do everything I can to maintain that reputation and even to surpass our previous contributions to the war effort."[20] On the surface, the municipal election, as usual, was not especially linked to patriotic issues, although Wilson's prominent war-related activities helped define his candidacy. Wilson was easily re-elected, 5,567 votes to 3,773, doubling his margin of victory. Thrilled at the outcome, the *Guardian* reminded readers that English-speaking voters were "in large percentage ... of the staunch, old, conservative British stock, who believe in the established tradition of British fair play."[21]

The English-speaking community assumed that if Wilson lost the mayoralty it would be due to the absence overseas of many of his patriotic (English-speaking) followers. One anonymous resident wrote the *Guardian* complaining that Verdunites on active service should be allowed to vote, since 90 percent of them were likely to vote for Wilson. Gunner William J. Swain, an artilleryman serving in Britain, wrote an appreciative letter to Wilson upon receiving his carton of cigarettes from the Mayor's Cigarette Fund. Swain told Wilson that he hoped to be "back in Verdun when they hold another election because I'd vote for you 100 times using a different name each time just to see you as Mayor of Verdun." The cigarette-supplying mayor was popular with the troops and also with the men's families. One Verdun women whose brother was overseas wrote Wilson: "Thanks so very much for your wonderful interest in the Verdun boys – you sure [are] a good mayor."[22] Wilson's support of the local and national war efforts did him no harm electorally, as he knew. Wilson was both a patriot and a politician, and each role served the other well.

During the 1945 campaign Wilson emphasized the expectation that Verdun would suffer widespread unemployment as a result of military demobilization. He stressed Verdun's need for an experienced administrator able to provide political continuity into the postwar period. Wilson claimed that this stability would benefit the returning men and the entire community. Some opposition to the mayor was generated as a result of his well-known CCF leanings. He was denounced as a "socialist" by a newly formed group calling itself the United Citizens' Association of Verdun as well as by the Verdun Voters' League, whose members included tenants and proprietors from both language groups.[23] But ideological opposition to Wilson seemed a hard sell in Verdun in 1945.

The population voted for continuity and re-elected Wilson by a count of 6,817 to 4,945, an increased majority once again. Wilson won every poll in Ward 4, won Ward 3, and did reasonably well in Wards 1 and 2. The votes of already discharged servicemen improved his showing. The Verdun Voters' League lamented the results, claiming that they indicated "a split between the two principal racial elements living in Verdun," which was only partly true.[24] The lack of meaningful criticism regarding Wilson's leadership had helped him garner support from a wide cross-section of Verdun's population, including even some east-end French speakers. Five of eight aldermen elected were French speakers; one alderman elected from Ward 3 and both from Ward 4 (including one to the executive committee) were English speakers.

Verdun's wartime municipal elections were quiet affairs, eliciting moderate interest compared to the highly charged provincial and federal contests described in Chapter 7. The war was infrequently an issue, and war-related matters affecting Verdun, such as war employment and soldiers' civil re-establishment, rarely surfaced. Wilson proved a popular and capable mayor. No grassroots movement was ever organized in an attempt to dislodge him from office. Still, his French-speaking opponents in each of three wartime elections obtained the support of most French speakers who voted, and Wilson's re-election was always due to the bloc voting behaviour of English speakers. It was more likely for a French speaker to vote for Wilson than for an English speaker to vote for one of Wilson's opponents. Language remained an important political issue in municipal elections, as it was in most social matters.

Enemy Aliens and National Registration

Even before Canada declared war against Germany on 10 September 1939, Wilson and Verdun's police director, Alfred Dubeau, had contacted the Royal Canadian Mounted Police and the Quebec Provincial Police for information "in connection with ... taking every precaution to safeguard public property and public utilities from damage during the present war crisis as well as for the maintenance of public order."[25] Even though there were few strategic facilities in Verdun (this changed in 1941 with the establishment of an important war plant; see Chapter 5), Wilson had ordered the posting of guards at public buildings and along the aqueduct that formed the city's northwest limits.[26] Spies, traitors, and saboteurs were widely believed to be active in Canada. To be better informed of potential threats, federal government policies, and civic responsibilities, on the day Canada declared war, Burgess wrote to the King's Printer for two copies in English of *Regulations Regarding the Defence of Canada* (at 25 cents each).[27]

The city continued to provide relief payments to men enlisting and to members of the militia called out for emergency "anti-sabotage service" until they had received their first service pay.[28] Municipal employees who enlisted received two weeks' salary and a promise of their jobs back after demobilization.[29] City hall not only encouraged a patriotic popular response to the war but welcomed the accompanying diminution in relief expenditures.

In the late spring of 1940, the rapidly deteriorating military situation in France heightened Canadians' fears of "fifth column" activity. In May, Verdun's branch of the Canadian Corps Association (CCA) announced that it had prepared a "black-list" of suspected Nazi sympathizers and warned that CCA members would be on the alert against disloyal utterances. Verdun's CCA branch also requested that area municipalities discharge all known pacifists and communists on their payrolls and reminded civic leaders that residents of German origin had to be watched closely. According to the 1941 Dominion census, only 376 German and 295 Italian ethnics lived in Verdun, many Canadian-born, totalling less than 0.1 percent of residents. The small number of enemy aliens limited intracommunity ethnic conflict, and municipal administrators showed civility and fair-mindedness in paying relief to the families of interned men. In September 1939, for example, Herman Schmid, a German national who lived with his wife and teenaged son on Fifth Avenue, was interned. Mrs Schmid obtained municipal relief payments (paid by Ottawa) from November 1939 to February 1940. Gino Martellani of east-end Regina Avenue was interned in June 1940, obliging his wife and two sons, aged six and two, to obtain municipal relief for the next four months.[30]

This vigilante mood during desperate times was reflected at the municipal level. On 27 May city council unanimously passed the following resolution: "Verdun hereby offers ... to the Department of National Defence its full cooperation towards the prevention of subversive propaganda against the state in this time of stress, when the loyal support of every true Canadian is required for the prosecution of the war."[31] The minister of national defence, Norman Rogers, reassured the city that steps had been taken to curtail the potentially harmful activities of enemy aliens but did not rule out accepting Verdun's rather vague offer of assistance. Meanwhile, Wilson insisted on greater vigilance from the Verdun police.[32]

Two weeks following Italy's declaration of war against Britain and France on 10 June 1940, the executive committee rescinded the right of M. Miniucci to operate a restaurant at the city-operated swimming pool, the Natatorium.[33] The only grounds for this action seemed to be the man's Italian origin. Nevertheless, for unexplained reasons, Miniucci was allowed to operate another concession at the Verdun Auditorium without protest from the community until the Department of National Defence took over the auditorium a year later. When the restaurateur sought compensation for his loss of business and Ottawa refused his request, the city paid him $600, which it insisted it was not obliged to do.[34] This denouement suggests that Verdunites did not feel threatened by nor vindictive towards citizens of enemy-alien origin. Nevertheless, soon after Italy's entry into the war, some local Italian merchants complained of slander organized against them. There is some evidence that the merchants were labelled as fifth columnists by their business competitors, indicating ethnic animosity could be manufactured for local personal gain.[35]

These incidents occurred during a particularly bleak period of the war. Verdun reacted with concern, perhaps even on occasion with prejudice and paranoia, only when Allied fortunes were waning. Yet no physical attacks were reported on enemy-alien minorities in Verdun, nor did the city support petitions from various groups requesting curtailment of the liberties of enemy aliens.[36] Although municipal leaders could not know this in 1939-40, no incidents linked to saboteurs or enemy propagandists occurred in Verdun during the war.

The city also had to deal with national mobilization for home defence and the inconveniences caused by this limited form of conscription. Although Wilson did what he could to cooperate with federal authorities, this sensitive issue elicited considerable debate in city council. In June 1940 Parliament passed the National Resources Mobilization Act (NRMA), which called for an inventory of the nation's material and human resources. National registration took place 19-21 August. All Canadians sixteen and over had to register with the government to obtain a national identity card, which they had to keep with them at all times. This card was necessary to secure employment, vote, or engage in other activities requiring official identification. Single men and childless widowers aged twenty-one to forty-five registered under the provisions of the act were liable to military mobilization for home defence.[37]

Nearly 50,000 Verdunites were required to register with federal authorities. Registration facilities were set up in each of the city's four wards. Verdun's two chief registrars were drawn from each of the French- and English-language communities.[38] The registration process went smoothly, despite the call of Montreal's mayor, Camillien Houde, to ignore the government order on the grounds that it was a prelude to conscription – a move that resulted in his arrest and internment. Thirteen boards were established across Canada to review requests for exemption or postponement from NRMA military service. One of the three members of Montreal's exemption board was Dr Charles Barr, a local dentist who was chief warden of Verdun's Civilian Protection Committee and a Liberal Party organizer in Verdun. Men engaged in farm labour or in essential civil or industrial work were eligible for exemptions, as were men with valid personal reasons, including conscientious objection. Each case was reviewed on its merits. Nationally, exemptions or postponements were granted in 89 percent of the cases.[39]

At a Verdun city council meeting in September 1942, a rare disagreement on war policy arose over whether policemen and firemen might obtain city support in applying for NRMA service exemptions. Edward Wilson and Alderman Robert Scurrah opposed exemptions from service for these men. The other council members, all French speaking, argued that these men were engaged in essential service to the community. They also reminded the mayor of the high cost of recruiting and training new members for the police and fire departments – a major motivation for attempting to defer their military service.[40] Several aldermen suggested that patriotism sometimes cost the city too much. For them, local issues superseded national ones, even in wartime.

Council divided along language lines on this issue; despite Wilson and Scurrah's vehement protests, council authorized Burgess to contact city employees who had been called to duty and notify them that, if they desired, the city would request their release from service. The aldermen were anxious to secure the discharge of the city's trained security and civil defence personnel, and some of the men were pleased to return to their civilian occupations. The executive committee approached the Department of National War Services to obtain a blanket exemption for the city's policemen and firemen. Although the authorities refused, it hardly mattered, since thirty-four of thirty-eight Verdun policemen and firemen obtained exemptions between 1942 and 1944.[41]

The executive committee's views were contrary to Wilson's strong desire to assist the national war effort – in this case, even over the interests of his own city. The majority of city council members were less zealous to incur such a sacrifice.[42] Yet their actions should not be interpreted as "unpatriotic." They did not necessarily oppose national mobilization or prosecution of the war; as responsible municipal officials, they looked to public safety first. For them, patriotism began at home, not overseas. Wilson and Scurrah, in contrast, represented the view that the national war effort came first; a lesser commitment would be a lesser form of patriotism. On this issue, British Verdun did not get its way.

The Mayor's Cigarette Fund

In December 1940, the city created the Mayor's Cigarette Fund for Verdun Soldiers Overseas, Verdun's most popular war charity. An inspired creation, the MCF was a unique and high-profile wartime symbol of Verdun's patriotism. It raised funds to purchase cigarettes for dispatch twice yearly to Verdunites on active service overseas. This fund, more than any other local patriotic charity, expressed the community's commitment to the war and particularly to Verdunites' role in it. Mayor Edward Wilson, nominal head of the organization, lent his name and the prestige of his office and allowed the city to manage the charitable donations of thousands of residents. The MCF was Verdun's most inclusive communitywide fundraising campaign, open to and benefiting people from all linguistic, religious, and class backgrounds. The only prerequisites were that the recipients be Verdunites and posted overseas.

Cigarettes were probably the most popular "comfort" craved by overseas servicemen. Families, friends, employers, church groups, and voluntary organizations sent them regularly. Two huge national fundraising organizations, the Buckshee Fund and the Overseas Cigarette Fund, provided cigarettes for general distribution to Canadian troops from stockpiles overseas. The national Imperial Order Daughters of the Empire alone sent Canadian troops 6.7 million cigarettes in the year ending June 1943, while the Red Cross dispatched a staggering 25 million in the war's first three years.[43] But Verdun was probably the only Canadian municipality (and certainly the only one of those approaching its size) to organize an ongoing fundraising campaign on behalf of residents serving overseas. Every dollar raised went towards the purchase of cigarettes for local servicemen, and later servicewomen, and in a tight community like Verdun, this proved a strong incentive for donating.[44] Wilson's fund followed a local precedent: during the First World War the city had established the Verdun Overseas Tobacco Fund.[45]

Wilson, City Manager Joseph French, and City Clerk Arthur Burgess administered the MCF, and its official treasurer was the city's chief accountant, L.J. Grondin.[46] For most of the war, René Patenaude, the mayor's secretary, organized and managed the fund. The *Guardian* described the work of compiling and updating the mailing lists and arranging for the cigarette shipments with several tobacco firms as a "gigantic task ... the magnitude of which cannot easily be realized." Patenaude maintained a file-card index of all recipients, into which he entered their ranks, units, and home addresses. The MCF incurred few overhead costs, as all work was done by volunteers or city employees.[47] For a serviceman to become a recipient, a relative or friend simply had to send city hall one of the registration coupons published weekly in the local press.

From March 1940 on, tobacco companies and the federal government facilitated the shipping of cigarettes. A special rate of one dollar, post-paid, for a carton of 300 cigarettes was available to anyone sending cigarettes or tobacco to a member of the armed forces serving overseas. Federal and provincial duties were waived. The MCF placed all orders directly with the tobacco companies, which ensured that they were filled and dispatched to intended recipients.[48] Paul Fussell, documenting the similar American practice of cheaply dispatching cigarettes to overseas servicemen, has noted that tobacco manufacturers assured steady orders by advertising the great morale value of their products. Purchasing cigarettes thus became an act of patriotism, and it was no less so in Canada. Subsequently, various Canadian tobacco funds' shipments went out in bulk and individual gifts were drawn from company stockpiles in the United Kingdom, northwest Europe, and Italy.[49]

Just before Christmas 1940, the very active Verdun unit of the Women's Volunteer Reserve Corps (WVRC) organized a "tag day" for the MCF – one of the most effective ways of obtaining donations. The "taggers" solicited money from passersby and, if a donation was forthcoming, pinned a strip of paper (the tag) in the form of a cigarette or other icon on the donor's lapel. This event yielded over $600.[50] The WVRC worked tirelessly on behalf of the MCF. It held major tag days every October from 1941 to 1944 and organized numerous special events to contribute to the MCF's coffers. The *Guardian* supported these initiatives and printed registration coupons, reports on the fund's affairs, and thank-you letters from Verdunites overseas. Verdun's bilingual newspaper, the *Messenger*, also ran MCF registration coupons, although surviving coupons in municipal archives indicate that families of Verdun's overseas servicemen were overwhelmingly English speaking and read the *Guardian*. The MCF was the best-publicized fund in the community.

In March 1941, Verdun's first shipment of 691 cartons of cigarettes left for Britain. Each package enclosed a note from city hall, which read in part, "This gesture reflects the admiration and gratitude we feel towards you." This reminder was no doubt sincere, but including it did no harm to Mayor Wilson's standing in the community.[51] Over the next few years Verdun's remarkable enlistment rate dramatically swelled the MCF's files and made constant fundraising imperative.

Supporting the Fund

The Mayor's Cigarette Fund was extremely popular in Verdun; no group or person was above contributing, and no amount was too small. Individuals, social groups, institutions, and the municipality itself organized collections, canvassing activities, and benefit events. Both federal and provincial entertainment taxes were waived for shows, films, and performances staged for a registered war charity, which the MCF officially became in October 1941.[52] Owing to the MCF's clear local affiliation, by 1941 it overtook the Red Cross in popularity among Verdun war charities. A major MCF tag day that October was hailed by the *Guardian* as "one of the most important events of the year."[53]

On 7 October 1944, Verdun High School's air cadets took up strategic locations in the city, acting as MCF taggers. Earlier, the *Guardian* had lauded the local character of the MCF: "The appeal is not an ordinary one. It is one that is made in the personal name of sons, husbands, brothers, sisters and other relatives of scores of people in the city. None ... would hesitate to hand over the price of the ... cigarettes if those boys and girls were to meet them on the street and ask them for the smokes. Those boys and girls are unable to do so, they are engaged in a grim, bloody business."[54] The air cadets raised $850 and, added to donations made by social organizations and businesses, made the MCF's net take over $1,700 on this day alone.[55]

The idea of supplying local men and women with comforts bought by Verdunites themselves struck a responsive chord. Almost every social and community group in Verdun, it seems, supported the MCF at some point during the war. For example, in December 1941, the Verdun Women's Club gave $50, the Verdun Horticultural Society parted with $12.50, and the Verdun Motor Boat Club donated $15.[56] In April 1942, the Verdun United Church ladies basketball team held a benefit game in aid of the MCF, while Catholic St Willibrord Parish organized a boxing tournament that yielded $100 for the fund. An evening's proceeds from the Verdun Dance Pavilion yielded $329; even the orchestra played for free.[57] Verdun's Canadian Legion and Canadian Corps Association branches were regular and generous contributors. So too was the Verdun branch of the Red Cross, of which Mayor

Wilson was the chairman, which itself canvassed the city for funds. The Verdun Operatic Society offered the comparatively huge sum of $175 in May 1945. The city also donated $200 to the fund's first year of operations.[58]

In 1942 St Willibrord's inaugurated its own cigarette fund for parishioners overseas, supported by the proceeds of various public church socials. But it did not forget Verdun's overseas Protestants or French speakers. "Realizing that many of our friends ... are not of our faith or language," wrote the parish priest, Father E.J. Lapointe, "we are ... doing something for 'Their Boys.'" Accordingly, the parish diverted more than $60 to the MCF in a gesture typical of Verdun's wartime community spirit.[59] On Christmas Day 1943 the 1,500 patrons of the Verdun Palace Theatre all directly contributed to the cigarette fund by attending the Hollywood film *Captains of the Clouds*, which depicted Canada's British Commonwealth Air Training Plan. The day's receipts of $414 were turned over to city hall.[60] Other businesses and employees' groups also contributed. Imperial Tobacco, a not-disinterested player, set up impressive displays (and collection boxes) for the MCF in the lobbies of movie theatres in Verdun and even in the Montreal district of Notre-Dame-de-Grâce.

Many French-speaking groups in Verdun contributed as well, although few seemed to do so before 1943. The Cercle Ste-Jeanne-d'Arc, the Club de Raquetteurs LaFontaine, the Ligue des Propriétaires de Verdun, and the Ordre des Filles d'Isabelle all donated. The *nationaliste* Société Saint-Jean-Baptiste, Notre-Dame-de-la-Paix Parish, from east-end Verdun, contributed $50 in October 1944. Notwithstanding the eruption of a renewed conscription crisis at the time or an earlier decision by Société Saint-Jean-Baptiste headquarters in Montreal to stop contributing to patriotic charities, Verdun's Société remained devoted to the causes of Verdunites at war. By 1944, many French speakers living in the central and eastern neighbourhoods of the city were regular contributors, and most notables from the French-speaking community, especially politicians, merchants, and professionals, responded to city hall's solicitations.[61] The MCF was not about language; it was about community.

Every summer from 1941 to 1944, children were granted permits to set up candy or lemonade stands on city streets or to hold neighbourhood concerts to benefit the fund. Some young people sold or raffled their toys to buy cigarettes for the troops. Surviving lists show that most of the youngsters were English speaking. Wilson sent encouraging letters of appreciation to the children organizing these efforts. In 1942 he wrote one girl, "I am sure that your parents must feel very proud of you and I want you to know that we are all very glad indeed to have the help of such splendid little workers. It must make you feel very pleased to realize that you have had a part in sending cigarettes to our Verdun soldiers, and to our sailors and airmen too, who are now on the other side of the ocean."[62] Jean Tarr, who led a small "Victory Club" that met every week in the west end, wrote the mayor in

October 1943: "Four of us girls are making letter racks, brooches, etc. etc. and we are going to sell them and give the money to some war fund. We were wondering if you could send us a permit to sell these things. We are between the ages of thirteen and fourteen." Wilson suggested the cigarette fund as a worthy recipient of their fundraising, and within a month a cheque arrived at city hall for $5.[63]

"A Wonderful Thing"

Within a year of the fund's creation, MCF files contained the names of 1,233 men, who received a carton of cigarettes in time for Christmas 1941.[64] By the summer of 1944, the MCF had raised over $10,000 and sent 2.8 million cigarettes to approximately 2,400 men and women overseas. Despite the growing number of recipients, the MCF was never short of cash. Over 1.5 million cigarettes went out in 1944 alone. In January 1945, over 3,000 Verdunites overseas remained registered with the fund, while hundreds of others previously listed had returned to Canada, been discharged, or become casualties. The MCF sent 3.7 million cigarettes, even to prisoners of war.[65]

City hall received hundreds of letters and cards of acknowledgment following each biannual shipment. Many of the replies evoked the same sentiment: pride in coming from a city that so strongly supported its overseas servicemen. The gifts were greatly valued in cigarette-deprived Britain and helped alleviate stress at the front. Tobacco products often became currency for the men, and extraordinary security surrounded the overseas depots established by such groups as the Canadian Legion and the Buckshee Fund.[66] Some servicemen, on leave or discharged, even visited city hall to thank the mayor personally for the city's generosity.

The words of Verdun's servicemen speak for themselves. Trooper W. Gibson, 27th Canadian Armoured Regiment (The Sherbrooke Fusiliers), wrote in the aftermath of some difficult fighting in Normandy: "a fellow smokes a terrific number of cigarettes when in action in a tank – it helps relieve his nerves."[67] Another soldier put his thoughts in simple verse:

When the road is hot and weary
and it's 10 minutes for a smoke
with cigarettes at a premium
and a sapper that is broke
13 more days to pay day
and the post man brings a gift
thanks a million friends
for giving a guy a lift.[68]

Pte W.D. MacDonald, Royal Canadian Ordnance Corps, who signed his lengthy letter "a Verdun Defender," admitted, "when we have plenty of smokes things in general are much easier to bear, but to be without a fag seems to darken the outlook on most everything."[69] One soldier stationed in Britain reported, "Not only are the cigarettes welcome because of the high cost of tobacco in this country, and (strictly between ourselves) the superiority of Canadian 'smokes,' but also because they are a great reminder that those back home are thinking of us as we of them." Petty Officer Frank Harris, Royal Canadian Naval Volunteer Reserve (RCNVR), serving aboard the destroyer HMCS *St Clair*, stated simply, "It makes one proud to be able to say, 'I come from Verdun.'"[70]

But perhaps the most poignant letter of thanks was penned on 20 August 1942, by a soldier who, the previous day, had survived the carnage on the beach at Dieppe. Lance-Cpl J. Flood, RCASC, wrote:

> I wish to take this opportunity to thank you for the three hundred cigarettes which I received tonight and I can tell you, Sir, [they] were a wonderful thing to get after coming back from our first taste of real war ... I suppose you all heard over the air we were in France on the morning of the 19th. It is a morning I will never forget. I seen my buddies killed one after the other on all sides of me. We did what we went to do and that is the mane thing, and I can tell you all the men were tickled when they new they were going. You never saw a happier bunch of men in all your life. There were quite a few boys from Verdun like myself and I am proude some Verdun boys were in it.[71]

Verdunites used their gift of cigarettes to indulge in a little intercity rivalry. Sgt George Cobb, Royal Canadian Ordnance Corps, whose unit contained a large number of Verdunites, recalled that "it was a password in our unit, 'Have one on the Mayor.'" "I honestly hope the surrounding municipalities of Verdun follow your example," remarked Gunner Jack Holt, RCA: "we have a few other chaps here from around Montreal and they often wish they could get some smokes from their city."[72] One soldier bragged "whenever I rec[eive] cigarettes from you I show (and share [with]) the boys, and say, 'Now there's the kind [of] town you should come from.' And that always calls for an argument. But they always admit Verdun must have something."[73] Most Verdunites overseas agreed. "A Verdunite in India" reported that he was "very proud to tell anybody down here what a wonderful city we have no matter how far from it I may be."[74] In 1941 Trooper F.H. Colligan wrote: "These tokens from our fellow citizens serve well to remind us that our home is not just our relatives, but the people around them and the atmosphere of the town in which they live ... [O]ur civic pride increases immeasurably. After the job is over I feel sure we will make better citizens for this appreciation of our home town."[75]

Some non-Verdunites were lucky enough to receive cigarettes, and were no less appreciative. Roland Gélinas, RCASC, attached to the 18th Canadian Field Ambulance, a Franco-American barely literate in English, wrote: "I am very thankfull to know that my name was given to the MCF of Verdun as I have not live in Verdun.

I really love that City. Along the waterfront it is very pretty. If I ever come out of this war as I am when I am writing the letter I will make Verdun my home." A note on the *Guardian* MCF coupon that was sent in on behalf of Gélinas states: "This fellow is an American from Chisholm, Maine who came here in June 1940 to enlist. He considers our home his home now."[76] Patenaude had duly registered him into the fund.

Other soldiers claimed more comfort from the knowledge that their community remembered them than from the cigarettes themselves. Following the receipt of his gift of cigarettes, Sgt P.A. Tremblay of the Royal 22e Régiment wrote, in English: "We are training very hard and are impatiently waiting for a 'tête-à-tête' with Herr Hitler. I guess that if he doesn't show up pretty soon, we'll have to go there and dig him out. Although there is a considerable distance separating us from our beautiful home-town, your kindness and sympathy give us courage and determination and we are all looking forward to the brightness of the future ahead. Thanking you again, I take pride in calling myself a son of Verdun."[77] One grateful airman wrote: "Words seem so inexpensive ... when you ... put them against actions of kindness such as this, but when we realize that our folks at home are behind us, doing things to help make things easier – well it puts more heart into the job we've set out to do and we swing into it with grim precision."[78]

Overseas Verdunites occasionally used the MCF as a convenient conduit of information and requests. Gunner L.S. Blampied sent along two snapshots of the English gravesite of a fellow Verdunite, Sgt F.J.E. Jennings, "killed due to enemy action." Blampied requested that the photos be turned over to Jennings's mother.[79] Some Verdunites used the fund to reach their own families. The *Guardian* published a letter from one man who complained he had received no letters from his family in a long time.[80] The newspaper insisted that it was the patriotic duty of all Verdunites to correspond with family members in the military. Readers no doubt understood that failure to do so might result in an embarrassing letter from a son or husband appearing in the local press. "I haven't heard from my home for quite a while," another soldier told the MCF, "I would appreciate it if you [would] check on this and tell them I am anxious to hear from them."[81] Yet another asked the MCF to prompt his parents to write him, as he had not heard a word in five months, despite repeated letters on his part.[82]

Some soldiers, while not forgotten, received few gifts from home because their families were poor. For these men, the MCF made an even greater difference. One Verdun woman in difficult financial circumstances wrote a grateful letter to city hall: "As I am a widow with my only son overseas, I am indeed grateful for your kindness in sending cigarettes to [him]. Forty dollars per month pension [Dependants' Allowance], and the little bit of work I can do, does not give me much chance to send him a lot. So I am indeed thankful for anything that is sent to him."[83] Following the fund's inaugural shipment, Sgt Leslie Frost, of the Black Watch, noted that the families of many Verdunites could not afford to send gifts: "We Verdunites who are over here so far from dear old Verdun were all taken by surprise at receiving these smokes and I don't mind telling you that there [were] many envious glances in our direction from those chaps who unfortunately were not from Verdun. I think the [Verdun] chaps who were most surprised were the ones who for financial reasons never get anything from home. They feel now that at least they have something to boast about."[84] Many Verdun soldiers had little money overseas. Lance-Cpl Jack Cape, Canadian Provost Corps, wrote that "smoking in [Britain] at the present time is too expensive for a private soldier."[85] Pte Raymond Brodeur, of the Fusiliers Mont-Royal, informed the fund that cigarettes were very expensive and "this constitutes the greatest expenditure from our salaries." He added: "You've greatly pleased one of your own, on active service for his country."[86]

The soldiers themselves believed that no municipality emulated Verdun's example. Pte Ernest Meilleur, Royal 22e Régiment, wrote: "Yours is the only city in the greater Montreal area to have made this generous gesture. I am proud to be part of such a noble city which looks after its citizens."[87] A year later another soldier reported, "so far as I know, no other city has looked after there [sic] fellows overseas as well as our city."[88] A supervisor of the YMCA's overseas war services also singled out the fund for special praise. "Organizations and groups such as yours," he wrote, "are doing a splendid job toward Canada's War Effort. It may not seem much to you but to we men who are dealing with the moral[e] of the Canadian Forces Overseas, it certainly is a wonderful job. It is to organizations such as yours that the Canadian people will turn their thanks when this war is over."[89]

In October 1945 the MCF's status as a war charity was renewed, but its fundraising activities were nearly at an end. The remaining cash on hand was used to purchase cigarettes for distribution to Verdun veterans in Montreal-area military hospitals.[90] The Mayor's Cigarette Fund ceased operations on 31 December 1946 and was officially terminated as a war charity on 7 February 1947.[91] But the effects of the war persisted long after the fighting had stopped and Canadian war charities had been dissolved. As late as Christmas 1949, the city of Verdun purchased fifty cigarettes for each of the sixty-five Verdunites still suffering in veterans' hospitals. Edward Wilson and Arthur Burgess personally delivered the gifts.[92]

Verdun's cigarette fund could have originated and received such overwhelming support only in a community with a strong sense of local identity and community spirit. The MCF contributed to a feeling of wartime cooperation among French and English speakers and united them in a shared view of local and national patriotism. At the local, grassroots level, so clearly represented by the MCF, Verdun's war was based in community cooperation, not competition. Moreover, the MCF cemented ties between Verdunites on the home front and those on the battle front. That Edward Wilson was the public face of the fund was appropriate and entirely in keeping with his patriotic spirit and concern for his fellow citizens.

HMCS *Dunver*: "Verdun's own Frigate"

In 1943 the Royal Canadian Navy named a warship after Verdun – sort of. The honour was fitting, given the large number of Verdunites in the navy and the heightened interest in Canada's role in the war at sea that this generated among thousands of residents. In addition to the oddity of the name itself, the process of naming the ship laid bare some of the local politics of language in Verdun. But more importantly, the warship representing this patriotic community enabled a broadly based, grassroots show of support for the ship and its crewmen and reflected the pride Verdunites felt for their city's and their townspeople's role in the prosecution of the war.

The Politics of Naming

In 1940 Commander Eric S. Brand, Royal Navy, suggested in a staff meeting at Naval Service Headquarters (NSHQ) in Ottawa that, despite an apparent willingness on the part of the Royal Canadian Navy to name its newly built corvettes after flowers, as was the practice in the Royal Navy, it might be best to name new Canadian warships for towns and cities since "flowers do not knit socks."[93] The obvious implication was that the naming of ships offered the opportunity to link Canadians directly to the naval war while at the same time improving shipboard conditions for sailors. A purposeful and carefully managed ship-naming policy was born. NSHQ ranked Canadian cities and towns with populations over 2,800 to create a list of potential ships' names.[94] A namesake ship could serve as a prize for the patriotic.

In November 1941, Verdun's MP, Paul-Émile Côté, wrote to Angus L. Macdonald, minister of national defence for naval services, to inquire about the possibility of naming a warship of the expanding RCN in honour of the city of Verdun. Côté wrote at the request of municipal officials. Macdonald responded that, as there was already a ship named *Verdun* in commission with the Royal Navy, it would be impossible to christen a Canadian ship "Verdun."[95] To avoid communications confusion, no names could be repeated among Commonwealth naval forces.

In the meantime, with so many Verdunites serving in the navy and one of them, Able Seaman Michael Scullion, a local hero for his role in the sinking of a German submarine, support was growing in Verdun for a namesake warship.[96] In September 1942, NSHQ informed Mayor Wilson that, "in view of the importance of your City in the Dominion of Canada," the navy had decided to name for Verdun one of its new class of antisubmarine frigates then under construction. Reminded of the impossibility of using the name "Verdun," Wilson was asked to dispatch three alternative names of "local significance" to NSHQ.[97] Verdun was one of more than seventy communities obliged to select alternative names. For example, a number of important Canadian cities shared names with others in Britain (e.g., London and Hull) that the Royal Navy had already employed in christening warships.[98]

Wilson, a shrewd and successful wartime consensus builder, was anxious to involve the entire community in every local patriotic undertaking and initiated a citywide contest to select the three names. Organized by the city and administered by the *Guardian,* the contest offered a first prize of $5 and was open to all Verdunites "irrespective of national origin, religious belief, sex or age"[99] – wording that suggests Wilson's desire to unite Verdunites across language lines. But the mayor's attempt to involve both linguistic communities in choosing the warship's name failed, which was hardly surprising given the *Guardian*'s management of the contest. The vast majority of the more than 150 submissions came from English speakers. Nevertheless, the contest had popular appeal. Nearly two-thirds of respondents were female, and only a handful were children. People living in all parts of Verdun participated, and many mentioned that they were members of St Willibrord Parish, which had a large number of men on naval service. Quite a few forwarded the name of Scullion, a fellow parishioner. Entrants often had relatives on active service, which explains in part the greater appeal of the contest to English speakers. Many participants mentioned the city's patriotic zeal and their views that all Verdunites were united behind the war effort. The few French entrants wrote their letters in English, and most suggestions for names were English or English-sounding.

The city selected as its first choice "Beurling," in honour of the Verdun fighter ace who had gained fame that summer in the skies over Malta. The second choice was "Crawford," the surname of one of Verdun's founders, and the third suggestion was "Dunver" – the simple transposition of the two syllables in "Verdun." The city forwarded these preferences to NSHQ in November.[100] Given its policy of not naming ships for individuals, the navy found only one suggestion acceptable: "Dunver."[101]

The navy's choice generated the linguistic controversy that Wilson had tried to avoid. The name "Dunver" appeared imprecise and offended several leading French-language groups in the city. The Ligue des Propriétaires de Verdun, a chronic thorn in the mayor's side during the war, complained that "Dunver" was "an odd word which means nothing to anyone."[102] The Société Saint-Jean-Baptiste, Section Notre-Dame-de-la-Paix, Verdun, dispatched an irate and colourful letter to city hall. Members were "energetically opposed to this travesty as ridiculous as it is dishonourable" on the grounds that "Dunver" was an English word that shrouded the substantial French character of Verdun – "un nom bien français." The Société's executive committee resolved unanimously that the organization's members "protest with the full strength of their patriotism against a name which they consider injurious and vigorously insist that the said frigate be christened 'Cité de Verdun' and that this grotesque farce be ended at once."[103] The naming of Verdun's warship had become a delicate political and linguistic matter, at least for the city's French-speaking elite. City hall wanted a name acceptable to both language groups and, although the new warship had already been officially named *Dunver*, petitioned the minister, through the local MP, Côté, to have the word "Verdun" incorporated into the name.[104]

In the meantime, and although the city was working behind the scenes to arrange for a name change, on 29 June 1943 city hall warmly received *Dunver*'s commanding officer, Lt-Cdr William Woods, RCNR, in company with his French-speaking executive officer, Lieutenant André Marcil, Royal Canadian Naval Volunteer Reserve (RCNVR). Woods was a British-born Verdunite residing in west-end Ward 4, and one of the highest-ranking servicemen from the city. It was highly unusual during the war for a resident to be in command of a namesake warship.[105]

On 9 September 1943, NSHQ decided that the name *Dunver* would be changed to an awkward-sounding "Verdun of Canada" or "Verdun Canada." This was a mere two days before the ship's scheduled commissioning date. *Dunver*'s officers, however, balked at the order, citing as their principal reason that "crests, plate and stationery have already been prepared at great expense." Moreover, superstitious crewmen did not want the name of their ship changed. Macdonald rescinded the order; Verdun's frigate would remain *Dunver*.[106] The delicate matter ended there, and no further outcry was recorded from local French-speaking groups.

The power of linguistic symbolism, typified by the *Dunver* naming affair, mobilized Verdun's French-speaking elite and revealed local polarization on some war-related issues. But the Société Saint-Jean-Baptiste was not contesting the decision to name a ship in Verdun's honour, only the form of the name. Its vociferous response did not imply criticism of Verdun's war effort. Moreover, there is no evidence that opposition to the ship's name represented the views of most French Canadian Verdunites.

The frigate's crew paid scant attention to the naming imbroglio. One rating has recalled that while "most of the crew were aware of the origin of the name ... at that time everyone was more interested in the ship itself and the job to be done."[107] Moreover, "officers and senior ratings made everyone aware of how [the] name came about [as a] moral[e] booster," and the crew seemed "very proud" to represent Verdun. On the other hand, another rating aboard *Dunver* has stated, "I don't think 'Dunver' inspired as much pride as 'Verdun' would have, or any other city with its proper name."[108] But opinions of the name paled in comparison to the impact its symbolism had on Verdunites.

Adopting Dunver

The 300-foot, 1,445-ton frigate was officially commissioned into the RCN in Quebec City on 11 September 1943. As early as that April, the naval services minister, Macdonald, had already invited the city of Verdun and its voluntary groups to "adopt" *Dunver* by dispatching gifts and personal items ("comforts") to the men serving aboard. He noted that adoption by a community "has been found to be very advantageous in keeping up the morale of ships' crews."[109] Verdun's Women's Volunteer Reserve Corps was the first group to respond to city hall's solicitations. The already-busy unit described itself as "very interested" and by June 1943 had begun "knitting for the men."[110] Adopting a vessel improved wartime community spirit and heightened a sense of civic participation in the war, as well as benefiting the ship's crew.

According to the first letter sent to Wilson from *Dunver*, from the executive officer, Lt Marcil, on 13 September 1943, "the officers and men are unanimously proud to man this ship that carries Verdun's name to sea and wish to express their gratitude for the interest and kindness that you and your citizens have shown them."[111] Less than two weeks later, Woods and Marcil were guests of honour at a large dance and reception in Verdun. Local politicians from all levels of government, municipal officials, and prominent citizens attended the dance, as did officers from the WVRC and many ordinary Verdunites. The WVRC was the principal organizer of the event and used the proceeds from the fifty-cent admission fee to purchase comforts for the crewmen of "Verdun's own frigate." Wilson provided Woods with a framed portrait of the king for the officers' wardroom and, more practically, the promise of immediate delivery of 40,000 cigarettes purchased by the Mayor's Cigarette Fund for distribution to the 130 crew members. The city also contributed $100 for the purchase of other amenities.[112] The evening was so well attended and such a success that Woods told the gathering, "this is one of the very great days of my life ... [A]s a citizen of Verdun [I] feel proud to live in such a truly loyal and patriotic community."[113]

This was only the beginning of the relationship. The navy suggested that people dispatch playing cards, cribbage boards, magazine subscriptions, radios and batteries, electric toasters, and irons. But the most commonly sent items were cigarettes, clothing, toiletries, sweets, razor blades, gramophones, and sporting equipment.[114] Verdunites sent many of these things and more, all paid for by local collections and donations. A further shipment of 40,000 cigarettes went out just before Christmas 1943 and, as a reminder of its sponsorship, the city presented *Dunver* with an official crest of the city for display aboard ship.[115]

In the autumn of 1943, Arthur Burgess looked for suppliers for such scarce consumer items as irons and a washing machine, which the city sought to send to *Dunver*. The intervention of the naval-officer-in-charge, Quebec, was required to locate a washing machine in October, but irons were impossible to procure. In April 1944 a second washing machine was ordered for the ship, and Burgess wrote Woods, "nothing would be too much trouble for us."[116] The WVRC raised the nearly $300 necessary to pay for the washing machines. In September a piano paid for jointly by the WVRC and the Verdun Salvage Committee was sent to *Dunver*.[117] While the city did not directly pay for many of these goods, it organized or facilitated sponsorship activities and acted as the clearing house for *Dunver*-related correspondence and information. Crewmen also viewed city hall as the official point of contact with the community.

In December 1944, the frigate's new commander, Lieutenant William Davenport, who had officially succeeded Woods in August 1944, wrote both Wilson and Burgess to inquire about the possibility of obtaining a sixteen-millimetre film projector for *Dunver* – an expensive item. Despite previous fundraising by the WVRC, there was not enough money. No permanent fundraising campaign, such as existed for the Mayor's Cigarette Fund, existed for *Dunver*.[118] In response to Davenport's appeal, the mayor approached some community groups and merchants for patriotic donations of about $25 each. By the end of January 1945 the city had ordered a new $600 film projector for shipment to *Dunver*. Merchants remained one of Verdun's few sources of substantial and ready funding; it was difficult for them to refuse a public request for $25 from the mayor's office.[119] Davenport visited Verdun in September 1944 and again in January 1945, and Lt Marcil visited in November 1944 during a Victory Loan campaign. During his visit Marcil showed municipal officials a White Ensign flown by *Dunver* during the ship's latest Atlantic crossing. A strong relationship had clearly developed between the ship and the city, between the home front and the battle front.[120]

The sailors appreciated the gifts. Former crewman Walter Finlay recalled: "we knew the citizens were thinking of 'their ship' and trying to make the crew happy. [The] washing machine was a big thing and it had lots of 'washing time.' Smokes, woolen goods, and candy bars were always nice to receive."[121] Crewmen were aware that their ship was named in honour of the city, and several later recalled with gratitude gifts and comforts sent to the ship. They were unanimous in describing *Dunver* as a "happy ship," one to be proud of.[122]

On one occasion, two Verdunites stationed in Halifax visited *Dunver* and benefited from the crew's gratitude. In July 1944 Wren Jean Nugent, WRCNS, wrote her mother that she had boarded the frigate several times, once with fellow Verdunite Wren Violet Drummond.

I was on the "hometown ship" [and] ... treated like a queen. Lieutenant Pearce showed me about the ship a little and then I met a home boy who finished the tour with me. I chatted with a few of the boys and officers and had supper with them ... Verdun has contributed a rug to the officers' wardroom and a washing machine which is a godsend for everyone. The boys want irons, and the officers request a phonograph-radio ... They also expressed the hope they might get a piano in due time. I was requested to give this information to the "Guardian" so that citizens will know that the officers and ratings of their namesake ship really appreciate what is being done for them and that they like the ship very much.[123]

Dunver's involvement in naval operations elicited considerable interest in Verdun. Burgess wrote NSHQ in 1944 seeking information on *Dunver* that might be suitable for local dissemination, only to be advised that no details could be released publicly.[124] "Little has been heard about the frigate 'Dunver' since the day she was commissioned," wrote the *Guardian* with obvious disappointment in October 1944. The ship was hardly inactive, however. That month, Naval Service Headquarters released the news that *Dunver* had led the escort group that shepherded the largest convoy of the war, totalling 167 ships, to Britain in July 1944. "Verdun has been honored by the choice of the 'Dunver' as 'flag ship' of the covering naval force," crowed the *Guardian*.[125] In February 1945 *Dunver* shared the credit with another warship and an aircraft from the Royal Air Force's Coastal Command for the sinking of the German submarine *U-484* in September 1944. "The City of Verdun has cause for rejoicing today," wrote the *Montreal Daily Star*, while the *Guardian* gushed out the news on the front page of its next edition.[126] Every favourable reference to *Dunver* in the press brought pride to Verdun. Copies of the *Guardian*'s reports of these incidents found their way to the ship and were proudly posted on bulletin boards. The crew was well aware that its actions were keenly followed in Verdun.[127]

Curiously, there existed a widespread misconception that Verdunites made up the majority of *Dunver*'s crew – a fallacy often repeated in the Verdun and Montreal press. As early as October 1943, the Montreal *Gazette* reported that "most" of the crew were Verdunites. "Many of the officers, non-commissioned officers and members of the crew serving under Lt. Comm. Woods are residents of Verdun," echoed the *Guardian* in early 1944. The *Guardian* reiterated this erroneous information throughout the war. The *Montreal Daily Star* claimed in 1945 that the crew members were "all Verdun and Montreal men." As late as March 1946, the *Messenger* commented that "a very large part of ... *Dunver*'s crew were men from this City."[128] In reality, apart from Woods, there were rarely more than half a dozen ratings and petty officers from Verdun aboard, although there were also a number of Montrealers.[129] The belief that the frigate was crewed by Verdunites helps explain some of the pride felt in the city whenever NSHQ reported its operations.

On 23 January 1946, *Dunver* was paid off and sold for scrap. The ship's bell was presented to the city in an official ceremony in December 1946.[130] In addition to helping win the Battle of the Atlantic, *Dunver* served a valuable home-front role as a wartime symbol around which all Verdunites rallied.

The Verdun Auditorium Armoury
Within two weeks of Canada's declaration of war, authorities from Military District (MD) 4 considered the Verdun Auditorium – then nearing completion – as a possible barracks, armoury, or other defence facility. A military delegation visited the site in September 1939, and shortly thereafter the federal Department of Public Works invited the city to consider leasing this large municipally owned riverside

arena for military purposes. The *Guardian* welcomed the potential presence of a military unit but reminded Verdunites that if the auditorium were occupied all use by local hockey teams would "go by the boards."[131]

The city council's executive committee, which controlled municipal finances, proposed a rental fee of $2,500 per month for at least six months, with renewal at the discretion of the federal government.[132] By the time of the official opening of the arena on 28 November 1939, however, the Department of National Defence (DND) had not leased it, and the building was used for hockey games and figure skating. The issue was shelved for the time being.[133] At a council meeting on 25 June 1940, the city once again offered the federal government use of the auditorium in aid of the war effort. In a sombre mood as a result of the recent severe Allied setbacks in Europe, Wilson stated simply: "we have offered all the property which the City of Verdun has to the government."[134]

Alderman Robert Scurrah, whose overt patriotism on council was rivalled only by the mayor's, proposed that the city offer the facility to the military for the duration of the war for one dollar per annum. The executive committee agreed to this on 2 July. The profit motive apparent in council's dealings with DND the previous autumn seemed to have been replaced by the genuine desire to assist in the prosecution of the war. Verdun offered Ottawa the "unrestricted use" of the auditorium and its surrounding land "for any military or defence purpose which [the government] may desire."[135] In October 1940 an officer from MD 4 asked the city to establish a "definite price, if any" for the rental of the auditorium. The unselfishness displayed in the summer by the executive committee gave way in somewhat less unnerving conditions to a more hard-edged business sense. The executive committee, soberly reassessing the remunerative potential of the deal, recommended to council the rate of $18,000 for the first year and $12,000 for subsequent years. The first-year rate included the cost of compensating sporting and entertainment groups that had contracted to use the venue in the forthcoming season.[136] Profit and patriotism proved easy bedfellows, and there was little dissent in council.

And yet DND hesitated. Thereupon Scurrah again proposed leasing the building to the government for one dollar per year plus maintenance costs, and city council hastily agreed, perhaps before Ottawa went looking elsewhere.[137] With this arrangement, the city would not derive profit, but would not incur any losses either. This might have been the council's idea all along. With the civic administration devoted to producing balanced budgets if not surpluses, the large expenses incurred in maintaining the building may have been a factor in the city's willingness, even eagerness, to turn the facility over to the military authorities. Even though the city earned $8,000 in revenue from hockey alone in the 1939-40 season, the overall deficit for operating the auditorium was $15,300 in 1940, and there were no indications that 1941 would offer much improvement.[138] Whatever the motives, municipal offers of cooperation with DND were always couched in patriotic terms.

In April 1941, the mayor offered DND the facility for the duration of the war plus an additional six months, for the nominal sum of one dollar "as [Verdun's] contribution to the national cause." The final deal retained the financial advantages for the city. According to the agreement, Ottawa assumed all the building's operating and maintenance costs and paid $7,500 interest annually on a sinking fund used to finance the auditorium, $1,434 annually for insurance and other premiums, and the cost of any structural modifications or repairs. On termination of the lease, the building was to be restored to its original state, "reasonable wear and tear excepted." The auditorium closed on 23 July 1941 to await its new military tenants.[139]

That autumn reserve army units from MD 4 moved into the auditorium for training. These included the 3rd Division (Reserve) Royal Canadian Army Service Corps and the 16th (Reserve) Field Company, Royal Canadian Engineers. The RCASC had relocated to Verdun from its inadequate barracks on St Antoine Street.[140] From the beginning, these units made a conscious attempt to integrate themselves into their host community. The engineers, for example, directed their recruitment efforts to Verdun residents, claiming that their unit offered "an opportunity for Verdun to have its own unit in the Reserve Army."[141] The RCASC employed the same strategy. One banner front-page headline in the *Guardian* proclaimed, "R.C.A.S.C. Appeals for Volunteers." Below it ran "an open letter to the men of Verdun": "Montreal is a Class A military objective – a Leningrad of the western world. *And you live in it.* Your family lives in it. Your business is here. Does anyone think Nazi Germany would not make another Warsaw of Montreal if she were able? ... That is why Verdun's own unit, the R.C.A.S.C., is building up a strong and vitally important branch of the Reserve Army."[142] The headquarters of the unit was referred to as the "Verdun Auditorium Armoury."

The Saturday night after the move, the RCASC invited the community to a dance in its new home, and an estimated 2,800 people attended.[143] Officers and men stationed at the auditorium also frequently participated in social events staged by local patriotic groups such as the Legion and the Red Cross. Others took part in local sports and competitions, musicals, entertainments, and various fundraising events. In May 1942 the RCAF established a temporary presence in the auditorium, when 300 airmen arrived for training.[144]

The troops quartered in Verdun were good citizens. In October 1942 the police director, Alfred Dubeau, stated that the city had had "no trouble whatever with the troops, I wish [to] stress that point. There may be a little bit too [much] merriment and singing at times, but we have no serious trouble."[145] No fighting or troublemaking on the part of the servicemen was reported in Verdun's press during the war, the absence of local bars and taverns no doubt contributing to the good behaviour. Though Verdun possessed no licensed establishments, its location next to a larger metropolis seemed to satisfy the recreational needs of most of the men, not all of whom were permanently stationed there. Verdun's calm was probably an anomaly, given that social friction and even violence sometimes developed between civilians and servicemen in communities across Canada.[146] Moreover, the influx of hundreds of soldiers and airmen must have helped local businesses.

Municipal employees assigned to the auditorium who had been "dispensed with" were the first to resent the arrival of the reserve army.[147] As the war continued, the most determined opponents of the auditorium's military use were local hockey teams, figure skating clubs, and other sports teams, drawn from both language groups. After only two seasons of play in the highly praised 5,000-seat structure, many Verdun teams had reverted to outdoor skating facilities; their recreational aspirations conflicted with the needs of the military (or with the city's fiscal priorities).

Some Verdunites became convinced that the reserve army was making too little use of the building. In November 1943, after a prolonged period of quiet disgruntlement from sporting circles, the former mayor Hervé Ferland, then an alderman, presented a motion in council that Verdun should ask DND to permit hockey teams to use the auditorium in winter. The situation had begun to annoy other aldermen and their constituents and had become a minor political issue; Ferland's motion received unanimous consent. Ottawa refused to share the auditorium, however, stating that this would interfere with ongoing military training. A further inquiry by Mayor Wilson was also rejected by Ottawa in September 1944.[148]

Wilson had been a strong supporter of the reserve army in Verdun and in 1941 had played a key role in attracting the military to his city. Although he never publicly criticized the reserve army, by 1944 his support for its presence at the auditorium appeared to waver in proportion to the negative effect its continued occupation of the arena exerted on community morale. As both mayor and practical patriot, Wilson saw that it was not in the best interest of his city to be denied the use of the auditorium, nor was it in the interest of the war effort to allow Verdunites to harbour misgivings about the military. As the issue picked up momentum in the winter of 1944-45, he knew that it could also do him electoral harm. Municipal finances were in much better condition in 1944 and, besides, the war appeared almost won.[149] The city wanted its arena back.

By 1945 a growing chorus of Verdunites questioned the value of the leasing arrangement. After VE Day, local interests publicly asserted themselves over national ones, even though municipal interests had also been a consideration in attracting the military to Verdun. Softball teams voiced their grievance with the reserve army for ruining their playing field in Lafrance Park, adjacent to the auditorium. It had been converted into a parking lot for heavy trucks, jeeps, and assorted other military vehicles.[150] In September 1945, with the Pacific War over and hockey season about to begin, city hall sought to regain control of the auditorium as quickly as possible so as to reap rental income from the many sporting and entertainment groups clamouring to use the rink. But the reserve army was not ready to break camp. It expected the auditorium to be useful in the demobilization period. Pressure mounted in Verdun for the return of the building. One columnist in the *Guardian* questioned indignantly why local teams were being denied use of Verdun's facilities now that the war was over. The city reminded Ottawa that, as hostilities had officially ended on 2 September, the lease on the auditorium would expire on 2 March 1946, and the city expected full compliance with its stipulations.[151]

In February 1946, Wilson and two aldermen went to Ottawa, partly at the suggestion of Paul-Émile Côté, Verdun's Liberal MP, in the hope of obtaining a timely termination of the lease. But DND replied that it simply would not be ready to give up the building until 1 September 1946.[152] The city had no alternative but to wait; the relationship between DND and the city had soured noticeably since the cessation of hostilities. Verdunites' early goodwill had changed to chagrin once Allied fortunes improved and the facility's underuse became well publicized, and a broad consensus existed in Verdun for severing the links. The patriotic sentiments of the city on this issue, at official and popular levels, did not extend beyond VE Day. Home-front patriotism had its limits.

THE CITY OF VERDUN was at war; Mayor Wilson, no less than his fellow citizens and the groups to which they belonged, made sure of that. While the involvement of the city entailed certain burdens on ratepayers and additional work for city employees, it also brought tangible benefits. The war reduced the number of men on the dole and enabled the city to transfer the costs of its new auditorium to Ottawa. Moreover, the Department of National Defence, not city hall, incurred the disenchantment of Verdunites for DND's seemingly overstaying its welcome. The Mayor's Cigarette Fund brought renown to Verdun and enhanced the city's reputation among its own residents and its neighbours. The MCF helped bridge divisions in the community and acted as a convenient magnet for the patriotic energy of hundreds of Verdunites from all backgrounds. The city's creation of the fund helped sensitize the population to the war and to the fact that Verdun's contribution in manpower was significant even on a national scale. The city's assumption of some responsibility for the welfare of the crew of *Dunver* showed that city hall's war effort extended beyond helping only Verdunites on active service overseas. Heightening the visibility of *Dunver* and its exploits in the community brought the war home to many Verdunites and, like the cigarette fund, enabled a wide cross-section of people to help achieve victory.

Sometimes support for the war masked the pursuit of a hidden agenda. Whispering campaigns against local business people of Italian ethnicity had more to do with economic competition than with a sudden patriotic response against a fifth column. The notion of profitable patriotism united the city council in its quest for a military tenant for the auditorium. And when the community felt that it was time for the military to break camp, diverse interest groups united in their efforts to terminate the lease. City hall and civic groups were able to achieve their own goals under the mantle of the city's considerable war effort. Also remarkable is the extent of linguistic harmony during the war. French speakers and English speakers jointly participated in fundraising ventures, and no protests were heard in Verdun against municipal expenditures or efforts in support of the war or against Verdunites' role in it.

4
The People's Response

Certain wartime activities allowed the entire population of Verdun to participate indirectly in the prosecution of the war. In November 1940 Mayor Wilson remarked that "the present war is everyone's war and every citizen is expected to do his share in bringing it to a successful conclusion."[1] Fears of subversive activity and the perceived threat of air raids were countered by the formation of the Civilian Protection Committee. The CPC's practice blackouts and air-raid precautions in Verdun improved shaken civilian morale and involved all residents in the home-front war. Salvage collections and Victory Loan campaigns also touched almost every Verdun household. They offered residents an opportunity for meaningful participation in the war effort, of vicariously engaging the enemy, of fighting from home. Women looking for a more active role joined the Women's Volunteer Reserve Corps, a paramilitary group that performed many war-related tasks and assisted with many local patriotic activities. And large numbers of Verdunites turned out for military parades and other exciting wartime events.

The Montreal press frequently commented on the determination and war-mindedness of Verdun's population. Early enthusiasm for some war-related campaigns, however, was more difficult to sustain after 1942. The people's commitment to the cause of civil defence, as to that of salvage, peaked early, when the war was at its worst for the Allies. War savings and Victory Loan campaigns were less sensitive to the progress of the war and benefited from the increasing incomes of many Verdunites. However defined, and whether focused on Verdun, Canada, or even Britain, patriotic expression was often the result of Verdunites' community-mindedness. The communal nature of Verdun's wartime activities united residents across linguistic, gender, and age barriers. These grassroots responses were at the heart of Verdunites' home-front war experiences, helped define and unite the community, and, ultimately, served the national interest.

The Verdun Civilian Protection Committee
Few people thought in September 1939 that Canadian territory would be seriously threatened by enemy action. The fall of France in June 1940 and the widespread belief that Britain faced imminent invasion drastically altered this perception. If Britain were invaded, or even if the Germans merely acquired air bases in the North Atlantic (in Iceland, Greenland, or the Azores), Canada would find itself on the front lines of a war then going extremely badly. Even inland cities were poten-

tially in danger. The distance from the nearest air base in German-occupied Norway to Winnipeg, following a polar route, was 5,700 kilometres. But because the Luftwaffe's fleet of bombers would have required additional fuel tanks for the journey, any planned German raid on Canada would have been a one-way trip.[2]

Cities on the east coast clearly had the most cause for concern. As early as 3 September, the day Britain declared war, Saint John, which already had a civil-defence organization, held a blackout exercise. Three blackout drills had taken place by mid-October. Halifax, too, had a trial blackout but by the end of November had relaxed its lighting restrictions. Surface naval attacks on east coast ports were considered unlikely, given the threat that German ships faced from land-based aircraft as well as the strength and disposition of the British fleet. By 1941, however, enemy submarines menaced Canada's Atlantic waters and coast, though they did not come in force until 1942. Even in British Columbia, Civilian Protection Committee (CPC) groups had been established by 10 September in Vancouver, Victoria, and Richmond.[3]

While maintaining an umbrella air-raid precaution (ARP) organization, Ottawa granted provinces the authority to form their own civil-defence establishments to coordinate the services of municipally organized CPC groups. On 12 December 1939 the Quebec government passed an order-in-council creating a provincial CPC and allowing municipalities to organize CPC units and appoint neighbourhood wardens. Montreal had begun preparing in October 1939 and sought to recruit 2,000 First World War veterans as ARP wardens.[4]

Even in the threatening summer of 1940, the likelihood of German air attacks on Canada was remote. But only with hindsight do we know that this would be so for the remainder of the war, and that the threat would disappear well before the end of hostilities. Eastern Canadian CPC organizations – mindful of Britain's agony during the German blitz – remained apprehensive and took ARP preparations seriously. Meanwhile, dire pronouncements from Ottawa kept CPC members on their toes. A 1940 Canadian Press wire story estimated every major Canadian city's response time to enemy bombers launched from ships off Canada's coasts. Verdun, like Montreal, would have seventy-five minutes to prepare itself following the first warning of the enemy's approach.[5] Anything was considered possible in wartime.

Protecting Verdun from Air Raids
In early June 1940, prominent Verdun citizens, acting on their own initiative and in cooperation with local veterans' groups, decided to set up a Civilian Protection Committee. That month Mayor Edward Wilson chaired the first meeting of the Verdun CPC at city hall, attended by aldermen, municipal officials (including the police director, Alfred Dubeau), business and community leaders, a Protestant clergyman, representatives from veterans' groups, and, by special invitation, the

provincial CPC chairman, J. Gordon Ross, KC, of Quebec City, as well as Charles Barnes, chairman of the CPC for the Montreal area. Ross reminded the meeting that the CPC was governed by the Defence of Canada Regulations and designed primarily to assist police and fire departments and other constituted authorities in protecting civilians from enemy air attack, sabotage, or subversive propaganda.[6] Given the widespread fears of possible fifth-column activity, the CPC's earliest objective was to act as a watchdog and to shore up shaken civilian morale. Especially in the group's first two years, members worked within an uncertain overseas military environment and with the belief that their skills might one day prove crucial.

CPC members were unarmed volunteers over forty whose equipment was supplied by the federal government. All Verdun CPC wardens later received photo-identity cards and were fingerprinted. They subsequently were obliged to take oaths as law officers acting under "war orders."[7] The city engineer, Henry Hadley, a First World War veteran, prepared a map dividing the city into eight CPC districts, numbered in ascending order, northeast to southwest, and stretching from the riverfront to the aqueduct. He further subdivided each district into ten zones. With a captain expected to lead a ten-man detachment in each zone, Hadley's plan required 800 volunteer wardens – a number far in excess of the 500 that Barnes had suggested as a minimum. Volunteers would be expected to train in first aid, serve as auxiliary firemen, turn out for practice drills, report any suspicious activity, patrol their neighbourhoods in times of emergency or during exercises, and, generally, to further local security arrangements and support the war effort.[8] The CPC therefore had to recruit.

A local CPC press release asked citizens "to maintain a tradition of public service unexcelled by any other city, especially in the defence of their country."[9] Mayor Wilson believed that volunteers should be "kindly disposed, polite and courteous ... in good health, possess a good character, coolness, initiative, sound judgement, and a good reputation."[10] This was a tall order. Joining the CPC seemed an ideal solution for middle-aged men seeking an outlet for their patriotism, especially those British-born whose mother country was being bombed relentlessly and in grave danger of invasion by August 1940. A large number of British-born men past the age of military service resided in Verdun, many of them veterans. According to the 1941 census, 6,205 Verdun men aged thirty-five to sixty-four were of British ancestry. Nearly two-thirds of them had been born in the British Isles or in overseas British possessions such as Newfoundland. Many future members of the CPC belonged to local veterans' groups, such as the Canadian Legion and the Canadian Corps Association.[11]

By 5 July a paltry total of seventy Verdun men had registered for service as CPC wardens, and from among these were selected eight district wardens and eight deputy district wardens. These sixteen top wardens were chosen partly because of their places of residence, since all wardens were required to live in their respective districts. The organizers preferred that wardens have previous military experience or membership in a "Civic Organization, Club, [or] Society." Two character references were also demanded.[12] Men of a certain social stature in the community were especially solicited, since they would command more authority among the population. The wardens and their deputies were charged with recruiting in their own districts and appointing zone captains.

Although the wardens were under the nominal command of the police director, Dubeau, real organizational control of the CPC belonged to Chief Warden Charles H. Barr, a well-known local dentist and bilingual Liberal Party organizer. Linguistic representation was important, and Barr's two deputies were drawn from each language group. Initially, three of the four east-end districts received French-speaking district wardens with English-speaking deputies, the other district being led by an English speaker seconded by a French speaker. In the west end, it was nearly the reverse, with three of four district wardens being English speaking, one with a French-speaking deputy. The remaining district had a French-language head and an English-speaking deputy. Thus six of eight districts were led by men from both language groups. In total, ten of the sixteen officers appointed that summer were English speakers. By February 1941 only the leadership of district 8, the westernmost, remained entirely English-speaking.[13] Although the rank-and-file wardens included French speakers roughly in proportion to their numbers in the population, leadership positions were filled with English speakers throughout the war. At the end of July 1940, the CPC reported 445 men on strength – a good start but still below the minimum authorized complement.[14]

A large CPC meeting took place at the Verdun Auditorium in late August 1940, while the Battle of Britain was raging. Six hundred "grim-faced Verdun men," mostly members of the CPC, assembled to hear an address by Barnes, who reaffirmed the need to combat the threat from fifth columnists and saboteurs. Provincial chairman Ross also spoke of the real possibility of air raids.[15] The seriousness with which Verdunites undertook ARP duties related perhaps more to Britain's plight than to Canada's or Verdun's, but they prepared for air raids anyway. The volunteer ARP wardens trained in firefighting and first-aid work. By October 1940, 275 Verdun men (171 English-speaking and 104 French-speaking) had signed on for the first-aid courses offered by the St John Ambulance, while 122 had reported for duty as members of the volunteer fire brigade, to be trained by city firemen.[16] ARP linked men (and later women) of both language groups in common concern for the security of their city.

Despite the eight-district division for the broader CPC organization, the specific ARP network divided Verdun into only five districts, each with an emergency shelter station in a school. Only the two westernmost and mainly English-speaking CPC districts, the largest in area, had their own designated ARP ambulance posts/

casualty clearing stations; the other six districts were doubled up, with one ARP shelter for each. Given Verdun's small surface area, this did not constitute a problem. City hall was designated CPC headquarters and the ARP control centre, while the Verdun General Hospital stockpiled first-aid equipment.[17] In April 1941 the five ARP zones replaced outright the eight CPC districts.[18]

In January 1942, Chief Warden Barr reported to Mayor Wilson on the strength of the Verdun CPC, which had fluctuated from year to year. The unit could count, he said, on 350 wardens, 200 Boy Scouts equally divided among the five casualty clearing stations, more than 100 members of the increasingly important Women's Auxiliary, all qualified in first aid, 50 members of the Women's Volunteer Reserve Corps, 35 fire wardens, and 28 members of the St John Ambulance. Moreover, during an emergency 180 civic employees would be made available for demolition duties, while the largest coal and wood dealership in Verdun, the firm of J.P. Dupuis, had volunteered the services of its 225 male employees in the event of need.[19] The CPC itself probably did not exceed 600 members at any time during the war.

Funding and Local Support

The CPC quickly achieved a high profile. On 1 December 1940 it organized a massive parade in Verdun of some 1,000 CPC members from eleven mainly waterfront communities in southwestern Montreal and along the south shore of the St Lawrence. Many CPC, civic, political, police, and military dignitaries from these municipalities were present at a reviewing stand set up in front of the Verdun Police and Fire Station on Lasalle Boulevard.[20] The organization of such a large parade in Verdun, and the impressive turnout, underscored the strategic nature of the St Lawrence River, Montreal's status as a potential target, and the protective measures taken by local civilian organizations. Verdun housed the Montreal aqueduct filtration plant – a hub for the metropolitan district and a critical element of infrastructure. The city pledged to protect it and the interests of the wider Montreal community.[21]

Verdun extended every possible support to the CPC but its enthusiasm for ARP matched its own self-interest, and, as the threat of air attack receded, the costs began to rankle. The CPC groups, no less than the underwriting municipalities, were unhappy with federal assistance. In November 1940, just before an impressive CPC parade in Verdun, the organization's Quebec executive had demanded full funding from Ottawa. At a meeting of the Union of Quebec Municipalities Wilson had proposed petitioning the federal government to cover CPC operating costs because, in his opinion, ARP was Ottawa's responsibility and not the municipalities'.[22]

In October 1940, city council allotted $500 for CPC uniforms – justified as "additional police and fire protection."[23] The CPC ordered 200 of them, the style described by Barr as a "one-piece belted khaki uniform which snaps in closely at the ankles." Wedge caps completed the outfit.[24] A year later, Barr complained that some men still lacked uniforms: "Ottawa [has] to date failed to contribute a cent to the Verdun C.P.C."[25] It was not until May 1942 that the unit obtained 100 new blue coverall uniforms from the federal government.

Following the entry of Japan into the war in December 1941, the federal government designated all Canadian coastal areas as risk category A (most vulnerable). The Montreal area was category B (definite risk).[26] Though thousands of miles from the nearest German or Japanese military installation, Verdun took no chances. The city's executive committee prepared a plan to ensure an effective emergency administration in the event of an air raid. The city manager, Joseph French, defined the roles and allocated the services of all municipal departments and patriotic groups active in ARP exercises.

The onset of the Pacific War worried city hall, and the Verdun CPC also found itself desperately short of emergency equipment. Following a meeting with Barr and Dubeau, Wilson wrote Charles Barnes: "we have not the intention of finding ourselves any longer in this miserable position of unpreparedness, and, without exaggerating our needs or displaying any tendency towards panic, we are firmly of the opinion that it is necessary for us to have *immediately* six auxiliary pumps and 3000 feet of hose ... [We] are convinced that the C.P.C. organization is useless without necessary equipment to adequately control any serious eventuality."[27] J. Gordon Ross informed the city that, as soon as the federal government made ARP equipment available, he would attempt to satisfy Verdun's most pressing needs. Ottawa did not deal directly with the municipalities but only with provincial CPC organizations; it furnished equipment to the cities on the recommendation of the latter.[28] In addition to water pumps and hoses, the municipality wanted warning sirens, first-aid kits, stretchers, steel helmets, coveralls, and armbands for its wardens. Except for the coveralls, these hopes were not immediately satisfied. Ross reminded the city that "in a great many cases, the Federal Government is having the same difficulty in obtaining equipment from the manufacturers as you might feel you have in obtaining equipment from us."[29] He had earlier described the provincial CPC headquarters as merely a "clearing house for ... equipment and all federal orders, literature, etc. for relay to the municipalities."[30] No one at the municipal or provincial levels was willing to assume responsibility for ARP shortcomings. Because of the widespread panic on Canada's west coast following Japan's entry into the war, the federal government had diverted a good deal of vital ARP equipment earlier earmarked for eastern Canada, including some for Verdun, to Victoria and Vancouver.[31] In no immediate danger, Verdun had to wait.

Mayor Wilson had always offered the full support of the city to the CPC, including financial aid, and relations were very amicable.[32] In May 1942 the municipally operated Verdun Salvage Committee turned over $2,270 to the CPC for "the purchase of necessary equipment for [its] wonderful work."[33] By this date, air attack was seen as unlikely and fears of fifth-column activity had abated, yet funding for the community-minded CPC still obtained a broad consensus in Verdun.

Only in February 1943, when enemy attack seemed more remote than ever, did Ottawa provide Verdun with 1,500 gas masks – among nearly two million that it distributed nationwide. The gas masks were divided among CPC workers, city employees earmarked for ARP work, and members of local voluntary organizations assisting with ARP duties. Judging by the membership numbers provided by Barr a year earlier, half the gas masks probably remained packed.[34]

Practising for the Real Thing

By April 1941, air-raid practices occurred every second Monday in Verdun.[35] On 12 May 1941, a casualty-clearing demonstration took place in the streets of the city. The main ambulance posts/casualty clearing stations in each district were the focal point of activity for CPC wardens, auxiliary firemen, first-aid workers (including many from the CPC Women's Auxiliary), street patrols, and many other participating groups. These included the Women's Volunteer Reserve Corps, Red Cross nurses, the St John Ambulance, Boy Scouts, and the Boys Brigade. The exercises were as realistic as possible. According to one CPC report:

> Railway flares – burning red for ten minutes – are lighted at intervals of about six minutes. The patrols, on spotting a flare (i.e. incendiary bomb), call the Control Centre from the nearest available telephone ... The Control Centre operator records the call and immediately calls the Ambulance Post in that District. The Post ... despatches an ambulance car which picks up two casualties and carries them to the Post. C.P.C. stretcher bearers meet the ambulance ... and carry the casualties inside where the nurse in charge, acting as Casualty Admitting Officer, records name, address, injury and disposition of case. Ten flares are lighted in each district; 20 boy scouts are used as casualties (two Scouts to each flare), giving the Red Cross and Ambulance Post staff plenty of practice.[36]

At its own suggestion, the Women's Volunteer Reserve Corps was under the occasional command of the CPC to assist during practice air raids and other simulated civil emergencies. The WVRC provided ten women to act as street patrols in each of the five casualty clearing stations. Other women served as ambulance drivers at first-aid posts (with private cars taking the place of real ambulances) and as telephonists at the city hall control centre. Although the CPC benefited enormously from the assistance of the WVRC, Barr deflected the WVRC's suggestion that Senior Commandant Joan Adams or another representative be admitted to the CPC executive. He refused to relinquish any ARP decision-making responsibility to the WVRC and stated flatly that all ambulance and first-aid posts would be "supervised exclusively by C.P.C. officers."[37]

On 9 June 1941, a trial blackout involving several Montreal-area municipalities was organized on orders from the Department of National Defence.[38] In Verdun this widely publicized drill involved over 600 people, including 260 CPC wardens, 125 Boy Scouts, 86 men from the police and fire departments, 83 women of the WVRC, 35 members of the Boys Brigade, 28 people from the St John Ambulance, and – according to the *Guardian*, though not the CPC summary of the event – cadets from local French-language Catholic schools. One of the emergency ambulance posts was fully staffed by two doctors, ten Red Cross workers, and three St John Ambulance men. With foot patrols from these groups ready to move, at 10:20 p.m. a two-minute "alert" signal was sounded from police sirens and nearby factory whistles. Residents and motorists were thereupon granted ten minutes to extinguish or mask completely all lights. At 10:30 another two-minute blast signalled the start of the enforceable blackout period. Street lights were also extinguished at this time. The "all clear" signal, consisting of a succession of short siren and whistle blasts, sounded at 10:45, when normal activity resumed.

During this exercise, only thirty-four residential light violations were noted by the monitors deployed to all Verdun's streets. Nine shops and two automobiles were also found to be showing light. This was an excellent record for a city of more than 67,000 inhabitants. The *Guardian* described the blackout as the "nearest to war Verdun has yet seen."[39] Verdunites were extremely cooperative and thereby legitimized the work of the local CPC.

The city and the CPC would not tolerate uncooperative citizens, but the city lacked legal certification from CPC provincial headquarters. Accordingly, despite the Defence of Canada Regulations, city hall could do little to prosecute blackout violators. Even six months later a frustrated Wilson wrote to Ross: "We should ... be pleased to hear what steps, if any, have been taken against those who infringed instructions during the latest blackout, or if there is any intention of taking such steps. We had several flagrant violations in Verdun and it is our opinion that proceedings should be taken, and if not – why not? You have been furnished with a copy of a list of all those who decided not to comply with the regulations laid down. We want to know what value such a list has and whether the blackout regulations mean anything."[40] Wilson's support for patriotic residents was matched by fury directed against those taking a more cavalier approach to the war. In March 1942 Burgess wrote to Marcel Gaboury, KC, who earlier that year had replaced Ross as head of the provincial CPC, and obtained legal authority for Verdun to enforce adherence. Gaboury, conscious of the need to maintain maximum public support for ARP operations, cautioned Burgess: "it would be advisable to prosecute only those cases of flagrant bad faith."[41] Provincial headquarters seemed to take a dim view of Verdun's zeal.

In the summer of 1941, perhaps because daily German bombing of Britain had ended after a nine-month blitz, interest in Verdun's civil protection began to wane. The CPC summary of the June blackout noted tellingly: "The blackout increased the attendance of C.P.C. Wardens by 25% over fortnightly turnout ... Trial blackouts should be staged once a month. Men who had lost interest in the C.P.C. organization turned out and several new members were obtained. It rejuvenated the organization."[42] Trial blackouts occurred at irregular intervals, usually in conjunction with island-wide exercises. Still, the Verdun CPC was far from dead. A Montreal-wide blackout on 22 February 1942 was considered especially successful in Verdun, with over 700 monitors on duty. The new Japanese enemy was scoring victory after victory in the Pacific, and fears were rising of attacks on the west coast of North America. The city clerk, Arthur Burgess, who acted as the CPC secretary, noted that "this blackout clearly demonstrated [the] increasing realization of all citizens of the approach to Canada of actual warfare."[43] But once the shock of Japanese successes had worn off, it became clear to citizens that the threat to Verdun had not increased.

On 20 October 1942, a very realistic training exercise saw aircraft mount a mock raid against Verdun. The demonstration formed part of a consciousness-raising effort during the third Victory Loan campaign. B-24 Liberator bombers, Harvard trainers, and even an American B-17 Flying Fortress participated in a simulated fifteen-minute bombing run over the general vicinity of city hall on Church Avenue. The roar of aircraft and the simulated explosions of bombs and anti-aircraft fire caused "mild panic" and sent some people scurrying for shelter. According to a press report, some "exploding somethings" were detonated and caused a "deafening" noise, much smoke, and four shattered windows in the city hall target area.[44] More mock air raids (minus the aircraft) were staged in October 1943, again to publicize the sale of war bonds.[45] The relevance of the CPC's ARP work had become irreversibly subordinated to its utility as a public relations exercise for other war causes.

Still, some Verdunites actually believed at one point that an enemy attack was in progress. At forty minutes past midnight on 5 September 1944 a mild earthquake rumbled through the Montreal area, woke some residents, and caused one case of slight "hysteria." "On Manning Avenue [in west-end Verdun]," wrote the Guardian disparagingly, "a woman and her two children were [found] kneeling on the curbstone praying, at the same time shrieking that enemy planes were bombing the city."[46] Obviously the dire warnings of the Verdun CPC had sunk in with some people.

In October 1941, Barr boasted that the Verdun CPC was the "best trained in the Province of Quebec."[47] Several months later Ross paid great compliments to both Barr and the unit and added that he had "received from no Mayor of any municipality more constant support and wise counsel than from Mayor Wilson."[48] In July

1943, an article in the *Messenger* claimed, "perhaps the most comprehensive system of Civilian Protection against enemy air raids in the whole province has been perfected in Verdun."[49] The same article noted that "few citizens realize the protection that has been organized to [safeguard] the lives and property of Verdunites." Perhaps by then residents simply did not feel the need for protection.

Barr had admitted as early as October 1941 that his organization's primary mission was to foster a "win the war" attitude among the population. Subsequent ARP exercises were meant mainly to instil civic interest in the far-off war. After mid-1943 the CPC was in rapid decline. During a trial alert in September 1943 and a blackout in October, the Verdun CPC admitted that its "Medical Services completely failed to function."[50] Apathy had set in. In December 1943 Barr admitted in a letter to Gaboury that his organization needed no more than fifty uniforms due to low turn-outs.[51] The city hall ARP control centre employed itself mainly in coordinating salvage collections.

Canadians still feared Germany's advanced V-1 rockets and V-2 missiles, especially as Radio-Berlin had recently threatened to bomb New York with them.[52] The *Guardian* warned: "While probabilities of enemy attacks from the air naturally grow smaller ... it is a common trait of the wild beast to make a last ... fell attack upon his enemy ... There is still a 'kick,' and a great deal more, left in the Nazi vulture ... Jerry may search to punish Canada for taking such a great part in the destruction of the Hitler regime of blood, terror and oppression. His birds of prey may still darken our skies and drop destruction and death upon our people, even right here in Verdun."[53] Notwithstanding the dire predictions, the writing was on the wall for the CPC.

In October 1944, the provincial office of the Civilian Defence Committee (CDC), as the CPC had been renamed, stopped issuing ARP equipment. Restrictions were lifted on storefront lighting, and blackouts became a thing of the past. Volunteers who had been issued personal items such as uniforms, flashlights, helmets, and whistles could keep these, while the Crown's War Assets Corporation offered heavier pieces of equipment, such as water pumps, hoses, and other firefighting gear, for sale to municipalities that had set up a CDC. The CDC was officially disbanded across Canada in mid-February 1945, and the Verdun unit held its last meeting that month.[54]

The Verdun Salvage Committee

The war continued unfavourably for the Allies in the year following the fall of France, and Ottawa responded by organizing the nation for an unlimited war effort. One of the measures that gained the widest publicity and ultimately involved perhaps the largest number of Canadians was the collection of salvageable raw materials, especially metal, paper, rubber, glass, and rags. The Department of National War Services organized the National Salvage Campaign in April 1941 to coordinate the recovery of salvage throughout the country for the duration of the war. It named provincial administrators, and hundreds of local salvage committees quickly sprang up across the nation. Although they were normally municipally led, some were organized by local social organizations such as the Canadian Legion or the Imperial Order Daughters of the Empire. The campaign's goals were to assist the war effort by increasing the supply of available raw materials, to allow ordinary Canadians to be a part of the war effort, and to collect funds for patriotic groups through the sale of salvaged material for industrial use.[55]

Some Verdunites had become concerned enough about salvage by 1941 to ask Mayor Wilson to organize a citywide collection program, as other Canadian municipalities had done. "Some of us are wondering when there will be a house to house collection of salvage," wrote one British-born woman in June 1941. "In some towns the Boy Scouts have done this on their own and made several hundreds of dollars which have been used to further the war. The other week I got after one of the Scouts so he came with another lad, and brought a little coaster wagon. He could not take all I had but took what the little wagon would hold and sold it. He got thirty-eight cents which he turned in to the Red Cross. A lot of stuff which could be sold for salvage is put out in the garbage."[56] In fact, the city had already made "temporary arrangements" to pick up salvageable material and later that summer organized a large salvage drive in conjunction with most other municipalities on the Island of Montreal. A salvage collection in Verdun at the end of July 1941, billed as "Aluminum Night," received wide publicity in the Montreal press. To help with the manufacturing of military aircraft, patriotic residents deposited more than 7,000 pieces of aluminum – mainly pots and pans – in Woodland Park. *Le Canada*, a Liberal Party organ, printed a photograph of Wilson holding some items of salvage. "According to the organizers," stated the caption, "Verdun is once again a leader among Quebec municipalities." The self-promoting Verdunites reminded readers that only 5,000 articles of aluminum had been collected in the city of Montreal.[57]

The first general scrap collection in Verdun (again, part of an island-wide campaign) was held the following week, with the CPC, WVRC, Boy Scouts, and other volunteers undertaking a systematic appeal, described in the press as "Canada's first door-to-door salvage effort to cover a complete municipality."[58] Newspaper accounts reminded people that one ton of scrap metal made 150 field-artillery shell cases; ordinary waste paper such as envelopes could be converted into food containers, first-aid kits, and cartridge wadding; and old clothes and rugs meant greatcoats and blankets for the men in uniform.[59] This inaugural Verdun salvage day yielded 150 truckloads of material totalling a reported 200 tons. The co-chairman of the National Salvage Campaign for Montreal wrote Wilson that "we had anticipated a mere two-thirds of the quantity collected" and that this constituted "a further indication of the civic-mindedness and the patriotic spirit of the people of

Verdun."[60] The *Gazette* published an editorial lauding Verdun's effort: "it's another feather in the cap of the city which, as far as the war effort is concerned, had no lack of feathers before."[61]

Verdun's salvage came almost exclusively from its working-class households, mainly small flats without yards. Ottawa encouraged farmers, scrap metal and junkyard dealers, and large commercial enterprises to clean up their properties and turn over reusable materials.[62] None of these were present in Verdun, which also lacked the industry, port facilities, and railway tracks and embankments that usually generated lots of scrap metal and other salvageable refuse. But densely populated, residential Verdun contained more than 16,000 dwellings in 1941, which made door-to-door canvassing among the three-storey tenement flats a potentially rewarding if laborious task. The large population meant successful salvage collections for more domestic materials such as paper and rags.

Starting a Salvage Committee

Although Verdun's Protestant schools and Boy Scouts had also collected salvage, a regular collection system was lacking.[63] Jean Cool, part-owner of a well-known trucking business in Verdun, felt it his duty to inform the city in January 1942 that, as a local garbage collector, he felt certain that a ton or two of scarce rubber was being incinerated every week through the carelessness of Verdunites. Intent on halting this waste, and perhaps seeking some business, he wrote: "I expect ... that city council will empower me to prevent this from re-occurring."[64] Perhaps prompted by Cool's offer of assistance, within days the city decided to take action. Verdun's territory was nominally covered by the Montreal and District Salvage Committee, but the city's executive committee decided that the municipality itself was best able to administer a formal local salvage organization. Accordingly, it formed the Verdun Salvage Committee (VSC), named Wilson its head, and appointed to it the eight city aldermen, the city manager, and all other ranking city administrators. The Verdun Salvage Committee Fund was officially registered as a war charity at the end of January 1942.

While the VSC was a community effort, the city took on the task of organizing, publicizing, and materially assisting in salvage operations.[65] For the remainder of the war, city hall acted as the focal point for the receipt and dissemination of salvage information and the dispatch of appropriate transportation to recover material. City-owned "Salvage Trucks" collected every Wednesday from Verdunites who had called the salvage committee office at city hall. Salvage was dumped and sorted at the municipal yard on Galt Avenue in the east end or in a large playground adjacent to the Verdun Auditorium. Municipal patriotism had its financial limits, however, and the use of city trucks and the time of those municipal employees required to sort scrap metal and other salvaged items were not free of charge. The VSC paid for these services.

In its first month, the VSC earned over $700 from the sale of forty-five tons of collected salvage to nearby scrap-metal yards, paper manufacturers, and other dealers. The city was disappointed to average fewer than 110 pickups per week that first month, as the VSC had hoped for at least 400. Salvage was considered vital; it was a question, said the *Messenger*, of "Save or Slave." Residents were implored to cooperate.[66] In March 1942 calls rose to an average of over 160 a week. But this was the high-water mark for the entire war. By July 1943 salvage pickups were cut back to once a month, although not a week went by until July 1945 that Verdunites did not call seeking to contribute their waste materials to the war effort.[67]

There were 1,722 local salvage committees in Canada by the end of 1942, including 520 in Ontario and 254 in Quebec. A year later, almost all provinces registered a decline in the number of salvage committees, with British Columbia dropping by over 30 percent. Quebec lagged far behind Ontario in salvage tonnage, both absolutely and proportionately. Though not necessarily an accurate measure of available salvage or of popular support for its collection, to the end of 1943 Ontario, with 33 percent of the population, had contributed 52 percent of the salvage collected by voluntary salvage committees while Quebec, with 29 percent of the population, had generated only 16 percent of the national take.[68] Verdun's contribution fit the provincial trend.

Salvage Drives

The Verdun Salvage Committee jealously guarded its mandate and wanted no competition for Verdunites' scrap; civic prestige was at stake. Within days of its creation, it sought to control the ad hoc salvage efforts of local Junior Red Cross groups, Protestant schools, and Boy Scout troops. It also informed local merchants that all future salvage collections or publicity had to make reference to the VSC. In April 1942 the VSC sought Ottawa's permission to hold exclusive jurisdiction to collect salvage in Verdun. Ottawa was unable to grant it such a right, although "duplication of effort" clearly was to be avoided.[69]

The local and Montreal press gave wide publicity to Verdun's second major salvage drive in late April 1942. Although under the auspices of the VSC, the CPC organized this collection, while local Scout troops and the Boys Brigade performed much of the physical labour. This pattern of cooperation was repeated during subsequent salvage drives. The timing of the drive took advantage of the traditional 1 May moving day in the Montreal area, which especially affected a city of tenants like Verdun. People seemed more prone to divest themselves of unwanted articles at that time of the year. On this occasion Verdunites turned up 160 tons of salvage – the largest single-day total of the war under the jurisdiction of the VSC. The haul was carted away by trucks loaned by nearly two dozen local firms, merchants, and individuals.[70]

By "special authorization from the National Salvage Committee," the local CPC received most of the proceeds from the sale of this salvaged material. All Canadian salvage committees were empowered to donate funds to war charities of their choice, such as the Red Cross or the Overseas Services of the Salvation Army. Strictly speaking, the CPC was not a war charity. But Verdunites could hardly oppose funding an organization devoted to their own welfare, even if ARP was rapidly becoming irrelevant. Besides, the city was helping fund the CPC, so these donations allevi-ated its financial commitments. A press release from city hall described Verdun as a "very important and vulnerable city" and the CPC as "in urgent need of funds."[71] Wilson recognized that salvage collections "would be very difficult undertakings without the help" of the CPC.[72] Almost all other recipients of VSC aid were local groups, including the Mayor's Cigarette Fund, the Red Cross, the WVRC, and the crew of HMCS *Dunver*.[73] In finding salvage for sale, Verdunites directly helped their own and, through them, the national war effort.

It was difficult for salvage drives to be cost-effective, however. Prices for sal-vaged materials were generally standardized by Wartime Salvage Limited, a Crown corporation. Given average prices in December 1942 of $15 a ton for scrap iron and steel and a mere $8 a ton for waste paper, a considerable amount of material was necessary to offset the high costs of carting and sorting. In that month, for ex-ample, the VSC spent $106 to pick up only eight tons of material worth $128, a whopping 83 percent of income lost to overhead expenses.[74] Expenditures were very rarely below 30 percent of receipts in Verdun during the war, and in eleven individual months between March 1943 and June 1945 costs actually exceeded re-ceipts. In February 1945, for example, the VSC paid nearly $51 to pick up salvage worth $30. Over the entire period of the VSC's active existence, from January 1942 to July 1945, nearly half of its earnings went to cover expenses (see Table 4.1).[75] This

Table 4.1

Verdun Salvage Committee statistical summary, 1942-45

Year	Salvage (tons)	Revenue ($)	Expenses ($)	Costs as % of revenue
1942	459	8,241	3,270	39.67
1943	164	1,616	1,213	75.06
1944	166	2,464	1,155	46.87
1945	84	1,302	597	45.85
Total	873	13,623	6,235	45.76

Source: Verdun Salvage Committee, Reports of Salvage Collections, February 1942-July 1945, box A-331, file 2, Verdun Borough Archives.

did the war effort little good. But salvaging was not always about the materials recovered or the funds raised; it allowed Verdunites on the home front the opportunity to feel as if they were contributing to the cause and assisting on the road towards victory.

The only really profitable salvage ventures were the widely publicized special salvage days organized once or twice a year, which often coincided with a Montreal-wide appeal. On these days, the VSC collected material that residents placed on the curb, much like a garbage collection. Often citizens had amassed the salvage over a period of time and saved it for these occasions. The year-round call-in and pickup program was inefficient, especially in winter, when salvage returns were very low. Well over half of all salvage realized in Verdun during the war had been collected by the end of 1942, as shown in Table 4.1. The next year saw the nadir of salvage collection, and by 1944 the VSC asked citizens to hold on to their diminishing amounts of available salvage until they were worth collecting.[76] Trucking costs had become prohibitive, and pickups had to be consolidated. Moreover, there was simply less salvage to be had.

The wartime demand for salvage was also used to advantage by the city. Salvage collections fitted in nicely with the goals of the City Improvement League of Greater Montreal, with which Wilson was involved. The removal of salvageable refuse improved property appearance, which furthered the objectives of the League. In May 1942 the League launched a major cleanup drive throughout the Montreal area, including Verdun, in which salvage campaigns played a major role. In 1944 the new director of the Verdun Fire Department (separate from the police department since the previous year), R. Proulx, also saw salvage collection as a convenient means of ridding the congested city of many fire hazards and seized on the idea of linking preventable house fires with unpatriotic conduct.[77] If women whose husbands and sons were away on active service inspected their chimneys and electrical systems, and ensured proper storage of inflammable cleaning materials, manpower in the fire department could be freed up for other tasks. By eliminating the risk of conflagration, women could "kill two birds with one stone; Fire at home; Hitler at the front."[78] Cleanliness was thus both patriotic and helpful to the city – which, as shown previously, was not averse to turning wartime circumstances to suit its own ends.

Women assumed the burden of much of the salvage effort. They saved, stored, and supplied fats, bones, paper, clothing, rags, glass jars, tin cans, and an assortment of discarded household items.[79] Children's salvage efforts, extremely important in Verdun and elsewhere in Canada, were frequently the subject of newspaper articles and advertising. Under the January 1943 headline "Nails for Nazis, Iron for Italy and Junk for Japan," the *Messenger* suggested that signs reading "Admission: One Nail" be posted on the doors of local schools, movie theatres, parks, playgrounds, and even churches. "Let's gather [the nails] ... and give our fighting men a chance to shoot them at the baby murderers who have been bombing women and children," shrilled the accompanying article.[80]

Verdun's salvage campaigns were regularly hailed for their military contribution, so essential in a city with a large number of residents on active service. "Waste Paper May Save Lives of Boys of Verdun," stated a headline in the *Guardian:* "If the present emergency is not met, some of the fighting men, some of them boys from Verdun, who are 'over there' fighting the battles of freedom and liberty, may lack something to help save their lives. That single thought should stir the people in the city to [a] greater and more persistent effort."[81] In 1944, Ottawa had anticipated the monthly need for 20,000 tons of scrap paper and, from that July until the war's end, waste paper became the VSC's top priority.[82] Paper was the object of collections in April and May 1945. Children became "Waste Papertroopers," ferreting out valuable old telephone books and the like. "Waste paper is still Canada's war material shortage No. 1," stated a Department of National War Services bulletin issued to all salvage committees. Verdunites were also reminded that "perhaps the bundle they supply may save the life of one of their own dear ones in the fighting forces."[83] Nearly 18,000 (paper) flyers were delivered to every Verdun residence and business reminding the population that all proceeds from the paper drive on 16 May 1945 would go to war charities serving local men. Every old newspaper or cardboard box donated would indirectly help a friend or loved one. Even though the war with Germany had ended over a week earlier, an impressive 47 tons of paper and other material was collected by 125 volunteers, most of whom were Boy Scouts.[84] The community's response to war-related activities improved when linked to local causes instead of those more national, and more nebulous.

By the end of 1943, Verdunites had given to the VSC approximately 11.27 tons of salvage per thousand residents, rising to over 12.5 tons by war's end, based on an average population of 70,000 in the period 1942-45. Even though the city had only one significant wartime industry and no rail facilities, these figures were slightly above provincial averages. Overall, Verdunites contributed 873 tons of reusable salvage, which sold for more than $13,000.[85] Verdun's salvage record was good but not particularly cost-effective, since the city refused to defray the costs of transport. The Verdun Salvage Committee was officially dissolved on 9 October 1945. It donated its surplus of slightly over $1,000 to the Red Cross and the Canadian Legion's Provincial War Memorial Building Fund.[86]

As with many other wartime activities, the communal nature of Verdun's wartime salvage campaign had united residents across linguistic, gender, and age barriers.

War Savings and Victory Loans

Canada's war was expensive, and Ottawa employed various means to finance it, the most obvious being increased taxation. Another was borrowing. As in the First

World War, the federal government appealed for public assistance. In February and September 1940 it mounted two successful War Loan campaigns that yielded $500 million. National campaigns also sold War Savings Certificates. These public sales of government bonds, savings certificates, and stamps, offered at 3 percent interest and redeemable well into the postwar period, yielded considerable sums.[87] When even these successful methods proved insufficient, Ottawa held its first carefully orchestrated Victory Loan campaign in June 1941. Mass publicity, ample use of the machinery of government, and the constant reminder that purchasing bonds was a patriotic duty combined to make this program a huge success. The nine Victory Loan campaigns held between June 1941 and November 1945 raised $12 billion, with slightly more than half this amount coming from corporations.[88]

War Savings in Verdun

In November 1940, the Verdun War Savings Committee (VWSC) was set up, chaired by Joseph French, the city's chief financial officer. Verdun's MLA, J.J.L. Comeau, Mayor Wilson, local merchants, and prominent citizens attended the group's inaugural meeting. The local elite usually ran wartime patriotic organizations, and the VWSC was no exception. Nine of the sixteen men present were French speakers – like most elected officials and the majority of Verdun's merchants, professionals, and landlords. The committee asked almost all Verdun businesses to act as points-of-sale for War Savings Certificates and delegated speakers to address local social groups and clubs (especially women's groups) to request their assistance, particularly as sales agents for war savings stamps and certificates.

The city and the Protestant and Catholic school boards immediately instituted payroll deduction plans for workers wishing to purchase certificates. Several larger businesses followed this lead, while all having at least five employees were urged to adopt the plan.[89] Within a month, all permanent city employees, the majority French Canadian, had subscribed to payroll deductions.[90] The National War Savings Committee included Verdun on its honour roll in 1941, along with most of the city's participating firms.[91] In January 1942 the city obtained consent from all 225 of its employees to deduct $1 a week from their salaries, in addition to voluntary contributions, towards the purchase of War Savings Certificates. This more or less obligatory imposition of war savings was not rescinded until September 1945.[92]

The selling of bonds was chiefly a female role, especially in English-language organizations. Within a year of the establishment of the VWSC, over thirty English-speaking women's organizations, including the Daughters of England, the Imperial Order Daughters of the Empire, the women's auxiliary of the Legion, the Verdun Women's Club, the Women's Volunteer Reserve Corps, the YWCA, and groups from almost every English-language church, were participating in the sale of War Savings Certificates in Verdun.[93] The city planned a meeting of the heads of these groups and similar French-language groups. Wilson wrote to each of the

English-language organizations, and Joseph French to their French-language counterparts. As a French speaker, he perhaps had more influence with this audience
than the British mayor. In any event, both language groups responded to the call
to invest in the war effort.[94]

Despite the disturbing military situation in Europe, the idea of investing in
Canada's war had to be sold to some citizens, many of them earning steady wages
for the first time in years. R.P. Jellett and Napoléon Charest, co-chairs of the Provincial War Savings Committee, attended the Verdun War Savings Committee's
first business meeting in December 1940. Jellett urged his audience to convince
workers that the purchase of certificates would not only help win the war but
would constitute a sound financial investment; otherwise deductions might be
viewed as merely another form of salary tax. Moreover, J.P. Dupuis, a member of
the VWSC and Verdun's leading merchant, reported that some of his more than
200 employees feared they might lose the bonds or see them destroyed in a fire.
Harkening back to the economic downturn that afflicted Canada after the First
World War, Jellett stressed "the importance for all wage-earners to ... creat[e] for
themselves a useful back-log of savings for the depression period which usually
follows a war." This was sound advice for a working-class community. Charest
congratulated the VWSC for its "enthusiasm" and added that it was "one of the
best organized ... in the Province."[95]

Even before the VWSC had been formed, in July 1940, when an invasion of Britain was believed imminent, the *Guardian* had exhorted Verdun's substantial British-
born population to invest in the war effort. During a coordinated nationwide
"theatre night campaign," participating cinemas admitted patrons free of charge
so long as they purchased at least fifty cents' worth of War Savings Stamps. The
Guardian's caption to a photo of the king and queen read: "Loyal Britishers throughout Verdun will prove their loyalty ... by purchasing War Savings Stamps at their
favourite local theatre." The city's four theatres sold $3,500 worth of stamps –
almost double the anticipated amount.[96]

War stamps were especially popular with schoolchildren. From December 1940
to the end of April 1941, the 5,300 students in Verdun's Protestant schools purchased $10,500 worth of stamps, averaging nearly $600 a week. Three years later
the total amount had reached $63,000, including some teachers' contributions. In
elementary schools, pupils gave their teachers small change, and, once twenty-five
cents had been amassed, a savings stamp was glued on a card provided by the
National War Finance Committee. When the card was full, it was sent to Ottawa in
exchange for a $5 certificate.[97]

One Verdun pupil, Bill Jameson, invented a catchphrase promoting the sale of
War Savings Stamps for his school newspaper: "Hey, gang? Keep on licking War
Savings Stamps – they're full of Vitamin V!" The slogan soon propelled him to
national prominence. The National War Finance Committee adopted the phrase

and distributed to schools across Canada thousands of posters showing the young Verdunite uttering his famous patriotic appeal. So popular was the slogan that it was picked up and used officially in the United States. Reflecting the importance allotted the civilian war effort, the *Guardian* treated this story almost as glowingly as it did that of overseas war heroes.[98]

Victory Loans

To the end of the fiscal year 1940-41, Ottawa had borrowed over $640 million from the Canadian public in the form of War Savings Certificate and Stamp sales. But this was hardly enough to keep pace with war expenditures, and the federal government hoped to raise twice this amount in 1941-42.[99] Accordingly, the first Victory Loan campaign was officially launched on 22 June 1941. The city of Verdun took out a Victory Loan advertisement in the *Guardian* under the headline "Verdun Defies Hitler": "thousands of Verdun Citizens are already on active service. Thousands more are helping by their work on the home front, willingly, eagerly ... Let us make our dollars talk democracy! Keep Verdun on the map as a fighting outpost for a democratic victory ... Verdun is always in front – we will not fail!"[100] Many local business people, such as the patriotic J.P. Dupuis, and social and patriotic groups, such as the Legion, sponsored ads in the press in support of the warbond drives. A strong sense of local identity and community pride permeated many of the messages. In June 1941, the local branch of the Lion's Club, formed that month, sponsored a bellicose advertisement: "When Verdun is aroused Hitler may well tremble ... Let's Show Canada what Verdun can do."[101]

Verdun women mobilized for this first Victory Loan drive. A well-publicized bond-purchasing rally in Woodland Park, which followed an evening parade through the streets with bilingual floats, attracted 3,000 women, including representatives of the Civilian Protection Committee Women's Auxiliary, the Girl Guides, the Imperial Order Daughters of the Empire, the Red Cross, the Verdun Sisterhood, the Verdun Women's Club, the WVRC, and many church groups, as well as the wives of several prominent elected officials, including Elizabeth Wilson. The only men officially participating were the pipers of the Black Watch band. Well-known women's rights activist Thérèse Casgrain was the main speaker, which lent importance to the event. All purchasers of war bonds immediately received a small Union Jack – a promotion in keeping with the outlook of most present.[102]

While Verdun met its subscription goals, campaign organizers expressed some disappointment that many Verdunites had purchased their Victory Bonds at work in downtown Montreal. Since these did not count as local purchases, the *Guardian* gently reproached these Verdunites for their lack of "local" patriotism.[103] Even in 1945, during the eighth Victory Loan campaign, the *Messenger* reminded Verdunites: "Buy in Verdun. When you make your investment, let Verdun get the credit. Don't buy in Montreal where you work, but buy in Verdun. It's your city.

It's a patriotic city. Verdun has sent the cream of her youth to the fighting front, Verdun must back them up."[104] Recognition of Verdun's patriotism seemed at times as valued as the actual subscriptions. The city's newspapers regularly called on readers to patronize local businesses, use local facilities, and promote Verdun's impressive war record. They constantly reminded residents that the differences between Montreal and Verdun were real ones and that the smaller city compared favourably to the larger.

Highlighting its willingness to assist the war effort as swiftly as possible, in June 1941 the city's executive committee agreed to French's plan to allow city employees to subscribe to Victory Loans on credit provided by the city. The city purchased the bonds from the government immediately and collected employees' money from payroll deductions. Employees obtained their bonds from the city on final payment.[105] During the second Victory Loan campaign, launched on 26 March 1942, city employees subscribed $10,000, $9,000 of it borrowed from city hall. The city loaned over $200,000 to its employees in this manner. For the duration of some loan campaigns, city employees pledged more than 15 percent of the amount of the city payroll.[106]

Overall, Verdunites attained 157 percent of their subscription objective during the March 1942 campaign. Substantial oversubscription became the norm for every subsequent Victory Loan drive, even when, by November 1944, the fixed objective exceeded $1 million, exclusive of payroll deductions.[107] Following the fifth Victory Loan campaign of November 1943, the National War Finance Committee awarded Verdun the honour of flying a three-star "V" pennant from city hall in recognition of Verdunites' contributions. A photo of the flag was proudly displayed on the front page of the *Guardian*.[108] Lt André Marcil, executive officer of HMCS *Dunver*, visited the city in November 1944 as the representative of the National War Finance Committee and presented Verdun with yet another Victory Loan flag.[109] Though not a wealthy community, Verdun was a full partner in the national war savings scheme, and Verdunites invested in the victory that their loved ones were helping to achieve.

The pressure to subscribe was very great. By all means possible, including thinly veiled and probably unneeded coercion, the city induced English and French speakers to purchase for victory. Speaking in support of the fourth Victory Loan campaign in May 1943, Edward Wilson, speaking mainly in French, told city employees packed into the council chamber that good Canadians bought Victory Bonds, whereas bad ones did not. In the mayor's mind, it was that simple, and many Verdunites agreed. A film was shown, in French, depicting the horrors that the Germans were visiting on occupied Europe. On the podium with Wilson were two Verdun survivors of the corvette HMCS *Weyburn*, recently torpedoed. One sailor was a French speaker and the other an English speaker, and both spoke of their difficult experiences and implored the city workers to contribute to the Victory

Loan. A show of hands was then requested of all those who would not purchase a bond. No one budged, and all present thereupon signed over more payroll deductions for the cause.[110]

With the exception of some larger institutional investments, the money to purchase bonds came essentially from Verdunites' savings. As the war proceeded, more Verdunites earned more income. More than 5,000 individuals, businesses, and local institutions made purchases averaging $2,000 each in November 1944's seventh Victory Loan campaign. This was 700 more purchases than during the previous campaign and constituted a large amount for a working-class community.[111] The eighth Victory Loan campaign, begun 1 May 1945, yielded $1.25 million from Verdun, as against the $1 million sought. Many of the sales were termed "gratitude" purchasing, seemingly the result of VE day euphoria. Ottawa's major selling points during this campaign were that Japan remained to be subdued, that speedily repatriating Canadian service people would be expensive, and that Canadians needed to save for the postwar period.[112] Like all Canadians, Verdunites wanted their men and women home as quickly as possible.

The ninth (and final) Victory Loan campaign took place in November 1945, long after the Pacific War had ended but well before all Canadian troops had returned from overseas. The huge Verdun quota of $2.25 million was subscribed 150 percent, making it by far the city's largest financial response to the campaigns. Verdunites had plenty of disposable income available by then, especially as few consumer luxuries had been available during the war on which to spend the good wages that they had earned in war industries. Verdun and the adjacent low-income Montreal neighbourhood of Point St Charles, combined, led the "west end" of Montreal during this last campaign, which illustrates the wartime socio-economic transformation of their working-class families and the level of their patriotic commitments.[113]

The War Savings campaigns in Verdun induced contributions and cooperation from all strata of the population. Individuals and workers formed the backbone of the drives' success, but businesses and employers, schools, and city hall were also major participants. The dense network of local community groups was able to reach large numbers of Verdunites and helped sell the government's war-financing schemes. Verdunites' responses generated a good deal of community pride, and the city and the local press used this pride to stimulate further sales. While some Verdunites undoubtedly purchased war bonds for patriotic reasons, others acquired them as good investments and as insurance against the expected postwar economic downturn. Patriotism and personal gain mixed easily.

The Women's Volunteer Reserve Corps

From 1941 on, nearly 50,000 Canadian women belonged to the Canadian Women's Army Corps, the Royal Canadian Air Force – Women's Division, and the Women's

Royal Canadian Naval Service, or served as nurses attached mainly to the Royal Canadian Army Medical Corps, the air force, and the navy. As well, women performed vital civilian service in Canada's defence industries, with approximately 250,000 directly engaged in war work at some point. Hundreds of thousands more toiled indirectly in support of the war, including work as agricultural labourers. In addition, hundreds of thousands of women of all ages worked as volunteers and fundraisers for charitable causes. A less quantifiable contribution consisted of the enormous personal and family responsibilities assumed by Canadian women, many of whom, because of enlistments, suddenly became heads of single-parent families or had to finance and administer their families' affairs on their own.[114] The public profile of women increased during the war. Women and women's groups debated national issues such as day care, wage equity, and price controls. One home-front group of service-minded women that has received comparatively little attention is the Quebec-based Women's Volunteer Reserve Corps. In Verdun, these women's activities were numerous and ranged from fundraising to training as civil protection auxiliaries.

Established in June 1940 by an enthusiastic and large group of Westmount women, the WVRC was a civilian organization that trained women in certain essential services, some well outside their established gender roles, and produced a ready cadre of useful volunteer workers devoted to the war effort. Their training included courses in first aid and motor mechanics as well as compulsory military drill. The uniformed, volunteer members of the WVRC adhered to a rank structure and generally acted in cooperation with government agencies or other groups organizing such ventures as air-raid precaution drills, Victory Loan campaigns, the distribution of ration booklets, and recruitment drives. A principal activity of Verdun's WVRC was raising money on behalf of such patriotic causes and charitable organizations as the Canadian Red Cross, HMCS *Dunver*, the "Wings for Britain" Fund, and the Queen's Canadian Fund in aid of British victims of German bombing.

Verdun's WVRC

In July 1940, a group of women in Verdun established a chapter of the WVRC, although the larger Westmount group acted as the organization's headquarters.[115] By August the Verdun WVRC numbered 161 members, who were required to purchase uniforms replete with "VERDUN" shoulder flashes.[116] On 22 March 1941 the Verdun group selected as its senior commandant Miss R.B. Joan Adams, originally from Cornwall, Ontario. Adams had moved to Verdun in the 1920s and quickly developed a reputation as a feminist and social activist. She was also the founder and principal of the Canadian Commercial College and had made a name for herself as an Independent candidate in the March 1940 federal election.[117]

Adams increased the status and improved the image of the WVRC. She did not view the unit's role as merely fundraising on behalf of the Mayor's Cigarette Fund or for other charities. Adams believed that assisting British civilians and providing auxiliary military services at home were the group's primary functions. As a result, WVRC women patrolled streets during civil-protection exercises and assumed at least some of the social authority denied them out of uniform. They paraded as a military unit and drilled in the basement of Verdun High School under the supervision of the reserve battalion of the Black Watch. Adams soon earned the nickname "the Little Colonel" and later admitted to being "aggressive" in the pursuit of her goals.[118]

This vigour did not go unnoticed. The Montreal press reported that the "Verdun unit is taking drill seriously. If and when the Government has need of women, there will be hundreds of physically fit and well-trained recruits in this unit alone. The 'men' are taking driving lessons and they have a large mechanics class as well."[119] In April 1941, the *Montreal Daily Star* also published an extremely laudatory article: "big business could in many cases take a lesson in efficiency and cooperation from this closely knit voluntary unit headed by [that] ... incredibly persevering and patriotic personality, Commandant Joan Adams. Throughout the years many stories will no doubt be told of the heroic efforts made by the women to help Canada in her task, but undoubtedly the daily work now being performed by the W.V.R.C. in Verdun will be one of the most interesting and dramatic – although just a handful of women the work they are doing could make any triple size organization proud ... [T]hey are few in number but the work they do makes thousands happy."[120]

This article put the unit's membership at 120 – down from 161 the previous August. Although its goal was 400, in the summer of 1941 it mustered only 187 members.[121] Despite the membership statistics mentioned in the press, Adams also claimed that the Verdun WVRC was one of the largest in the Montreal area. With ninety-nine women making up a full company, she recalled that, at one point, her unit boasted nearly three companies. In April 1941 the WVRC's mainly English-speaking membership was 1,500 in the Montreal area, including the parent branch in Westmount and others in Verdun, Montreal, Pointe Claire, and Lachine.[122] Certainly the expense of purchasing uniforms discouraged some working-class Verdun women; many required at least some assistance to do so. Uniforms were compulsory: "either you wore the uniform as a soldier or you didn't," recalled Adams.[123] Increased war work also diminished time available for voluntary efforts. Moreover, any sense of social elitism attached to the group, as suggested by the Westmount headquarters, would have put off many Verdun women, just as it discouraged local membership in the Imperial Order Daughters of the Empire. The WVRC's impressive strength in Westmount, with less than half of Verdun's population, indicates its attractiveness to middle- and upper-class women.[124]

The given and family names of some WVRC members, occasionally mentioned in the local press, indicate some (probably bilingual) members of French ancestry.

Years later Adams could not remember any French Canadian women; she believed that social pressures prevented their more active participation. The Verdun unit's assistance to British causes or organizations did little to attract French-speaking Verdunites, who opted for voluntary war work of a more local or national nature.

Women who had volunteered for duty in organizations such as the WVRC were among the first women to go on active service when the military established women's branches in each of the services.[125] Ottawa looked to these civilian groups to provide a nucleus of trained and drilled women for its new formations. Joan Adams believed that the WVRC proved to the military authorities that women could act as valuable, fully fledged members of the military community. The women of the WVRC gave the impression of being more official, professional, and perhaps useful than the female volunteers knitting for the Red Cross or canvassing for war charities. By the spring of 1942, at least seven Verdun women had traded in their WVRC uniforms for the real thing. Others followed.[126]

Motives and Activities

Though a 1942 article in the *Guardian* estimated that most WVRC women were wage earners, with perhaps 80 percent of them in munitions work, Adams has recalled that many did not have regular employment.[127] She claimed that most of the women were thirty-five to forty years old and had joined the WVRC for patriotic reasons or because they had relatives and friends serving in the military. The WVRC offered these women a way to support their men in uniform and did not necessarily reflect a desire to raise the status or alter the orientation of women's work. A Verdunite serving in the WVRC wrote a revealing poem in September 1941 which read in part:

We remember we're just women
And not as strong as men,
But big enough to hold the fort
'Til they come home again.

We are just a bunch of women
Not out expecting praise,
But raising dollars where we can
To shorten Hitler's days.

We can't be out there fighting
In that land across the sea,
But we can do our bit right here
In the fight for Liberty.[128]

The author, Private Linstead, joined the WVRC out of patriotic fervour and a desire to serve as an auxiliary to the men of her community, not as a woman striving to highlight the potential wartime contribution of her sex.

Adams, however, perhaps an anomaly in her own organization, strongly affirmed that the WVRC demonstrated the utility of women in activities outside their gendered sphere. In a 1942 address before a meeting of the Notre-Dame-de-Grâce Women's Club held in Victoria Hall in Westmount, Adams emphasized the importance of raising women's consciousness regarding their crucial wartime role. A consistent defender of women's rights, she described her own uphill battle to have WVRC women in Verdun assert themselves as community leaders. She claimed that many Verdun women were unused to participating in and being identified with a socially prominent women's organization. They required instruction and encouragement regarding their functions in the WVRC and in the community at large.[129]

The Verdun WVRC made its valuable wartime contributions firmly within the context of male social primacy. Its members' social standing and even the organization itself were assumed to be temporary. By January 1942 the Verdun unit provided its members with courses in signalling and Morse code, unusual training for civilian women.[130] But it is difficult to assess whether the practical experience and social confidence deriving from membership in the WVRC translated into a lasting social consciousness for these women. Wartime was an exceptional situation, demanding increased social and personal commitments from both men and women. Donning uniforms or acting as auxiliaries to male-dominated activities might not necessarily have affected the self-perceptions of many Verdun women.

Nor was Verdun society particularly conducive to female assertiveness. Mary Davidson, in her study of Verdun in the early 1930s, remarked on the patriarchal organization and strict gender-role definition existing in Verdun's numerous British-immigrant families.[131] By today's standards, outright gender defamation appeared regularly in the pages of the *Guardian* during the war. Fillers at the end of columns and jokes or anecdotes routinely disparaged or ridiculed women. One October 1942 "gag" headline read "How to Shoot Your Girlfriend," and was really about photography techniques. The same month the newspaper ran a series of short editorial vignettes entitled "Thoughts on Women." One read, "So many bare female legs seen on the streets these days are so pale, hairy, lumpy, bruised, scarred or shapeless that the male pedestrian has no trouble keeping his mind on his business." In October 1945 the sight of three female army lieutenants in uniform on Verdun's riverfront boardwalk impressed the *Guardian*'s "Roving Reporter," but only because of the way their uniforms fit their bodies, not because of the ability, authority, or professionalism that their jobs implied.[132] Examples of this attitude abound in this newspaper and seem to represent both the times and the views of the reading audience.

In its first two years, the WVRC boasted an impressive list of accomplishments, including numerous tag days and fundraising events, assistance in war savings, salvage and blood drive campaigns, and the offering of courses in first aid and other militarily useful subjects. Members also acted as essential auxiliaries during civil-defence exercises. As the Canadian war effort accelerated and the war itself increased in complexity, the WVRC became less visible in Verdun. When its high-profile senior commandant, Joan Adams, left to join the CWAC in 1943, it lost its most energetic leader. The local group's status was hurt by her departure, and, as the military situation improved, enthusiasm for the organization waned. By 1943 the local press paid the WVRC diminishing attention, partly because of the existence of so many other patriotic organizations and war charities. The group's work in adopting HMCS *Dunver*, however, kept it in the public eye. Though still strongly representative of women's efforts, the WVRC increasingly took on the role of an auxiliary to men's organizations such as the Civilian Protection Committee. In the last two years of the war, the shrinking Verdun WVRC continued to provide valuable assistance to Canadians serving overseas, both directly and indirectly, by contributing to other organizations.

The Women's Volunteer Reserve Corps wound up its activities not long after the cessation of hostilities. Little material assistance was ever offered the WVRC by the government, and Adams later credited the tireless efforts of its members for the organization's success. Like their counterparts in Britain, these women "were the human mortar which was filled in between the bricks of officialdom."[133] During their service, these women's efforts helped make a difference to the lives of many service people and civilians overseas and brought renown to Verdun throughout the Montreal area.

Special Civic Events

Aside from organized campaigns and voluntary groups, Verdunites had many opportunities to show their support for the war effort. Verdun's English-speaking majority and strong British character helped define the city's posture towards the war and its reactions to news from overseas. The more perilous the military situation for Britain in the spring and summer of 1940, the more personally intense became the patriotism of many residents. For example, on 24 May 1940, the *Guardian* published a front-page morale-boosting article as well as a special prayer for victory aimed directly at Verdun's very worried British population. With almost every edition, it reaffirmed the city's British character, so different from most Quebec municipalities. For Empire Day in 1941, it published a full-page advertisement, "Loyal Canadians," sponsored by local English-speaking businesses: "This page has been made possible by the Citizens and Firms in the City of Verdun who re-affirm their loyalty to the British Empire and their firm intentions to Buy and Sell British and Canadian Merchandise."[134] Despite the ad's obvious commercial goal, Verdun's special connection to Britain was unmistakable.

In July 1941, Ottawa issued a "Call to Arms," making it known that victory depended on the efforts of "all true Canadians." It urged "stout-hearted able-bodied men" to enlist immediately. At the invitation of Brig-Gen E. de B. Panet, district officer commanding, Military District (MD) 4, Mayor Wilson formally and gravely read the proclamation to an estimated 15,000 people (nearly a quarter of the population) in Woodland Park. Alderman Albert Rolland read it in French.[135] Panet made the same request of other communities in his district, but so strong a showing could only have enhanced Verdun's reputation as an especially responsive and patriotic city.

In August 1941, a "recruiting convoy" visited Verdun. The showpiece was a Canadian-built Universal carrier, a tracked, lightly armoured troop transport, and the *Montreal Daily Star* published a photo of Wilson, French, the city engineer, Henry Hadley, other municipal officials, and the MLA, J.J.L. Comeau, sitting and standing in the vehicle. "Verdun's enthusiasm for Canada's war effort was demonstrated again last night when thousands of men, women and particularly children of Quebec's third-largest city turned out for the demonstration ... The show was preceded by a tour of the city staged by the convoy with sirens screaming and people running through the streets ... From the crack of the first torpedoes to the roar of the finale, the mimic war put on by the soldiers was as popular with Verdun's war-minded citizens as it is wherever it goes."[136] The next day, the *Star* again highlighted Verdun's patriotic mood and war consciousness. The city possessed the "enviable double record" of leading Canada's war effort and of building "outstanding" recreational and municipal facilities without increasing municipal debt. Although enlistment figures broken down by municipality were unavailable, the paper assumed that Verdun proportionately led the country. "Following up an enviable Great War record of service, the men, women and children of the suburban city are making a contribution to the war effort that should prove a shining example to other communities in the Dominion. It is on the home front that the widest participation in the war effort is evident in Verdun, from war loan drives to school children selling candy in aid of relief funds." Wilson and French were working "day and often night" on behalf of the cause.[137]

The same month the Quebec Tourist Bureau asked Wilson to arrange for the city to paint the famous "V for Victory" emblem on Verdun's principal intersections ("V...–," the three dots and the dash being Morse code for the letter "V"). While considered "a patriotic undertaking," these signs were also meant to enhance Quebec's image with visitors from the still-neutral United States. Oddly, the Tourist Bureau believed that American tourism would increase "if we demonstrate our 100 percent commitment in heart and soul towards victory." Verdun happily obliged by painting a large victory sign on the street at the west-end waterfront intersection of Lasalle and Bannantyne, near the Natatorium swimming complex. The Montreal press claimed that Verdun was the first area municipality to use its streets and flower beds to promote victory. Later, in response to a solicitation from MD 4, the city also painted victory slogans on selected sidewalks.[138]

To commemorate the second anniversary of Canada's declaration of war, Ottawa organized a national Reconsecration Week, complete with special military displays, solemn church services, and public pledges. Verdun decorated all its public buildings with patriotic bunting and called on residents and merchants to do the same. The entire text of that year's Reconsecration Proclamation was read into the minutes of city council, and Wilson wrote to the local clergy, school boards, and public bodies to reconsecrate themselves to victory. He proudly invoked Verdun's "exemplary tradition" of high wartime morale.[139]

To mark Reconsecration Week 1942, Verdun and MD 4 combined to stage a large military parade. Participants included the Royal Canadian Army Service Corps and Royal Canadian Engineers, quartered at the municipal auditorium, the Civilian Protection Committee, the WVRC, and veterans' groups. City hall saw the occasion as "an expression of the intense feeling in [Verdun] to prosecute the war to the utmost." Panet took the salute from a reviewing stand at Verdun and Desmarchais, in the heart of the city. Thousands lined the streets and followed the procession. At a rally in Woodland Park, Panet described Verdun as "one of the most patriotic municipalities in the entire Dominion." The popular Wilson exhorted all citizens to engage in war work of some kind and received "applause and cheering ... most enthusiastic and vigorous." Selections chosen by the military and local bands included "There Will Always be an England" and "Tipperary."[140] Panet's presence confirmed Verdun's image as Quebec's leading patriotic city.

Perhaps nowhere in Canada was the memory of the famous Second Battle of Ypres, fought in April and May 1915, more vigorously observed than in Verdun. Many Verdunites had participated in the battle and, given the city's First World War record in general, these observances acted as a significant reminder of local wartime service. Since 1920 Verdun had held an annual military parade and remembrance ceremony on the Sunday closest to 22 April, Ypres Day. The Great War Veterans' Association and, from 1926, the Canadian Legion branch organized the events.[141] These became well known in Montreal for their many participants and onlookers.

With another war looming in Europe in the late 1930s, Verdun's veterans (joined by others from Montreal) increasingly observed Ypres Day. In April 1939 an estimated 4,000 veterans participated, along with marching bands (including the obligatory pipes and drums of the Black Watch), local dignitaries, and representatives of various civic and social organizations. Nearly 20,000 cheering spectators, including many from elsewhere in the Montreal area, lined the parade route and attended the ceremony at Verdun's First World War memorial.[142] In 1940 Ypres

Day took on the added poignancy of wartime remembrance and included representatives of the Canadian Active Service Force and many other military units from all services. Brigadier J.P. Archambault, district officer commanding, MD 4, took the salute.[143] As the war continued, the impressive spectacle only grew in size and meaning. In 1942 a record 50,000 people reportedly attended.[144]

In Verdun, the tradition of granting the use of city streets for military parades found wide popular approval. No wartime public gatherings were larger than the Ypres Day parades. The war served as a catalyst for the success of the parades, and no other events held the same attraction. Their significance should not be underestimated, as they symbolized the stature of the veteran and military presence in the community. The occasions were solemn and dignified, and the extraordinary annual Ypres Day constituted a public display of prevailing values and attitudes. Wartime parades gave sanction, authority, and legitimacy to the participants as well as to the groups that they represented.[145] The parades highlighted not only the soldiers of two world wars, but Verdun, its residents, and their demonstrated patriotism.

The Ypres Day parades confirmed and publicized Verdun's reputation in the Montreal area as a steady source of British-inspired patriotic sentiment and military enlistments. MD 4 seemed to choose Verdun disproportionately often as the locale for military gatherings and demonstrations. Verdun's Britons, none more than Edward Wilson, increased their profile during the war, when their emotional ties to their beleaguered homeland grew more pronounced and prominent. This mood generally dovetailed with both national sentiment and federal war policies. The city's patriotic spirit did not emanate only from its British-born or English-speaking residents. French-speaking Canadians, too, volunteered their time and services, participated en masse in civil defence, salvage collections, and the purchase of war bonds, and attended military parades and displays.

VERDUN'S WAR was fought on the home front and overseas by men and women born on both sides of the Atlantic and representing both of Canada's principal language groups. The message from Verdun was unity in war and community participation for victory.

5
Institutions and Industry

During the Second World War Verdun was home to a large number of diverse social organizations. Many emerged from the city's sense of local identity and community, others were based on language, class, religion, or gender, and some united various social elements. Some were branches of larger organizations while others were linked through association with the socially prominent; the names of well-known Verdunites sometimes appeared on different groups' letterheads.[1] The city supported many of these bodies in some way or other, often by making available municipal facilities for meetings or special events.

In the 1930s and 1940s Verdun contained the densest concentration of British-patterned social groups in the Montreal area, made up significantly of British-born residents. Charitable and patriotic organizations included the Army and Navy League, the Canadian Legion, and the Imperial Order Daughters of the Empire (IODE). Recreational associations included many sporting clubs, choirs, and dramatic societies. Among the nationalist fraternal orders were the Sons of England, the Ancient Order of Hibernians, and various Scottish clan organizations. Though composed mainly of a Canadian-born rank and file, political and civic organizations such as the Co-operative Commonwealth Federation, Conservative, and Liberal clubs, the Verdun Voters' League, and the Verdun Workmen's Association had mostly British-born leaders. Another group popular with the English-speaking community was the Young Men's Christian Association (YMCA).[2] Most of these organizations actively participated in the war effort.

The two largest and most active French Canadian charitable or fraternal organizations in Verdun were the Société Saint-Jean-Baptiste and the Société Saint-Vincent de Paul. Mgr J.A. Richard, founder of Verdun's largest French-language parish, Notre-Dame-des-Sept-Douleurs, had been a cleric in Verdun for nearly half a century by 1939 and wielded great influence. Consequently, many high-profile French-language social organizations in Verdun were Catholic, while other, less visible groups such as the Gouttes de lait were social in outlook.[3] Notwithstanding Verdun's English-speaking majority, the Ligue des Propriétaires de Verdun and the local chamber of commerce were also almost entirely French speaking.

French Canadian social organizations and institutions were significantly fewer and less diverse than their English-language counterparts. They appeared less active in support of the war effort, but then Catholicism often prevented them from too close an involvement with nominally Protestant organizations such as the

YMCA. Moreover, especially early in the war, English Canadian and British groups aided British more than Canadian causes. In fact, Verdun's French Canadian support for the war went mainly to local initiatives in support of Verdunites of either language.

A large part of Verdunites' war efforts consisted of voluntary and charitable work, with leisure time going to patriotic pursuits. The goal of voluntary service was to "support the Fighting Forces and win the war."[4] Most volunteers were women. Many worked for registered war charities such as the Red Cross, or on behalf of official auxiliary war services such as the Salvation Army.[5] Thousands belonged to smaller, less conspicuous organizations that contributed their resources to larger groups. For example, Verdun's St George Society often donated the proceeds of its social activities to the Mayor's Cigarette Fund. Many volunteers were inspired by patriotism; others sought distraction and social interaction. Most were moved by genuine devotion to the war and concern for those on active service.

One thing is certain: mutual aid was a well-established tradition in Verdun. With so many local men in uniform, volunteering energy and resources on the home front usually meant indirectly (and perhaps directly) helping a family member, neighbour, or friend on active service. "War work and community work went hand in hand," wrote the historian of Winnipeg's domestic war effort.[6] This truth made giving in Verdun easier.

Volunteering through community social groups brought people closer together in aid of the war effort. This was also true of paid labour. With the opening of the Defence Industries Limited (DIL) plant in east-end Verdun in 1941, residents participated even more closely in the war's prosecution. Verdun men and women from both language groups and of different generations found employment there and the resulting improvements in family finances helped Verdunites to support the city's enormous contribution of overseas manpower materially and financially. Whenever possible, this large defence firm forged links with the community and co-operated with the fundraising efforts and other activities of groups like the Red Cross and the Women's Volunteer Reserve Corps.

While hundreds, perhaps thousands, of Verdunites worked at the DIL plant, the precise number who belonged to wartime voluntary associations is difficult to ascertain. In his study of wartime urban development in Halifax, Jay White writes that "producing quantitative figures on the precise dimensions of [citizens'] involvement would entail meticulous research into the activities and membership rolls of many organizations."[7] Unfortunately, many of the records of local groups and institutions, small and large, are fragmentary or, in most cases, simply nonexistent. This chapter attempts at least a qualitative assessment for Verdun with respect to selected larger patriotic organizations operating there during the war – the Red Cross, Canadian Legion, YMCA, and Société Saint-Jean-Baptiste – as well as the organized responses from churches and school boards. These groups have been chosen because they represent various dimensions of Verdun's social organizations and, through them, of Verdunites in general. While English-speaking organizations often interacted during the war, French- and English-language groups had little to do with one another.[8] Some patriotic groups, such as the Red Cross, contained both French and English speakers. If patriotic impulses contributed to social unity, they also highlighted differing, though not necessarily conflicting, approaches to the war effort.

After the war Verdun's city clerk, Arthur Burgess, wrote that so many voluntary organizations were active in Verdun during the war that "each ... is worthy of an historical record."[9] What follows is only part of that record, though perhaps a representative one.

The Verdun Red Cross

More than any other wartime body, the Red Cross rallied a wide cross-section of Verdun society to its cause. The reasons for this are clear. It possessed a long and distinguished record of public service in the face of war and disaster and had built up a solid public reputation. It was an inclusive group, seeking and accepting the assistance of all Canadians. Moreover, its appeal was distinctly humanitarian, non-partisan, and non-sectarian. Few could argue with its wartime role of alleviating suffering. The Red Cross grew to be Canada's most recognizable war charity and earned an exalted position in the ranks of wartime organizations. Red Cross volunteers – the majority female – raised funds, prepared articles of clothing and medical supplies for overseas servicemen and prisoners of war, staffed blood donor clinics, and assisted with a multitude of wartime community programs.

Organizing

Within a week of Germany's invasion of Poland on 1 September 1939 and before Canada was officially at war, representatives of about a dozen Verdun social organizations, including women's groups, church groups, mutual aid societies, and fraternal associations, met at city hall to set up a local chapter of the Canadian Red Cross Society. The provincial Red Cross headquarters, located in Montreal, called the meeting, and the groups attending included the IODE, the Verdun Sisterhood, the Gouttes de lait, Assistance maternelle, the Dames de charité, and the women's auxiliaries of the Royal Canadian Legion and other veterans' organizations.[10]

Two weeks following this first meeting, the provincial organization formally granted a charter to the Verdun chapter of the Red Cross. By this time Catholic and Protestant church organizations, the International Order of Foresters, the Verdun Community Club, the YMCA, and other community groups had pledged to work on behalf of the Red Cross. Each group, such as the Chalmers Church Red Cross and the IODE Red Cross, was designated a "unit" or "work group." These were self-guided and administered by the Verdun branch on behalf of provincial headquarters. The city generously supported this patriotic venture. The Red Cross chapter received use of city hall for its executive meetings, while the police-station gymnasium on Lasalle Boulevard at Willibrord, in the east end, accommodated its office space and warehouse. In addition, the city supplied furniture.[11]

The chapter's executive committee consisted entirely of local political, community, and business notables; the Red Cross was prestigious, especially in the early years of the war. Edward Wilson was president, and Alderman Émile Ste-Marie was vice-president, replaced later by Alderman Albert Rolland, a close associate of Wilson's. Others on the committee included Joseph French, Arthur Burgess, Henry Hadley, Dr Charles Barr, head of the Civilian Protection Committee, and J.P. Dupuis, Verdun's leading merchant. Yet Verdun's women did much of the organizing and most of the work. Elizabeth Wilson, the mayor's wife, chaired the separate Ladies' Committee and was the real head of the organization.[12] Edward and Elizabeth Wilson led Verdun's war by example.

Before the war was two months old, the Verdun branch possessed an astonishing thirty-five units totalling 1,200 women volunteers.[13] The Quebec average at the end of 1939 was about 860 volunteers per branch, although national statistics seem to have been exaggerated, or at least elastic.[14] The Verdun branch was one of Quebec's largest and was said to be the most productive on the Island of Montreal. By February 1941 it claimed 1,400 regularly active volunteers, which amounted to one in forty-five Verdunites, or, since virtually all the volunteers were female, one in eighteen females over the age of fourteen.[15] One study of the lives of Quebec women during the war estimated that in July 1942 there were 35,000 women knitting and sewing clothing or rolling bandages for the Red Cross; perhaps 80 percent were French speaking. They were scattered across 190 provincial branches, averaging by that time about 185 active volunteers per branch. In the light of these figures, Verdun's membership was impressive.[16]

The *Guardian*, forever fomenting competition with other area municipalities, wasted no time in gloating that the Verdun branch had been "organized quicker and more completely than any other on the Island of Montreal."[17] Before the month was out, Miss E. Huntley Duff, from the executive of the provincial headquarters, concurred, stating that "the City of Verdun has shown the way by a truly magnificent example unequalled in the Province of Quebec."[18] In February 1940, less than two weeks before the death of her husband, the governor general, Red Cross patron Lady Tweedsmuir visited the Verdun branch to the delight of the organization's hard-working volunteers.[19]

The home addresses of the Red Cross's executive committee indicate that most came from Verdun's elite. Of the twenty-three officers and executive committee members in July 1944, ten had French surnames, thirteen had English names, and all but four lived in the noticeably more affluent west end. Nine of the ten men and women with French surnames lived there.[20] This linguistic mix of committee members remained fairly constant throughout the war. Despite this seemingly patrician bearing (in Verdun terms), the Red Cross enjoyed wide appeal among all classes.[21]

Verdun's French Canadian social organizations supported the Red Cross. They participated in all of the Red Cross's successes, including fundraising, producing goods, organizing the blood clinic, and serving on the executive committee. Verdun's three largest French Catholic parishes maintained active Red Cross units during the war.[22] This stands as a small example of the unheralded support for the war found in French Canadian society, in Verdun and elsewhere. In February 1941 the Verdun Red Cross trained 514 English-speaking and 282 French-speaking women in home nursing and in dealing with war emergencies. Hundreds of local women continued to be trained in home nursing and first aid throughout the war, although the numbers gradually diminished. At the end of 1943, 276 were enrolled.[23] One Quebec woman has recalled that because of their larger families, many French-speaking women had less time for voluntary service.[24] Thus their participation rates may have had less to do with wartime politics or patriotic commitment and more to do with family demographics and income. In Verdun, they participated roughly in proportion to the linguistic balance in the community.

Activities

Verdun's first Red Cross fundraising drive in November 1939 was a resounding success. The $7,200 collected from a community not yet fully recovered from the Depression was more than double the target of $3,000. All of the city's nearly 17,000 households were canvassed by some 700 volunteers, 450 of them women. Patrons at movie theatres, concerts, and miscellaneous social events were also solicited. Some 10,000 Verdun households contributed.[25] Once a member of a household had donated to the appeal, a small Red Cross sticker was affixed to the door or window of the dwelling. Later, a follow-up call was made on every home not displaying such a sticker. Donors gave in proportion to their modest incomes and included men, women, and children from both language groups and all areas of the city.

Organizers of the provincial Red Cross campaign singled out Verdun for its thorough canvassing methods and remarkable oversubscription. The *Montreal Daily Star* noticed too; it said that the Red Cross appeal "gripped the people of Verdun" and mentioned only the Verdun branch.[26] The average contribution in Verdun – a densely populated city containing many children and low wage-earners – was not high. Well-off, English-speaking Westmount, with less than half Verdun's population, contributed well over $33,000 to the drive in the same period.[27] In the following year Verdunites gave more than $10,000, representing over 17,000 individual subscriptions.[28]

In early 1943, with virtually full employment across the country, provincial headquarters assigned the Verdun branch a fundraising quota of $14,000. By this time,

Table 5.1

Verdun Red Cross, funds collected, 1939-44

Year	Amount ($)
1939	7,245.09
1940	10,275.69
1941	1,389.25[a]
1942	12,124.02
1943	19,324.85
1944	16,839.19
Total	67,198.09

a The low amount for 1941 cannot be explained from available
   evidence. It is possible no specific funding appeals were
   organized that calendar year.
Source: Box A-331, file 5, Verdun Borough Archives.

local Red Cross organizers had divided Verdun along linguistic lines for fundraising in an attempt to secure the best possible results. They named English- and French-speaking campaign managers to coordinate the drive. Each was to target public institutions such as schools, parishes, churches, hospitals, and other community organizations. The managers supervised individual Red Cross units, most of which could be identified as either English or French speaking.[29] Each unit canvassed its members, parishes, or neighbourhoods. In this way, existing local, associational, or personal bonds furthered the appeal. The cooperation and generosity of both language groups ensured that fundraising quotas were always fully or oversubscribed (see Table 5.1).[30]

Throughout the war years organizers donated the proceeds from various benefit shows and events staged in Verdun to the local Red Cross. Children's fundraising activities were often prominently publicized. The stories of youngsters patriotically giving of their time and energies provided good newspaper copy and heart-swelling accompanying photographs. Many Verdun children set up candy, baked goods, or lemonade stands to raise money for the Red Cross. The first large wave of such ventures in Verdun took place during the dark days of August 1940, when Britain's fate seemed grim. The names and addresses of the children participating indicated that almost all were English speaking and lived in east-central Verdun on the densely populated numbered avenues.[31] Their parents had encouraged them to join in the war effort. Although children's stands could be found on street corners throughout the war, sugar rationing, announced in 1942, limited production of some of the more traditional confections. What is more, not all proceeds went to the Red Cross; later in the war children had a greater choice of charities, frequently in unintended competition with one another.

Edward Wilson, mayor of Verdun 1939-60. Born in Lancashire, the left-leaning but intensely patriotic Wilson was heavily involved in war-related activities and proved to be a shrewd consensus builder during the war. *Verdun Borough Archives*

Joseph Rienzo French, Verdun city manager, 1933-64, a French-speaking Catholic and Verdun's top unelected official. A strong supporter of Mayor Wilson, he helped mobilize the city's resources solidly behind the war effort. *Verdun Borough Archives*

Arthur Burgess, Verdun city clerk, 1929-62. British born and heavily involved in patriotic activities in the city, he was instrumental in preserving the city's archives pertaining to the war. *Verdun Borough Archives*

The "Verdun Gang" of the 1st Medium Regiment, Royal Canadian Artillery, taken in England probably in 1941. Indicative of their large numbers overseas and sense of hometown identity, Verdun members of this unit sent this photo-postcard home to friends and relatives. *Courtesy Joseph Way*

A family of soldiers from Second Avenue: from left, Thomas Snow, Robert Snow, Bernice Snow, Ted Snow, Archie Bain, and unidentified friend, April 1941. Note typical Verdun tenement housing and few parked cars in this lower-income municipality. *Courtesy Paul Moreau*

Flying Officer George Frederick Beurling wearing the ribbons of the Distinguished Service Order, the Distinguished Flying Cross, and the Distinguished Flying Medal and Bar. Only twenty at the time this photograph was taken in 1942, Beurling had already downed twenty-nine enemy aircraft and was one of the war's leading Allied aces. *Department of National Defence*

George Beurling speaking at his homecoming ceremony at the Verdun Auditorium, 10 November 1942. "This is no place for me ... I'm a fighter pilot," stammered Beurling, to uproarious applause. *Library and Archives Canada, PA-176977*

Adoring Canadians treated fighter ace George Beurling like a matinee idol. Nowhere was this more so than in Verdun, which organized a massive homecoming celebration for him at the Auditorium on 10 November 1942. Nearly 5,000 people crammed into the building. *Department of National Defence*

FACING PAGE, BOTTOM
Flight Lieutenant George Beurling meets highly decorated Alf Hamer, a sixty-nine-year-old British-born veteran of three previous wars. The occasion is the opening day of the sixth Victory Loan drive, 11 May 1944. Verdun's "thermometer" indicator showing the progress of local donations was mounted at Church and Verdun avenues. This photo was published in the Montreal *Daily Star* under the title "Two Heroes of Verdun." *Verdun Borough Archives*

A display donated by Imperial Tobacco for the Mayor's Cigarette Fund in the lobby of the Fifth Avenue Theatre, May 1941. Standing are the theatre managers; seated are Mayor Wilson and canvassers from the Women's Volunteer Reserve Corps whose husbands were overseas. *Verdun Borough Archives*

A "tag" worn by Verdunites having contributed to the Mayor's Cigarette Fund during special fund-raising campaigns. *Author's collection*

A typical coupon for the extremely popular Mayor's Cigarette Fund as published in the *Guardian*. City hall collected more than 6,300 names of residents serving overseas, who received cigarettes twice annually. *Verdun Borough Archives*

His Worship Mayor Edward Wilson and the City Council are pleased to announce that applications are now being accepted by the

MAYOR'S CIGARETTE FUND

FOR DISTRIBUTION OF CIGARETTES TO

VERDUN SOLDIERS OVERSEAS

Including shipments to Verdun airmen overseas as well as to Verdun sailors aboard ships assigned to service in Eastern Atlantic or Mediterranean waters.

If a member of your family is on active service OVERSEAS, clip out and fill in this coupon, mailing it to the MAYOR'S CIGARETTE FUND, CITY HALL, VERDUN. It should be noted that cigarettes can be sent only to those Verdun soldiers, airmen and sailors whose relations furnish their names and addresses to the Fund, as there is no other method of obtaining this information. If your name has already been sent in, please do not duplicate.

Regimental Number ... *D 76 053.*
Rank and Name .... *C.Q.M.S. FAUBERT. J.L.*
Full Details of Unit *C' COMPANY.*
.... *ROYAL. MONTREAL. REGIMENT.*
.... *MACHINE GUN.*

Relative's name *MRS. J.L. FAUBERT.*
Relative's address ..*767 Third Ave. VERDUN.*
What relationship ...*WIFE.* ... Telephone No. ....

Lt-Cdr William Woods, Royal Canadian Naval Reserve, commanding officer of the antisubmarine frigate HMCS *Dunver*, signing the Golden Book of the City of Verdun in the mayor's office, June 1943. At right is the ship's executive officer (second-in-command), Lt André Marcil, a Montrealer. *Verdun Borough Archives*

A souvenir shot of HMCS *Dunver* off the coast of Nova Scotia when the ship entered service in the autumn of 1943. The navy took similar photos of virtually every warship (frequently adding the same superimposed billowing clouds) and sold prints to crew members. *Department of National Defence*

FACING PAGE, BOTTOM

The Verdun Salvage Committee collection and sorting depot on the waterfront behind the Verdun General Hospital, 16 June 1943. From left, Georges Ladouceur, deputy warden of the Civilian Protection Committee (in the CPC coveralls), Dr Charles Barr, chief warden of the CPC, and Mayor Edward Wilson. The Salvage Committee hired trucks from local merchants to collect the salvaged materials. *Verdun Borough Archives*

MEET THE COMMANDER

OF THE

VERDUN FRIGATE!

Lt. Commander Wm. Woods, R.C.N.R.
(of Verdun),

AT THE

NAVY DANCE

SPONSORED BY THE

WOMEN'S VOLUNTEER RESERVE CORPS

(VERDUN UNIT)

WOOD HALL FRI. SEPTEMBER 24
AT 9.00 P. M.

To Provide Comforts for the Officers and Men of
Verdun's Own Frigate.

Under the Distinguished Patronage of

HIS WORSHIP THE MAYOR and COUNCIL

CAPT. J. E. W. OLAND, D.S.C., R.C.N.

Naval Officer in Charge of the Port of Montreal

COMMANDER F. DAVIS, R.N.

Naval Control Officer and Other Staff Officers

Special Features :-

—Navy Band of H.M.C.S. "St. Hyacinthe"
—Star Artists
From the Royal Canadian Navy Musical Revue.
—"Meet The Navy"
Now playing at His Majesty's Theatre.
—Frankie Modler and His Orchestra
—Presentation to Lt. Commander Wm. Woods
of gifts for the officers and men of the Frigate, donated by the City of Verdun and
the citizens of Verdun through the W.V.R.C.

ADMISSION 50¢

To help publicize the fifth Victory Loan Campaign, in October 1943 a yellow Harvard training aircraft was installed next to Verdun's impressive First World War cenotaph, located in the city's east end. *Verdun Borough Archives*

FACING PAGE
A poster for a highly successful fundraising dance organized by the Women's Volunteer Reserve Corps in honour of the crew of HMCS *Dunver* in 1943. Lt-Cdr William Woods, a Verdunite, remarked to the gathering, "This is one of the very great days of my life." *Guardian* (Verdun), 17 September 1943

Verdun Defies Hitler!

THE CLARION CALL SOUNDS TO BUY THE TOOLS
of WAR, for VICTORY and PEACE!

Thousands of Verdun Citizens are already on active service. Thousands more are helping by their work on the home front, willingly, eagerly.

Hitler sneers at us, pushes his panzer divisions and wafts his luftwaffe across the world, with a ruthless efficiency that takes no account of human feelings or human life.

Guile, cunning, treachery, contempt for moral values . . . plus a people driven by compulsion to do his will.

Can Democracy meet this challenge . . . on its own terms? It's for YOU to say, Verdun and hundreds of Canadian cities, towns, villages, must give the answer.

Let us make our dollars talk democracy! Keep Verdun on the map as a fighting outpost for a democratic victory!

BUY
VICTORY
BONDS

BUY
VICTORY
BONDS

The Mayor and Council of your City have implicit faith that all citizens will answer this call to the very utmost of their ability.

Verdun is Always in Front — We Will Not Fail!

HELP FINISH THE JOB—BUY VICTORY BONDS!

Capitalizing on a strong sense of local identity, city officials and the *Guardian* regularly linked national fundraising campaigns to Verdunites' pride. This advertisement for Victory Bonds is especially effusive and probably originated with city hall. *Guardian* (Verdun), 30 May 1941

Miss R.B. Joan Adams, in the uniform of commandant, Women's Volunteer Reserve Corps, Verdun Branch, March 1941. The outspoken and ultrapatriotic Adams later joined the Canadian Women's Army Corps. *Courtesy Joan Adams*

Women from Verdun's Red Cross chapter preparing material for dispatch overseas, 2 October 1943. The Red Cross was an inclusive organization crossing linguistic, religious, and class barriers. *Verdun Borough Archives*

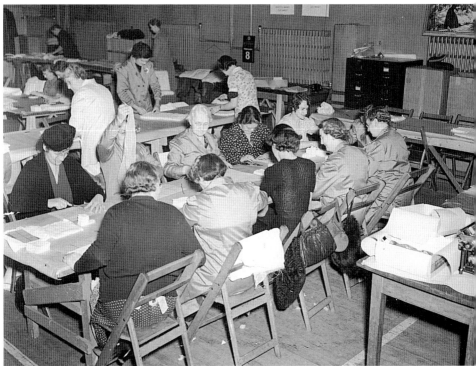

These children sold candy apples and other sweets at the corner of Rielle and Verdun avenues, 20 September 1941, to aid the Queen's Canadian Fund, a charity assisting British victims of German bombing. Queen Elizabeth's photograph is prominently displayed as is an American flag, despite American neutrality at the time. *Verdun Borough Archives*

A typical wartime display in the lobby of a Verdun business, 2 February 1942. The girls of Barbara's Knitting Club made and dispatched comforts to assist British children evacuated from areas targeted by German bombers. Helping Britain came easily to Verdun's large British-expatriate population. Standing next to Mayor Wilson is Mrs Barbara Tasker. *Verdun Borough Archives*

Some 200 Verdunites lost their lives during the Second World War. Gordon Hutton was killed during the gruelling campaign in Normandy and is buried in Brettville-sur-Laize Canadian War Cemetery. "Not only today but every day in silence we remember." *Author's collection*

Verdun's Red Cross women volunteers made bandages, medical supplies, and bedding for hospital use, clothing for refugees, and warm clothes, such as toques, gloves, sweaters, and socks, for servicemen (see Table 5.2).[32] Some of the women worked at the police gymnasium, but many did so at home or in their unit's regular meeting places. Their work was usually an extension of their traditional maternal social roles as caring, nurturing providers, and their immense efforts were valued highly by Canadian servicemen overseas.

The Chalmers United Church Red Cross unit in the east end, established immediately on the outbreak of war, serves as an example of Verdun women's contributions. This group met every Wednesday at the church, "where [by 1941] eight sewing machines were kept in operation." Most of the knitting was done at home. At the end of 1940, seventy-one women of the congregation worked in this unit, although on average only thirty-five attended the weekly sessions. These women produced 19,000 articles, including quilts and afghans, for members of the armed forces and for British victims of air raids. They did not officially wind up their activities until January 1946.[33] Although the Chalmers women believed that theirs was Verdun's best Red Cross unit, in April 1940 the largest group was from St Willibrord Parish, which covered the city.[34]

The Canadian Red Cross Society provided relief parcels for Allied prisoners of war, perhaps its greatest contribution to alleviating the suffering of thousands. Red Cross volunteers prepared and packaged parcels that included food, medicine, various amenities, and cigarettes. Over eight million were dispatched – one-quarter of them prepared in Quebec.[35] In February 1944 a repatriated prisoner of war appeared at the annual meeting of the Verdun branch to recount vividly how much these packages meant to recipients. Sgt André Michaud, a Verdunite, had been captured at Dieppe as a member of the Fusiliers Mont-Royal. He gave an "inspiring" address and responded to numerous questions. He assured the gathering just "how grateful the men were for the service rendered by the Canadian Red Cross Society, without which service life in the Camp would be intolerable."[36]

Another of the Red Cross's crucial wartime tasks was to collect blood. At the end of 1943 there were 71 clinics and 314 subclinics in Canada, two-thirds of which had opened in the previous twelve months. The closest clinic to Verdun was on Ste Catherine Street in downtown Montreal. By January 1944, Verdun's enthusiastic responses to routine, Montreal-wide solicitations for blood persuaded the Red Cross to create a permanent blood-donor clinic in Verdun. The idea of local clinics drew a positive response across Canada, including in Verdun. "So much is this service upon the hearts of the people of Canada that almost every community from coast to coast without a Blood Donor Clinic has been clamouring to provide one," stated a Red Cross pamphlet published that year.[37]

The new clinic galvanized a cross-section of Verdun society. A local French-speaking pharmacist, T.E. Gaucher, offered to organize the clinic and publicized

Table 5.2

Verdun Red Cross, items sent overseas, 1939-44

Type of article	Year						Total
	1939	1940	1941	1942	1943	1944	
Hospital supplies	3,697	13,992	6,155	1,783	3,335	3,734	32,696
Surgical dressings	–	–	–	6,150	320,886	247,850	574,886
Knitted goods, military	692	11,907	8,126	9,482	3,489	2,619	36,315
Knitted goods, auxiliary services	40	–	1,392	929	400	48	2,809
Civilian clothes	1,921	6,481	8,938	5,438	2,890	5,184	30,852
Miscellaneous donations	–	497	566	375	420	104	1,962
Miscellaneous items for the navy	–	–	–	750	250	–	1,000
Miscellaneous items for Russian relief	–	226[a]	–	5,330	–	–	5,556
Total	6,350	33,103	25,177	30,237	331,670	259,539	686,076

a Probably refers to Finnish war relief.
Source: Box A-331, file 5, Verdun Borough Archives.

his intention in a full-page advertisement in the local press. The mainly English-speaking Lion's Club volunteered to sponsor and staff the proposed facility. The *Guardian* agreed to act as a clearing house for information, suggestions, and offers of assistance. Edward Wilson, acting both as president of the Verdun Red Cross and as mayor, endorsed the proposal wholeheartedly. The superintendent of Protestant schools in Verdun, H.E. Grant, noted that "the population of Verdun consists mostly of Old Country people with a high percentage in the armed forces. Naturally, their relatives would appreciate a clinic in Verdun and ... their response would be very good."[38] The *Guardian* printed over two dozen quotations in support of the clinic from merchants, clergymen, and heads of local institutions and social organizations from both linguistic communities.[39]

After more than nine months of planning, preparation, and lobbying, in November 1944 the Red Cross opened a blood-donor clinic using space donated by Defence Industries Limited in its munitions plant in Verdun's easternmost neighbourhood (discussed below). DIL provided interim staff until the Lion's Club fielded properly trained volunteers. The overburdened Montreal clinic transferred the files of all registered Verdun donors to the new site.

To sensitize residents, the *Guardian* published the story of Victor St André, a handicapped Verdun tailor described as "small and slight," who had donated blood fifty-one times during the war. Though unable to don a uniform, this French-speaking member of the Lion's Club was hailed as a selfless participant in the war effort.[40] By the autumn of 1944, Canadian and Allied troops had suffered enormous casualties, especially in Normandy and northwest Europe, and there was the promise of many more to come. Yet less than three months after these hopeful beginnings, DIL notified the Red Cross that a new contractual commitment with the Department of Munitions and Supply necessitated use of the clinic's space. This was odd given that DIL production would cease in March. The Red Cross could not find new accommodations and Verdun lost its much-coveted clinic early in 1945.

The proliferation of national and local charitable organizations and patriotic causes taxed the community's resources. There were limits to the availability of volunteers, and the increased wartime work opportunities for women also eroded the time available for charitable efforts. By 1941 this competition had begun to adversely affect the Verdun Red Cross. At the end of that year, the local branch was down to twenty-six units with 668 volunteers – a loss of over half in less than a year. Twelve months later there were only nineteen units and 496 workers.[41] While the branch managed to increase the output of medical supplies and clothing for overseas servicemen and refugees every year up to 1944, it did so with fewer units and a depleted staff. By 31 December 1943 the Verdun Red Cross could muster 467 volunteers spread over twenty-two units, the slight increase in units masking their shrinking sizes.[42] At the start of 1945 the chapter at Chalmers United Church numbered forty-six women, down 35 percent in one of the city's most patriotic churches.[43]

This shift reflected not a diminution in the volunteering spirit, but merely its wider diffusion. Early in 1943 Elizabeth Wilson believed former Red Cross women volunteers were choosing to work instead for the auxiliary units of regiments or services in which their male relatives were enlisted. This affiliation provided a personal meaning and immediacy to their efforts that was usually unavailable in Red Cross work. The great number of Verdun enlistees thus acted as an indirect drain on local Red Cross resources. Mrs Wilson also noted that many Red Cross volunteers had taken jobs in war industry.[44] It was difficult for them to be both wage earners and volunteers, especially given responsibilities in the home.

The Verdun branch of the Red Cross attracted the largest number of regular and occasional volunteer workers and program participants of any war-related or patriotic organization in the city. Although membership declined during the war, Red Cross activities continued to be the focal point of the war effort for hundreds of Verdunites of all backgrounds, almost all of whom were women.

The Canadian Legion

Following the First World War, Verdun became well known in the Montreal area as a veterans' community. By 1939 it possessed four separate veterans' groups: the Army and Navy Veterans in Canada; the Canadian Corps Association, Verdun Section No. 1; the Canadian Legion, Branch (No. 4) of the British Empire Service League; and the Canadian National Railways War Veterans' Association. In addition, with nearly 900 Newfoundlanders living in Verdun,[45] the Newfoundland War Veterans' Association established a branch in the city in 1942. The largest group – the Canadian Legion – played a major patriotic and social role in Verdun during the Second World War. While the Verdun Legion is introduced here, later chapters examine some of its main activities, such as its efforts to ameliorate the wartime housing crisis and to assist in the civil re-establishment of discharged soldiers.[46]

In 1919 a branch of the Great War Veterans' Association, at the time the largest veterans' group in Canada, was formed in Verdun. Perhaps a staggering 20 percent of the city's population had been in uniform during the First World War. In 1926, as a result of a national amalgamation of returned servicemen's organizations, Verdun's Great War Veterans' Association branch became a branch of the Canadian Legion. In 1929 Governor General Viscount Willingdon officially opened the local Legion's impressive headquarters: the Great War Memorial Hall, located in the centre of the city at Verdun and Willibrord Avenues.

Branch No. 4 was a workingman's institution. J. Arthur Mathewson, KC, its legal advisor, wrote in 1939 that "most of the fathers of the Branch were men without financial resources and without great influence."[47] Its executive consisted almost exclusively of former "other ranks," not officers, as was often the case in other branches. The president for most of the war was Arthur H. James, who succeeded F.C. Stapley in 1940. In October 1939 there were 4,197 Legion members in Quebec.

At the end of May 1940 there were 4,573 members in fifty-three branches, a wartime increase of 10 percent in a matter of months. The Verdun branch numbered approximately 450 members.[48]

The Verdun Legion's frequently changing executive committee in the period 1919-39 shows not a single man whose mother tongue was French. During the Second World War the Legion continued to be led exclusively by English speakers. A listing of the fifty-five active branch members who had died between the wars shows fifty-three English surnames and two French surnames. Although the branch was almost entirely English speaking, there were at least some French-speaking members. A commemorative program for its twentieth anniversary (1939) offered French translations of selected passages, and a congratulatory message from Mayor Edward Wilson appeared in both languages.[49]

In the 1920s and 1930s Verdun's Legion was a leader in the national organization's struggle for improved government pensions and disability allowances for veterans. The Legion also assisted numerous financially strapped Verdun veterans and their families and felt that "the Branch ha[d] won an honoured place in the Community of Verdun."[50] The authors of a study of First World War veterans' rehabilitation termed Verdun a "notorious" case in the eyes of the federal government. In 1935 the federal government established a committee to investigate unemployment among Canadian veterans. Verdun's veterans' groups zealously investigated the plight of their unemployed, destitute members, providing the government commission with many sad case studies.[51] By 1939, with its large membership, modern facility, and devotion to its community, the Legion had become a pillar of Verdun's English-speaking society.

During the Second World War Ottawa designated the Canadian Legion as one of the few official auxiliary services. The others were the Knights of Columbus, the Salvation Army, and the YMCA. All these organizations worked together and benefited from federal support for their activities in Canada and overseas. The Legion's patriotic credentials included its twenty-year struggle on behalf of veterans. Moreover, Legion members clearly knew more about the nature of war and the demands required of a wartime society than any other group. First World War veterans accepted it as their right and duty to examine critically Canada's war effort. Many veterans also felt that they had bequeathed a sacred trust to all those who would follow them – to uphold the principles for which they had fought.

Verdun's Legion branch, like its parent national body, passed many war-related (and warlike) resolutions, placed its facilities and expertise at the disposal of the nation, and offered its services and financial assistance to many patriotic and charitable causes. Much of No. 4's correspondence was directed at city hall, where the Legion generally found a supporter in Edward Wilson. Every week the *Guardian* reported on the Legion's social and recreational activities, and it frequently mentioned Legion donations to such local groups as the Civilian Protection Committee and the Mayor's Cigarette Fund. The Legion's wartime visibility was enhanced by its well-orchestrated parades and commemorative ceremonies, especially the observances of Remembrance Day and Ypres Day. These events served as platforms for the Legion to promote its patriotic views and to remind citizens of their civic obligations. Verdunites were a receptive audience.

One of the Legion's major wartime contributions was providing material assistance and comfort to the needy or distraught families of overseas servicemen and returning veterans – a critically important but "silent" role.[52] Canadian cities found themselves short of housing during the war and many military families lived in demeaning conditions. By 1945 Verdun's population had swelled by some 10,000, with few new homes to accommodate them. Concerned that the housing crisis eroded civilian and soldiers' morale, the Legion attempted to find shelter for veterans' and servicemen's distressed families. It publicly questioned why Canadians should be asked to fight tyranny overseas when their loved ones could not find decent, affordable housing at home. Families facing eviction registered with the Legion in the hope of finding shelter. Chapter 6 reviews Verdun's housing crisis and the Legion's prominent response. The Legion also comforted bereaved families – a task increasingly common in Verdun in the last two years of the war.

The Dominion Command of the Canadian Legion vociferously supported conscription and total national mobilization – a position that it adopted at its Dominion conventions in the 1930s and confirmed during its convention in Montreal in May 1940. The Legion urged the immediate national conscription of manpower, wealth, and industry and remained hostile to Ottawa's refusal to adopt these measures.[53] During the 1942 plebiscite to release the federal government from its previous pledge not to impose compulsory overseas service, the Verdun Legion campaigned locally for the "yes" side (even though the Legion considered the government's strategy a half-measure). Its views obviously represented much of English-speaking Verdun, since the city voted 63 percent in favour of the measure.[54]

While identified with the welfare of Canadian service people, the Legion's aggressive stance and rhetoric on conscription and other wartime issues also confirmed it as essentially English speaking and Empire minded, as reflected in the views and membership of the Verdun branch. Throughout the war the Verdun Legion proved a strong and able supporter of Verdunites in uniform and helped define the community's wartime self-perception, but it did little to improve local language relations.

The YMCA

To meet the needs of an English-speaking Protestant population that had doubled in the previous decade, the Young Men's Christian Association opened a branch in Verdun in 1929. The next year it completed an impressive recreational and sporting facility – known as the Southwestern Branch, for Verdun's location on the Island of Montreal – in the east end of the city. The city cooperated with the YMCA in every way possible, and the "Y" soon occupied a prominent place in local social, recreational, and sporting life. Not long after it opened, nearly two dozen other community groups began using its building in some capacity, especially for swimming and as a meeting place.[55] With 900 members by 1932-33, the "Y" rapidly became the largest community organization in Verdun (although some members lived in the nearby Montreal parishes of Côte St Paul and Ville Émard). The Southwestern Branch was a "Family Y," one of only a handful in Canada that allowed female members.[56] During the Depression the YMCA implemented many useful programs to assist unemployed and impoverished Verdunites, and its stature in the community grew. At the end of 1941, Verdun's ever-growing "Y" boasted 1,330 members.[57]

There had always been a good deal of cooperation between the "Y" and the local Protestant school board and churches, but there was little interaction between the Southwestern YMCA and Verdun's French-language community. The "Y" was an English-language institution with a previous history of evangelical Protestantism. French Canadian Catholics traditionally had shunned the organization and continued to do so, even though it had replaced its mission-oriented character with a greater concern for community sports and recreation. A listing of the sixty-three groups using the "Y" during the first year of the war indicates that the single French-language organization associated with the "Y" was the Église Bethany, a Protestant church. Of the 195 boys and girls enrolled in the YMCA's Summer Vacation Club in 1937, only two attended French Catholic schools, while another twenty-one were Catholic English speakers. Moreover, the YMCA attracted mainly more financially secure families. Half of these youths lived west of Desmarchais Boulevard (the traditional dividing line between the poorer, mainly French-speaking east end and the somewhat better-off, mainly English-speaking west end), and only 7 percent came from east of Church Avenue, arguably the poorest section of Verdun.[58]

At the outbreak of war in 1939, Verdun's branch, following the YMCA's national policy, "made available its physical facilities and its personnel to whatever extent they might be needed for the duration of the ... conflict."[59] The large influx of young men into the armed forces meant that suitable training, sporting, and recreational facilities in the Montreal area were in great demand. With its modern swimming pool, Verdun's "Y" proved very popular with the military. From mid-September until the end of January 1940, 3,249 uniformed personnel, many based in Montreal, used the pool, gymnasium, and lounge. In the early months of the war it was common to see soldiers marching towards the Verdun YMCA. Like other branches across Canada, it provided any man in uniform free membership privileges.[60]

The YMCA's women's volunteer committee offered weekly teas, socials, and dances to troops stationed in or passing through Montreal. Similar groups were established at other nearby YMCA facilities. Women members of Verdun's "Family Y" also established a Red Cross unit and provided home nursing courses.[61] Miss Betty Allen – a survivor from the first British ship lost in the war, the passenger liner *Athenia*, which a German submarine torpedoed on 3 September 1939 – spoke to a large audience at the "Y" about her experiences. The event aroused considerable interest since twenty-one Verdunites, most returning from visiting British relatives, had been aboard the ill-fated vessel, and two residents were killed.[62] Highlighting the early wartime contribution of the Verdun YMCA, Walter Kemball, executive secretary of the Southwestern Branch, was selected to chair a committee of Montreal social groups set up to coordinate all recreational services in Military District 4.[63]

The YMCA transformed many regular recreational activities into war-related, patriotic work. For example, boys from the modelling club and other arts and crafts groups spent thousands of hours making wooden model airplanes for use by RCAF instructors. The Verdun Arts and Trade School allowed the groups to use its power tools to speed up production. Verdun High School students later did the basic woodworking of the models, while the "Y" modelling club continued to finish and paint the airplanes.[64] Like-minded Verdun youths from different organizations thus worked together in a war-related cause.

The Verdun YMCA also helped to maintain morale at nearby Defence Industries Limited. Walter Kemball felt that an arrangement with DIL-Verdun would promote better war use of the branch. In early 1941, the National Council's R.S. Hosking met with a representative of DIL's parent firm, Canadian Industries Limited, to consider organizing recreational and sporting activities for war workers – a service that the "Y" was providing at the DIL plant in Brownsburg, Quebec.[65] DIL-Verdun was initially reluctant to invest in recreation, but the "Y" convinced the firm of its merit. From 1942 on the YMCA arranged many sporting competitions between the Brownsburg, Montreal Works, Verdun, and Villeray DIL plants.[66]

The war allowed the YMCA to enhance its already-strong leadership in Verdun's Protestant community. The "Y" integrated wartime activities into its regular schedule of events and acted as the focal point for the patriotic endeavours of many English-speaking Protestants. But unlike the Red Cross, the YMCA did not bridge social barriers in the interest of common patriotic pursuits.

Churches and the War

Verdun was a city with many churches, Catholic and Protestant, French and English; there were no non-Christian places of worship. In January 1940, there were five Catholic churches (four French and one English), fifteen Protestant churches (one of them French-language Baptist), and two mission halls, including the Salvation Army citadel. At the end of the war Verdun had one more English Catholic church, one more French Catholic, and one fewer Protestant.[67] The churches had played a significant social role before the war, often serving as the focus of social, charitable, and recreational activities. Many parishioners looked to them as a source of identity; religion remained a powerful force, both as a unifying and as a divisive element. Schooling, hospital care, and social assistance services were virtually entirely segregated by religion.

Churches of both languages raised money for patriotic causes, provided space for Red Cross units and other groups doing war-related relief work, and comforted the anguished, the fearful, and the lonely.[68] But Verdun's English-language churches contained many British-born and first-generation Canadians and contributed earnestly to the war effort. It was said of Rev Donald H. MacVicar, minister of Chalmers United Church, that "those of his congregation who came to know him found in [him] a source of strength, support and friendship that served them faithfully during the long years of the Second World War." The churches' support to those left behind remains a little-publicized but integral part of their wartime role. At the bottom of the honour roll of June 1944 for St Willibrord Parish was the following message:

> To the parents of all those "Boys" of our Parish who have made the supreme sacrifice, we, the priests and parishioners of St Willibrord's, assure them of a continued remembrance in our Masses and prayers that Our Lord may grant them eternal rest.

> To the parents of those serving either here or overseas, we know that they join us in our daily prayers that Our Lord will watch over them and bring them safely home; If it be His will that they should not return we, with them, humbly beg of Him that He grant them to leave this world in His grace and friendship.[69]

Most English-speaking congregations and parishes maintained honour rolls of parishioners who enlisted. "In this war, as in the previous, Chalmers gave of its best in both combatant and non-combatant services," stated one commemorative booklet.[70] All of the English-language churches in Verdun could have said as much.

Nor did the churches forget the troops' material needs. Chalmers set up a Soldiers' Comfort Fund with two collection boxes at the church's front entrance. These boxes kept the war in the minds of the congregation. Between 1942 and 1945 the fund sent Chalmers "boys and girls" serving overseas some 720 cartons of 300 cigarettes and 297 parcels of chocolate. In 1946 the fund ceased to operate following a "welcome-home party" for returned members of the congregation.[71]

In January 1943, St Willibrord's organized a similar Overseas Cigarette and Comfort Fund. By the summer of 1945, it had sent overseas more than 3,800 cartons of cigarettes – averaging more than three per enlistee – and delivered some 450 "comfort packages" to the disproportionately large number of parishioners serving in the navy, many based in Canada and ineligible for discount-rate cigarettes.[72] St

Willibrord's had one of the largest chapters of the Catholic Women's League, a charitable welfare organization with 1,460 members in the Montreal area. Like the Red Cross, League members made clothes, collected books and magazines, and raised money, mostly for Britain. Other recipients included the Merchant Marine and the St Willibrord Boys' Overseas Christmas Fund.[73]

St Willibrord's seemed always to act in such matters independently of other Catholic (but French-language) parishes and other English-speaking (but Protestant) churches. Despite being the odd parish out, with about 10,000 parishioners by the end of the war it could raise substantial funds. If English and French Catholics differed, it was not over the war but rather over administration of the Verdun Catholic School Commission (see below). Catholic and Protestant English speakers were often united in common patriotic purpose, though acting separately through their churches. Other wartime community efforts, such as salvage collection or the Mayor's Cigarette Fund, brought all these groups together.

Verdun's war was shared by Catholics and Protestants. Following the war, Edward Wilson wrote of the remarkable enlistment record and patriotic contribution from St Willibrord's: "no part of the population did more than our English-speaking Roman Catholic youth. To them ... the City of Verdun owes a lasting debt."[74]

Language, more than faith, shaped the participation of churches in the local war effort. According to the 1941 census, 74 percent of Verdun's Catholics were of French origin, almost all of whom spoke French as their mother tongue. Of the remainder, more than one-third were Irish, with almost all the rest being English, Scottish, Italian, or Polish.[75] Verdun's French-language parishes offer virtually no records or other evidence of their wartime efforts. Of the commemorative booklets issued for each parish since 1945, only one even mentions the war.[76] Other than what can be gleaned from other sources regarding their Red Cross work or fundraising campaigns, the sources are mute concerning their wartime roles. But since the clergy administered Catholic schools, those schools' war efforts shed light on parish views.

Schools at War

According to the 1939-40 annual report of the Montreal Protestant Board of School Commissioners, in all schools in its jurisdiction, including those in Verdun, "the principals and teachers have been vigilant to inspire and maintain a patriotic spirit among the children."[77] War-related activities, excursions, plays, and films became a regular part of the curriculum. War Savings Stamps and Certificates were sold in schools, Junior Red Cross groups were formed to raise money and to prepare clothing bundles for beleaguered Britain, and drives for newspaper, metal, and glass salvage were organized, with every Protestant school converted into a salvage depot. Teachers gave lessons in democratic ideals and "practical patriotism." "In almost every respect," stated the board's 1940-41 annual report, "the daily programme of the schools has accommodated itself to the influence of the War."[78] And so it was in Verdun's seven Protestant and, to a lesser extent perhaps, thirteen Catholic schools.

Students attending Verdun's Protestant high school were certainly war conscious. The 1940 *Annual* of Verdun High School (VHS) contained students' essays and poetry devoted to war themes, invoking mainly defence of democracy and maintenance of the British Empire as justification for Canadian participation in the war. Still, this volume seems restrained, given that the country had just gone to war. In 1941 the tone was far more warlike. The editor, Bruce Raymond, wrote, "As might be expected, the War situation has influenced almost unbelievably the contributions to the *Annual*. Articles on democracy, War Heroes and War Histories were received ... and the best of these have been printed."[79] The students' sense of the costs of the war to their community was also more apparent. Mildrid Culkin, the 1941 associate editor, dedicated the *Annual* to those Verdunites who thus far had died in the war. "There are many persons in our community ... whose hearts are heavy with sorrow because of a loved one lost in this great conflict."[80] An honour roll of former students from VHS (which had opened in 1933) on active service began with the 1942 *Annual*. By 1945 it contained nearly 700 names.

The *Annuals* also noted that all grades in Verdun Protestant schools had contributed to war charities such as the Spitfire Fund, the Queen's Canadian Fund (to assist British victims of air raids), the Red Cross and, by 1943, the Aid to Russia Fund and the Navy League Fund. In the summer of 1942, thirty-two students from Verdun High School went with thousands of other Canadian high school students to western Canada to assist with the harvest.[81]

The 1944 yearbook of St Willibrord High School provides a somewhat different picture. References to "King and Country" and the "British Empire" are conspicuously absent, probably because of the sensibilities of the large Irish element in this parish; "God" and "Jesus" replace them.[82] This publication includes no warlike essays or patriotic photo collages. Yet the war is ever present. Louise Matthews, whose favourite expression was said to be "c'est la guerre," wrote: "Because I'm patriotic I must remember to bring pictures of my brother for the military Honor Roll, and good reading matter to sustain the morale of our fighting men. We're going to offer a decade of the beads every day for those who appear on the Honor Roll."[83] The Sodalists, a lay charitable society, also "organized groups to attend Mass and receive Holy Communion on specified days, for the intentions of specified soldiers of our Parish serving overseas." Seventy-five men were remembered in this way and "informed of this activity." Some thirty of them wrote letters of thanks.[84]

The war affected school enrolment in Verdun. As part of a Montreal-area trend, high school numbers dropped suddenly, while those for elementary school climbed. The 1941 VHS *Annual* listed 67 graduating students, of whom only 55 obtained their diplomas; that compared to 83 graduating students the previous year, a decline of 19 percent. Many of the senior class identified military service as their ambition. The 1942 *Annual* listed only 50 students in the graduating class with many of the young women expressing a desire to become military nurses. In 1943 there were again only 50 potential graduates, while in 1944, 66 were listed and 56 graduated.

In the foreword to VHS's 1941 *Annual*, Principal J.A. Weatherbee wrote about the sacrifices being borne by Canada's youths, including many alumni. His message was that the promise of a good future was well worth fighting for.[85] Protestant school board superintendent H.E. Grant stressed the importance of obtaining a high school leaving certificate, even though "it is not difficult now for any bright teenage boy or girl to find a job in an office or in industry." As well, "there are at present many disappointed youths who, because of failure to gain matriculation, are unable to qualify for commission in the Army, Navy or Air Force." (In fact, few Verdunites attained officer rank, and insufficient education was often the reason.) Grant's tone was not inspirational but pleading; the lure of a uniform or a job in war industry, sometimes needed to bolster a family's finances, was exacerbating an already high dropout rate.[86] With a steady influx of people into the Montreal area and an improvement in many family economies, school enrolment shot up dramatically later in the war. In 1945, 92 of 104 students graduated.[87]

Students' essays in the VHS *Annuals* were almost all British oriented. The British prime minister, Winston Churchill, received praise frequently, as did US president Franklin Delano Roosevelt. The Canadian prime minister, William Lyon Mackenzie King, was never mentioned. Regarding conscription, the editor in 1943, William Weintraub, wrote a not-very-subtle piece in French, entitled "Jean-Paul s'enrôle," which barely concealed his disdain for French Canada's response to the war.[88]

High school during the war had a martial air. Many male students participated in cadet programs, which allowed them to look and feel like part of the war. In 1941, 200 enrolled in the Verdun High School Army Cadets – more than one-fifth of the school and about 15 percent of the Protestant board's cadet strength. The next year, as a result of student preferences, the board converted its program to air cadets. In fact, in November 1941 the Air Cadet League of Canada had already formed a squadron at VHS, heralded by the local press as an important initiative.[89]

Verdun was proud of its air cadets. On the evening of 16 January 1942, an estimated 2,500 people attended ceremonies at two movie theatres in Verdun, the Fifth Avenue and the Park, at which Air Chief Marshal Sir Frederick Bowhill, head of the Royal Air Force's Ferry Command, presented squadron colours to 69 Squadron (Verdun High School), Air Cadets.[90] By May 1942, 150 of VHS's over 900 students were enrolled in 69 Squadron. The air cadets played a prominent role in local parades, demonstrations, and other civic and military events. For example, on 10 November 1942 they participated in the gala ceremonies at the Verdun Auditorium for the triumphal homecoming of fighter ace George Beurling. That autumn the Protestant school board instituted compulsory air cadet training in all its high schools. In 1944 VHS's air cadets numbered 143 seniors (aged fifteen to eighteen) and 84 juniors (aged twelve to fifteen), for a total of 227 out of a school population of about 1,100.[91]

The Verdun Catholic School Commission (VCSC) also cooperated with municipal and federal war efforts. The two elementary and two high schools (one each for boys and girls) of St Willibrord's were English speaking, while the remaining nine Catholic schools were French speaking. Throughout the war there were no English speakers on the VCSC's executive committee, and by December 1941 this had become a sore point with the underfunded English-speaking Catholics.[92] This friction helps explain the absence of a united Catholic response to the war, as well as St Willibrord's independent program of war charities.

The participation of Verdun's French-language residents in the war effort can be measured through their schools. The main French-language high school, École secondaire Richard (named in honour of the omnipresent Mgr Richard of Notre-Dame-des-Sept-Douleurs Parish), organized an army cadet corps, and all schools participated in Red Cross and other fundraising activities and in special salvage collections. In March 1941 the VCSC asked all Catholic schoolchildren to contribute one cent to the Canadian War Services Fund, of which Mayor Wilson was local campaign chairman. It opened its schools for national registration in August 1940, for meetings of Verdun's Civilian Protection Committee and the Verdun section of the National War Finance Committee, and as distribution points for the government's ration-coupon booklets. The VCSC donated cash to the Knights of Columbus War Services and purchased more than 100 war maps for the upper grades in its schools.[93]

"It is ... impossible to overestimate both the moral and material values of the contribution which the schools are making" to the war effort, stated the 1941-42 annual report of the Montreal Protestant Board of School Commissioners.[94] Yet some commissioners feared that the war, and perhaps the schools' role, was harming some young people. "No other group in the community are giving so much of their lives and spirit to Canada's War Effort as Canada's children," stated the 1943-44 report. "Who can measure the effect on these children ... [of the] unrest and the war psychology which pervades the community?"[95] The board's efforts to make schoolchildren aware of the conflict might not, in the longer term, make them better or well-adjusted citizens.

La Société Saint-Jean-Baptiste

In the 1927-28 Verdun city directory, the Société Saint-Jean Baptiste described its role: "All French Canadians should join our organization. This is about national pride the measure of which will have consequences for our patriotic solidarity in the struggles ahead. In Verdun are two of the finest sections of the Société St-Jean-Baptiste in Montreal."[96] A decade later, the Société, with three parish chapters in Verdun, faced a series of struggles on wartime issues such as conscription, immigration, and helping men on active service.

As early as July 1937, the Outremont branch of the Société had passed a resolution against a Canadian contribution in manpower, armaments, or money in any overseas war. The next month the large Montreal headquarters branch complained against federal plans to increase defence spending and called on Ottawa to limit such expenditures.[97] Not surprisingly, on 2 September 1939, the day before Britain declared war on Germany, the Société, in a letter to Prime Minister King, implored the government to remain neutral in the upcoming war.[98]

Officially the Société Saint-Jean-Baptiste de Montréal tried to remain neutral. According to the organization's official historian, Robert Rumilly, when the Société was asked early in the war for its cooperation by Lt-Col Eugène Nantel, head of auxiliary services for Military District 4, it suspected the government wanted to use the Société's apparent influence with French Canadians for Ottawa's own propaganda purposes. Yet not helping to organize Montreal-area auxiliary services would leave French-speaking servicemen at the mercy of English-speaking, Protestant organizations such as the Salvation Army and the YMCA. Consequently, the Société collected French-language books and magazines for locally stationed French Canadian troops and regiments, and sent representatives to meetings of various auxiliary services.[99]

Nevertheless, the Société was more concerned with the welfare of French speakers on military service than Rumilly's interpretation allows. In June 1940 the Société officially registered its Comité d'aide aux soldats as a war charity and asked Ottawa to expedite its application so that it could hold a tag day at its annual Saint-Jean-Baptiste Day parade on 24 June 1940. That summer, despite the passage of the National Resources Mobilization Act and its implications for possible conscription, the Société devoted most of its weekly radio broadcasts to publicizing and vaunting the efforts of its Comité d'aide aux soldats.[100] This suggests an early positive involvement in the domestic war effort.

Once conscription for home defence had begun in earnest in the winter of 1941, however, the Société's leadership cooperated only grudgingly with the auxiliary services. The basically unilingual-English nature of the armed forces also discouraged the organization, which wound down fundraising activities and the Comité d'aide aux soldats by mid-1941. After the divisive and acrimonious conscription plebiscite of April 1942, the Montreal Société ignored soldiers' welfare, except for giving some remaining Comité funds to the Régiment de Maisonneuve and dispatching songbooks to military camps in Quebec.[101] Its definition of patriotism involved local defence and non-compulsion, and this clashed with the attitude of mainly English-speaking social groups. Relations between city hall and the Société's Verdun chapters were kept to a minimum. The mayor himself would have had difficulty accommodating an organization whose aims English-speaking circles widely considered to be contrary to the prosecution of the war.

The Société's support among French-speaking Verdunites is difficult to measure. Membership appears to have been small in the three parish branches, and its local influence is also unclear. Its campaign against married women working in war industries, for example, promoted in alliance with the Catholic clergy, seems to have been ineffectual. As its leaders, and even its members, came from the local French-speaking elite, the organization seems to have possessed only a limited appeal for working-class French-speaking Verdunites.[102]

During the war, all three Verdun branches kept low profiles compared to other local groups. They maintained their regular activities but rarely contributed to war-related campaigns, with the occasional exception of the Mayor's Cigarette Fund. The *Guardian* mentioned the Société infrequently. On 20 October 1939, a small item reported an oyster party in the basement of Notre-Dame-de-Lourdes Church, with all proceeds being donated to the parish. By this time most English-speaking groups organized social events, such as an Imperial Order Daughters of the Empire card party advertised in the same edition, to raise money for such patriotic causes as the Red Cross. Nevertheless, Société Saint-Jean-Baptiste branches across Quebec together averaged about $20,000 in purchases each Victory Loan drive. Many branches also sold War Savings Stamps.[103]

At the outset of the war – a conflict in which Rumilly claims the Société did not approve of French Canadians participating – this organization was willing to cooperate with military authorities and to provide French Canadian enlistees with comforts and amenities. But the slide towards conscription portended by the National Resources Mobilization Act and the basic unilingualism of the Canadian military led the Société to end its support for military causes. While Verdun's French speakers generally agreed with the Société's views on conscription, they continued strongly to support local initiatives in aid of Verdunites on active service. Indeed, even the Verdun Société branches felt the pull of local identity and contributed to the Mayor's Cigarette Fund throughout the war.[104]

Defence Industries Limited and Economic Renewal

Until the summer of 1940, Ottawa had been remarkably slow and complacent about placing defence contracts with Canadian industry. C.P. Stacey has noted that "nothing could be much more unwarlike than the chronicle of contracts awarded through the winter of 1939-40," which at least assured the armed services a plentiful supply of corn syrup and toilet paper.[105] After the crushing defeat of Allied arms in western Europe in June 1940, Britain placed urgent orders for Canadian war matériel and

Ottawa suddenly abandoned its lacklustre production effort. The Canadian economy moved to an unlimited war footing.

C.D. Howe, the dynamic minister of munitions and supply, authorized the widespread construction of new defence plants and the conversion and modernization of some existing civilian facilities.[106] Canada's industrial base grew in scope, diversity, and technological complexity. Canadian war production proved of inestimable value to the Allied cause and was nothing short of remarkable for a nation of 11.8 million people. Canada produced over 400 naval escorts and minesweepers, 391 merchant vessels, 16,000 military aircraft, 850,000 military vehicles of every description, 251,000 machine guns, over 900,000 rifles, and more than 72 million rounds of artillery and mortar ammunition.[107] Much military industry centred on Montreal, and the area's number of factories, levels of employment, and gross value of production all rose substantially as a result. Montreal was already Canada's largest city and port and served as headquarters for much of the nation's transportation industry.[108]

Throughout the war the Department of Munitions and Supply helped finance defence contractors, providing grants and loans to upgrade or expand facilities. It also entered the defence business: by the end of 1943 it owned and operated 33 Crown plants (as well as owning and managing 16 Crown corporations), owned 92 Crown plants operated by private companies, and coordinated production at 299 privately owned and operated war facilities.[109]

Ammunition Production

At the outbreak of war only the government-run Dominion Arsenal at Quebec and the private manufacturer Canadian Industries Limited were capable of producing small-arms ammunition in Canada (that is, ammunition with a bullet diameter of one inch (2.5 centimetres) or less). Canadian Industries Limited did so almost solely for retail sale, mainly for sporting purposes. Yet by 1943, according to the official historian of Canada's industrial war effort, the manufacture of small-arms ammunition "became an outstanding feature of the nation's munition programme."[110] Verdun played a central role in this success.

In 1939 Verdun was still suffering from the ravages of the Depression. Since relatively few Verdunites who enlisted had been unemployed, the jobless rate remained fairly high until mid-1940. War industries had not yet hit their stride. Municipal authorities, seeking to exploit the economic opportunities occasioned by the war, petitioned federal and provincial departments and agencies to ensure Verdun's share of the anticipated industrial expansion.[111] Eager to attract investment, Verdun also sought to lessen its relief payments to the unemployed. In April 1940, for example, Arthur Burgess wrote to the War Supply Board in Ottawa (which gave way on 9 April 1940 to the new Department of Munitions and Supply) about Verdun's First World War-era munitions plant, the former facility of British Munitions and, later, the Dominion Textile Company.[112]

The War Supply Board noted the several Verdun firms capable of manufacturing defence-related goods, and in August 1940 Ottawa offered capital assistance to Defence Industries Limited (DIL) to re-establish a munitions factory in Verdun. A wholly owned subsidiary of Canadian Industries Limited, DIL had been incorporated as a private company on 14 September 1939, "for the purpose of segregating from the normal commercial business of Canadian Industries Limited the production of munitions for the Allied Governments."[113] DIL initially consisted of two small plants and 250 employees, all Canadian Industries Limited staff, producing limited quantities of TNT and cordite. The federal government and Allied nations were the sole recipients of DIL's products. The company did not sell its munitions, since the government owned the means of production and incurred all manufacturing costs, but rather collected fees from Ottawa for managing and operating the plants. Direct government financing allowed for massive expansion and the construction of capital projects. According to a study of the DIL plant in Ajax, Ontario, the company became virtually an "agent of the government."[114]

With orders for war supplies increasing rapidly, in December 1940 the Verdun press triumphantly announced reactivation of the British Munitions plant. Renovation work, tooling, and equipment installation began the next month, although a serious shortage of machine tools caused some delays. Consequently, the plant became operational only in May 1941, and then only at partial capacity. Such delays were common in Canadian war industries, and most munitions plants encountered early tooling problems.[115]

DIL developed a large network of defence facilities across Canada. The firm manufactured small-arms ammunition in its Montreal Works in the city's north-central Villeray district, as well as in Brownsburg, north of the city. Facilities in Beloeil and Shawinigan (Quebec), Windsor (Ontario), and Winnipeg produced explosives, cordite, and related chemicals; Pickering (Ontario), St-Paul l'Hermite (the Cherrier plant), and Ste-Thérèse (the Bouchard plant) filled shells; and, more ominously, Cornwall made mustard gas.[116] Like all war industries, DIL-Verdun obtained its production contracts and operating guidelines from the Department of Munitions and Supply.

Although DIL used the main buildings constructed by British Munitions in 1916, it completely transformed the triangular, 27.5-acre lot in east-end Verdun. By 31 December 1943, Ottawa had invested or committed to invest more than $17 million on buildings, renovations, and modernization, and $32 million for fixed assets. This amount was the most capital investment given any producer of small-arms ammunition or any other DIL plant. Very few Canadian war plants in any industry, especially those operated by private firms, benefited more.[117] Some forty new buildings went up, including a ballistics-testing range, and rail sidings linked the plant to the railway system of neighbouring Point St Charles. Floor space doubled to 516,000 square feet.[118]

The Verdun plant immediately assumed a large role in the nation's production of small-arms ammunition. DIL-Verdun specialized in .303-inch ball ammunition for Lee-Enfield rifles, Bren light machine guns, and Vickers machine guns in standard service with Commonwealth and other Allied forces. The plant's original planned output was 50 million rounds per month of .303-inch ball ammunition – "a bullet composed of a bullet jacket and a lead core assembled with the cartridge case ... filled with either powder or cordite."[119] This estimate proved unrealistic and the production average to May 1943 was closer to 45 million per month. Nonetheless, DIL-Verdun produced more of this type of ammunition than any other munitions plant in Canada, including even the Dominion Arsenal at Quebec, which each month supplied close to 40 million .303-inch rounds of all varieties. In mid-1943, existing government stocks and usage projections led to reduced orders, and Verdun's production rate dropped to about 30 million per month.[120]

DIL-Verdun produced over 1.5 billion cartridges during the war, an enormous output by any standard. This total included 1.2 billion rounds of .303-inch ball ammunition, 183 million rounds of .303-inch tracers, 94 million rounds of 9-mm ammunition, and 84 million rounds of .30 calibre.[121] The factory also produced millions of rounds of various kinds of experimental .303-inch ammunition, with mixed results, as well as some .45- and .50-calibre ammunition.[122] During a visit to Verdun in 1946, C.D. Howe, by then minister of reconstruction and supply, stated that it had been one of the largest small-arms ammunition manufacturers in the Allied nations. Canada produced slightly more than 4.6 billion rounds of small-arms ammunition during the war, of which 3.3 billion was of .303-inch calibre. DIL-Verdun's 1.38 billion .303-inch ball and tracer rounds constituted almost 42 percent of all .303-inch rounds made in Canada and nearly one-third of *all* Canadian small-arms rounds.[123]

Employment in Verdun

At its height in early 1943, the small-arms ammunition industry employed over 30,000 workers nationally, including private industry and the Dominion Arsenals in Quebec City and Lindsay, Ontario.[124] At the peak of its production in early 1943, DIL employed 32,500 people across Canada, manufacturing small-arms and artillery ammunition, related components, and other products. The Verdun plant employed 6,805 people at the crest of its production in December 1942, or about 21 percent of DIL's workforce (see Table 5.3).

The Department of Munitions and Supply's February 1941 projection of labour requirements for Verdun anticipated a majority of unskilled workers, most of them women. Of 7,500 forecast jobs, 3,225 were expected to be unskilled, 1,200 semi-skilled, 225 skilled, and 225 clerical, and fully 2,625 were not categorized.[125] In July 1943, of the 27,100 Canadians manufacturing small-arms ammunition, 14,400 were

Table 5.3

Employment at DIL-Verdun, 1941-43

	Male	Female	% Female	Total
July 1941	1,166	591	33.63	1,757
February 1942	1,809	1,382	43.30	3,191
July 1942	2,622	2,366	47.43	4,988
December 1942	3,268	3,537	51.97	6,805
July 1943	2,089	2,184	51.11	4,273

Source: Composite drawn from information provided from the following sources (which do not always accord): Economics and Statistics Branch, Department of Munitions and Supply, "War Employment in Canada – Geographical Report," 5th ed., 15 January 1944, RG 28 A, vol. 187, LAC; "Geographical Distribution of Labour Requirements for War Production," 27 January 1942, 30 May 1942, and 26 January 1943, RG 28 A, vol. 182, LAC; Report of the Arsenals and Small Arms Ammunition Branch, 21, RG 28A, vol. 26, file 1, LAC. The total figure for July 1943 is listed as 4,949 in "War Employment in Canada."

women (53 percent of the total). About 16 percent of these 27,100 were in Verdun.[126] The sex ratio of workers at DIL-Verdun resembled the national average; women constituted the majority of workers in Verdun from August 1942.

The city raised the question of preferential hiring for Verdun residents as had occurred during the First World War. At the time of DIL's opening in May 1941, city council petitioned MP Paul-Émile Côté to ensure that Verdunites obtained "a reasonable proportion" of the new jobs. Côté replied that he had been working towards that end since early 1941 and that, following discussions with the Department of Munitions and Supply, he could promise that "preference will be given those Verdunites whose qualifications will match those required."[127] This promise seems to have been kept, if later press commentary can serve as a guide.

As early as December 1940, the *Guardian* noted that Verdunites would receive hiring preference and gleefully anticipated "one of the biggest booms to this city that has ever occurred."[128] A month later, the Verdun Unemployment Relief Commission announced that it would close on 1 July 1941 owing to dwindling unemployment and, specifically, the opening of the DIL plant.[129] Economically, the city and its inhabitants benefited directly from the war: municipal finances improved considerably as relief rolls dried up, and thousands of Verdunites moved out of poverty.

Labour-management relations at DIL-Verdun appeared to the *Guardian* in 1946 as having remained "friendly" during the war.[130] Given the number of labour disputes in Canada at that time, the point seemed noteworthy. Although the workers in Verdun did not strike, there is some evidence that not everything was

satisfactory. Alderman Émile Ste-Marie told the executive committee of city council in February 1942 of many complaints from DIL workers that they were not
being paid as well as their colleagues in Ontario doing similar work. Although
the city intended to form a special committee (Aldermen Ste-Marie and Robert
Scurrah) to investigate, no more was heard of the matter at the municipal level.[131]
Nevertheless, a wartime labour board conciliation committee looked into some
of the Verdun workers' allegations. Despite the reaching of general agreement
between labour and management, delays in implementing change infuriated
labour organizers, including Robert Haddow, a Verdunite. Haddow felt the conciliation committees were government puppets and an "insult to the workers."[132]
Even if the complaints were accurate, however, the workers in Verdun never disrupted production.

DIL accentuated Verdun's housing shortage. As early as January 1942 the city
realized that a considerable number of DIL's workers were not Verdunites. Since
the federal government did not provide workers' housing, city council feared that
a large influx of workers and their families might exacerbate local tensions and
ultimately hamper war production. It asked federal authorities to designate the
city a priority zone under the terms of the 1938 National Housing Act (NHA) and
wartime restrictions on building materials. This would also have spurred local
development. Ottawa remained aloof, and a shortage of housing persisted well
into the postwar period.[133]

Despite DIL's presence, Verdun remained overwhelmingly residential, as municipal authorities preferred. DIL was Verdun's only significant war industry, although such local enterprises as lumber and coal yards and industrial laundries,
employing relatively few workers, indirectly aided the war effort. In June 1942 the
city refused to allow RCA Victor to start a woodworking plant because the building under consideration stood amid residential housing recently erected under
the NHA. In an attempt to impress on Verdun the importance of the RCA plant,
the Department of Munitions and Supply made it clear to a delegation of city
officials, which included Edward Wilson and three aldermen, that this woodworking plant was to be engaged solely in war work. But the city remained reluctant to
compromise quality of life. Unless federal and municipal goals coincided, Verdun's
immediate needs took priority over those of the war.

Ottawa looked for an alternative location, but ultimately insisted.[134] In August
C.D. Howe wrote Wilson that the site of the proposed RCA plant was "urgently
required for the execution of important war contracts." The almost-apologetic
Howe wrote: "I appreciate your reluctance to permit the establishment of an industry in close proximity to a residential area. On the other hand, we must realize
that war brings with it many inconveniences. I would not ask you to issue a permit
... if it were possible to find satisfactory building space elsewhere." The city granted
the permit the same day, but only "in view of the urgent representations and direct

request of the Hon. C.D. Howe."[135] Once unemployment had more or less disappeared, industrial expansion seemed to portend more disadvantages to Verdun than benefits.

The local munitions works allowed non-combatants to assist in the war. With so many Verdun homes having men and women in the armed services, many local workers felt that they were tangibly supporting their relatives and friends in uniform. Yet Verdun's press paid relatively little attention to the DIL plant. Even taking into account wartime caution, the *Guardian* published few reports on DIL's immense importance to Canadian war industry or on Verdunites' substantial role there.

The interaction between DIL and the wider Verdun community is difficult to gauge. The reserve army units using the Verdun Auditorium as an armoury occasionally received permission to set up recruiting tables on the company's premises. The Verdun chapter of the Red Cross set up an on-site blood-donor clinic and, on one exceptional occasion in 1942, the Women's Volunteer Reserve Corps solicited donations on behalf of the Mayor's Cigarette Fund from the thousands of DIL workers leaving and entering the plant during shift changes.[136] DIL did not seem to need its host community as much as Verdun needed it as an employer, and in fact, the city gave the company relatively little support. In the spring of 1942, the aptly named Silver Bullet Club – a recreational group of DIL employees – obtained municipal permission to use a nearby playground for its softball teams. But later that year the city refused DIL use of city hall for occasional company dances and social gatherings: "all available [space] is being increasingly required for war services and allied charitable purposes. Moreover, the city does not wish to prejudice the owners of local halls who pay taxes to operate."[137] While the city wished to help maintain war workers' morale, DIL was not a charity and was expected to pay its way.

At the end of 1943, during the peak period of Canadian war production, C.D. Howe announced a cut in Canadian production of small-arms ammunition owing to lower-than-expected usage. This followed a May 1943 decision that had scaled back production in Verdun by one-third. These decisions seriously affected the DIL plants in Verdun and Villeray. Some 3,500 of the company's workers nationwide were to be let go by 31 March 1944, with other war industries expected to absorb only about 1,800 of these people. Notices posted at the Verdun factory informed workers that up to 35 percent of them could expect to be laid off in the following three or four months, which is precisely what happened.[138] Most seem to have found work in Montreal, and the layoffs produced no serious social repercussions.

Large numbers of Verdunites worked in other war industries throughout the Montreal area. For example, when Canadian Pacific announced in March 1943 that its east-end Angus Shops would cease production of the Valentine light tank (for delivery to the Soviet Union), many among the 2,000 workers to be laid off were expected to be Verdunites.[139] A few weeks later, a forty-eight-hour strike by Montreal Tramways workers proved both acrimonious and extremely inconvenient. It disrupted thousands of workers' regular transit schedules and hurt defence industries as well. The *Guardian* stated its local impact: "There is probably no other outlying municipality where so many men and women ... are engaged in Canada's great war effort, as in the City of Verdun, proportionally to its population."[140]

As the war in Europe wound down, it became obvious that DIL workers would be casualties of retrenchment in the defence industry. At the end of 1944 the payroll at DIL-Verdun had dropped to 1,800, down 74 percent from December 1942. By the end of March 1945, production had virtually ceased. Within two months, only Dominion Arsenal was producing small-arms ammunition in Canada.[141] The cessation of hostilities in Europe in May 1945 brought significant job losses to Verdun. The DIL plant shut down permanently in July. The government declared it surplus in August and turned it over to the War Assets Corporation for disposal.[142]

Thousands of Verdunites had worked at DIL and the city sought to replace these jobs. Even before Germany's surrender, various options were considered for Verdun's war plant. Côté suggested using it as a technical school to retrain veterans or former defence workers. He also hoped that part of it might become an armoury or drill hall, which many in Verdun wanted.[143] The main goal was employment to counter an anticipated economic slump. Wilson hoped to avoid a return to the hardships of the Depression years.

Due in no small part to Côté's strenuous efforts, the city and War Assets agreed to transform the DIL property into a minor industrial park. Within months War Assets had leased to private investors many lots and buildings suitable for manufacturing. The federal Real Estate Advisory Committee believed that a policy of offering leases would hasten the development of Canadian industry and allow companies to make quick inroads into national and international markets. Verdun selected industrial tenants thought likely to generate the most employment.[144] By November 1945, twenty-six light industries, including machine shops, furniture makers, printers, and makers of pharmaceutical products, rubber goods, and small appliances had signed up. An estimated 2,500 jobs were expected to result, many of them for Verdunites; the press hailed the possibility as "a great stabilizing power in the community." Verdun's working-class population had grown slightly apprehensive since the closure of Montreal-area war industries and the demobilization of thousands of servicemen.[145] But all augured well for Verdun. By May 1946 the DIL site had attracted thirty-nine firms, expected to employ over 2,900 people.[146]

On 20 May 1946, Minister of Reconstruction and Supply C.D. Howe inspected the former DIL grounds, renamed the Verdun Industrial Plant, and proclaimed the relocation a harbinger of greater things to come. Accompanied by a large delegation of politicians and officials representing three levels of government, Howe noted that Verdun's conversion of a munitions factory for civilian use showed great foresight, and he gave much of the credit to Paul-Émile Côté.[147] Edward Wilson boasted that the city's industrial future was assured.[148] On 23 May 1946, the *Guardian* published a special supplement – "A Source of Prosperity for Verdun" – and praised the conversion, something of a pioneering effort, as the leading example of its kind in Canada.[149] The war had helped improve Verdun's image as a progressive and far-sighted city, the *Guardian* was sure, especially in the eyes of the Montreal-area business community. Why else would so many industries agree to locate in Verdun? The war and its aftermath seemed to have brought employment security to Verdun and injected an air of confidence and optimism.

ALL ELEMENTS in the community, notwithstanding other differences, had wanted a war industry. The city had sought and obtained a plant, to the joint benefit of the local population and the overall war effort. After postwar conversion to civilian use, the DIL lot continued for some time to serve the city's economic interests, and this legacy, as much as the site's outstanding wartime achievements, reveals its lasting worth to the community.

The unpaid war work by thousands of Verdunites left a different legacy, as Verdunites from both language and religious communities responded in large numbers to the wartime calls for money and volunteer work sounded by social organizations and war charities. Their involvement was extensive in terms of the number and backgrounds of residents engaged and the diversity of activities undertaken. The Red Cross attracted the most volunteers – mainly women – and was the most successful in bridging Verdun's linguistic and religious divides. Larger English-language social organizations such as the Legion and the YMCA devoted considerable resources in aid of Verdunites at home and in uniform. Verdun's churches and schools were also active participants in the war on the home front. While Protestants led the way, the Verdun Catholic School Commission involved itself in most patriotic undertakings and normally cooperated with government authorities.

A lack of data makes it impossible to discern the level of involvement by Verdun's few significant French Canadian social organizations. Feelings of political alienation caused by the conscription debate may have dampened the official enthusiasm of certain groups and individuals, as occurred with the Société Saint-Jean-Baptiste. But even this organization's local branches subscribed to Verdun causes, and the city's French speakers, despite religious differences, helped raise money for mainly English-language groups. Both language groups became most active when these endeavours directly benefited Verdunites, especially those serving overseas.

6
Family and Social Dislocation

The Second World War profoundly affected Verdun and its residents in many ways, not all of them positive. For those who lost close relatives on active service, the war shook the foundations of their lives. For those who assumed greater familial and financial responsibility at home, the war proved a social and personal burden, although this also had a socially liberating effect on some women.[1] The war influenced everyone, even though its effects might have been barely perceptible to some.[2] Life may have gone on, but the war changed the way most people lived, worked, shopped, and enjoyed themselves. For every family shattered by the war, two or three derived financial advantage from it; frequently the war caused both material gain and emotional loss.

Wartime conditions could be stressful for those on the home front. A housing shortage seriously eroded many Verdunites' quality of life. Verdun's enlistments sometimes produced financial hardship for those left behind. The departure of the principal breadwinner could devastate family finances and morale, and some Verdunites were forced to accept social assistance. Rationing caused consumer anxiety. Children's behaviour was also affected, and many Verdunites worried about the rise in juvenile delinquency. In 1944 Verdun was even the scene of a serious social disturbance that implicated many youths and servicemen. Many of these social issues were interrelated, and their class and linguistic dimensions were magnified by the extraordinary circumstances of war.

Housing
One of Verdun's most serious and widespread wartime social problems was an acute housing shortage.[3] Until the end of 1942, Verdun benefited from various assistance programs for low-cost housing offered under the National Housing Act (NHA) of 1938. The onset of war did not change the city's pre-NHA practice of selling cheap, empty lots for the building of modest bungalows or duplexes. Most of the lots had been seized from their owners by the city for non-payment of taxes during the Depression. No other city in Quebec or Ontario took advantage of the NHA's financial incentives and tax concessions to the extent that Verdun did. More dwellings were constructed in Verdun in 1940 than in any year since 1928.[4] West-end Ward 4, particularly the Crawford Park neighbourhood bordering Lasalle, experienced a building boom in the early war years.

Ottawa recognized early that the war eventually would cause a housing shortage and social distress. Federal authorities quickly began regulating the distribution of building material and the labour supply allotted to housing construction. Since the expanding defence industries received first priority, fewer residential structures were built and fewer still were of an adequate size and quality to meet market demands. By 1940 the increasing urban industrial workforce, bolstered by a large-scale influx of men and women from rural areas seeking jobs, presaged a national wartime housing shortage, especially in lower-income areas with a wage-earning population. This influx, 250,000 into the Montreal area alone, coupled with early wartime inflation, drove up rents across Canada.[5] W.C. Clark, the chairman of the federal Economic Advisory Committee on Housing Policy, reported to cabinet in November 1940 that, since the demands of the war economy overrode normal housing needs, "Canada must accept an increasing amount of 'doubling-up' and overcrowding ... with all the [resulting] social disadvantages." Clark stated that "the outlook in this connection is not bright and we should not gloss over the evils that will result and the unrest and public criticism that will follow."[6] These predictions proved all too accurate, as housing construction remained secondary to the overall needs of the war effort. Nonetheless, in 1941 only 93 of 1,572 Verdun households canvassed during a national study on housing needs reported having more than one family resident. This was the lowest "doubling up" rate (5.9 percent) of any city over 30,000 in Canada.[7] Verdun was overwhelmingly a city of four- and five-room flats, and these could not support more than one family and one or two boarders at best. For the most part, doubling up could be only a last resort in Verdun.

Landlords and Tenants, to 1943

Many local landlords attempted to profit unduly from the wartime scarcity of housing. In the first few months of 1941, many Verdunites complained bitterly to city hall about sudden and substantial rent increases. Rent controls had been established in officially designated congested areas in September 1940 by the Wartime Prices and Trade Board's Rentals Administration, which investigated reports of illegal or unjustified rent increases. Sympathetic but powerless municipal authorities directed aggrieved tenants to the Rentals Administration, which wrote mayor Edward Wilson in February 1941 that it had recently received "a large number of complaints" from Verdunites about inflated rental demands.[8]

The situation proved a serious social problem for low-income Verdunites, who already resided in one of the cheapest rental districts in the Montreal area. Some First World War veterans unable to afford higher rents were among those forced to vacate their flats. Other groups that denounced local landlords represented a mix of patriotic and social organizations including the Canadian Legion, the Verdun branch of the Canadian Housewives' League, the Verdun Tenants' Association, and individual wives of overseas servicemen.[9] Because the majority of English speakers were tenants, the groups representing their interests were English-language based.

Traditionally, 1 May was the date when leases expired in the Montreal area, and congested Verdun normally witnessed a moving frenzy on that day. Verdunites on the move usually stayed in Verdun. Trucks and vans blocked the narrow streets while thousands of men and women manoeuvred furniture and personal belongings up spindly, winding exterior staircases to their new rented accommodations. Not infrequently, tempers flared, and anxious moments were experienced when some people were obliged to vacate their flats with nowhere else to go. This had been a common and sad sight during the worst days of the Depression.

Notwithstanding some unfortunate situations in early 1941, when cash-strapped tenants were forced to accept inadequate accommodations, Edward Wilson believed that overall there was "no serious situation in Verdun this moving season." The mayor's view was confirmed some months later by the local branch of the Canadian Legion, which was aware of only a handful of unresolved housing problems involving families of servicemen or veterans.[10] But the rent gouging and the tightening supply of available housing were just hints of more serious problems to come.

Construction in Verdun continued throughout 1941 and 1942, despite limitations imposed in 1942 on the NHA and the growing scarcity of construction material and labour. Verdun was proud of its 458 dwellings erected in 1942, which was quite a feat, given growing wartime restrictions.[11] Before the end of that year, however, owing to population growth, very little housing was available in Verdun, a situation mirrored throughout the country. Moreover, some 91 percent of Verdun dwellings were occupied by tenants – the highest proportion of any city in Canada.[12] Making matters worse in this densely populated city, an increasing number of unscrupulous landlords, forbidden by federal Wartime Prices and Trade Board (WPTB) regulations to raise their rents to a level that the market could easily have sustained, refused to renew leases. They preferred instead to demand lucrative bribes ("key money") or other incentives from people desperate for housing. Some landlords imposed other illegal leasing conditions, such as the payment of a year's rent in advance. Others, chafing under WPTB rental ceilings, sent tenants renewal leases indicating a rise in rent for the forthcoming year but without stipulating the actual amount of the increase until the tenant had signed the lease. The Verdun Tenants' Association vocally opposed these ploys, but with only limited success.[13]

As early as March 1940, the Canadian Corps Association in Verdun had complained to the office of the provincial attorney general and to the city about landlords who refused to rent their flats to the wives and families of overseas servicemen. The property owners were worried that they would be unable to pay their rent.[14] The families of enlistees were among the most vulnerable to eviction, a fact deplored by the patriotic Montreal Soldiers' Wives' League (MSWL), a welfare organization run by well-heeled women, frequently the wives of top-ranking military personnel. Founded in 1899 at the time of the South African War, the MSWL had as its motto "To bring the wives, other relatives, and friends of soldiers into closer touch and sympathy, that they may help one another in times of trouble and distress." In April 1942, eyeing developing housing problems for the working-class families of Montreal-area servicemen, the MSWL interviewed the mayors of Montreal and Verdun, and the city manager of Westmount, to inquire about "temporary shelter for any dependants of men in the Forces who may not have secured homes by the first of May." All agreed with the MSWL that these families merited special consideration, though few promises were made. In Montreal, soldiers' families in need could phone city hall and register for temporary shelter until proper accommodations could be secured. In response to the MSWL, Verdun's Mayor Wilson was "most co-operative and promised *preferred* treatment" [original emphasis] to soldiers' families needing shelter. P.H. Lane, the head of Verdun's welfare committee, knew of six military families in need in 1942 but did not expect that number to rise substantially. Mayor Wilson was "indignant" to learn that certain landlords were refusing to rent to soldiers' wives and families, probably on account of hoping to charge higher rents to well-paid defence industry workers. Wilson insisted on being sent the names of any such landlords in Verdun. Residents in need could telephone Lane for assistance.[15]

The MSWL also coordinated the housing complaints of Montreal's numerous regimental, corps, and service association's women's auxiliaries. These women took on assertive leadership roles among Montreal-area soldiers' families and, as the war progressed, helped many families in dire straits, often in Verdun. In the spring of 1942, for example, the MSWL helped 156 families across the metropolitan area. The women noticed a general reluctance on the part of landlords to rent to other than the "head of the family," which put soldiers' wives in a difficult position. The women of the MSWL visited landlords to persuade them, almost always successfully, to accept soldiers' families. The MSWL also advanced money to impoverished women for moving expenses and advised certain families, probably the victims of irregular practices on the part of the landlords, to stay put when their leases expired. The families with no alternatives were split up, scattered, or relocated far from their communities, in summer cottages, for example.[16]

In late 1942 and early 1943, the MSWL assisted another thirty Montreal-area families to find housing, relocating six of them to the country. But many increasingly glaring problems remained. In Verdun, the RCAF Women's Auxiliary reported to the MSWL the plight of a family on Verdun Avenue living in an "old store [with] bad sanitary arrangements." The Victoria Rifles Ladies' Association alerted the MSWL to the travails of Mme Maisonnet, who lived with her seven children in a Wellington Street store. Mrs Thompson was described as living in a "condemned" and "damp basement flat, in bad repair" on west-end Osborne Avenue. Mrs Ledoux of east-end Church Avenue was obliged to "room with [a] friend – children in foster home – 3 in one home, one in another – furniture stored."[17] The situation would worsen sharply before the end of the war.

The Verdun branch of the Canadian Corps Association linked this profiteering to the opening of the DIL ammunition plant, which was expected to draw hundreds of families to Verdun and tighten the housing market. "It is not the British spirit to take advantage of any tenants because the Nation is at War," wrote Harry Shaver, the branch president, to city council.[18] His reference to a "British spirit" seemed to imply that most local landlords, being French speakers, were not fully committed to the war effort. The language dimension to this growing crisis exacerbated tensions between the English-speaking tenant class and the local French-speaking petite bourgeoisie.

Some of the class tensions occasioned by landlords' rent demands might have been of non-Verdun origin. Most resident Verdun landlords lived in the same tenement block as their tenants, usually in the coveted bottom flat with access to a small patch of yard and an unfinished basement, and friendly landlord-tenant relations were not unusual. But 30 percent of Verdun landlords – a figure that includes corporate property owners – were not Verdun residents. These owners of investment properties could not be expected to be imbued with the community spirit and sense of neighbourliness for which Verdun was recognized.

The difficulties existing between the language groups over wartime issues remained manageable, but they may have increased tension at the end of the war between returning soldiers finding their families in distress and those landlords who made illegal rent demands. A careful gleaning of both the *Guardian* and the *Messenger* has unearthed no conclusive evidence of landlord-tenant animosity based on language. But the local press generally employed a cautious approach to linguistic matters throughout the war, and the absence of documentation does not preclude the existence of problems.

According to the *Guardian* there was little activity in Verdun on moving day 1943, since "there were no places for dissatisfied tenants to move in to ... rewards of $25, $50 and even one of $100 were [offered] to any person who could find a house or flat [for them] to rent in this city. Any moving that did take place was by tenants who exchanged the flats they were living in ... for a residence occupied by tenants who also wished to change."[19] By July 1943 the city estimated an outright shortage of 500 dwellings in Verdun – there was not a single vacant flat, and only thirty-two vacant commercial properties. Sixty-two Verdun stores and shops were serving as dwellings, sometimes with more than one family. Doubling up had become more common. No dwellings capable of reasonably accommodating families with five or more children had been built since 1942.[20]

By March 1944, seventy-three Verdun families had resorted to renting commercial space on Wellington Street, Verdun Avenue, Church Avenue, and other streets, converting them as best they could into dwellings. City hall was concerned about the health and hygienic conditions confronting these 172 adults and 222 children but did little to ameliorate their situation. The same local social groups that during the Depression had fought to improve the living conditions of Verdun's disadvantaged residents found their services in demand again during wartime. But despite petitions from the Greater Verdun Community Council and the Verdun Women's Club, the municipal administration offered no solutions.[21] At least the store dwellers had shelter.

Evictions, 1944

By moving day 1944 the troubling issue of evictions had surfaced in Verdun. Many poorer Verdunites and residents of working-class districts of Montreal – often the families of servicemen – faced forcible removal; even the controlled rents had far outstripped what they could afford. Many working-class families needed two incomes to make ends meet.[22] Across the Montreal area approximately 5,000 eviction notices were served on tenants, very few of whom had found suitable or affordable new places. The plight of these people very quickly became Montreal's most pressing social issue. Changes to WPTB guidelines prevented landlords from evicting tenants with a good rental record unless the landlord or the landlord's relatives in demonstrable need of shelter were going to use the premises.[23] But these measures were often circumvented.

Seventy-six families faced eviction in Verdun, many because their principal breadwinner was on active service. Continuing its leading role in the fight against local property owners, the Verdun Tenants' Association tried legal means to prevent evictions. Although some situations were resolved happily, the *Guardian* published many sad stories of patriotic, and sometimes bereaved, Verdun families without shelter.[24] One incident attracted considerable local attention and indignation that May: the eviction of the Glasgow family, which had lost two sons killed in action in 1942. The *Guardian* appealed to Verdunites to take this impoverished family into their homes, though the outcome is not known.[25]

Wartime evictions received greater attention when they involved a serviceman's family. Most housing agitation, like that of the Legion, seemed intended as much to repay patriotism as to alleviate suffering. Though an effective wartime stratagem, it implied a hierarchy based on contribution to the war effort. The local press rarely mentioned the dozens of other families facing eviction that had no members on active service. Only the combative Verdun Tenants' Association, which had won the respect of the tenant class during the Depression, seemed to take up their cause. Patriotic community groups, the press, city hall, and even the WPTB assigned priority in settling eviction cases to servicemen's families. In October 1945 Eric R. Gold, coordinator of the federal Emergency Shelter Administration, visited Montreal to investigate the housing crisis. Gold's report to Donald Gordon, chairman of the WPTB, stated clearly: "Our Administration will have to be completely hardboiled and turn a deaf ear to pleas of civilian families for assistance."[26] In Verdun, numbers of "civilian families" lacked shelter and the visible crutch of patriotic sacrifice. They too were war's casualties.

In 1944 classified advertisements began to flood the *Guardian* from people seeking to rent or exchange flats and even single rooms. The conversion of a former mission hall on Woodland Avenue into ten dwellings attracted 400 inquiries.[27] Many people were desperate enough to purchase unbuilt small bungalows in Verdun on the basis of blueprints alone. The *Guardian* reckoned that if the number of dwellings built increased tenfold they all would be sold in very short order.[28] Some Verdunites, as a last resort, appealed publicly to the generosity and community spirit of their fellow citizens. One discharged serviceman, who identified himself merely as "troubled," wrote the *Guardian*: "For the past two years we rented an unfurnished room, ground floor and it is cold and damp. The doctor has told us that we must find something warmer ... We have advertised for several weeks and tried all agencies, but without success and with the winter coming we don't know what to do. There are just two of us and we still hope to find a small, warm place as we want to stay in Verdun. Perhaps someone will hear our plea."[29]

Edward Wilson was outraged with the federal government for not resolving the housing crisis, and with the profiteering and lack of feeling of some local property owners. Wilson described the situation in Verdun as "detrimental to public health, family life and the efficiency of war workers and the general community" and promised that no resident would be without shelter on 1 May 1944, even if it meant establishing temporary housing in municipal facilities. City council dispatched several resolutions to the federal government, but to little avail. By the end of 1944, the city estimated Verdun's population at nearly 74,000 (including about 4,000 away on active service) and its immediate housing needs at no fewer than 1,000 dwellings.[30]

The poorest Canadians suffered most from the housing shortage. A 1944 survey showed nearly 90 percent of tenants in the lowest income group paying a disproportionately high rent in relation to their income. Many Verdunites fell into this category. In this respect, wartime differed little from the Depression. The urban planner Humphrey Carver noted in a 1948 study of Canada's housing crisis that the poorest wage earners bore the brunt of the housing shortage and rent gouging – a frustrating and humiliating experience for thousands of working-class Canadians.[31] One very disgruntled recently discharged veteran, who sought to move to Verdun in 1944, wrote to the *Messenger*:

For 3½ years I served this country to the best of my ability. Discharged, I returned looking forward to being with my wife and child. My present employment necessitated my locating in Verdun. Locating in Verdun! I wonder how many readers realize what that simple statement means ... Yes, I can get a flat ... or even a house if I want to pay up to $300 for the key, pay a year's rent in advance or build. I am not in a position to do any of these. Had I remained behind like so many others [and] taken a job in a war plant ... I would have a place today. Just how long are we, the younger generation, supposed to swallow this stuff about "fighting for democracy" and "saving our freedom"? Take any hundred men who have served in this war and ask them, you'll get your answer.[32]

The home front could prove a bitter pill for a discharged soldier who had sacrificed several years in the service of his country. There were limits to what the veterans were willing to accept. As the housing situation worsened, social tensions mounted.

The Housing Crisis, 1945-46

From February 1945 until well after the war had ended, housing remained one of the issues to which the *Guardian* devoted the most attention – an indication of its social significance. With an increasing pool of discharged servicemen in Verdun, the Legion asserted itself as the protector of servicemen's families facing eviction. It organized meetings, sent delegations to city council to enlist municipal support, wrote letters to government officials, and investigated every eviction case brought to its attention. At a highly charged Legion meeting in January 1945, one man wondered aloud about the angry attitudes of returning soldiers towards landlords who had evicted their families. Violence could not be ruled out. A letter from one destitute Verdun woman was read aloud: "My husband and two sons, and my two sons-in-law, are in the service. My daughters are making their home with me while their husbands are away. Five from one family doing their bit, now we are ordered to get out and nowhere to go. Is this what our boys are fighting for? ... Those who are staying at home and making big money are buying the houses and putting the servicemen out on the street. We have lived here for 12 years and always paid our rent regularly, looked after the property and kept [it] in good condition."[33] Mounting public frustration revealed cracks in wartime Verdun's cohesive community consensus. The sentiment grew in Verdun that, as Wilson believed, the federal government was letting down the very persons who had given so much to help win the war.

In February 1945, the *Guardian* published another painful letter from a Verdun woman who wished to remain anonymous.

I was evicted three years ago and since have occupied an abandoned store for which I pay $25 per month. Each winter I use six tons of fuel. The thermometer is usually at 45[°F] in the morning and may reach 66 during the daytime. My family (three school children) have no bath other than the swimming pool in summer. During the last three years a couch ... has been my bedroom, with a plentiful supply of mice for company. I have my three sons in the services since 1939. Three of my daughters are helping in the war effort by working in munitions plants. One of them has already had a nervous breakdown, owing to environment. I feel my duty to King and Country has far exceeded its limits. Where would King and Country be without sons such as mine, and what on earth are they fighting for? Of late I have begun to appreciate the word "sucker" when applied by a Zombie to a man in uniform ... Could I have foreseen what has happened to us since 1939, believe you me, my three boys would have donned overalls instead of khaki.[34]

This woman's plight reflected the home-front experience of other financially distressed Canadians. Her letter also expressed working-class fury that, while young men were risking their lives, the government seemed unable to alleviate their families' deplorable living conditions. The letter is representative of the more extreme social malaise occasioned in Verdun by the war and shows that some of the women and children "left behind" suffered severe social dislocation. The patriotism felt in the early war years had waned by 1945 among Verdun's hard-hit urban poor. Some servicemen's families felt that the war was beginning to cost too much on a personal level.

Another letter to the *Guardian* written in March 1945 by a Verdun woman identifying herself only as "Fifth Avenue" again showed that the government, not necessarily the war, was the object of the people's wrath. She wrote that her forty-one-year-old husband had enlisted because he

thought so much of Verdun, his family and home. He is somewhere in Germany offering his life to defend all these. Here is his reward, Sir, an eviction notice, all very legal, property being sold. But what about us? Where are we to go? ... I have been told by some kind people to store furniture in my mother's basement and take rooms. Nice thoughts for the home it took twenty years to gather. Is this the security men are dying for? Perhaps we would still have a home had my husband thought less of his country, stayed in his job, earned big money and let the government look after the war. Apparently, they cannot look after the fighting men's families. The kind government says write cheery letters, keep up their morale. How? By telling them we may be living in a garage in the spring? This being the reward for fighting for one's country, we can easily understand why we have Zombies and Draft dodgers. Another eviction case on our street. The man has been overseas five years and ... his wife works in a defence plant. So this is democracy![35]

The housing crisis hurt the morale of some men overseas, as the Legion claimed it would. A 1944-45 army survey clearly demonstrated that the housing crisis was a leading cause of anger among returned servicemen. Friction also developed between discharged soldiers and well-paid defence workers.[36] One desperate Verdunite serving overseas wrote the mayor for help in finding his family a place to stay. Sgt A.F. Hébert, RCAF, wrote Wilson in 1945: "We had a very nice place on Bannantyne Avenue when I joined up in the summer of 1940, but had to give it up. My wife and little girl have since been living with her parents. Since the first of the year she has been trying to get a flat of any kind just as long as it is home for us. So far her efforts have been fruitless ... I would very much appreciate it if you could try and locate something for her."[37]

All these letters indicate that lack of housing had created a significant social problem in Verdun and that many Verdunites and recently discharged veterans believed that their war effort was not being matched on a social level by the government. But the federal government, overwhelmed by the magnitude of the housing crisis, did attempt to assist servicemen's families. The NHA was revised in 1944 to facilitate wartime building, with hopes of instigating about $1 billion worth of construction nationwide. Ottawa also announced, before the June 1945 federal election, that 35 percent of all dwellings to be built in the immediate future were to be set aside for soldiers' families.[38] Ottawa could not place a higher priority on housing policy than on the prosecution of the war, but its support seemed too little, too late for many Canadians, especially discharged servicemen unable to secure lodgings. There were many of these in Verdun. In February 1946 not one of Verdun's nearly 18,000 dwellings was vacant, and only nine stores remained unoccupied. In April 1946 hundreds of Verdunites still lived in stores, boarders lucky enough to find a room were routinely overcharged, hundreds of flats were overcrowded, and reasonable rents were virtually unobtainable. Communities across Canada suffered similarly.[39]

PC 9439 (19 December 1944) set up Emergency Shelter Regulations of which the primary feature was the Emergency Shelter Administration (ESA) under the control of the WPTB. The ESA controlled the housing moves of people within designated cities and could confiscate any building at any time for any purpose. The ESA could also revoke eviction notices. Its role, however, was not to build dwellings, but to coordinate the distribution of existing shelters. Ottawa did not impose the ESA on municipalities until July 1945. Until then it was a "voluntary measure" to which interested municipalities applied.[40] Congested cities such as Victoria, Vancouver, Hamilton, and Ottawa voluntarily delegated responsibility for housing to a federally appointed emergency shelter administrator.

The Verdun Legion, which claimed to speak for the entire community, pressed city hall to place Verdun in the ESA's hands so as to halt landlords' excesses. Despite Wilson's support, city council declined to approve the measure. Moreover, the ESA included Verdun in the Montreal area, and as it had appointed no administrator for Montreal, it could not assign one to Verdun without special arrangements with the WPTB.[41] The executive committee represented the city's landlords, who vehemently opposed the idea; its members also sat in the committee of the whole of city council. Even Wilson, a home-owning member of the executive committee, could not persuade the landlord class to change its position in the name of the greater good. Thus the housing crisis was not always Ottawa's fault; sometimes the blame lay closer to home.

The Ligue des Propriétaires de Verdun officially protested to the federal government the potential loss of control over the landlords' own property. As a result, both proprietors and tenants were on record as decrying Ottawa's policies, but for exactly opposite reasons. The Ligue considered the ESA "excessive and unjustified" and a violation of democracy.[42] Because many of its members were Verdun residents, not absentee or corporate property owners, these views indicate class divisions within Verdun. While the Ligue did not represent the views of all Verdun property owners, its attitude helped create tension between landlords and their less prosperous tenants, a situation worsened by the overarching linguistic dimension to the dispute. The Verdun Legion, wholly and publicly opposed to the goals of the mainly French-speaking proprietors, grouped together an overwhelmingly English-speaking and tenant-class membership. The Verdun Tenants' Association, too, was mainly English speaking.

Class divisions and wartime occupational and attitudinal differences between military families, mainly English speaking, and civilian landlords, mainly French speaking, brought relations to a breaking point. For a time in the spring and summer of 1945 it seemed that the city would explode in anger and that hundreds of returned men would demand immediate remedies to their housing problems or, more ominously, seek revenge against dishonest landlords whose actions had harmed their families. By autumn 1945 up to 60 percent of eviction notices nationally were served on servicemen's families (many of the men still being overseas), and Ottawa expected this to bring "serious trouble."[43] Historians Desmond Morton and Jack Granatstein have referred to the "ugly tension between veterans and civilians" produced by the shortage of accommodation in Canada.[44] In March 1945 the Verdun Legion even went so far as to request of Ottawa special leave for servicemen whose families were threatened with eviction so that they could "guard their homes and their dependents against those who would evict them." Notwithstanding this request, which implied the potential for violence, in August 1945 the Verdun Legion counselled distraught returned men not to resort to violent or extreme measures. The Legion feared, as did the *Guardian*, that continuing extortion by some landlords requesting "key money" would lead to vigilante attacks against them.[45]

Although disavowing violence, the Legion suggested that servicemen's families faced with eviction should simply refuse to move. Just days before the dreaded 1 May 1945, Robert DeWitt, recently elected president of Verdun's Legion branch, told these families: "Sit tight on May 1 and we'll do everything possible to keep you in your homes. If your landlord comes don't let him in ... It will take six days for the landlord to issue a writ ... and we'll immediately take protest action. We did that last year and ... people are still in their homes."[46] While he refused officially to sanction illegal protective pickets around these families' flats for fear of violence, DeWitt insisted that "we won't see soldiers' wives abused" and arranged for a group of veterans to be on call at the Legion Hall on 1 May in case any landlords acted too aggressively. Arthur James, the Verdun Legion's immediate past president, stated that "if your son is overseas then your lease is frozen as far as we're concerned." Verdun was home to one-third of the 150 servicemen's families facing eviction in the Montreal area brought to the Canadian Legion's attention.[47] The Legion was also perplexed by the government's ability to find money, materials, and labour to wage war while it seemed unable to locate resources to solve the nation's housing dilemma. The strain on hundreds of Verdun families, of servicemen or not, was terrific. Nevertheless, the local media reported no serious incidents of violence.

In May 1946, at least fifty Verdun veterans and one "police dog" converged on the staircase and on the sidewalk in front of a flat on Fifth Avenue to protect a fellow veteran from bailiffs intent on evicting him and his family. Even in violation of the law, the protesters acted under the banner of patriotism: a Union Jack strung across the steps served as a patriotic barrier that no one dared defy. A contingent of police, ordered by city hall not to intervene, and hundreds of onlookers were also on the scene. The incident took on the proportions of a cause célèbre in the Montreal area. Although the *Guardian* expected bloodshed following a "very precarious and dangerous" forty-eight-hour standoff, the Legion found the unfortunate family a flat in the nearby Montreal neighbourhood of Côte St Paul. Though a small victory, in this dramatic and highly publicized instance, the veterans clearly had had their way.[48]

Housing for Veterans, 1941-46

Notwithstanding the views of its local detractors, the city of Verdun devoted considerable attention throughout the war to easing the housing strain. In the spring of 1941, Parkdale Homes Development Corporation, a residential development contractor, began purchasing undeveloped areas in the westernmost neighbourhood of Crawford Park for the nominal sum of $25 a lot.[49] This company undertook most of Verdun's wartime construction, which took place mainly in Crawford Park, the most suitable sector for residential expansion. The dwellings were primarily small cottages, virtually all of the same basic pattern, as well as some duplexes. The city cooperated by extending and paving Crawford Park's streets and improving its infrastructure.

The number of new houses begun in Verdun was significantly lower after 1942, mainly because contractors could not secure scarce building materials. Nevertheless, the *Municipal Review of Canada* noted that year that Verdun was not "waiting

Table 6.1

Housing construction in Verdun, 1940-44

Year	Building permits	Family dwellings
1940	183	388
1941	276	486
1942	292	456
1943	173	300
1944	162	236

Source: "Building Permits Issued," 1 December 1944, Survey on Housing Situation, 14 December 1944, box A-331, file 3, Verdun Borough Archives.

for the post-war period, but has already made a big start in the building of permanent homes for the people."[50] In December 1944 Arthur Burgess informed the provincial government that Verdun, "notwithstanding war conditions, [has achieved] considerable dwelling construction since 1939" and had been singled out by Ottawa as "an example of success under the National Housing Act."[51] Table 6.1 shows wartime housing starts in Verdun. The number of overall dwellings per building declined by 32 percent between 1940 and 1944, owing to a greater emphasis on low-cost, single-family homes after 1942. At the end of 1944 Burgess estimated that, even though nearly 1,800 lots suitable for residential construction remained in Verdun, 90 percent of the six-square-kilometre city already had been built up.[52]

Verdun's successful housing development helped alleviate the desperate shortage of shelter from 1944 to 1946. Between January 1940 and February 1946, 1,787 dwellings were built in Verdun, mostly bungalows and duplexes. Sixty percent of these went up before the end of 1944, a notable accomplishment, as Burgess pointed out to provincial authorities.[53] Without this far-sighted building program conditions in Verdun would have been intolerable at war's end. In 1945 Ottawa unveiled a postwar housing program, part of its Veterans' Charter, which offered veterans cheap mortgages and easy repayment terms. Verdun was apparently the first Canadian city to initiate housing construction under this scheme. In July 1945 the city announced that Parkdale Homes would build eighty-eight homes in Ward 4, with thirty-five reserved for ex-servicemen – well above the proportion that Ottawa had decreed for former military personnel. The small cottages were to be ready that autumn. These were the first of hundreds of identical "veterans' homes" that eventually dotted west-end Verdun (and neighbourhoods across Canada) and came to characterize Crawford Park as a virtually separate veterans' community.[54]

City hall took a leading role in ensuring construction of the greatest possible number of dwellings in wartime Verdun. The policy of Edward Wilson and Joseph

French was to convert empty city-owned lots into taxable real estate as quickly as possible. They were remarkably successful, given wartime conditions. By April 1945, total valuation had increased by $5 million since the start of the war.[55] In March 1945 Verdun had set aside large tracts of empty fields in Crawford Park and elsewhere for veterans' housing, and it sold the lots to developers (almost invariably Parkdale Homes) for the usual small sum of $25 each, on condition that construction began within sixty days. Outside these designated zones the city agreed to sell lots to developers at the generous rate of 50 percent of whatever the city had originally paid for them.[56]

Wartime Housing Limited, a Crown corporation, did not interest Verdun, because, as the city explained, of the temporary nature of its dwellings. City council preferred to sell lots to private firms offering affordable, permanent homes.[57] The greater value of permanent homes increased municipal valuation rolls. Yet, at the end of March 1945, with moving day fast approaching, the city met with delegations representing the Society of Verdun Servicemen's Families and the Legion, both of which urged it to seek prefabricated temporary housing from Wartime Housing Limited. Recognizing the urgency of the situation, the city sought to acquire some of these structures. But none was to be available for months and the city abandoned the idea, perhaps with some relief.[58] The city's view throughout the war was that Ottawa should vastly increase subsidies to wage-earning renters or purchasers of low-cost, permanent housing.

At the height of the local housing crisis in April 1945, and after Verdun learned that Ottawa would provide no temporary housing, the city entered into a contract with Parkdale Homes for the immediate erection of 100 flats on Egan Avenue in Ward 4. The city insisted that the first thirty-six rentals be reserved for Verdun servicemen or their families, including the families of those killed on active service. This was a strong patriotic and community-minded commitment by the city. So anxious was Verdun to stimulate construction that it sold these lots for a nominal sum of $1 each. The *Messenger* hailed this move with the headline "Verdun Leads Canada in Providing Shelter for Returning Veterans." But it also noted sombrely an "unprecedented scramble" to find housing in Verdun. Similar arrangements for low-cost flats were contracted throughout the summer. In part as a result of the city's high enlistment rate, the urgent need to house repatriated service people altered west-end Verdun permanently.[59]

VERDUN'S WARTIME housing shortage – later crisis – was serious but manageable. The Verdunites most affected by the crisis were among those least able to cope and often included low-wage earners and the families of servicemen. The city did all that it could to facilitate housing construction and ease the social strain. Wilson did his utmost within wartime restraints to support families of Verdun servicemen and worked closely with local interest groups, especially the Legion, to that end. The only blot on the city's record seems to be its failure to request a special arrangement with the WPTB to place Verdun under ESA administration, despite Wilson's willingness to do so. The landlords' firm grip on those aspects of civic administration that most directly concerned them could not be broken.

In a working-class community that had offered so many of its young men to the war effort, it was perhaps inevitable that some Verdun families would find themselves in straitened circumstances. Whatever the motivation for voluntary enlistment, active service often entailed serious familial dislocation.

Family and Society

While the Second World War may have solved some of the social and economic ills that beset Canada in the 1930s, it created, accelerated, or magnified others. The war years challenged existing social values, perhaps most noticeably those concerned with the role of women. For the families of servicemen, morale was often difficult to sustain: stress, fear, and anxiety took their toll on parents, spouses, and children. Yet the booming war economy at least helped make life more tolerable. Many families prospered, though not all Verdunites shared in this economic renewal.

Servicemen's spousal allowances and meagre service pay were often not enough for their dependants. In the autumn of 1942 the wife of an army private received a monthly Soldiers' Dependants' Allowance of $35, plus $12 each for their first two children, $10 for a third child, and $8 each for fourth, fifth, and sixth children. In addition, overseas servicemen were obliged to remit half of their pay to dependants in Canada. For a private this amounted to at least $20 a month, though rarely more than $22.50. A private's wife with three children therefore could expect $89 to $91.50 a month in allowances.[60] But the federal government's Marsh Report of 1943 calculated that a couple with three children under twelve required no less than $122.85 a month to make ends meet.[61] A serviceman's wife with children needed to supplement her income, as her Dependants' Allowance was clearly insufficient. In 1943 Robert England, who helped plan and implement Ottawa's civil re-establishment strategies during the war, admitted that the allowances, "in the case of a small family ... are not quite feasible if the family is resident in a large city."[62]

They Also Serve Who Only Stand and Wait

The Department of National Defence recognized that many young mothers and some aged parents were experiencing hardship because their husbands and sons had enlisted. It set up various administrative boards, such as the Dependants' Board of Trustees and the Dependants' Advisory Committee, to provide special and often emergency assistance to servicemen's families suffering financial or medical misfortune. Many cases came before these bodies, usually through a local welfare or social agency.

In wartime Montreal the Family Welfare Association, a Protestant charitable group, assisted and counselled needy families of overseas soldiers. In 1941 this agency helped cover medical or child-care expenses for 245 Verdun soldiers' families, often made up of aged or ill parents or unemployable spouses with children; these families also received advice on budgeting and managing debt. These 245 families accounted for some 10 percent of Verdun servicemen at that time. The Family Welfare Association spent over $18,000 assisting Verdunites in 1941 and a similar amount in 1942.[63]

Some women sought marital and emotional advice from the association, symptomatic of their long separations from their husbands. Joan Adams, wartime head of the Women's Volunteer Reserve Corps, noted that many marriages and relationships in Verdun simply could not stand the strain. This became especially difficult for children, in her opinion, when the personal relationships entertained by some soldiers' wives, fiancées, or girlfriends became the subject of gossip at school or in community organizations. The emotional stress was very hard on these families.[64]

By 1943 the absence of so many Verdunites overseas had placed an increasing number of families in financial hardship or even destitution. Active service claimed many families' wage earners, sometimes forever. During a 1943 fundraising drive by the Montreal Welfare Federation (made up of many social agencies, including the Family Welfare Association), J.W. MacGillivray, a Verdun businessman and local chairman of the appeal, noted that "we in Verdun understand the needs of any welfare organization." Although employment was at an "all time high," many Verdunites left behind lived in distressed circumstances. Recalling the city's strong community spirit during the Depression, MacGillivray asked residents once again to help their less fortunate but no less patriotic neighbours. Moreover, servicemen could better perform their duties overseas knowing that their families were being cared for at home.[65] In helping one another, Verdunites could support the war effort.

In 1942 Verdunites contributed $1,900 to the Welfare Federation, meeting the city's quota, but giving only one-tenth of what the federation returned to the community in aid. In the first eight months of 1943 the Family Welfare Association looked after at least 143 Verdun servicemen's families facing indebtedness, a seriously reduced standard of living, or crippling medical expenses. Some of these families also received special grants from the Department of National Defence's Dependants' Board of Trustees.[66]

In March 1944 the number of Verdun servicemen's families receiving aid remained over 200. Only six families, however, had their incomes and spending strictly supervised by the Family Welfare Association. "In view of the large number of Protestant families of enlisted men in Verdun," wrote the *Guardian*, perhaps surprised, this low figure constituted a "tribute to the [financial] management by the wives" left behind.[67] Money management offered women enhanced social status and visibility. The view that many servicemen's wives were unable to cope with the intricacies of planning a family budget was common across Canada, however.[68] In reporting on the good works of the Family Welfare Association in Verdun, the *Guardian* regularly insinuated that many women left behind could not adequately organize family finances to supply the needs of their families. But financial difficulties rarely resulted solely from an inability to manage available funds or balance a budget.

The *Guardian* applauded local Protestants' patriotism and lack of extravagance. Clair McLaughlin, a prominent local merchant, and Elizabeth Wilson co-chaired the 1944 fundraising effort in Verdun. McLaughlin stated that "nobody in Verdun needs to be told that [some] soldiers' families cannot cope with unforeseen problems." Verdunites, though wearying of the many charitable appeals, still donated $2,941, or 111 percent of the fund's objective for Verdun. Verdunites were aware that their largesse would flow back into their community, possibly even to families that they knew. This made the costs of patriotism easier to bear. The Family Welfare Association presented Elizabeth Wilson with a trophy for heading a "women's division" with the best results in the Montreal area.[69]

In 1941 only 15 percent of the Family Welfare Association's Montreal-wide caseload had concerned servicemen's families. But by 1944 the proportion had risen to 43 percent, or 1,164 families. Montreal's enlistment rate had grown by 1944, and more jobs were available for non-service families, while women with children often could not work. In its annual report for 1944, the association listed 392 case files in Verdun on which it spent $13,000, for an average per-household cost down considerably from the earlier war years. In other words, more soldiers' families were receiving less help. In March 1944 about two-thirds of family welfare cases in Verdun related to servicemen's families – a much higher proportion than elsewhere in Montreal.[70] Almost all Verdunites in uniform served in the lowest-paying ranks, and Verdun's unusually young population meant that more local servicemen's wives or mothers cared for more children at home than was the case in other neighbourhoods. But though the absolute numbers had risen, in 1944 a far lower overall proportion of Verdun servicemen's families were seeking such aid than in 1941. Increased labour demand, especially from 1941 on, speeded financial recovery for many families whose members were able to work. One French-speaking Verdun women recalled that her war labour helped restore her family's finances, which had been devastated by her husband's six years of nearly uninterrupted unemployment.[71]

Financial hardship was just one type of war-induced social burden for families. The war also dramatically accelerated the caseload of the Verdun Protestant Hospital, one of Canada's leading psychiatric institutions. Since Canadian troops were not committed to sustained ground combat until the invasion of Sicily in July

1943, and since relatively few Canadian casualties were incurred during the first few years of war, the stress resulting from the loss or feared loss of relatives and friends was not at first noticeably high in Verdun. In the hospital's 1940 annual report, the medical superintendent, Dr C.A. Porteus, stated that the war "has not resulted so far in actually increasing the number of those admitted as patients to this hospital." A year later there had been only a slight increase in admissions: "Analysis of the individual cases does not reveal that the war, with its coincident depressing background ... has been a specially determinant force in developing mental disorder."[72] After three years of war, however, cracks developed. In 1942 the hospital recorded 429 new admissions – the largest number in a single year since the hospital opened in 1886. Still, Porteus downplayed these statistics. He noted that it was difficult to blame mental disorder on the war, although it might have encouraged symptoms, such as nervous breakdowns, to manifest themselves.[73]

In his 1943 report Porteus preferred to emphasize the many patients discharged, not the new record of 461 patients admitted. Still, he hinted that a shortage of personnel due to enlistment and stringent federal regulations allocating labour might have speeded up the release of patients.[74] In 1944, with Canadians from all services heavily committed in Europe and elsewhere, the hospital admitted 477 new patients. The *Messenger* referred to the "expressions of anxiety" common in Verdun following the Allied landings in Normandy, since "it was known at once that Verdunites were in the vanguard, as Verdunites are to be found in many regiments."[75] Hundreds of Verdunites had been killed or wounded to this point in the war. Porteus could no longer minimize the war's role in creating so many new stress cases, particularly among female relatives of serving personnel, who made up a large percentage of the new arrivals. Over 2,100 patients were treated in 1944, for an increase of 10,301 patient days over 1943.[76] Although new admissions dipped below 400 in 1945, they went way up in 1946 to 502. Porteus acknowledged that even though the shooting war had stopped, war-related social problems, especially the enduring housing crisis, led to depression and much despair.[77]

The patients admitted to the Verdun Protestant Hospital suffering from nervous collapse as a result of the war came from all over the Montreal area and even further afield. It is not possible to determine how many were Verdunites. But because this Verdun hospital acted as a regional psychiatric centre for the English-language community and witnessed some of the emotional and psychological stress induced by the war, its experiences are part of the fabric of wartime Verdun.

Children's Needs

Servicemen's children, too, frequently needed medical help, but of a more material kind. Despite Verdun's large English-speaking and working-class populations, its Well Baby Clinic had closed in 1935 after a dispute between the Child

Welfare Association of Montreal (CWA), a public charity, and the city council's executive committee over funding responsibilities. The Well Baby Clinic had operated without rental charges from a school basement, where mothers could consult two full-time public health nurses as well as physicians available twice weekly. Although the clinic was heavily subsidized, families had paid a small membership fee. In 1940 CWA officials met with Mayor Wilson and his wife, Elizabeth, head of the Verdun Red Cross, to discuss the re-establishment of a clinic, but little came of the meeting despite the Wilsons' being "extremely interested" in improving Verdun children's welfare. Many local families and their pre-school-age children were in critical need of assistance, a situation magnified for some by the enlistment of the principal breadwinner.[78]

In the absence of a municipal government commitment, a man's military "family" could help look after his small children. Nothing was done until May 1943, when Montreal's Naval Auxiliary Association approached the CWA with a plan to establish a trial three-month Well Baby Clinic in Verdun, to serve the thirty-seven local families in need who had a member serving in the navy. With 28 percent of the Association's case load, Verdun had the largest number of such families in the metropolitan area – not surprising given the many sailors from Verdun. That summer local cases increased to forty-eight. As a result of the Naval Auxiliary Association's initiative, a physician and a public health nurse were available at four designated times on a trial basis from the existing clinic in neighbouring Point St Charles. Nurses also made eighty-two visits to Verdun families, and staff offered vaccinations and other medical services.[79]

Upon hearing of this trial program, Edna Somerville, the welfare convenor for the Black Watch (Royal Highland Regiment) of Canada, contacted the Montreal Soldiers' Wives' League in the hope that it would cooperate with the CWA to extend the service to all Verdun servicemen's families in need. "The need for a Well Baby Clinic in Verdun ... is a very pressing one." she wrote. "Verdun, with its large English population has contributed so well to all the forces and these families deserve that their children should have the care afforded to them in their part of the city."[80] Accordingly, the MSWL dispatched a circular letter to the women's auxiliaries of all military units in the Montreal area noting that the trial arrangement offered by the Naval Auxiliary Association and the CWA "proved to be so well received and of such benefit that it is felt it should be expanded to include the other Services."[81] The MSWL requested that each organization provide it with the number of English-speaking families in Verdun in their association lists and the number of children under five in those families. While this last piece of information was not usually to hand, and not all associations responded, the 476 men listed combined for at least 130 children under the age of five.[82] Though the plan highlighted to a metropolitan audience Verdun's immense manpower contributions and the welfare needs of some of the servicemen's families, nothing came of it.

Another means of helping working mothers with pre-school-age children was the establishment of day nurseries. Detractors saw these as upsetting the traditional family structure: women should stay at home and look after their children, and those who took jobs while they had small children at home were negligent. Certainly the Catholic Church in Quebec opposed day nurseries as socialistic and encouraging child abandonment; French-speaking munitions workers preferred to leave their children with neighbours and relatives.[83] Six wartime day nurseries were established in Quebec, most operating in English and all in the Montreal area, through a federal-provincial 50-50 cost-sharing initiative.

On 1 May 1943, the largest of them opened in St Willibrord's parish hall in Verdun. The densely populated city, especially since the opening of the DIL plant, had an obvious need for such a facility. Perhaps indicating a linguistic division in church policy, St Willibrord's was willing to host the day care. Nevertheless, the children's welfare was not completely without a religious dimension. The first interim director of Dominion-Provincial Day Nursery No. 2 was Miss Patricia Sheeran, a teacher, nurse, and Catholic. She was succeeded by Mrs Rae McKeown, formerly of the Catholic Welfare Bureau. McKeown's hiring might have had more to do with her experiences in doling out Catholic welfare, since she had no training in child care and was obliged to take a course.[84] The St Willibrord's facility had spots for sixty-two children aged two to six.[85]

This arrangement allowed more Verdun women with children to work than otherwise would have been the case; the day nursery was an instant success. In its first month of operation, forty-four children were registered, belonging to thirty-two mothers. Three-quarters of the women worked in war industries, as the federal government insisted be the minimum. By August sixty-two children were registered belonging to forty-one mothers, 85 percent of whom were defence workers. Staffing increased to six paid workers assisted by fourteen volunteers.[86] By the time it closed on 15 October 1945, Verdun's daycare had averaged by far the largest daily attendance of the six in Quebec, thirty-six children, with the next highest average being twenty-three. Verdun's working women protested the day nursery's closure but, as elsewhere across Canada, to no avail.[87] The success of St Willibrord's daycare showed that Verdun's English-speaking women with pre-school children were more than willing to continue working, notwithstanding social pressures, perhaps especially if the family's principal breadwinner was away on active service.

Children's perspectives of the war are often difficult to obtain. Few grasped the wider issues that so affected their lives. Mary Peate, in her recollections of growing up in wartime Montreal, believed that many young people were conscious of the government's efforts to involve them in the struggle and that many found burdensome their wartime roles as fundraisers or collectors of salvage. Their participation in patriotic causes seemed an obligation dictated by their parents or other adults. For adolescents, however, wartime constituted a social and experiential norm against which many measured the period that followed.[88]

Wartime culture permeated children's lives. Chapter 5 discussed the war effort of Verdun's schools and the alarming number of high school students who abandoned their education early to enlist or to work in war industries. In addition to collecting War Savings Stamps, joining cadet corps, and participating in salvage and fundraising drives, many prewar hobbies and pastimes took on a martial tone. Films, comic books, toys, games, trading cards, mail-order paraphernalia of every description, and even the backs of cereal boxes were designed with war-related themes or motifs.[89]

The war also affected Verdun sporting circles when a shortage of players led to the disbanding of the Verdun Bulldogs of the Quebec Senior Hockey League in the autumn of 1940. There were far fewer registrants for senior hockey throughout the Montreal area because of recruiting. Enlistment also badly depleted Verdun's football leagues. By adopting nicknames such as "Corvettes" or "Dreadnoughts," hockey and football teams fought vicarious wars.[90] The war increased stress and anxiety levels in some children. One ten-year-old Verdunite, Wilson Dornan, learned of the outbreak of war over the radio and became extremely frightened and agitated, believing that his home might be bombed. But as time passed, Dornan recalled that for him and perhaps most children, the war years settled down into a routine of "more or less business as usual."[91]

Crime and Juvenile Delinquency

Wartime, with its constant reminders of patriotic behaviour, was at first conducive to a "law and order" mentality. Non-conformity or criminal behaviour, while contrary to peacetime social norms, seemed especially harmful to the national war effort. Verdun was not beset by serious crime during the war. While the incidence of crime and juvenile delinquency increased, wartime conditions permitted exaggeration of an issue widely seen as destabilizing, divisive, and unpatriotic. The press, community groups, and public officials overstated the problem.

According to police statistics and figures from Verdun's Recorder's Court, in 1939 serious criminal infractions in the city were rare. There were very few cases of burglary, auto theft (few residents owned automobiles), or assault, though there were ninety-one cases of loitering and twenty-five cases of disturbing the peace. Illicit gambling and backroom slot machines were considered Verdun's greatest criminal problems. In 1940 burglaries and auto thefts were reported to have decreased 50 percent over the previous year. In 1941 even fewer burglaries and only fourteen instances of disturbing the peace were recorded in Verdun. Few offences more serious than disturbing the peace were investigated by the police in 1942.[92] These are hardly the statistics of a crime-infested city, especially one with a population above 67,000 in 1941.

Wartime enlistment removed at least some of Verdun's older juvenile offenders from city streets. The local press had dubbed one organized group of teenagers the "Galt Avenue Gang." Opinions about these troublesome youths changed once they enlisted, at which time their fighting spirit and destructive energies were hailed as positive personal qualities, when applied to the proper cause. Their past misdeeds, including loitering and disturbing the peace, were explained in the press as nothing more than youthful exuberance. According to the *Guardian*, the gang could "by no stretch of the imagination have been termed anything but young lads 'full of the devil' ... None of them had any real bad traits or tendencies to do any actual harm ... And now the 'Gang,' or the greater number of them, ... are in all the services of His Majesty's forces, in training ... or chafing under the strain of having to wait to make the age limit."[93] The list of gang members on active service showed ten names, all British in origin. Their ages ranged from sixteen to twenty-one, with most being eighteen or nineteen. As evidence of the group's organized patriotism, each member received a silver disc from the gang on enlistment, a gesture much approved by the local press.

In September 1942, the *Guardian* reported, under the headline "Evil Minded Give Verdun Wide Berth," that the city "enjoys the enviable position of being probably the most law-abiding and peaceful community of its size ... in the Dominion, if not on the American continent."[94] Police spent half of their time doing "social work": "readjusting family troubles, giving a word of friendly warning or stricter reprimand to a young fellow slipping ever so little from the straight and narrow way, or getting off the street and into his own home without fuss or scandal a decent citizen who may have dined not wisely but too well. This type of social work ... in Verdun often reaches an average of 50 cases a week all done without fanfare or publicity."[95] The local perception of Verdun as a safe, conformist, and patriotic municipality seemed justified by the crime statistics as well as by the helpful attitude of the city's policemen, themselves mostly Verdunites. But this idyllic self-portrait, representative of a strong sense of community, did not last much beyond 1942.

By April 1943, a growing number of reported criminal transgressions had created apprehension in the city, and the *Guardian* suddenly took on an alarmist tone. For the first time since the outbreak of war public safety was called into question.[96] Police statistics for May 1943 showed fighting, vandalism, loitering, and disturbing the peace as increasingly common, especially among youths. The *Guardian* contended that most of these hooligans were not residents, but it offered no evidence. The local press could not or would not believe that Verdunites themselves might be responsible for local disturbances.

Serious crimes committed in Verdun in 1943 consisted of two "highway robberies" and two hold-ups, eighty-two burglaries, twenty-seven auto thefts, fifteen cases of indecent assault, and one of carrying a concealed weapon.[97] Crime was on the rise. Rowdiness became more common, especially at night along the riverfront boardwalk. In April 1944, several serious disturbances involving gangs of youths congregating at the riverfront induced the city to institute regular police patrols of the boardwalk by two or three plainclothes officers and a motorcycle patrol.[98] City hall was determined to prevent Verdun from being a wartime battleground for disaffected youths.

The crime rate rose throughout the country during the summer of 1945. The cessation of hostilities relaxed the "patriotic" social discipline of the early war years. The return of thousands of young servicemen from overseas signalled a rise in antisocial behaviour. Concern had been expressed in Canada that the demobilized soldiers, desensitized to violence by their training and experiences, might constitute a disruptive social force and menace to public safety. In 1946 adult offences rose 12 percent nationwide over 1945, although they dropped 10 percent in Québec.[99]

By early 1945, the community perceived a growing criminal problem in Verdun, widely attributed to discharged soldiers. That summer a number of assaults on women took place; without evidence, the press quickly suspected returned servicemen. Police patrols increased. Indeed, not all Verdunites were able to readjust smoothly to civilian life. In the ensuing year the *Guardian* reported a dramatic rise in the number of loiterers and panhandlers, some known to be discharged soldiers.[100] Although the war initially had been blamed for increased criminality, in the short term it was the postwar repatriation of thousands of servicemen that brought increased crime to Verdun.

Most Canadian and American studies of the home front during the Second World War refer to the rise in juvenile delinquency.[101] The contemporary perception was very strong that juvenile delinquency was the direct result of interrupted family cohesion. Hundreds of thousands of fathers had disappeared from the home and thousands of mothers were absent at jobs, sometimes employed on evening or night shifts. The lack of parental supervision was feared to encourage juvenile delinquency among "latch-key children" or "eight-hour orphans." In June 1942, as a result of enlistment and female employment, more than 5,000 children in Montreal were believed to be improperly supervised.[102] Growing delinquency was viewed as the result of overcrowded housing and the general tension and strain of wartime conditions. Stealing, vandalism, truancy, and general "anti-social behaviour" were the usual transgressions of delinquents.[103]

Many Verdunites were disturbed to learn in April 1940 that juvenile crime had risen 19 percent in the previous year, at the same time as adult crime was on the wane.[104] The trend continued until it was believed to have reached crisis proportions in the summer of 1943. Available statistics indicate, however, that this view was an exaggeration. National rates of juvenile delinquency peaked in 1942 and coincided with the vast increase in the employment of female labour in war industry. Yet the steady decline in the national rate throughout 1943 and 1944 preceded the return of these women into the home, indicating that the causal effect of female labour participation was overstated. Moreover, because most men eighteen to thirty, traditionally the most likely source of crime, were on active service, more time was devoted to policing youths. This increased the number of juvenile arrests and prosecutions (many for simple curfew violations) and inflated the apparent rate of juvenile crime.[105]

In 1943 minor vandalism became common in Verdun's public parks and against private property, and the situation worsened during the summer.[106] Of twenty-one people arrested in Verdun in July 1943, seventeen were juveniles taken into custody for relatively petty offences. In August 1943, however, a roving gang of some fifty young rowdies disrupted a "sing-song" concert for young people at Woodland Park, near the waterfront. Police were called to quell the disorder. This incident demonstrated that an organized gang of delinquents operated in Verdun. Future wartime sing-songs were tainted by the threat of violence, and one woman, Béatrice Ste-Marie, who was a child living on Third Avenue during the war, has recalled that attendance was considered risky.[107] In January 1944, thirty of thirty-four people arrested in Verdun for various offences were youths. In June 1944, forty of fifty-two offenders taken into custody were juveniles, most of them picked up for loitering and disturbing the peace.[108] The local press, citing police sources, alternated between alarm and reassurance. The frequency of delinquent acts depended on the season. The onset of winter lowered rates of juvenile loitering and vandalism; there was less to vandalize in winter, especially in public parks.

Boredom was viewed as a further possible cause of juvenile crime. The city hoped that sports and games would subdue mischievous young people. Sports constituted an important and inexpensive community activity and helped relax wartime tensions. In 1942 the Verdun Municipal Playgrounds Commission recorded its busiest year to that date. It issued nearly 1,500 permits for sporting matches at local parks, while 1,233 players were registered in municipally organized leagues and 305 in independent leagues.[109] The city saw to it that its playgrounds remained popular. In the summer of 1944 city hall increased the commission's budget by $5,300 to improve sporting facilities and offer more activities. Between 1939 and 1945 the number of Verdun playgrounds increased from five to eleven.[110] In cooperation with the city, Verdun's YMCA branch expanded its many youth-oriented activities, all of which the *Guardian* viewed as "wag[ing] war on delinquency."[111] The city's campaign met with the approval of a broad spectrum of local groups including the Greater Verdun Community Council, the Knights of Columbus, the Ligue indépendente catholique and the Société Saint-Jean-Baptiste.[112] A united response addressed a common problem.

While wartime Verdun experienced some increase in juvenile delinquency, the municipality was no hotbed of criminality. The overwhelming majority of young people were not delinquents. The city attempted to deal with juvenile crime, even though public safety was not threatened or eroded. Though the war exacerbated some social or familial circumstances that facilitated a drift to juvenile crime, it was not a substantial cause of criminal behaviour.

The Verdun "Zoot-Suit" Disturbances

Though not directly linked to local levels of crime or juvenile delinquency, one spectacular violent incident rocked wartime Verdun and became etched into the city's collective memory. On 3 June 1944, Verdun was the scene of a "zoot suit" riot that pitted more than 100 sailors stationed in Montreal against a lesser number of young civilian men and teenagers, many of them "zooters" or "zoot-suiters." Zoot suits had a garish, even shocking, combination of colour, cut, and pattern. They consisted of a long, loose coat with excessively wide, padded shoulders, ballooning pants pegged at the ankles, a shirt with wide collar points sometimes accompanied by an oversized bow-tie, a wide-brimmed hat and a long, hanging watch chain. This fad was most prominent in the United States and Canada, although some youths in Britain were also adherents.[113]

Most contemporary observers concluded that the zoot suit was foremost a symbol of youth rebellion and defiance. Antisocial behaviour such as drinking and loitering was often linked to zoot-suiters, and some roving zooter gangs were criminal and violent. Given the tense wartime atmosphere and government exhortations for social cohesion, zooters' actions and appearances seemed unpatriotic. Their attire contravened Wartime Prices and Trade Board guidelines for the rationing of fabrics and textiles, while their non-conformist attitude seemed to suggest antipathy to established social behaviour.[114] Considerable ill-will towards the apparently unpatriotic zoot-suiters developed among servicemen stationed in or near large urban areas, where concentrations of zooters could be found.

In Montreal these two groups sometimes clashed violently, and these collisions were occasionally worsened by perceptions of linguistic differences.[115] A serious outbreak of zoot-suit-related violence took place during the night of 27 May 1944 in St Lambert, on the south shore of the St Lawrence River opposite Montreal. *La Presse* noted that the zooters were mainly of Italian origin, although there were also a few French speakers among them. The soldiers and some local youths who opposed them were English speaking. Further altercations took place on 31 May, and fighting spread to the south shore landing of the Jacques Cartier Bridge, where a group of mainly French-speaking soldiers stationed in nearby Longueuil were set upon by a mixed-language band of zooters, fifty-three of whom were arrested.[116] Isolated incidents occurred daily in the Montreal area until at least 7 June, including the well-publicized beating of a sailor and his wife by zooters.

Meanwhile, at the end of May there had been disturbances in Verdun along the riverfront boardwalk as well as on Wellington Street. The *Guardian* referred to the incidents as "baby riots" and "demonstrations of racial feeling." Although the combatants appear to have been divided by language, it is unclear whether servicemen were involved.[117] Despite nearly five years of war and several passionate election campaigns that had often divided Verdunites along ethnic lines, this was the first reported wartime incident of linguistic discord in Verdun on a scale large enough to warrant police intervention.

A much more serious outburst rocked Verdun in the late evening of Saturday, 3 June. At roughly the same time, some 400 overwhelmingly English-speaking sailors sought out and attacked zooters in downtown Montreal, especially along Ste Catherine Street. The men were apparently avenging the sailors attacked by zooters during the previous week. According to the *Guardian*, the trouble in Verdun began when "some of the over-excited sailors ... drifted to Verdun and when they met with some youths who were wearing what looked like zoot suits, started to chase them. Fights developed in a pool room on Wellington Street."[118]

Well over 100 sailors left Montreal on foot and made their way, "en formation de parade,"[119] to the Verdun Dance Pavilion on the waterfront next to Woodland Park, where they confronted perhaps sixty youths, not all of whom were zooters. Hundreds of non-zooter patrons were at the pavilion, and sailors mistook some of them, wearing prewar, pre-WPTB suits, for zooters. Dozens of naval shore patrolmen, army provosts, and Verdun police arrived to break up the melee, watched by a large number of Verdunites. The brawl lasted for more than an hour and was over by about 11 p.m.

The interior of the Dance Pavilion sustained some damage, and many minor injuries were reported. Four civilians were arrested, while the military police detained some sailors. Naval shore patrols monitored the explosive situation in Verdun long into the night. At first the local police force was overwhelmed by the magnitude of the violence, and many injured zoot-suiters, especially those who were stripped of their outfits by the sailors, were simply driven to the nearby police station to await the arrival of friends or relatives.

The *Montreal Daily Star* described the fighting in Verdun as "vicious." *La Presse* emphasized the language dimension, and noted that "the brawling was serious in Verdun."[120] The *Guardian* looked approvingly on the servicemen's vigilante actions and insisted that linguistic tensions had helped produce the violence. It treated the fighting almost as an innocent prank, accompanied "by a number of rather humorous incidents ... [and] some laughter." Its account was restrained compared to the detailed report in the *Messenger*, which was far more sympathetic to the zoot-suiters and assumed them to be mostly French speakers. In an English-language article, the *Messenger* attacked the ill-disciplined sailors, who "seemed quite willing to descend to Gestapo methods to enforce their own particular 'way of life' upon fellow citizens."[121] The *Guardian* would never have compared Canadian sailors to the Gestapo. Mirroring the views of most English-speaking Verdunites, the *Guardian* fervently opposed the zoot-suiters for what they were believed to represent: a dissenting view of the war effort, and a generally French-speaking one at that. Referring to the zoot-suiters as "clown-like," the *Guardian* claimed the suits were the "symbol of insolence and army evasion, frivolity in time of war" and blamed the zooters themselves for the violence.[122]

Appearances could be deceiving, however. Not all zooters attacked by the sailors were French speakers, and many did not even live in Verdun. The *Messenger* named three zooters who were arrested or injured: two were French speaking and one English speaking, while only one was from Verdun. All were between the ages of seventeen and twenty. One was arraigned in court and told by the magistrate to visit his tailor so as to "avoid further trouble."[123] No incident specific to Verdun had ignited the fighting; the sailors' march on Verdun was an outgrowth of brawling in Montreal. That the Dance Pavilion was a known haunt of zooters was sufficient to attract the sailors.

Yet Verdun's English speakers generally identified zoot-suiters as French speakers. In 1943 one grade eleven student at Verdun High School wrote a short fictional conversation (mostly in French-accented phonetic English) based on the zoot-suit craze. The piece suggested that the typical zooter was French speaking. Many Verdunites remember well the June 1944 fighting at the pavilion and usually discuss it as a language issue. One former resident, who was fifteen at the time of the disturbances, recalled the events vividly and stated that the zooters were considered "the Frenchmen."[124] This perception encouraged a hardening of attitudes in Verdun against the unpatriotic zooters, and was a contributing factor to the fighting. But a post-riot investigation indicated that this view was mistaken.

Testimony taken at the navy's official board of inquiry into the Montreal-wide incidents, on 5 June, showed that the zooters whom the sailors attacked in Montreal and Verdun came from many ethnic backgrounds. Five of eight witnesses who were asked about the zooters' language or ethnicity insisted that they were predominantly of Italian ancestry; two claimed that the zooters were mainly French speaking, while another believed that they were of all nationalities. Several witnesses also mentioned that some zooters were "Jewish" or "Syrian," and most agreed that there were many English speakers among them.[125] Despite contemporary notions and enduring popular perceptions, Verdun's zoot-suit disturbances did not neatly divide French speakers from English speakers. The belief that they did so was a product of, and tainted, perceptions in Verdun of wartime social relations.

Verdun's municipal administration was alarmed at the sudden rash of violence and acted swiftly to defuse tensions. The executive committee petitioned Ottawa and the naval authorities in Montreal to investigate the matter and to take steps to prevent men under their command from engaging in renewed violence in Verdun. The city received letters of assurance from Minister of National Defence J.L. Ralston, Minister of National Defence for Naval Services Angus L. Macdonald, and MP Paul-Émile Côté promising a thorough investigation beyond the naval inquiry.

Edward Wilson, who lived only 250 metres from the Dance Pavilion and had gone to the Verdun police station at the time of the disturbances, met with Commander F.H. Davis, naval controller of the Port of Montreal. Davis promised measures to prevent similar situations in future.[126] Immediately after the fighting the navy declared the Dance Pavilion off-limits to naval personnel, cancelled leave for a week, and imposed a sailors' curfew starting at 9 p.m.[127] Since civil-military relations in Montreal were becoming increasingly tense, the navy was serious about curbing further violence involving its men.

Wilson enlisted members of Verdun's Catholic and Protestant clergy to restrain latent linguistic and social animosities, even though it was known that few of the sailors and only some of the zooters of 3 June were Verdunites. Linguistic relations in Verdun were occasionally somewhat more strained than indicated by city hall's cordial façade. In a letter released to the press immediately following this incident the mayor wrote:

> In Verdun, as elsewhere, one can see more and more that youth is losing its respect towards the public ... It follows that to efface this intolerable attitude that is now growing in alarming proportions among certain groups of young boys and even among girls, it is necessary to adopt energetic measures. Consequently, the City Council has already taken efficient steps to punish leaders of gangs ... measures should be taken to improve community spirit in our municipality and awaken and impress our youth with the necessity of respecting our various religious beliefs. The end that we are anxious to attain is that of national unity at all times and in particular during the time of the present war. For, if there is one thing which must be safeguarded above all others, it is that spirit of mutual goodwill for which the City of Verdun has always been renowned.[128]

The French translation of this letter, published simultaneously in the *Messenger*, underscored its real intention: the phrase "improve community spirit" was replaced with "improve racial harmony."

Wilson may have been acting also to ensure that non-Verdun quarrels remained that way. No further zoot-suit battles took place in the city. The brawling was an aberration and the "mutual goodwill" between the two language groups held fast. In any event, Verdun was the scene, not the origin, of the quarrel. But the local riot was symbolic of the dichotomies inherent to Canada's war: those in uniform, those not; those English speaking, those French speaking.

Some Verdunites were outraged by the zoot-suit incidents. A frequent contributor to the *Guardian*, Reverend Ernest S. Reed, rector of St John the Divine Anglican Church, had strong opinions on the matter. Until the zoot-suit riots Reed generally had been an erudite voice of moderation on a variety of social and patriotic issues. But his "Church Editor's Column" of 15 June 1944 was anything but moderate. He referred to zoot-suiters variously as "hoodlums," "hooligans," and "chisellers of the lowest kind." In calling for "sterner measures" against these youths, whom he blamed entirely for the recent violence, he wrote: "If there are those who object to military service, let them be honest ... But young people who are making good wages in war industries and who spend their leisure time sniping at those in the armed services fall into a very different category [from conscientious objectors] ... There may be even more sinister influences behind these disturbances. If any groups are using 'zoot-suiters' to nefarious ends, let these groups be exposed. Those who, by their teaching or practice, set creed against creed, race against race or group against group are the most despicable kind of fifth columnists."[129] Reed clearly perceived a language dimension to the disturbances; he blamed the zooters and, by extension, seemingly unpatriotic French-speaking youths for the fighting.

The owner of the Dance Pavilion, Rolland David, implied that the animosity between the sailors and the zooters had more to do with social and civil-military differences since, he claimed, both sides contained English and French speakers. Rivalry for the affection of young women was also a significant contributing factor.[130] As a dance-hall owner accustomed to dealing with youths, David was familiar with the backgrounds of many of his clients. He was on the scene during the fighting and insisted that the language factor was exaggerated as an explanation for the fracas. David warned the naval inquiry that henceforth it would be dangerous for sailors to walk the streets of Verdun alone, as many local zooters and their friends and relatives would seek to avenge them. He believed that sailors risked being "knifed or hav[ing] their heads split open."[131]

The Montreal and Verdun zoot-suit riots became known to Verdunites serving overseas. In September 1944, one artilleryman wrote in a letter of appreciation to the Mayor's Cigarette Fund, "at the present time Jerry is on the run and the boys aren't giving him any time to rest ... But if our loyal friends the zoot-suiters don't want to fight for their country, we will have to do it alone ... If you need any reinforcements in Montreal to fight the Draft Dodgers, apply for them [in] France, you will get more than you need."[132] The view of zooters as draft dodgers was popular among servicemen and current among the civilian population. The zoot-suit disturbances constitute evidence that not all was well in the Montreal area between servicemen and civilians, between French speakers and English speakers, and between youths and their elders. Verdun was not immune from the effects of these tensions.

The Consumers' War

If zooters and juvenile delinquents were seemingly more overtly unpatriotic, other citizens, too, less visible, broke wartime regulations and contributed to social discord. Even before Britain or Canada had declared war on Germany, the Verdun branch of the Canadian Corps Association (CCA) told city hall that some local merchants had raised food prices, especially for sugar, in response to the crisis in Europe. Some retailers allegedly extorted a minimum purchase of other goods from clients before agreeing to sell them sugar. The CCA, already concerned about the families of First World War veterans struggling on relief, accused the merchants of "war profiteering." City council informed federal and provincial police, while the municipality itself, relying on women shoppers for most of its information, undertook to monitor local retailers' prices. The city served notice to consumers, too, reminding them that the hoarding of essential commodities would be "unhesitatingly" reported to the federal authorities. Verdun also urged Ottawa to grant municipalities the powers to enact special by-laws to "combat this abuse."[133]

City hall strongly condemned illegal pricing, a practice that Mayor Edward Wilson considered vile and unpatriotic. In October 1939 Sarah Upton, a representative of the embryonic Verdun Housewives' League, sought the city's help in organizing resistance to merchants' profiteering. Arthur Burgess, the city clerk, responded that the city was already cooperating with the Royal Canadian Mounted Police in the matter. Upton's attempts to organize Verdun women suggests widespread public opposition to unscrupulous and unpatriotic local business practices.[134]

As a result of the Canadian experience during the First World War, Ottawa adopted immediate measures to limit profiteering. At the outbreak of hostilities it established the Wartime Prices and Trade Board to prevent hoarding and profiteering, and to regulate and monitor retail prices and the distribution of commodities and materials. By 1941 its main task was to control inflation.[135] Until the autumn of 1941, however, it played only a discreet role in regulating purchases. Then in October, following a rise in the cost of living estimated at 17.8 percent since the start of the war, the WPTB imposed a comprehensive system of wage and price controls effective 1 December 1941. This move reflected Ottawa's goal of consumer and commercial stability and restraint. The Maximum Prices Regulations set a ceiling on prices of goods and most services as they existed in the month-long control period of 15 September to 11 October 1941. The WPTB also wielded the power to enforce the price ceilings. These complicated administrative measures, affecting the lives of all Canadians, proved successful; inflation was kept to an acceptable 2.5 percent for the remainder of the war. For example, food prices increased only 6 percent, rents rose a mere 1 percent, and clothing increases averaged below 2 percent.[136]

Since Canadian women did nearly 85 percent of all household spending on retail merchandise, they also monitored prices and investigated suspected offences. In the first few months of the war retail prices rose approximately 13 percent. From December 1941 until the end of the war some 16,000 Canadian women, organized into Women's Regional Advisory Committees, acted as voluntary price wardens and supplied consumers with WPTB guidelines. Ruth Pierson has suggested that, in fulfilling their accepted and expected social roles as shoppers, these women, drawn from various class and linguistic backgrounds, were "indispensable" in checking inflation.[137] To June 1942, however, only 147 merchants nationwide were prosecuted as a result of consumer vigilance.

In 1942 Canada introduced full-scale rationing of scarce and essential goods and services. The WPTB administered the system and issued all consumers with ration coupons to surrender at the point of sale. Purchases of gasoline were regulated in April, sugar followed in July, and tea and coffee were rationed from August 1942 to September 1944. Butter was controlled from December 1942 on, and in May 1943 meat was regulated at one kilogram per person per week. Many customers patronized a single supplier in the hope of obtaining small, unsanctioned favours. One Verdunite, Wilson Dornan, recalled a butcher shop that gave his family certain privileges since they were regular customers.[138]

The WPTB set up over 500 offices across Canada, including one in Verdun in 1942. Wilson headed the local ration board, first housed in city hall. He then recruited "responsible" citizens to carry out the board's functions, which included price monitoring and distributing booklets of ration coupons. Volunteers based at eleven schools ran neighbourhood distribution points for the booklets.[139] Merchants were required to undertake a daily coupon count and administer a complicated accounting procedure in which commodity sales had to match wholesale deliveries. The coupons became so onerous to handle and collate that in March 1943 chartered banks began collecting the coupons from merchants and sorting them in local branches. The scheme was known as "ration banking." Shopkeepers opened coupon accounts in which they deposited their customers' ration coupons. The bank then issued merchants a voucher for the coupons, a form of "surrogate currency" enabling them to reorder rationed items from distributors. By the summer of 1943 the Royal Bank of Canada branch in Verdun handled the comparatively enormous amount of 400,000 ration coupons a week, which underlines the density of Verdun's population.[140]

A black market developed with the diversion or theft of products, dishonest record keeping, and overpricing of commodities. Despite its large population, however, Verdun appeared to have remarkably little black-market activity. The press reported very few cases of evasion of ration control. Perhaps the absence of significant industrial or wholesale enterprises made the city unattractive to racketeers. But on an individual level, Verdunites were no different from other Canadians, and some residents sought to turn the system to their own advantage. In 1943 Verdun detectives broke up the local black-market trade in automobile tires. Some citizens resorted to hoarding. Immediately following the imposition of gasoline rationing in April 1942 two raids in Verdun netted illegal caches of hoarded gasoline. A year later a resident was fined $100 for hoarding sugar, condensed milk, and canned goods.[141] Verdunite Peter McClask, owner of a small printing business, was arrested late in the war for possessing printing plates, dyes, and other materials used for printing counterfeit gasoline ration coupons. He was fined a hefty $1,500 – more than the annual salary of many workers at the time.[142] Rationing affected some citizens by reducing municipal services. In October 1942, the Montreal-area controller of electric power ordered Verdun and other municipalities to dim street lighting by as much as 20 percent to save electricity. To install streetlights in Verdun's recently developed areas, the city had to curtail lighting for the riverside boardwalk, hockey rinks, and parks, and even along Verdun Avenue, a main thoroughfare. The controller's order created some distress and provoked opposition from the Council of Women of Montreal. That group feared that at a time when police services were pared and juvenile crime was on the increase, reducing lighting was potentially hazardous for women on the streets after dark. Without denying that rationing was a necessary wartime expedient, it questioned the wisdom of this particular measure. Despite this request, City Engineer Henry Hadley reported in November that street lighting had been reduced as required.[143] Verdun had had to conform, and for local women, sports teams, and nighttime pedestrians wartime nights would no longer be as enjoyable as they had been.

THE SECOND WORLD WAR affected Verdun society in a variety of ways, some more profound than others. The housing crisis caused widespread demoralization in Verdun and aroused much bitterness in this community of tenants against dishonest and insensitive landlords as well as against the federal government. By 1945 a growing number of Verdunites, especially low-income, overburdened mothers, had begun to view participation in the war more as a lengthy struggle against social marginalization and less as a duty automatically answered. The situation contained the potential for violence. But far-sighted municipal authorities had implemented a wartime development plan that eased the burden somewhat. Without the city's interest and determination, housing conditions would have been far worse. The thousands of returning service people did not have to wait long before Crawford Park was converted into a comfortable veterans' enclave.

Even though most Verdun families benefited from increased employment, the war also brought financial distress, personal hardship, emotional duress, and tragedy for many. Servicemen's families were among the city's most disadvantaged residents, a situation that wartime patriotism found particularly odious. Verdun casualties numbered in the hundreds; while hardly insignificant, they were not as heavy as the city's enormous enlistment rates might have suggested.[144] More noticeable was the disruption of family finances and cohesion caused by the departure of thousands of men on active service.

Juvenile delinquency increased during the war, but its incidence seemed unduly magnified by its characterization as unpatriotic. The city became alarmed at this perceived rise in antisocial behaviour and provided Verdun youths with improved outlets for their energy. These initiatives were hailed in the community, which seemed satisfied with municipal responses to the social problems occasioned by the war. The local outburst of violence between zooters and sailors was the result of wider issues than those of Verdun's own making.

Despite the great potential for wartime division along class and linguistic lines, Verdun society remained generally cohesive. Hardships were borne and the social fabric remained intact. The war brought both prosperity and some dislocation, but neither in sufficient quantity to alter the city radically. Verdun was changed by the war, but Verdunites away on active service had no difficulty recognizing their home town on their return.

7
The Political War

Studying electoral behaviour in wartime Verdun is revealing. The elections served as a focus for the community's issues, divisions, commonalities, and local culture – in both languages. The emotive power of wartime elections, added to Verdun's socioeconomic and cultural makeup, risked straining the city's "bonne entente" and laying bare its structural divide. But this did not happen.

Verdun's electors voted on eight occasions during the Second World War. Two were federal elections, in 1940 and 1945; two were provincial, in 1939 and 1944; three were municipal, in 1941, 1943, and 1945; and the plebiscite on conscription was held in 1942. The provincial and federal contests all dealt with the divisive issue of conscription and other war-related matters, while the municipal elections focused on local finances and improvements. As discussed in Chapter 3, war-related political issues rarely filtered down to the municipal level. But an examination of Verdun's wartime politics provides insight into the effects of national issues on community harmony and cohesion. The community's political responses were the measure of local social dynamics.

The provincial electoral boundaries of Verdun coincided with its municipal limits, but the federal riding of Verdun included neighbouring Lasalle, which had about 4,000 residents in 1940 of whom perhaps 60 percent were French speaking. By 1939 Verdun's French- and English-speaking communities had coexisted for several generations. Whomever most of the English-speaking majority supported stood the best chance of winning a seat in Verdun. Traditionally, the city's English-speaking, working-class majority had voted Conservative in both federal and provincial elections. During the Depression, the social programs of the Co-operative Commonwealth Federation became popular in Verdun, where the party achieved its greatest level of support in Quebec. Yet in the 1935 federal contest Verdun elected a Conservative, one of only forty in Canada and five from Quebec. In the 1935 and 1936 provincial elections Verdun returned a candidate representing the Union Nationale, which had replaced the provincial Conservative party. But the war altered Verdun's traditional electoral behaviour.

The 1939 Provincial Election
The surprise election called by Premier Maurice Duplessis for 25 October 1939 created a great stir in Quebec and across Canada because of its underlying implications for wartime national unity. Ostensibly, the election was fought over the

federal usurpation of provincial rights and the legitimacy of Ottawa's conduct of the war effort. In fact, the major issue turned out to be the sincerity and validity of Ottawa's promise not to impose conscription. Strong opinions on this matter were mobilized in Verdun.

MLA Pierre A. Lafleur had represented the city in the Legislative Assembly first as a Conservative (1923-35) and then as a member of the Union Nationale (UN), which had formed the government in 1936. Lafleur had always received substantial support from English speakers and was sensitive to their wartime mood, which was ill-disposed to his party's lukewarm war stance. The conservative *Guardian* noted that Lafleur had "pledged his loyalty to King and Country and held that the Government of Quebec was [as] loyal as any other in the country." Lafleur stated his opposition to conscription but promised to keep an open mind on the subject. He distanced himself from his party and from its leader, and reminded the *Guardian*'s readers that his wife of forty-two years was English speaking as well as the founder and regent of the small Verdun chapter of the Imperial Order Daughters of the Empire. Accordingly, Lafleur offered his "energy and that of [his] wife" in fulfilling his mandate.[1]

Lafleur's chief opponent was the Liberal J.J.L. Comeau, principal of the Verdun branch of O'Sullivan's College, a business and commercial school. Both the English- and French-speaking Liberal organizations in the riding endorsed Comeau in a show of Liberal unity that had not always been evident in Verdun.[2] Comeau's early identification with a vigorous national war effort earned him the strong support of the English-speaking electorate. His insistence on the need for Empire solidarity won the hearts of many British-born residents. Reflecting the community's mood, but also wariness of the UN's *nationaliste* strain, the *Guardian* warned that a Liberal defeat would encourage the "hideous armies of Nazism." Comeau's fortunes rested with the heretofore mainly Conservative English-speaking community. "The question arises," noted the *Guardian*, "as to whether the west end of Verdun will vote Liberal. Stalwarts in the Comeau camp claim that this is one time they [English speakers] can cast their ballots for a Liberal without suffering any pangs of conscience."[3] "Let every English-speaking voter in the Province of Quebec forget ... party politics in this election and join hands with the right-thinking French-Canadian element that is determined to end the reign of tyranny and extravagance it has known," read one of Comeau's advertisements.[4] Comeau had one significant advantage over Lafleur: he had served three years with the Canadian Expeditionary Force in the First World War. A community of veterans and Britons could scarcely ignore this virtue.

Although the Liberals hoped that the English-speaking community would vote for them *en bloc*, the candidacy of another high-profile veteran threatened to split its vote. Robert L. Calder, a well-known Montreal lawyer, civil libertarian, and active opponent of the Duplessis government, was the province's only Co-operative Commonwealth Federation candidate. The bilingual Calder had served as an officer in the Black Watch during the 1914-18 war, and advertisements and articles emphasized his enviable military record. These attributes did much to offset his party's potential unpopularity in Verdun owing to the CCF's early hesitation in fully supporting Canada's war effort. Calder firmly opposed conscription, however, and felt that Canada should limit its participation in the war to voluntarism and the provision of arms and foodstuffs to the Allied cause.[5] As a result, the CCF supporters among the city's many British-born workingmen were choosing class identification over their ties to the mother country.

The political vitriol increased as the election drew nearer. Comeau accused the UN of "treason" and asked the electorate, "Does the Union Jack still mean anything to you?" Lafleur tried to address some of the issues consuming his English-speaking constituents. He referred to Adolf Hitler as the "mad dog of Europe" and insisted that he would resign from the UN if it formed the next government and enacted laws prejudicial to Allied victory – a promise few UN candidates made. Lafleur also desperately reminded voters that "Verdun has always been Conservative" and implored them not to "let the party down." But the issue of the war overrode party allegiances. The approving headline in a special pre-election issue of the *Guardian* screamed, "Comeau says Duplessis Hitler Ally."[6]

The Liberals easily swept the riding. Comeau polled strongly throughout the city, whereas Lafleur's support dwindled rapidly and decisively outside the predominantly French-speaking east-end wards. The CCF did reasonably well in English-speaking neighbourhoods, winning several polls and coming close in many others in Wards 3 and 4. The final tally showed Comeau with 4,449 votes (51 percent), Calder with 2,513 (29 percent), Lafleur with a dismal 1,415 (16 percent), and Georges Daoust, representing the moribund Action Libérale Nationale, with 362 (4 percent). Comeau was said to be the first Liberal ever elected from Verdun.[7]

Neither Verdun's French nor its English speakers voted *en bloc*. English speakers deserted the UN, ensuring Lafleur's defeat. Since the CCF received its support overwhelmingly from English-speaking voters, this means nearly as many English speakers voted for the CCF as for the Liberals. At this early stage of the war, then, ideology mattered as much as patriotism to many working-class Verdunites. Among French-speaking Verdunites, support was split equally between the Liberals and the UN. Provincewide, the Liberals obtained 52.7 percent of the popular vote to the UN's 40 percent.[8] Verdunites from both language groups had joined the rest of Quebec in rejecting the Duplessis government in favour of Adélard Godbout. For the politically eventful first five years of the war, Verdun's representative in Quebec City was an ultrapatriotic, French Canadian First World War veteran sitting on the government side. Comeau did not disappoint those who had voted for a candidate pledged to support the war effort.

The 1940 Federal Election

Amid opposition charges of maladministration of the war effort, Prime Minister William Lyon Mackenzie King dissolved Parliament in January 1940 and called a general election for 26 March. This announcement found Verdun's federal Liberal and Conservative constituency organizations in disarray. By mid-campaign, the Montreal press reported that "Verdun appears to be the political storm centre of the Montreal district."[9] The spirited campaign in Verdun attracted eight candidates – one Liberal, three Independent Liberals, a Conservative, an Independent Conservative, a CCFer, and an Independent – the most in any riding on the Island of Montreal.

When war was declared, Jules Wermenlinger, the Conservative MP for Verdun, had stated that Canada "will have to go to whatever limit is necessary to win," which did not rule out conscription. But by the time the election was called considerable opposition had developed in local Tory ranks to this politically ineffective Verdun shop owner. Although Wermenlinger ultimately secured the backing of the riding association, his shaky position within his own party was underscored by the fact that an Independent Conservative candidate, Sam Currie, challenged him for Verdun's Tory vote.[10]

The Liberals had troubles of their own. The local party was wracked by factionalism. Despite attempts to unite the half-dozen widely divergent Liberal groups (based on language, ideology, and personality), rivalries among them were too deeply entrenched and recriminations too heated. The united front created the previous October by the provincial Liberals could not be repeated by the federal Liberal groups. The normally conservative *Guardian* labelled the situation "badly muddled," and language embittered the struggle.[11] Verdun's English-speaking Liberals hoped to emulate the Liberals in Sherbrooke, where a French-speaking candidate ran provincially and an English speaker federally. With the election less than four weeks away, the Liberals had not yet settled on a candidate. The party's national council finally broke the deadlock by choosing Paul-Émile Côté, a young Verdun lawyer, as its official candidate. It was an odd choice. Côté was neither fluent in English nor well known in the city, even in Liberal circles. He had been mentioned only once in the *Guardian*'s frequent earlier references to possible Liberal candidates.[12]

Côté's nomination dissatisfied many Liberals. Within days, two English-speaking and one French-speaking Independent Liberals threw their hats into the ring. Côté stressed national unity (which only the Liberals could offer) and moderation in the war effort, and attached his political fortunes firmly to the coattails of Prime Minister King. During a campaign rally, Côté said, "I am not in favour of conscription ... I will fight tooth and nail against any attempt to bring in the draft."[13] This was a somewhat risky statement to make in a predominantly English-speaking and traditionally Tory constituency, notwithstanding the fact the national Conservatives themselves had not yet adopted conscription as a policy.

Robert Scurrah, an outspoken and zealously patriotic alderman from Ward 4, ran as an Independent Liberal, claiming to represent Verdun's English-speaking Liberals. Almost pathologically anti-French-Canadian, Scurrah's campaign used defamatory and inflammatory rhetoric. He insisted that language alone should determine voting behaviour. In blurring the differences between language and politics, Scurrah exemplified the difficulties of obtaining social and political cohesion in wartime Verdun. Although an extreme case, his exaggerated views suggest linguistic tensions in the city that were exacerbated by the emotional strain of war. His campaign was the closest thing to hate-mongering witnessed in Verdun's wartime politics. His full-page advertisement in the 22 March 1940 issue of the *Guardian* began by reminding readers that Verdun's English-speaking majority "alone can control this election." The way he saw things, "Verdun, with 65% of its electors of the English-speaking race is one of the few Quebec communities which should, by all rights of fairness ... and of Democracy, have an English-speaking representative at Ottawa ... For the past five years, the English-speaking majority that makes up this municipality has neither had a representative at Ottawa nor at Quebec. How can we express those opinions and feelings that are our birthright under the British flag?" Scurrah believed in the existence of a French Canadian "intrigue" to deny the "solemn" agreement entered into among Verdun Liberals to nominate an English speaker to stand for federal office.

The French-speaking candidate running as an Independent Liberal was Hervé Ferland, the colourful former mayor. Ferland came out firmly against conscription and was the candidate most closely identified with a lukewarm war stance.[14] Given his popularity among the city's French-speaking poor, his candidacy contained the potential to siphon off votes that otherwise might have been Côté's. The *Guardian* simply ignored his candidacy.

R.L. Calder, the CCF candidate who had finished in second place in Verdun in the recent provincial election, benefited from a certain level of popular sympathy but experienced difficulty in translating this into votes. The CCF's support was weak. The party failed to make inroads into the French-speaking electorate, which was influenced in large measure by adamant clerical opposition to the CCF's socialist outlook.[15] As well, the party's leadership came entirely from English Canada, and its support base clearly lay outside Quebec. Its failure to attract more English speakers was due to its only grudging support for the war and to the unlikelihood of the party's electoral success. Given Ferland's strong support among east-end French speakers, many English speakers felt it important to concentrate the English-speaking vote.

One of the most unusual candidates anywhere in Canada in this election was R.B. Joan Adams, founder and principal of Verdun's Canadian Commercial College. She was a prominent local social activist and feminist and later headed the local branch of the Women's Volunteer Reserve Corps. She ran as an Independent on the basis of a "straight women's" platform, which included the demand for women's pensions at age sixty-five, better legal protection for women and children, improved housing and increased allowances for mothers with at least one son serving overseas, and assistance to non-pensioned war widows.[16] She pointed out that her election would highlight Verdun as a progressive community, award the city national attention, and help force the Quebec government into granting female suffrage. She was the only woman candidate in the province and one of nine across Canada.

Adams fervently supported a strong war effort. She listed the "successful prosecution of the war" as her "first duty" and began one speech at Verdun's Legion Hall by stating that "a man who hasn't enough courage to fight for his country isn't much of a man."[17] Blending patriotism with maternal feminism, and proclaiming, "A United Front for War, a United Front for Women, Women of Verdun Unite," Adams insisted that Verdun's MP must be imbued with "sufficiently noble British ideals ... We Verdun people are proud of the accomplishments of our soldiers, but we are also proud of the quiet way, without show or hysterics, that our women bear the brunt of the evils of war."[18] Adams gave feminism a patriotic face in Verdun and made clear that women's contributions to the war effort would not go unnoticed.

Adams's views, and her very candidacy, appear to have affected the electorate, not to mention her political opponents. Fearing that she might attract a large number of female votes, some of the other candidates suddenly felt it expedient to pander to Verdun's female voters. Scurrah reminded women that he sought "the ladies' vote," while Wermenlinger promised to support "all measures appertaining to women's rights." Ferland put the plight of Verdun's many non-pensioned widows of veterans on his political agenda.[19] At the very least, Adams's campaign sensitized voters and politicians to women's unequal social status. Her unprecedented feminist challenge was not always appreciated. The stodgy *Guardian* paid her little attention and on 22 March devoted a brief article to her without once mentioning her name, referring to her instead as "the only woman candidate in Verdun." Even though she later claimed that her political organization was staffed almost entirely by women volunteers, many Verdun women did not support her candidacy, instead agreeing with a common male view that women had no place in political life.[20] In the end, she received scant support on election day, indicating that the electorate remained generally unmoved by gender issues.

On 26 March 1940 Mackenzie King's Liberals won a decisive victory. They swept all sixteen seats on the Island of Montreal. Verdunites participated in this landslide by overwhelmingly rejecting the Tory incumbent and choosing Liberal Paul-Émile Côté, aged thirty, as one of Canada's youngest parliamentarians (Table 7.1). Côté received an unimpressive 31 percent of the vote, most of it from English speakers. The results nevertheless signified a shift in voting behaviour. The *Guardian*

Table 7.1

Verdun federal election results, 1940

	Civilian vote		Military vote		Total	
	Number	%	Number	%	Number	%
Paul-Émile Côté, Liberal	8,361	30.93	67	11.92	8,428	30.55
Hervé Ferland, Independent Liberal	7,092	26.24	92	16.37	7,184	26.04
Robert L. Calder, CCF	3,770	13.95	81	14.41	3,851	13.96
E. Jules Wermenlinger, Conservative	3,489	12.91	210	37.37	3,699	13.41
R.B. Joan Adams, Independent	1,805	6.67	19	3.38	1,824	6.61
Charles Halpin, Independent Liberal	1,150	4.25	43	7.65	1,193	4.32
Sam Currie, Independent Conservative	780	2.89	33	5.87	813	2.95
Robert Scurrah, Independent Liberal	583	2.16	17	3.03	600	2.16
Total	27,030	100.00	562	100.00	27,592	100.00

Note: There were 40,000 eligible voters.
Source: Guardian, 29 March 1940; *Montreal Daily Star,* 2 April 1940.

stated in an editorial, "In the election of Côté, Verdun [has] changed its entire political physiognomy within the brief space of a year. Many thought the C.C.F. might take the seat, but that was only wishful thinking for the vote shows that the people almost treated it as a lost cause ... Mr. Côté's stand on the war issue coincides with that of his party and doubtless this had much to do in causing a large portion of the Conservative vote in the west-end of the city to swing to his favour."[21]

Verdun was a reluctant Liberal constituency. Only sufficient English-speaking (formerly Tory) support for the Liberal candidate ensured the defeat of the ever-popular Ferland, who placed a respectable second.[22] This realization resulted in a shift away from the CCF, which, nominating only ninety-six candidates nation-wide, had no chance of forming the government. The CCF received fewer votes in Verdun than it had obtained there in 1935. Yet more than half the votes cast for the CCF in Quebec in 1940 (spread over only three constituencies) were from Verdun.[23]

An examination of the 1940 soldiers' vote yields some useful information on Verdun. Servicemen voted at special polls established on military bases in Canada and overseas, and their votes normally were transferred to the constituency of their last civilian place of residence.[24] Of roughly 90,000 eligible Canadian ser-vicemen, 63 percent cast their ballots in the election. Overall, 49.8 percent voted for the Conservatives, 41 percent for the Liberals, 5.3 percent for the CCF, and 4 percent for other parties and independents.[25]

On the Island of Montreal, the Liberals won a plurality of the 4,621 military votes cast. Verdun was easily the constituency in which the greatest number of soldiers cast ballots. Verdun's 562 military votes outdistanced the large riding of St

Lawrence-St George by 86. (It is not known how many Montreal-area servicemen were eligible to vote.) As Table 7.1 shows, Verdunites on active service voted quite differently from their fellow townspeople. The Conservative candidate was the most popular among Verdun soldiers, while the winning Liberal placed a distant fourth. For many, being in uniform dictated their electoral behaviour, and the Conservatives obtained greater support from military voters for advocating a more vigorous national war effort. On the other hand, unlike their civilian co-citizens, the soldiers might not have been as aware of the weakness of Côté's candidacy, which obliged many normally Conservative voters back home to support the Liberals. Ferland's surprising popularity suggests a larger number of French speakers on active service than has been assumed, although his name was arguably the most recognizable on the ballot. This might have induced some without knowledge of his war stance to vote for him. Half of all Montreal's CCF military voters (81 of 162) came from Verdun, a similar proportion to the civilian vote for this party. This confirms that Verdun was the centre of CCF strength in Quebec. Some Verdunites remained conscious of their working-class origins despite Tory appeals to the men in uniform.

The 1940 federal campaign demonstrated some general electoral patterns in Verdun that persisted throughout the war. Both language groups split their votes; no party was able to garner the support of the great majority of either. The Liberals were the only party able to depend on meaningful electoral support from both English and French speakers. The CCF remained a political threat, especially as the war continued and its popularity dramatically increased with overseas servicemen. Class and military service also combined to increase its local support, especially as more Verdunites enlisted.

The 1940 election took place early in the war, just months before the military situation deteriorated for the Allies and measures were introduced in Canada to bring the country to a near-"total war" footing. Although Côté disappointed many English-speaking Verdunites during the later debate on conscription, nearly two years passed before that debate demonstrated that the city remained strongly divided politically along language lines.

The Conscription Plebiscite, 1942

The outbreak of war in 1939 had raised the contentious question of conscription for overseas military service. Prime Minister King repeatedly promised in messages aimed particularly, though not exclusively, at French Canada that his government would not impose conscription. The fall of France in June 1940, however, obliged his government to re-evaluate its war policies; Canada could no longer contribute to the war merely on a "limited liability" basis. In these difficult circumstances, on 21 June the House of Commons hastily passed the National Resources Mobilization Act, which introduced plans for a national inventory of all

Canada's resources, both human and material. It also introduced compulsory military service for home defence for Canadian men of certain age groups and civil status. Nevertheless, King pledged once again that the NRMA would not lead to conscription for overseas service. Only general service volunteers would serve outside the Western Hemisphere.

National registration proceeded without serious disruption, despite minor but widely publicized criticism in Quebec. But, as the months passed and the Allied military situation worsened, calls for full-scale compulsory military service grew more insistent from the Conservative Party (and some Liberals), much of the English-language press, and diverse segments of the English-speaking public. In contrast, French Canadian public opinion seemed almost unanimously opposed.

In response to this mounting pressure, in January 1942 the government announced that a national, non-binding plebiscite would be held on 27 April to ask Canadians if they would release the government from its commitment to avoid conscription. At the same time, King renewed his personal vow not to impose compulsory service unless it became essential. The plebiscite campaign was loud and acerbic. Nowhere was this more so than in Quebec. For months Montreal was the scene of strenuous, sometimes raucous, and always divisive debate. In mixed-language Verdun, the dispute might have led to an explosive social situation. But there is little evidence that this was the case.[26] Verdunites' calm response demonstrated mutual understanding when it was never more necessary, or at least showed that social harmony relied on linguistic moderation.

In February 1942, nearly two years following his election, Paul-Émile Côté spoke for the first time in the House of Commons. He used the occasion to state his opposition to conscription. He termed Verdun's linguistic balance a "veritable miniature of Canada" and went on to say that Verdun had "more than once been cited as [an example] to all communities seeking progress in union, understanding and tolerance."[27] He reminded the House that he represented a patriotic, bilingual community and objected to any national policies that might divide it along linguistic lines, since this would ultimately damage Canada's war effort. Echoing previous Liberal Party pronouncements, Côté remarked that those clamouring for conscription were more harmful to the war effort than those seeking to avoid the measure. "The constituency which I have the honour to represent, and where there are people of various races and creeds, strongly supports maintenance of the voluntary system of enlistment for overseas service ... I am all the more willing to express the views of my constituents on that subject as I am and will remain a supporter of the anticonscriptionist doctrine." Though professing support for the government's decision to hold a plebiscite, Côté's attitude was distinctly cool; he failed to indicate whether he would appeal for a "yes" vote. His statement that his constituents did not favour conscription was disingenuous and only partly correct, as he undoubtedly knew. The strong British element in Verdun favoured the measure. In a March 1942 editorial, the *Guardian* exhorted readers to vote in the affirmative: "the only course people who love their country can take."[28] It knew its readership. Until the plebiscite, it printed similar editorials every week.

The 17 April edition of the *Guardian* led with the front-page headline "Leading Citizens Call for Affirmative Vote." The accompanying article noted that these "leading citizens" were drawn from "both races" as well as from all faiths and political parties. Their endorsements followed, urging support for the government. Several comments took the form of veiled barbs against those, obliquely identified as French speakers, who were opposed to the measure. Edward Wilson said, perhaps unhelpfully, "We are British in Verdun and proud of it." Charles Barr, head of the Civilian Protection Committee, stated, "You can quote me as saying that every man in the C.P.C. is voting 'yes.'" Joan Adams, of the Women's Volunteer Reserve Corps, chimed in, "Every woman in the W.V.R.C. is 100% for the affirmative." Côté, who was not quoted, was said to be seeking a "yes" result in the riding.

But Côté's support was limited. By his own later admission, it was not until King's "magnificent" radio address of 7 April that Côté fell into line and urged a "yes" vote.[29] He believed that a "no" vote would destabilize King's position and allow viewpoints less sympathetic to French Canada to gain ascendancy in the government. In a French-language radio broadcast on 23 April Côté told listeners that they should vote "yes" because a victory for that option, he believed, would delay the conscription debate in the House longer than would a "no" vote. This was faint support. The MP's final formal statement before the vote was also very restrained. He reminded the electorate that the alternative to King's moderate strategy was an even worse option; voting "yes" was essentially the lesser of two evils.[30] Many among Verdun's English-speaking former Conservatives, sensing Côté's lukewarm attitude, may have regretted their Liberal vote in 1940.[31]

Verdun's Liberal MLA, J.J.L. Comeau, was far more enthusiastic about endorsing a "yes" vote, unusually for a French-speaking Quebec legislator. Just days before the plebiscite he issued a patriotic press release calling on Verdunites to vote with the government. He expressed confidence in the "sound judgement" of his constituents, who would not be swayed by "young ultra-nationalists" in their midst. Canada needed all the manpower at its disposal to prepare for the struggle ahead; all "no" votes would provide "comfort to the enemy." His English-language advertisements preached to the converted.[32] A two-page spread urging a "yes" vote appeared in the last edition of the *Guardian* before the plebiscite. "The City of Verdun is Full of Valiant, Full-Blooded Canadians who will Vote Yes in Defence of Canada and their Homes," blared the advertisement, which was supported by Comeau, Côté, Wilson, and other community leaders, as well as by the Legion and the Canadian Corps Association.[33]

City council tried to remain impartial and unanimously refused to endorse the anticonscriptionist Ligue pour la défense du Canada's petition that municipalities adopt a resolution in favour of a "no" vote. Given municipal restrictions on the posting of campaign material, city hall also ordered the police to remove "no" placards posted illegally throughout Verdun.[34] The Ligue pour la défense du Canada, organized specifically to lead the "no" campaign, received no assistance or sanction from Wilson's administration. The mayor's open support for the "yes" side clearly demonstrated the city's position on the matter. A day before the plebiscite Verdun held its popular annual Ypres Day parade. The parade, held in ideal weather, attracted a record-setting estimated 50,000 spectators and 2,000 military and paramilitary participants. Wilson and Comeau used the occasion to promote a "yes" vote by appealing to patriotism. Although the extent to which this emotive display swayed Verdunites is impossible to judge, the timing was no accident. The Verdun Legion, which organized the parade in cooperation with the city, had changed the date from the third to the fourth Sunday in April.[35] The event served as a blatant propaganda vehicle for the "yes" side.

Even though nearly 30,000 French speakers resided in Verdun, no significant anticonscription organization seems to have existed there. Neither the *Guardian* nor the French- or English-language Montreal press referred to any political speeches by prominent anticonscriptionists in Verdun at this or any other time. One "no" rally took place just before the vote in a church basement in the city's east end, although the *Guardian* disparaged it as a failure, stating that it attracted only 250 people despite seating for 1,000.[36] No local politicians or notable citizens were associated with the "no" cause. As a riding, Verdun was a "yes" community. Most French speakers knew how they would cast their ballots; there was no need to antagonize the majority of their fellow citizens and neighbours. Living side by side meant the pursuit of accommodation, or at least the stifling of unneeded provocation. Contemporary sources revealing popular attitudes in Verdun regarding conscription, other than press or municipal-level views, are rare. French-language voices especially are missing.[37]

The national result of the plebiscite was a victory for the "yes" side, which obtained 64 percent of ballots cast, even though 73 percent of Quebecers (and probably at least 85 percent of French Canadians) voted "no." The turnout in Verdun was the largest in the city's history. Verdunites voted 20,855 "yes" (63 percent) to 12,253 "no" (37 percent), making Verdun one of only nine ridings in Quebec – all in the Montreal area – to have voted in the affirmative. The *Guardian* noted with disapproval that the proportion of "yes" votes in the city was less than anticipated. The appeals of Comeau and Côté had gone largely ignored, as most French-speaking Verdunites voted "no." A ward-by-ward breakdown published in *La Presse* shows an unmistakable and predictable voting pattern in Verdun. Almost all polls in Ward 1 were won by the "no" side, though most by fairly narrow margins. The same is true of Ward 2, although the "yes" side took a sprinkling of polls. Ward 3, where proportionately more families of Verdun enlistees resided than in any other ward, voted very solidly "yes," with most polls won by margins of 3-1 or 4-1. And Ward 4 voted overwhelmingly "yes," with many polls running 6-1 and 7-1 in favour. One Ward 4 poll on Melrose Avenue, near the demarcation point with Ward 3, registered a vote of 61-0 for the "yes" side with no spoiled ballots – one of only two polls in Canada without "no" votes. Ward 4 resembled most polls in Westmount, Notre-Dame-de-Grâce, and other distinctly English-speaking neighbourhoods and municipalities in the Montreal area.[38]

No other neighbourhood in the Montreal area contained so large a mixed-language population in so compact a space with such a potential for discord. Yet Verdun experienced no reported political demonstrations or altercations pitting one language group against the other. There were no voting-day demonstrations or incidents to report, just a quiet victory for the "yes" side.[39] The plebiscite results were dictated by language and ethnicity, which was not surprising. More important, Verdunites' level-headed approach to divisive wartime political issues helped maintain basic social cohesion.

Verdunites were conscious of the fact that many of the city's households, both English and French speaking, had contributed men to the armed forces. In an effort to support those serving, and in many cases out of an ulterior sense of patriotism towards both Canada and Britain, Verdun's English-speaking community voted massively in the affirmative. English speakers made up 58 percent of the population of Verdun and included a higher proportion of residents of voting age than did the French-speaking population. Accordingly, the plebiscite result of 63 percent affirmative did not necessarily imply significant support for the measure among the city's French speakers. On the other hand, especially in Ward 3, many French speakers clearly voted "yes," probably in support of relatives on active service. But most French-speaking Verdunites refused Ottawa's request and confirmed the basic political and cultural differences that separated them from their English-speaking neighbours.

After the plebiscite, French-speaking Canadians became resigned to the inevitability of conscription and awaited its eventual imposition; many English speakers clamoured for its adoption. Section 3 of the NRMA was amended in June 1942: Bill C-80 provided for the possibility of conscription for overseas service, with the governor-in-council deciding the timing of its enactment. During the House of Commons debate on the bill, Côté opposed his government's plan to amend the NRMA. He felt that the plebiscite results did not empower Ottawa to amend legislation in advance of the demonstrated need to do so. Like other anticonscriptionists, Côté also worried about the negative social consequences that Bill C-80 might entail. Concerned Quebec legislators, moved by memories of the 1917-18 disturbances over the issue, advised the government to move more slowly in the direction of adopting conscription. Côté, speaking in the House for only the second time since his election in 1940, and for the first time in English, claimed unconvincingly that Verdunites did not seek conscription.[40] It is impossible, however, to distinguish between "yes" voters who sought immediate conscription and those who merely wanted to empower the government against future need.

The House voted 158-54 in favour of Bill C-80, with forty-five Quebec MPs voting against it. The *Guardian* noted dryly that Côté was one of only two members from the solidly Liberal Island of Montreal to vote against the government.[41] Côté's position would not have surprised those who had listened to his February pronouncements. Verdun's MP voted with his conscience, not according to the desire of the greater part of his constituency. As a compromise candidate, he compromised his party loyalty, though perhaps not his personal integrity. Whatever the case, he disappointed Verdun's English-language majority.

The 1944 Provincial Election

The province had rejected Maurice Duplessis and the UN in 1939 on the basis of federal promises never to impose conscription. The passing of the NRMA in 1940, the plebiscite of 1942, and the creation in the autumn of 1942 of the Bloc populaire canadien as a French Canadian nationalist political party at both the federal and provincial levels had significantly altered the mood of the Quebec electorate by 1944.

Many French speakers displayed at least some resentment towards national war policies. In August 1942, twice as many French speakers as English speakers polled (89 percent to 44 percent) believed that Canada already was doing its utmost to win the war. In February 1943 five times as many French speakers as English speakers polled (32 percent to 6 percent) believed that Canadians had been asked to make too many sacrifices for the war effort; four times as many English speakers as French speakers (54 percent to 13 percent) believed that Canada was not doing enough.[42] Although he remained more or less aloof from the conscription debate, Duplessis relentlessly attacked Liberal premier Adélard Godbout for his failure to protect Quebec's autonomy from the centralizing tendencies of the federal government. Godbout was portrayed, and widely seen, as having acted as Ottawa's lackey during his five years in office. The Union Nationale strategy was to ensure the public judged Godbout for the federal Liberals' sins, and not allow the election to be about public administration, where Godbout's Liberal party had performed reasonably well. On the other hand, Quebec's economic and labour woes were troublesome political issues. The Liberals were at the end of their mandate when Godbout called an election for 8 August 1944.[43]

The provincial government refused Quebecers on active service outside Quebec the right to vote. Although other provinces had made provisions for overseas votes, Godbout's Liberals decided that the difficulties involved made the proposition impractical. Edward Wilson, a CCF supporter, fumed at the decision, especially since the CCF had obtained the support of most of Saskatchewan's soldiers in that province's June 1944 election.[44] It was difficult to predict how the effective disenfranchisement of Verdun's large and mainly English-speaking military contingent would affect the election, especially since a wartime influx of French speakers had altered Verdun's overall linguistic balance.

For the first time in a Quebec provincial election women were allowed to vote. The *Guardian* expected women to support the governing Liberals, who had granted them the vote in 1940. In fact the Liberals solicited the female vote, stating in some of their campaign advertisements that the outcome of the election "lay in their hands." Verdun's Liberal candidate suggested that appreciative women should vote for him.[45]

Verdun's contest attracted five candidates: Bloc populaire canadien (an outgrowth of the Ligue pour la défense du Canada), CCF, Independent CCF, Liberal, and UN. The Liberal incumbent, J.J.L. Comeau, was dropped by his party in favour of Lionel A. Ross, a French-speaking Verdun lawyer and head of the Société Saint-Jean-Baptiste branch in east-end Notre-Dame-de-la-Paix Parish. One of the reasons for Comeau's dismissal seems to have been his extremely pro-war attitude, which by 1944 was regarded as a potential disadvantage with Verdun's growing French-speaking electorate. The linguistic differences manifested in Verdun during the plebiscite campaign, and the emergence of the Bloc populaire canadien as an electoral option for French-speaking Quebecers' discontent, had forced the Liberals to seek a new candidate. Although the CCF remained a threat to the Liberals, it was comfortably assumed that the majority of English speakers would support whomever the Liberals chose. In any event, Ross claimed that he would uphold Comeau's earlier pro-war stance.[46]

Pierre Lafleur retained the UN nomination. But other candidates, such as Hervé Ferland (Independent CCF) and Louis Hurtubise (Bloc populaire canadien), eroded the UN's support base in east-end Verdun. Lafleur scrupulously avoided mentioning his party, Duplessis, or even the war in his English-language campaign advertisements. He emphasized his past record of service to Verdun and concentrated on Liberal failures in economic and fiscal planning. This was standard UN strategy in English-language campaign literature.[47]

The CCF hopeful was Lionel P. Lebel, who was personally endorsed by federal CCF leader M.J. Coldwell. Lebel was not well known in Verdun, and Edward Wilson's strong support strengthened his hand considerably. Throughout the campaign, Lebel's name rarely appeared in the press or in advertisements without the name of Wilson being invoked. The two men were pictured prominently together in the *Guardian*'s last pre-election issue. The accompanying caption insisted that the CCF stood for "complete and final victory over the Axis enemy." The CCF's major interests in this provincial election, however, were public ownership of utilities and labour and social reform. Lebel was the first French speaker to run for the CCF in Verdun.[48] The CCF believed that it had a very good chance in Verdun and the Liberals had identified the CCF as their greatest rival for Verdunites' votes. The *Guardian*'s election coverage was more extensive in 1944 than in 1939 and 1940. Nevertheless, its passion did not seem at first to be shared by all Verdunites. An editorial of 27 July stated:

> The political campaign locally is heating up, but there is still evidence of apathy on the part of ... the electors ... A score of issues and side-issues have been injected into the provincial campaign. It appears that locally, however, the issue will be overwhelmingly patriotic. The great majority of local voters will consider the question: How can I best assist the prosecution of the war by my ballot? ... This is above all a patriotic constituency. So long as the war is on; so long as Germany and Japan are on their feet and swinging; just so long will most local electors be impatient with issues of a minor character.

This newspaper considered issues such as provincial autonomy, language, and French Canadian nationalism divisive and irrelevant. A second editorial on the subject, "The Issues in Verdun," appeared the next week:

> As an independent newspaper we ... have presented the views of all candidates as they themselves have presented them to us ... [But] there is lurking in the shadows, not daring to expose itself to light, a sinister voice which if heeded would, like a cancer, destroy the very heart of Quebec ... The first duty of any government at Quebec is to keep faith with those dying men who have staked their hopes on full freedom for all. Must our battle-scarred men, whose blood turns rivers red, bring back their Cup of Victory only to find there is nothing to fill it with except dissension and strife? ... It is unthinkable that the loved ones of these fighting men will sit idly by and surrender these freedoms to this sinister octopus whose tentacles attempt a strangle-hold on this province.[49]

The vicious and ongoing fighting in Normandy during the previous two months, which killed or wounded scores of Verdunites, had heightened war consciousness in the community and hardened the *Guardian*'s fiercely patriotic attitudes. Many Verdunites could not countenance the thought that, at the very moment of these heavy local losses, a suspiciously antiwar government or coalition government would assume power in Quebec.

Table 7.2 shows the 1944 election results in Verdun. Only 60 percent of eligible voters cast their ballots, and the Liberal, Ross, was elected. Although he polled satisfactorily in all wards, his margin of victory was not impressive. His percentage of the vote was the lowest among Liberals contesting primarily English-speaking ridings, where Liberals obtained on average 60 percent of the vote. The *Guardian* boasted: "Verdun has rendered its verdict ... In this city we demand unity in Canada

Table 7.2

Verdun provincial election results, 1944

	Votes	%
Lionel A. Ross, Liberal	8,691	36.68
Lionel P. Lebel, CCF	5,881	24.82
Louis P. Hurtubise, Bloc populaire canadien	3,259	13.75
Hervé Ferland, Independent CCF	3,009	12.70
Pierre A. Lafleur, UN	2,854	12.05
Total	23,694	100.00

Source: Montreal Daily Star, 9 August 1944; *Guardian*, 10 August 1944.

above all else. Verdun will have no part in ultra-national, separatist and subversive movements."[50] Neither the Bloc nor the UN made serious inroads among the French-speaking minority in Verdun, although Duplessis and the UN won the election. Ross would represent Verdun in opposition.

The poorly funded CCF made an excellent showing, but, since the party fielded only twenty-four candidates in the province, a majority of English-speaking voters chose the Liberals, the single avowedly pro-war party with a chance of winning the election. Lebel fared poorly in the east-end wards but picked up support in Ward 3 and won nearly half the polls in Ward 4 – an impressive level of support that undoubtedly owed much to Wilson. Verdun's CCF vote amounted to nearly a quarter of all CCF ballots cast in the Montreal area. Verdun was the only Montreal constituency in which the party placed second.[51] The feeling within the CCF hierarchy was that Ferland had acted as a spoiler by siphoning off votes from Lebel.[52] This is most unlikely; despite CCF fears expressed during the campaign, Ferland supporters almost certainly voted for the man, not for the party. The colourful former mayor and alderman had developed a bedrock of support in French-speaking east-end Verdun made up of electors who voted for him whatever his political allegiance. Avowed CCF supporters would not have voted for Ferland, and Lebel's direct loss of votes to him was negligible at most. Rather, Ferland's candidacy split the French-speaking vote in east-end Verdun and disadvantaged the UN and Bloc more than the CCF, for which few French speakers voted in any event.

The dénouement to Ross's election victory annoyed many Verdunites who had voted for him. On 1 March 1945, Ross voted in favour of a motion introduced in the Quebec legislature by ultranationalist René Chaloult, which condemned federal government conscription policies. Back in Verdun, erstwhile Liberal MLA Comeau, shunted aside by the party in favour of Ross, was outraged and accused Ross of breach of trust. Comeau demanded his resignation or public apology:

"Nothing less will erase from the hearts and minds of patriotic Verdun the shame and humiliation of having [its] name ... coupled with such a brazen betrayal ... Verdun has a record second to none in the British Empire for Patriotism, for Loyalty, for True Canadianism."[53] Many English-speaking Verdunites felt let down by their French-speaking Liberal representatives – first Côté in 1942 and then Ross in 1945. But victory in Europe was in sight, and the war ended before the political repercussions worsened. It remained to be seen whether the Liberals would suffer in the upcoming federal election for the wartime actions of their Verdun members.

The 1945 Federal Election

The period from the autumn of 1944 into the winter of 1945 was a difficult one for Prime Minister Mackenzie King and the governing Liberals. An election was near, and the Liberals worried about their chances. A perceived manpower crisis in November 1944 forced the adoption of a limited policy of conscription for overseas service, which angered nationalistic French speakers without satisfying ultrapatriotic English speakers. In addition, serious electoral difficulties for the federal Liberals seemed likely after Maurice Duplessis's return to power in August 1944, the resignation of Minister of National Defence for Air Charles G. Power in November over the dispatch of conscripts overseas, and the threatened development of a parallel, antigovernment Liberal movement in Quebec. The election of the CCF in Saskatchewan in June 1944 and that party's generally strong showing in national public opinion polls also served notice that election results would be difficult to predict.

Liberal electoral strategy concentrated on the future, particularly on a proposed new social order based on guaranteed social welfare measures, such as mothers' allowances, old age security, and national minimum standards in housing, health care, and nutrition. Most of the grumbling about conscription in the federal Quebec caucus had abated when King announced on 13 April that a federal election would take place on 11 June. After the war in Europe ended on 7 May conscription was no longer a contentious issue. The government had announced that the measure would not be imposed for Pacific service.[54]

The 1945 election campaign in Verdun, as in most of the country, was fought mainly on repatriation, civil re-establishment, and the postwar social order for Canada.[55] Perhaps 7,000 Verdunites had served during the war, and these issues were naturally of great concern to city residents. Despite the emotional relief that it brought, the end of the war also reminded people of the economically dismal prewar period. Demobilization and the shutdown of armaments industries ended the war-inspired livelihoods of thousands of Verdunites. Repatriated service people flooded the city during an acute housing shortage. The 1945 federal election in Verdun (a riding that also included Lasalle's 5,500 residents) represented a microcosm of wider national anxieties.

The incumbent, Liberal Paul-Émile Côté, accepted his party's nomination. In a show of unity, and not withstanding his stance on Bill C-80, his nomination committee included representatives from both local English- and French-speaking Liberal associations as well as from Verdun merchants and professionals.[56] While many English-speaking Liberals seemed prepared to forgive him, Côté still obtained much of his electoral support from French speakers. His stock had risen with this group since 1940 as a result of his strong opposition to conscription. For most of the 1945 campaign he simply (and safely) stood on the Liberals' wartime record and insisted on the need for government stability and continuity into the postwar period. Côté had antagonized many English-speaking voters whose support he knew was essential; faced with a serious challenge from the CCF, he kept a relatively low profile during the campaign.

Edward Wilson had won an unprecedented fourth term as mayor in early April 1945. He almost immediately announced his candidacy as CCF standard-bearer in the June federal election. Wilson's municipal campaign had stressed political continuity to deal most effectively with expected social difficulties. He could not repeat this strategy at the federal level, however, since he sought to unseat a government MP. Suddenly, a vote for change was desirable. Wilson believed that if the government had found the money to wage war, then it could pay the price of peace as well, including generous allotments for soldiers' civil re-establishment. CCF leader M.J. Coldwell spoke on Wilson's behalf at a rally in Woodland Park on 28 May. The Lancashire-born Wilson was a socialist and an avowed patriot, with the credentials to prove it. His opponents attacked the CCF's "revolutionary" views but refrained from overtly criticizing its popular candidate.[57]

The CCF had always enjoyed strong support in Verdun, and the high-profile Wilson was Côté's main rival for English speakers' votes. Yet a pre-election article in the *Messenger* suggested that the CCF had little chance in Verdun. It would be difficult for Wilson "to go before a constituency like Verdun as the representative of a party which declared that 'Canada must refuse to be entangled in any more wars fought to make the world safe for capitalism'; a party which declared 'We must make it clear to London ... that we intend to fertilize no more crops of poppies in Flanders fields'; a party whose leader, Mr. Coldwell, stated publicly that he would rather see his son in jail than in uniform."[58] Despite the high regard in which Wilson was held in Verdun, his work was cut out for him.

The official Progressive Conservative candidate was Wilfrid Pagé, a Verdun automobile dealer, who was supported by a representative group of local businesspeople. Pagé too was threatened by Wilson's candidacy and reminded voters that the vigorous prosecution of the war in which so many of their friends and relatives had fought had not been the preoccupation of the CCF.[59] But every Verdunite knew it had been Wilson's obsession. Pagé based his advertising campaign in the *Guardian* on the Tories' national campaign, emphasizing its "creed" of "Freedom, Security, Opportunity and British Partnership," and made numerous references to the Tories' upholding of the "British tradition."[60] While hardly designed to appeal to an already suspicious Quebec audience, these slogans proved attractive to some British-born voters. In emphasizing the Conservatives' imperial tendencies, Pagé stood to gain more votes among these Verdunites than he might lose among already hostile French speakers. In contrast, Côté used the generic national Liberal twelve-point platform as the basis of his campaign. Its high-sounding social, economic, and reconstructionist proposals seemed to have far greater relevance than the Tories' increasingly dated, traditional platform.

By mid-May, ten candidates (more than twice the Quebec average) had entered the contest, including Henry Turcotte of the Social Credit Party. Opposition to Côté had grown since his nomination. Three Independent Liberals ran, and clearly all was not well within Liberal ranks. Former MLA J.J.L. Comeau, the main Independent Liberal candidate, was virulent in his attacks on Côté: "Mr. P.E. Côté, [is] the man who betrayed his electors on the one solemn vote taken to determine the degree of our war effort. This choice is an insult to Verdun, to our armed forces, to our war dead ... The plebiscite vote in Verdun, 65% [actually 63 percent] Yes, was the will of the people, given on Mr. Côté's own request as well as mine. Refusing to honour it in Parliament was [an] unforgivable crime."[61] He assailed Côté without respite for the entire campaign, and Liberal circles feared that he might pry away enough English-speaking support from Côté to split the Liberal vote.

Another Independent Liberal candidate, Donald Elvidge, ran as an ardent Verdunite and a veteran – good enough reasons, he felt, for his community-minded and patriotic fellow citizens to vote for him. His style added an interesting local flavour to a campaign based on national issues. "In this electoral fight," his political advertisement begins, "I am facing a number of powerful adversaries, but a soldier of Verdun never shows the white feather, no matter how great may seem the odds against him." He slammed Côté as unpatriotic for his negative vote on Bill C-80 and dismissed the Tories as being "as ever for the Big Interests, and the Big Interests have nothing in common with the hard-working people of Verdun." Referring to Henry Turcotte's candidacy, he felt that it would "take an awful lot of education to make a Social Credit[er] out of the hard-headed boys of Verdun."[62]

The 11 June election very sharply reduced the Liberal majority in Ottawa (the party won 125 of 245 seats) but was a landslide victory for Côté in Verdun (see Table 7.3). All other candidates lost their deposits. Seventy-one percent of eligible electors cast their ballots, and Côté easily obtained the largest share. He even received a greater proportion of votes than the 41 percent that his party polled nationwide. Pagé's vote percentage was more than double the Progressive Conservatives' overall share in Quebec (a hopeless 8.4 percent), while Wilson's popular vote (19.8 percent) was higher than the CCF's national average (14.7 percent) and ten times greater than its provincial average.

Table 7.3

Verdun federal election results, 1945

	Civilian vote		Military vote		Total	
	Number	%	Number	%	Number	%
Paul-Émile Côté, Liberal	14,777	46.70	770	30.03	15,547	45.44
Wilfrid Pagé, PC	6,664	21.06	309	12.04	6,973	20.38
Edward Wilson, CCF	5,490	17.35	1,293	50.39	6,783	19.83
Louis P. Hurtubise, BPC	3,000	9.48	46	1.79	3,046	8.90
Sam Bailey, Labour Progressive Party	811	2.56	42	1.63	853	2.49
J.J.L. Comeau, Independent Liberal	364	1.15	20	0.78	384	1.12
Walter Wilson, Independent CCF	242	0.76	33	1.29	275	0.80
Henry Turcotte, Social Credit	172	0.54	8	0.30	180	0.53
Donald Elvidge, Independent Liberal	87	0.27	40	1.56	127	0.37
J.M.O. Royer, Independent Liberal	38	0.12	5	0.19	43	0.13
Total	31,645	99.99	2,566	100.00	34,211	99.99

Note: There were 48,000 eligible voters. Percentage totals do not equal 100 because of rounding.
Source: Guardian, 14 and 21 June 1945; *Montreal Daily Star*, 12 and 19 June 1945.

The enormity of Côté's victory surprised observers in Verdun and Montreal. The virulently anti-CCF *Montreal Daily Star* had deliberately ignored Edward Wilson's campaign yet managed to express surprise at his defeat. The French-speaking Pagé's second-place finish was also mildly surprising. There appeared to be more English-speaking Conservatives than socialists in Verdun, or perhaps Verdunites wanted their popular mayor to stay in Verdun and attend to local matters. The utter defeat of Comeau and the fact that many English speakers continued to support Côté were unexpected. The Liberals' postwar social plans had appeal, while it was clear that the CCF would be unable to form a government, despite running 205 candidates across Canada. The combination of votes from most French speakers and many English speakers had enabled the Liberals to win Verdun with ease.[63] The best means of securing the welfare of Verdun's returning soldiers and their families seemed to lie with the Liberals.

An examination of Verdun's military vote in 1945 yields some valuable insights. Only 46 percent of the 750,000 service personnel eligible to vote bothered to do so in 1945, compared with 75 percent of eligible civilians. While it is not known exactly how many Verdunites serving at home or abroad were eligible, 2,564 Verdunites in uniform voted. Verdunites on active service retained a strong interest in their community. Nationally, the military vote translated into 35 percent for the governing Liberals, 32 percent for the CCF (double its national average), and 26 percent for the Progressive Conservatives (2 percentage points lower than their average across Canada).[64]

The election produced huge gains for the CCF among military voters. The party's support in Verdun was remarkable. The soldiers' vote for the CCF was far higher in Verdun, 50 percent, than the Quebec military average of only 14 percent (and a civilian CCF vote of a mere 2 percent in Quebec); it was also significantly higher than the national military average of 32 percent. One in five Quebec military votes for the CCF was cast by a Verdunite, and Wilson was the party's only candidate on the Island of Montreal to outpoll his rivals among soldiers. The men and women of Canada's military forces at home and overseas were concerned about their futures. The social security legislation advocated for years by the CCF (some of which the Liberals adopted before the war was over) appeared sensible and timely.

What made the CCF even more appealing to Verdun's military voters in 1945 was its candidate. Edward Wilson embodied all that the city was doing for its volunteers. They identified him personally with the Mayor's Cigarette Fund – a high-profile initiative very popular with them and the community. Edward Wilson had exploited his popularity with the troops overseas and knew that it could be translated into votes; they owed him. Using the carefully updated mailing list of the Mayor's Cigarette Fund, Wilson dispatched a letter to the city's overseas volunteers complimenting them on the splendid job that they had done and baldly seeking their electoral support. Enclosed with the letter was a leaflet outlining CCF policies for postwar Canada.

Some Verdunites replied to Wilson's appeal, pledging their support as well as that of other Verdunites in their units. Sgt G. MacWilliams, Royal Montreal Regiment, wrote, "I am doing my utmost to get all the Verdun boys here to vote for you." Another man, Sgt R. Lemieux, RCASC, wrote from England, "You can rest assure[d] that the fifteen Verdun Boys in this Camp are voting for you. And another thing, the majority of Canadian Soldiers are in favour of [the] C.C.F."[65] Verdun servicemen did not hesitate to vote for the man who had offered the firmest support of any candidate to the struggle they had just been through, and who symbolized a commitment to that which was about to begin.

DESPITE COMPETING social and political wartime viewpoints, neither English speakers nor French speakers in Verdun cast votes solely on the basis of cultural identity; the issues mattered as well. Most of Verdun's English speakers assumed a political stance based on national policies and were prepared to subordinate other issues to winning the war. But they usually split their vote among pro-war parties, including the CCF. French speakers were more likely to divide their electoral allegiances between the pro-war Liberals and parties or independent candidates professing a more restrained approach to the war, such as the UN. The conscription plebiscite of April 1942 also demonstrated that English-speaking

Verdunites had more in common with English speakers nationwide than with their French-speaking neighbours.

The war significantly altered Verdunites' voting behaviour; the city forsook its Conservative past in favour of the Liberals. During the war the Liberal Party won four hotly contested federal and provincial elections and one national plebiscite in Verdun, emerging as the only political choice acceptable to sizeable elements of both the French- and English-speaking communities. The November 1944 decision to send a limited number of conscripts overseas did not affect the Liberals' popularity with Verdun's French-speaking voters, nor did that party's retention of Côté as a candidate lead to a significant loss in support among English speakers.

Language, not ideology (despite some continuing support for the CCF), came to define the wartime politics of the Verdun electorate at all levels of government. But, except for municipal elections, Verdunites rarely voted in language blocs. Both language groups split their votes, with the Liberal candidate always receiving enough support from each group to ensure his election. The successful candidates in Verdun's wartime elections – Comeau, Côté (twice), and Ross – were all French speakers representing a mainly English-speaking riding. This made political sense, since an English-speaking candidate might not have fared quite as well with the French-speaking community. In their advertising campaigns in the *Guardian*, all candidates catered to the concerns and outlooks of Verdun's English-speaking community. This fervently patriotic newspaper was itself an essential ingredient in every election campaign in Verdun and remains a key source for analysis of wartime elections. Verdun's wartime politics also produced some rare outspoken French-speaking imperialists such as Comeau and the Conservative Pagé. Their views were not popular with most French speakers. The 1942 plebiscite results showed a language schism in Verdun, but existing social harmony was not upset by wartime politics.

8
Peace and Reconstruction

The Second World War accelerated social change within Canada.[1] Even before the last shots had been fired, social reform, most vividly elaborated in the Marsh Report of 1943, had risen to the top of the Canadian political agenda.[2] By 1944 the housing crisis, industrial conversion, civilian employment, and rising criminality competed with the war itself as the objects of Canadians' concerns. The story of Verdun's war is not complete without the city's reaction to the cessation of hostilities, its losses and grief, and the repatriation and civil re-establishment of thousands of its citizens in uniform.

War's End
Hostilities with Germany formally ended on the morning of Monday, 7 May 1945. The next day, which the Allies proclaimed Victory-in-Europe Day, was the occasion of national celebration. But war-weary Canadians could not wait until the official day of celebration and reacted to the news of the German surrender with spontaneous outpourings of joy. That Monday morning, many Verdunites streamed into Montreal to participate in the boisterous celebrations in that city's business district and along its main downtown thoroughfare, Ste Catherine Street. There was some irony in this. Although Verdunites had jealously maintained and even strengthened their notion of community during the war, and had imbued this spirit with a proud patriotism, at the long-awaited moment of victory many of them boarded buses and streetcars to merge more or less anonymously with tens of thousands of other celebrants drawn from all over the Montreal area. United by a feeling of fierce municipal loyalty during the years of war, Verdunites nevertheless celebrated the return of peace as Montrealers, as Canadians, as victors.

Verdun's youths generally observed VE Day in their own neighbourhoods. Verdun High School students left their classes the moment they heard the news of the German capitulation and headed into the streets of Verdun (and Montreal) to celebrate. Hundreds of local residents watched as schoolchildren paraded during the noon hour in the heart of the city, along Wellington Street, Church Avenue, and other streets. Some children sang "Rule Britannia," many carried flags, and most beat pots and pans and whatever else would noisily announce the German surrender, and the children's presence, to people still in their flats. Others set off firecrackers and small flares. Motorists blared their horns, long-forgotten air-raid precaution sirens sounded, and church bells pealed. Effigies of Hitler, stuffed with newspapers and some set aflame, swung from trees, lampposts, and streetcar wires. Although violence and property damage characterized the VE Day celebrations in Halifax, Montreal, and elsewhere, no mischief was reported in Verdun.

Like telephone exchanges across Canada, those in Verdun were jammed that morning as people excitedly relayed the news to each other. Many families, especially those with members on active service, decorated the galleries (known as balconies to non-Verdunites) and railings of their homes with some combination of the Union Jack, the Red Ensign, the Stars and Stripes, bunting, streamers, ribbons, and portraits of the royal family, Winston Churchill, and other war leaders. Most businesses closed for the day. Verdun's celebrations were a fitting and moving tribute to a happy and momentous occasion. Many Verdunites would soon be home again.[3]

The front page of the *Guardian*'s 10 May 1945 edition was subdued. It patriotically displayed portraits of the king and queen and Winston Churchill. With a tone of disappointment, this newspaper curiously described local victory celebrations as "remarkably quiet" and without "cheering or boisterous crowds." It offered the excuse that the announcement of peace had taken residents by surprise. The *Messenger* was far more upbeat, describing Verdunites' collective response as "an unprecedented outburst of rejoicing." Both language groups appeared well represented among the throngs of people participating in the local festivities. The *Messenger* noted (in French) that "even the English, usually so phlegmatic, lost their self-control and joined the rest of the population at this time of joy." All Verdun's churches, Protestant and Catholic, French language and English, offered thanksgiving services and solemnly remembered those who had fallen in the previous six years.[4]

Even though many local men had volunteered for Pacific service, Verdunites apparently paid scant attention to the Pacific war.[5] For the vast majority of them, as for Canadians generally, the conflict that really seemed to matter was the struggle against Hitler. Victory-over-Japan Day, announced 15 August 1945, was celebrated in Verdun like VE Day, though perhaps more tamely. City council declared a two-day civic holiday 15 and 16 August. Firecrackers, scattered bonfires, burning effigies, children's noise, and the setting off of fire alarms marked the definitive end of the Second World War. Some French-speaking children gathered to sing "La Marseillaise." Although the weather was poor and no large crowds were in evidence, the police were out in force to prevent the kinds of disturbances that had marred VE Day in Montreal. Some loitering youths in west-end Verdun were quietly dispersed; there was no trouble. In the course of the following week, a celebratory Black Watch concert took place in Woodland Park, and restaurateur Léopold Lacroix organized a small victory street dance on Hickson Avenue in east-end Ward 1.[6]

The community was left with the mainly pleasant task of welcoming home the thousands of Verdunites who had served overseas and helping them restart their lives.[7] From June 1945 to June 1946 over 600,000 Canadians were discharged, and hundreds of Verdunites returned to their community every month. Family reunion parties were commonplace. During this period Verdun was continually dotted with "Welcome Home" banners and other indications that families and friends were being reunited. Douglas Whyte, discharged from the RCAF, returned home to First Avenue in the summer of 1945 aboard *Ile de France*. His mother had strung up a "Welcome Home" banner in their flat and organized a party attended by relatives and friends, including some former servicemen who had preceded him home. René Bisson, RCASC, was met at Montreal's Bonaventure Station by seven family members. He has recalled the joys that the occasion brought to all of them and the manner in which Verdun was impressively decorated with bunting, decorations, and flags, including some papal standards.[8] An otherwise elated Verdunite, Sgt Joseph Fantie, remarked upon coming home: "They should never have rationed hamburger. Ever since VE Day I've been dreaming of coming home to a minced meat dish – the way my mother prepares it."[9] As late as June 1946 one French-speaking family from the east end welcomed their son with a particularly "banging reception," complete with a welcome sign installed on the sidewalk with letters two feet high.[10] And so it was across the city for a year following the war's end.

A Shared Grief

Casualties among Verdunites were not insignificant. A close reading of wartime local press accounts, parish honour rolls, school board casualty lists, and reports prepared by such local organizations as the YMCA indicates that about 200 Verdunites were killed or died while on active service and that about 600 were wounded, many permanently disabled to some degree. The city's first fatalities were two residents lost in the sinking of the passenger liner *Athenia* on 3 September 1939. One was Hannah Baird, a stewardess, considered Canada's first merchant navy and female loss of the war.[11] Among the last from Verdun to die were some servicemen killed in traffic accidents in Britain in July 1945. Verdunites suffered death, injury, and capture almost everywhere Canadian arms were deployed. By the summer of 1943 between five and ten local casualties were listed in the *Guardian* every week, and, like newspapers across the country, its columns were scanned with trepidation by the friends and neighbours of those on active service.[12] At first air force and navy personnel were overrepresented in these casualty lists, but, following Canadian participation in the invasion of Sicily in 1943 and particularly in the wake of the Canadian army's extremely costly campaign in Normandy in 1944, hundreds of Verdun soldiers became casualties. One soldier wrote in September

1944, "I am now away from my Battalion which took a beating for a time. We have lost quite a few Verdun Boys."[13]

In October 1946 the *Guardian* noted that at least 102 Verdunites had been killed in the army, 43 in the air force, and 26 in the navy.[14] These figures were more indicative of Verdunites' particular enlistment trends than of the national casualty rates recorded for each service. Fewer RCAF aircrew from Verdun meant lower casualties in a service that suffered disproportionately heavy losses. Conversely, naval casualties in Verdun were higher than the national average because of the unusually large number of residents on sea duty. Every Canadian warship (and many merchant vessels) sunk or damaged seemed to contain Verdun crewmen listed in the press as lost or saved. Among Verdun's 4,000 or more soldiers, fatalities were slightly lower than the national average. Verdunites might have been spared in this regard because of the absence of a locally recruited regiment. Had such a regiment been in the Canadian army's Order of Battle, disaster could have struck the community. In Belleville, Ontario, for example, the war memorial lists 160 men from the city and region who were killed during the war, many of them members of the locally recruited Hastings and Prince Edward Regiment. This was an enormous loss for a region of only 30,000 people.[15] Verdun generally escaped this unhappy fate, although dozens of Verdunites were killed or wounded while serving in Montreal's Black Watch, which suffered appallingly high casualties.

Notwithstanding the lack of a locally based regiment, several Verdun families lost two sons. Many families lost one member and had another one or more wounded. The Glasgows from Ward 3 paid a heavy price. In 1942 two sons, Charles and William, both serving in the RCNVR, were killed within one month of each other in submarine attacks. A third son, John, remained on active service in the navy.[16] The Glasgows' bereavement became widely known in Verdun, and their loss took on symbolic overtones for the remainder of the war. The local press often described the Glasgow brothers as representative of the patriotic response offered by Verdunites and the deaths of two of them as typical of the city's sacrifice. Few Verdun households were as shattered by the war as was this impoverished family, which in 1944 was evicted from its flat. But the local elites also shouldered their burdens and grief. Edward Wilson's son-in-law, Warrant Officer Alex Stevenson, RCAF, was shot down and captured. The son of Dr Charles Barr, chief warden of the Civilian Protection Committee, was killed in the RCAF, as were the sons of Henry Garritty and Norman Hill, long-time trustees of the Verdun Protestant School Board.[17] Many Verdun parents were left childless, wives widowed, and youngsters rendered fatherless.

The dense local network of social and church organizations helped ease the pain. So did the nature of Verdun society, which was based on the common experiences of class and local identity. Even the manner in which people lived in Verdun helped. The adjoining flats and their shared balconies meant most people knew their neighbours very well, and a ready-made support network existed for a stricken family. One telegram delivery boy recalled the grief that engulfed a street or neighbourhood when he delivered the news of a death overseas. He claimed that this public manifestation of common mourning occurred only in the "poorer districts, where people looked after each other better."[18] Verdun certainly fit this description and, as a society, may have been better equipped than other communities to cope with wartime loss.

Homecomings

Thousands of soldiers and airmen were repatriated even before hostilities in Europe had ended.[19] From March to May 1945 the *Guardian* and the *Messenger* noted the arrival at Montreal's Bonaventure Station of trainloads of repatriated or discharged local servicemen, many of them recovering from wounds. One such article began: "Limping, burned and blinded, many Verdun fighters fresh from the battlefronts of Europe are today safely back with their relatives and friends."[20]

The *Guardian* reminded Verdunites to be sensitive to the signs of "shattered nerves" that some returning locals were likely to manifest. Many returned traumatized by their war experiences. One common theme in the local newspapers was the hope that fellow citizens would treat Verdun's veterans in a manner worthy of the sacrifices they had endured. The press mentioned the "hell and horror" of their overseas experiences and the "privations, hardships and suffering" that might have altered the men's and women's personalities or sown the seeds of lingering pain and psychological distress.[21] This was a rather different tone from the bombastic and aggressive statements and articles that had appeared regularly during the war.

The homecomings were causes for rejoicing, but they were not always easy. One discharged Verdunite simply exclaimed that the men were "ready to forget all we've gone through."[22] A Verdun RCAF veteran, John Neal, wrote years after the war that "it [was] impossible to recreate instant civilians when the uniform [was] gone. We could not simply press the 'off' switch. I came ... close to being alcoholic."[23] Some couples had not seen each other for as long as five years. Young children knew their fathers barely or not at all. Only the veterans themselves seemed able to understand war's full brutality, and many of their experiences and much of their pain remained internalized.[24] In October 1945 the *Guardian* published a moving article detailing the many needs of Canada's repatriated soldiers, especially those wounded. In soliciting subscriptions to the ninth (and final) Victory Loan campaign, the newspaper stated, "Verdun ... is now called upon to look after its own sons and none can shirk what is their most sacred duty and obligation ... Verdun more than any other city, with its great percentage of returned men, will no doubt see to it that [they] are taken care of."[25] The money needed from Verdunites was obtained. This continuing generosity may have been encouraged by the sudden reappearance of relatives, friends, and neighbours who bore the marks of the war on their bodies and in their minds. Perhaps many discharged men and women subscribed to the campaign.

As Verdunites had closed ranks to support their men and women overseas during the war, so too, as the *Guardian* had predicted, did they assist repatriated veterans. One successful postwar fundraising effort was the Daniel Fund. Norman Daniel was nineteen in February 1945 when he was blinded after stepping on a land mine in the Netherlands.[26] He was said to be Canada's youngest serviceman to lose his eyesight during the war. Daniel returned to Verdun in the winter of 1946. A popular star athlete, he was well connected in many local circles. Community-minded individuals established a trust fund so that he might further his civil re-establishment training at St Dunstan's, in Brighton, England, the most advanced rehabilitation centre for the war blinded of the British Commonwealth and perhaps the world. Daniel came to symbolize the wartime sacrifices of all Verdunites. The Daniel Fund gave poignant expression to a long-held community view that Verdunites took care of their own. Local groups donated to and worked on behalf of the fund. Individual contributions were deposited in charity boxes displayed in many local businesses. Benefit concerts and sporting events were also organized to finance the fund. The Montreal Canadiens fastball team played a Verdun all-star team at Willibrord Park, with the proceeds donated to the Daniel Fund. Included in the Canadiens' line-up were Bill Durnan, Butch Bouchard, Kenny Reardon, Maurice "Rocket" Richard, Elmer Lach, and Hector "Toe" Blake. Over $200 was collected. The original objective had been $1,000, but by the end of June 1946 the fund had swelled to $3,500.[27] In massively oversubscribing to the Daniel Fund, Verdunites again demonstrated their strong sense of local identity.

Although many repatriated veterans arriving at Bonaventure Station required transportation home to Verdun, few local families had automobiles.[28] In August 1945, Wilfrid Pagé, a local automobile dealer and unsuccessful Progressive Conservative candidate in Verdun in that June's federal election, organized the Free Transport League to shuttle people home from the train station. Gasoline rationing had ended in May 1945, and the League intended that as few Verdunites as possible would be among the "forgotten men" having to take public transit home from the war. The similar Montreal-wide Voluntary Transport League had been organized in 1944 to meet the needs of repatriated wounded men and others needing assistance. By June 1946 its 700 drivers had met 221 trains and provided 12,596 rides to 69,178 men and their kin. Much of this group's activity centred on Verdun.[29]

At the end of the war Gen H.D.G. Crerar, commander, First Canadian Army, stated that "there can be no more stabilizing influence in any community than the presence of 'all ranks' of a unit that represented that locality overseas."[30] Although no regiment was specifically recruited in Verdun, the city modestly welcomed home the 150-man 4th Field Company, RCE. The company's headquarters had been in neighbouring Point St Charles, and many of its original members were Verdunites. This unit, overseas since December 1939 with the 1st Canadian Infantry Division, was ordered to demobilize at the Verdun Auditorium, which had housed various reserve army engineer units since 1941 and had since become temporary home for several others that had been mobilized, including 4th Field Company.

In late September 1945, the Verdun press excitedly reported news of the unit's impending arrival at Halifax aboard the troopship *Nieuw Amsterdam*. This was Verdun's only opportunity to receive a returning body of men still organized as a unit. "Verdun ... has had an outstanding record of contribution and loyalty," wrote the Montreal *Gazette*. "Now it is receiving back some of those it so generously gave."[31] In principle, Ottawa's repatriation system was one of "first-in, first-out"; most Verdunites who had enlisted in 4th Field Company in 1939 had already returned home in individual drafts. With a hint of intercity rivalry, the *Guardian* noted that the Royal Montreal Regiment (which included many Verdunites) had received a "royal welcome" in Westmount the previous week and strongly suggested that Verdun should muster the same enthusiasm for "its" engineers.[32] The men formed up at Bonaventure Station before 9 a.m. on 1 October and were bussed through Point St Charles to the Verdun cenotaph at the intersection of Wellington Street and Lasalle Boulevard. From there the unit marched in battle dress but without arms down Wellington Street to Church Avenue and then, turning left, to the auditorium. Along the way, crowds were thin due to the wet, windy weather and the early hour.

At the auditorium the men's families had assembled. To simplify their reunions, the men entered the building in alphabetical order and formed ranks facing their kin, also organized alphabetically. All of Verdun's political dignitaries were present, and Mayor Wilson gave a very brief word of welcome. So did Maj-Gen Ernest-Jacques Renaud, district officer commanding, Military District 4, and Lieutenant-Colonel Wallis, commanding officer of the "Verdun unit." The national anthem was played and the men were dismissed into the arms of their families. The Voluntary Transport League dutifully drove many of the men home.[33] The modest event was a fitting symbol of thanks and respect not only to those men present but for all veterans from the community.

Verdun also welcomed another group of overseas arrivals in the twelve months following the end of the war: several hundred war brides. Not long after the dispatch of the 1st Canadian Infantry Division overseas in December 1939, the *Guardian* began publishing references to overseas Verdunites visiting relatives in Britain. As early as 1940, it noted that some local men already had taken British wives. Even before the war had ended, dozens of war brides had preceded their husbands home to Verdun. The Quebec Division of the Red Cross reported on the war bride arrivals in Montreal, and virtually every group from March 1944 onward contained women heading to their husbands' Verdun addresses. Most

Verdunites who married overseas, however, were repatriated to Canada after VE Day singly or with their units, and had to await the arrival of their spouses until shipping space could be found.[34]

Between 200 and 300 Verdunites had married overseas. The *Guardian* estimated that the number of these marriages was small compared to the percentage of Canadian service people who were married overseas.[35] A number of Verdun's French-speaking soldiers married British women. Pte R. Montpetit met his future wife during an air raid. She and their baby son arrived in Verdun in the autumn of 1944. The English wife of J.A. Robidoux, of the Royal 22e Régiment, and the Scottish wife of David Durocher also arrived in 1944.[36] Very few of Verdun's war brides were other than British born. The new arrivals found familiar accents, attitudes, and even shops offering British-style food and clothing. Press accounts suggest a warm reception. Yet war brides did not always enjoy their initial contact with working-class Montreal life. They were frequently cramped in substandard housing and stuck living with in-laws until the housing situation improved. One veteran, his war bride, and their two children lived with the husband's married sister in a flat in Verdun. The unfortunate bride wrote to the Montreal Soldiers' Wives' League, asking, "Please can you refer me how to find out about returning home. I have two children and I am expecting another. We have one room here, and have been told that we must find another place. Whereas we can't – places are hard to get and I wish to return to England."[37]

Thanking the Veterans

In September 1945, the *Messenger* recommended in successive front-page editorials that city hall should publicly and materially thank Verdunites who had served in the military, as well as the families of those who had not returned. It suggested convening the veterans and the bereaved at the auditorium so that the city could give each a $100 Victory Bond, as some other (smaller) Canadian towns had done. Such recognition would have cost Verdun between $600,000 and $700,000. In addition, an increasing number of residents complained that the city had failed to provide a suitable public commemoration for Verdun's veterans and war dead. Verdun had trumpeted throughout the war that it led the nation in enlistments; it was time to honour its heroes. City hall, however, seemed far more interested in the soldiers' re-establishment and the conversion of the Defence Industries Limited facility to civilian use. Civic leaders remained very patriotic but worked for future economic growth, jobs, adequate housing, and social betterment, as Wilson had promised in the 1945 municipal election campaign. Nevertheless, the *Messenger* adamantly pointed out that *all* Verdunites owed their citizen-soldiers a lasting debt, which an official material or financial tribute might partially repay.[38]

Some local groups acted. For example, the Verdun Community Club, a charitable and community organization, granted $50 to every former member who had returned from service.[39] In February 1945, the Verdun Labour Progressive Party Club (the Communist Party under a thin veil) started raising funds to grant a $50 Victory Bond to as many badly wounded Verdunites as possible.[40] Verdunites never reached a consensus on how to recognize veterans' services or how to compensate them for their sacrifices, and city hall did not perceive the men's financial welfare as its responsibility. After all, Ottawa had prepared a comprehensive and widely hailed package of veterans' benefits.

The merits of erecting a new war memorial provoked a minor debate in Verdun. The city saw it as an unwise expenditure, as did Verdun's Legion branch and most local veterans. Concerned more with a stable future than with commemorations, the veterans sought instead a more practical testimonial, such as an educational or job-training facility. Others in the community, strongly supported by the *Guardian*, felt that the raising of an armoury and a Verdun regiment would be an ideal tribute.[41] But this was hopelessly unrealistic at a time of massive military demobilization. In February 1946 the Greater Verdun Community Council requested that the city erect a memorial community centre. Not unnaturally, local sporting groups suggested a new outdoor stadium.[42] The city decided instead to add a phrase – "Also dedicated to the memory of those who fell during the Second Great War 1939-1945" – to Verdun's cenotaph. In this decision, Verdun fell into line with most other Canadian municipalities. No major spate of monument building occurred in Canada after 1945, unlike that which followed the First World War.[43] It seemed time to plan the future instead.

Verdun participated successfully in the postwar national industrial reconversion. As seen in Chapter 5, numerous light industries were established on the site of the former DIL facility. From June 1944 on, local economic expansion and the jobs and prosperity expected to flow from it were at the top of Mayor Wilson's agenda. An article prepared by city hall in December 1945 for the *Canadian Corps Magazine* described Verdun's reconversion program as "a real boon to the City and ... to its citizens, particularly those being discharged from the armed forces." In the meantime, the city filled available municipal positions with qualified Verdun veterans.[44] The city's goals and those of its repatriated men were the same: continued employment, income security, and social stability for the city.

In 1946 the federal government published a 300-page volume known commonly as the Veterans' Charter. It contained all the legislation passed up to that point, mostly in 1944 and 1945, dealing with re-establishment and rehabilitation. All veterans were entitled to war-service gratuities (calculated according to length of service), rehabilitation grants, and re-establishment credits to help buy a home, business, or equipment to make a living. Veterans were eligible for a land-settlement scheme, free vocational or university education, insurance plans, medical treatment, pensions, and other benefits.[45] Canadians overseas armed themselves with booklets such as *The Common-Sense of Re-establishment* (published June 1945), which outlined these government rehabilitation schemes and financial benefits. The Verdun Legion, like Legion branches across the country, acted as a clearing house for information concerning veterans' benefits, allowances, and pensions. The local Legion also provided a counselling service to help returnees avoid swindlers who targeted them and their sometimes large service annuities and gratuities. Within months of VE Day, fraudulent investment or housing schemes had bilked some unwary Verdun veterans of their re-establishment money.[46]

In January 1945, the *Guardian* published a negative editorial on Ottawa's plans for educational and training benefits for returned service people, based on the correspondence of a Verdunite then serving overseas. The unnamed soldier believed that the government's emphasis on university education, as opposed to technical and vocational training, was clearly aimed at a particular social class. He stated that his own prewar experience in Verdun, as well as the inclinations of other men with whom he had spoken overseas, indicated the desire for a wider range of practical courses to prepare them for "jobs that can be done with their hands."[47] While vocational training schemes for veterans had been evolving since the First World War,[48] and even though this man exaggerated veterans' general lack of interest in a university education, his working-class views may have coincided with those of many other Verdunites. The men of Verdun had shown the volunteering spirit. Following the war they wanted the government to address their own perceived needs, not spout middle-class values. John Neal, however, a Verdun RCAF veteran who before enlisting had worked in the Canadian National Railways locomotive shops in nearby Point St Charles, was able to attend McGill University as a result of Ottawa's program. His education allowed him to avoid "a less satisfying life." But few other Verdunites seem to have followed suit.[49]

IN 1946 VERDUN HIGH SCHOOL's *Annual* offered the view that "world peace is today's aim," as well as "a better life for ordinary folk."[50] The war was over, and no war-related section appeared in the school's publication that year. The air cadet band was allotted only a small photo on the last page, just before ads from sponsors. None of the poetry or short stories had a military theme. None mentioned the British Empire or the royal family – noticeable topics in every edition since the first in 1935. The new world and the new Canada had a new mood, and the young people of Verdun, fervently patriotic during the war, clearly reflected this postwar attitude. It was time to move forward, to embrace the potential of the future.

Conclusion

Verdun had been a close-knit and proud community before 1939, and the war intensified these feelings by offering its residents a powerful sense of achievement. Despite all that had taken place since 1939, social and institutional continuity remained very strong in Verdun. Yet from the perspective of 1945 the prewar era seemed distant. The war hastened Verdun's physical development and, in the short term, sharpened the city's image and self-confidence. Arthur Burgess wrote in December 1945: "The fame of the City of Verdun is known from coast to coast, and beyond, for its magnificent contribution in both World Wars, both in the number of enlistments for active service and in the intense work of its citizens for all forms of patriotic activity."[1]

Verdun's manpower contribution and well-organized domestic war effort had afforded it national prominence and became its calling card. The city had furnished Canada's best-known military hero of the war, George Beurling. Verdun's Defence Industries Limited plant had been the top producer of small-arms ammunition in the country, and the remarkable Mayor's Cigarette Fund and other local initiatives had established Verdun as one of Quebec's and Canada's premier patriotic communities. In recognition of the city's growing wartime stature, in April 1944 a prominent article on its military and civilian war effort had appeared in *Canada's Weekly*, a magazine produced in London, England, for overseas military personnel.[2] Already conspicuous throughout the Canadian military establishment overseas, Verdunites obtained even greater recognition in the widely circulated journal.

The war also improved Verdun's city finances and family economies. An article in the April 1943 issue of the *Municipal Review of Canada*, prominently reprinted in the *Guardian*, noted that "when Wilson became mayor [in 1939] Verdun was suffering from a hard dose of depression and past maladministration," but that, as a result of several years of war, the "working-class city has become one of the most prosperous communities in the Dominion."[3] While this was an exaggeration, the war had brought overall economic benefits to Verdun. Relief payments to unemployed Verdunites ended in 1941 as thousands of residents found work in war industries or enlisted in the armed forces. The resulting increase in disposable income available to most Verdun families strengthened the local economy and expanded the city's tax base. The city's net debenture debt per capita dropped by 28 percent between 1939 and 1945. Despite the housing crisis, the war stimulated urban growth and population expansion, both of which boosted the local economy. The sale of nearly 1,600 vacant lots for property development further aided municipal finances. Between 1941 and 1946 erection of more than 2,000 dwellings increased valuation rolls considerably. Existing streets were widened and extended, and new ones built.[4]

Between 1939 and 1945 municipal revenue from property taxes rose by 14 percent without a rate increase, revenue from water taxes went up by 27 percent, and revenue from local sales taxes rose by 33 percent. Overall the city's income increased by 38 percent during the war.[5] At the height of the war the *Messenger* marvelled at Wilson and French's ability to balance the budget and show a surplus: "evidence," it reported, "that all have worked together in this time of stress and crisis to keep the public services at their highest level, while protecting the money of the taxpayers and looking forward to post-war conditions."[6]

In January 1946 a feature article in Toronto's *Financial Post* represented Verdun as an altered city with great economic potential. Verdun had been previously "almost obscured ... by its proximity to Montreal," but the early postwar period had demonstrated that it was no longer merely a suburb of the greater metropolis. Verdun had experienced an "industrial boom" during the war, and "living conditions and general standard of living have been moving steadily upward." At the start of 1941 the city had had only twenty-two small manufacturers with 343 workers, whereas the wartime DIL plant had employed 6,800 at its peak, and its postwar reconversion to light industry was expected to generate several thousand permanent jobs.[7] There would be no going back to the depressed conditions of the 1930s.

A renewed sense of confidence reigned. The war had put Verdun on the map, and perceptions of the city, within and without, were very positive. Wilson's efficient administration, which had come to power only months before the war started, brought renown to the city and infused it with the hope of fulfilling the grander destiny predicted by civic boosters in the 1920s. Despite their apprehensions about the economy, Verdunites had shown their ability to surmount difficult challenges. Their experiences of the previous fifteen years seemed to prove that onerous social conditions could be survived; postwar life could hardly be more burdensome than the Depression or the war years.

Verdunites expressed faith in their city's future. On 28 September 1944, the *Guardian*'s headline announced: "Wellington Street to Grow to Great Business Location on Island of Montreal." The accompanying article claimed that projected modernizations would probably make Verdun's busiest street one of the leading shopping districts in Canada. By 1946 Verdun believed itself on the verge of significant economic and population growth. A buoyant city hall described Verdun as "one of the most progressive" urban centres in Canada. Riding the crest of wartime publicity, and in the hope of attracting investment, Verdun's optimistic city leaders promoted its beautiful riverside location and its extensive municipal services, playgrounds, and sporting facilities, especially the modern auditorium and the Natatorium swimming and diving complex.[8] Much of this optimism was the result of local wartime growth, pride in the civil and military accomplishments of Verdunites, and an enhanced sense of community. But the war years had not defined these characteristics so much as reflected them.

Verdunites had remained remarkably united in pursuing a vigorous war effort, especially whenever a patriotic cause allowed them to help fellow residents serving overseas directly, rather than just supporting general military or economic policies or the broader war aims of the Allies. French- and English-speaking Canadians, including the British born, had acted together as Verdunites. Community spirit created an atmosphere conducive to aiding local men and women on active service. The Mayor's Cigarette Fund is the best example of this focused attention. Community identification also spurred some Verdunites to enlist.

Despite occasional differences along ethnic, linguistic, religious, and even class lines, the war does not appear to have deepened existing social divisions in Verdun. Linguistic relations remained reasonably harmonious. Though they were not without tension, the war years also revealed a commonality of outlook, or at least shared local experience and interest. French and English Canadian Verdunites prosecuted the war at home and overseas together, and felt its consequences similarly. Community and class identity seemed as influential in social relations as the existence of sometimes-competing linguistic blocs. A shared identity as Verdunites may have helped bridge the barriers between French and English speakers.[9] It is also possible that ever-present shrill wartime patriotism discouraged overt opposition to the war. Nevertheless, conscription for overseas service apart, there is little evidence that French speakers much opposed their city's patriotic response to the war. The sense of pride that accompanied external recognition of Verdun's contributions on the home and battle fronts was not linguistically segregated.

The city of Verdun, and especially its energetic mayor, Edward Wilson, wholeheartedly backed the war effort. Such support was unusual for a Quebec municipality, and Verdun had over 30,000 French speakers by 1945 and a city council made up mainly of French Canadians. Municipal expenditures in support of patriotic endeavours caused not a ripple of dissent in council. Nor was the city averse to profitable patriotism. For example, council found a military tenant for the auditorium, an expensive building to maintain.

Perhaps the shared "national experience" of war in Verdun forced existing social animosities below the surface.[10] Rather than leading to obvious linguistic discord, in Verdun the war signalled an era of relative harmony and consensus. Verdunites separated by language, ethnicity, and religion shared common space in their congested city; compromise was absolutely necessary to personal and social accommodation. This social stability, if perhaps not cohesion, was never clearer than at the time of the conscription plebiscite of 1942; even though language and ethnicity governed political responses, the campaign resulted in no reported untoward incidents. In the divisive linguistic context of wartime Canada, a close study of bicultural Verdun forces some re-examination of historians' traditional views of language relations at this time. By forcing social accommodation, Verdun's linguistic duality actually helped ensure community harmony, not antagonism.

More than 6,300 Verdunites served overseas during the war. French speakers on the home front contributed generously to the many causes that supported these men and women even though 80 percent of Verdunites overseas were English speakers. French speakers were proportionately equal or near-equal partners with English speakers in many war-related activities, including working for the Red Cross, raising money for the Mayor's Cigarette Fund and the crew of HMCS *Dunver*, helping with civil protection, salvage efforts, and Victory Loan campaigns, working in war industry and, ultimately, enlisting.

The *Guardian* did not accord the military contributions of French speakers in and out of uniform the publicity that they surely merited. This newspaper was written by and for an English-speaking audience whose core was British born. The paper set a tone of smug self-assurance in its view that French Canada's responses to the demands of total war were unduly weak, and that French speakers in uniform should hardly be glorified for performing what in effect were their basic obligations as citizens. The *Guardian* rarely hinted at the thousands of French speakers who contributed to Verdun's war effort. Yet despite its occasional outbursts against French Canadian nationalism, this newspaper often extolled the virtues of the linguistic harmony reigning in wartime Verdun. In October 1942, six months after the conscription plebiscite, the *Guardian* referred to the "splendid community and co-operative spirit which has and still exists among [Verdunites], irrespective of nationality or creed."[11] In any event, linguistic enmity was considered unpatriotic, and if the *Guardian*'s attitude can serve as a guide, many English-speaking Verdunites felt it incumbent on French speakers to refrain from contradicting the wartime priorities of the local English-speaking majority. Thus could social peace be ensured. Still, Mayor Wilson was proud to state in 1945 that during the war there existed "the most cordial and friendly relations between all sections of the community. We have not only preached the Bonne Entente in Verdun, we have practiced it as well."[12] Verdunites, understanding the dynamics shaping social relations in their city, seemed less prone to extreme political views and social behaviour fuelled by linguistic animosities.

Verdun's unique mix of size, urban form, class, language, and religion, and its sense of community identity, both define and explain its responses during the war. The city's unusual British character, its working-class population, and its strongly entrenched, cross-linguistic community pride were all major determinants of Verdunites' domestic and military contributions to the war effort. Historian Sidney Aster has written of Canada's home front during the war that "patriotism, solidarity, community, stability and purpose were more often the rule than the exception."[13] Verdunites from all walks of life experienced the trials of the Second World War, adhered to its conditions, and faced its challenges. To this extent the war acted as a unifying force, which embodied a spirit of community and localism.

This examination of Verdun, in effect a wartime municipal biography, has viewed Canada's war from the perspective of these local experiences, seeking to provide insights into issues usually viewed from a national level. Other Canadian wartime community studies undoubtedly would find both commonality with and divergence from Verdun's story. But Verdun's war was also very much Canada's war. The national wartime experience was no more than the collection of smaller individual, group, and community responses, with many similar traits but none identical. The effects of the Second World War were felt at the community and individual levels. It is from these levels that Canadians responded and helped make possible the war's successful prosecution. Verdun's residents, at home and overseas, did what they had to do and what was expected of them, nothing more. Like wartime Canadians in general, they were just ordinary heroes.

Notes

Introduction: Studying the War at the Local Level

1 Desmond Morton and J.L. Granatstein, *Victory 1945: Canadians from War to Peace* (Toronto: HarperCollins, 1995), 255; Jeffrey A. Keshen, *Saints, Sinners, and Soldiers: Canada's Second World War* (Vancouver: UBC Press, 2004); Magda Fahrni, "Under Reconstruction: The Family and the Public in Postwar Montréal, 1944-1949" (PhD diss., York University, 2001).

2 With the fusion of all neighbouring communities to the city of Montreal on 1 January 2002, Verdun lost its independent municipal status and became a borough.

3 Keshen, *Saints, Sinners, and Soldiers*, is the best available. Sectoral approaches include Michael Stevenson, *Canada's Greatest Wartime Muddle: National Selective Service and the Mobilization of Human Resources during World War II* (Montreal and Kingston: McGill-Queen's University Press, 2001); Peter S. McInnes, *Harnessing Labour Confrontation: Shaping the Postwar Settlement in Canada, 1943-1950* (Toronto: University of Toronto Press, 2002); Ruth R. Pierson, *"They're Still Women after All": The Second World War and Canadian Womanhood* (Toronto: McClelland and Stewart, 1986); Ruth R. Pierson, *Canadian Women and the Second World War,* historical booklet 37 (Ottawa: Canadian Historical Association, 1983). André Laurendeau, *La crise de la conscription 1942* (Montreal: Les éditions du jour, 1962), and Paul-André Comeau, *Le Bloc populaire 1942-1948* (Montreal: Éditions Québec/ Amérique, 1982), employ a cultural and linguistic approach to the war's impact on Quebec. Ethnicity is covered by Norman Hillmer, Bohdan Kordan and Lubomyr Luciuk eds., *On Guard for Thee: War, Ethnicity and the Canadian State, 1939-1945* (Ottawa: Canadian Committee for the History of the Second World War, Ministry of Supply and Services, 1988).

4 The best basic work on Ottawa's direction of the war is C.P. Stacey, *Arms, Men and Governments: The War Policies of Canada, 1939-1945* (Ottawa: Queen's Printer, 1970). A comprehensive overview is J.L. Granatstein, *Canada's War: The Politics of the Mackenzie King Government 1939-1945* (Toronto: Oxford University Press, 1975). See also J.L. Granatstein and J.M. Hitsman, *Broken Promises: A History of Conscription in Canada* (Toronto: Oxford University Press, 1977); and Daniel Byers, "Mobilizing Canada: The National Resources Mobilization Act, the Department of National Defence, and Compulsory Military Service in Canada, 1940-1945" (PhD diss., McGill University, 2001).

5 Previous surveys of Canada's war offer little on the organization of these and other undertakings at a local level. See, for example, W.A.B. Douglas and Brereton Greenhous, *Out of the Shadows* (Toronto: Oxford University Press, 1977), and J.L. Granatstein and Desmond Morton, *A Nation Forged in Fire* (Toronto: Lester and Orpen Dennys, 1989).

6 A.F.J. Artibise and Gilbert A. Stelter, eds., *The Usable Urban Past,* Carleton Library no. 119 (Toronto: Macmillan, 1979), 2.

7 Mark Walsh, "The Micro Approach: Municipal Records and Canadian Studies," *Canadian Issues* (Association for Canadian Studies) 10, 4 (1988): 67.

8 Sidney Aster has described the national war experience of Canada and other nations as "integrative" and "consensus building." Aster, ed., *The Second World War as a National Experience* (Ottawa: Canadian Committee for the History of the Second World War, 1981), 2.

9   See Don Higginbotham, "The New Military History: Its Practitioners and Their Practices," in *Military History and the Military Profession*, ed. David A. Charters, Marc Milner, and J. Brent Wilson, 132-44 (Westport, CT: Praeger, 1992), and Richard Preston, "Canadian Military History: A Reinterpretation Challenge for the Eighties," *American Review of Canadian Studies* 19, 1 (1989): 102-3.
10 Jay White, "Conscripted City: Halifax and the Second World War" (PhD diss., McMaster University, 1994). Keshen, *Saints, Sinners, and Soldiers*, offers glimpses of many Canadian cities.

Chapter 1: Forging a Community
1   Denis Gravel and Hélène Lafortune, *Verdun: 125 ans d'histoire 1875-2000* (Montreal: Archiv-Histo, 2000), 12.
2   Julien Déziel, *History of Verdun 1665, 1876-1976* (Verdun: Centennial Committee, 1976), 10.
3   Ibid., 65-6.
4   The threat to Verdun's municipal independence recurred spasmodically until 1921. That year the provincial legislature established the Montreal Metropolitan Commission, of which Verdun was a member, to oversee the finances of Montreal's smaller neighbours. Arthur J. Burgess, City Clerk, "Cité de Verdun: La plus grande banlieue residentielle de Montréal," 15 March 1962, unpaged typewritten report, in box A-525, file 5, "Histoire de Verdun," Verdun Borough Archives (hereafter VBA). Between 1905 and 1914 twenty-six separate annexations by Montreal swallowed up sixteen municipalities. See Paul-André Linteau, *Histoire de Montréal depuis la Confédération* (Montreal: Boréal, 1992), 202-3 and 353-4.
5   Déziel, *History of Verdun*, 72.
6   Burgess, "Cité de Verdun"; Déziel, *History of Verdun*, 64.
7   Burgess, "Cité de Verdun"; 1911 Census, vol. 1, 546.
8   Mary Davidson, "The Social Adjustment of British Immigrant Families in Verdun and Point St Charles" (MA thesis, McGill University, 1933), 14.
9   The Verdun Motor Boat Club and the Grand Trunk Boating Club had wharves in Verdun. Two other wharves were able to accommodate light river traffic: one at the foot of Second Avenue in central Verdun and one at the foot of Riverview Avenue in the west end (a section of the city barely inhabited until after the First World War). The Verdun Yacht Club was established in the 1930s.
10 Davidson, "Social Adjustment," 13-14.
11 "Population de la municipalité de Verdun," file 52, "Population," box 237, VBA.
12 The 1911 Census, vol. 2, 434, indicates that 2,437 (20.9 percent) of Verdun's 11,629 residents were born in the British Isles. These British-born immigrants represented 42.8 percent of Verdun's residents of British ancestry (p. 278).
13 *Montreal Daily Star*, 25 September 1924, states that 2,500 Verdun mothers sent sons overseas, while the edition of 6 October 1924 gives the figure of 4,000.
14 Verdun branch (No. 4) of the Canadian Legion to Verdun City Council, 22 July 1940, box A-331, file 6, VBA; *The 1939 Anniversary Programme of the Verdun (No. 4) Branch of the British Empire Service League*, 31 October 1939, 9. Courtesy of Sydney Ashford.
15 David Carnegie, *The History of Munitions Supply in Canada* (London: Longman's, Green and Co., 1925), 76-81.
16 City of Verdun, Council Minutes (hereafter cited as "Council Minutes"), 13 March 1916.
17 Council Minutes, 26 June 1916.
18 *Guardian* (Verdun), special supplement, 23 May 1946; Carnegie, *History of Munitions Supply*, 148-9.
19 Council Minutes, 22 April 1919. For a review of the social effects of the First World War in Canada, see Desmond Morton, *Fight or Pay: Soldiers' Families in the Great War* (Vancouver: UBC Press, 2004).

20 Council Minutes, 8 January 1917.
21 *La Presse* (Montreal), 13 December 1917.
22 Robert Shipley, *To Mark Our Place: A History of Canadian War Memorials* (Toronto: NC Press, 1987), xx.
23 *Montreal Daily Star*, 6 October 1924. The name "Verdun" became famous during the First World War as a result of the successful and costly French defence of that city. This famous battle added poignancy to the name of its Canadian counterpart. Many people long believed thereafter that the Canadian city had been named for the French one. Curiously, correspondence emanating from Verdun city hall occasionally furthered this misbelief. See, for example, Council Minutes, 24 June 1918.
24 *Montreal Daily Star*, 25 September and 6 October 1924; *1939 Anniversary Programme*, 9. The *Guardian* (Verdun), 9 October 1942, stated that Mrs Leavitt had three grandsons enlisted during the Second World War. The Canadian government awarded each widow or mother of a wartime fatal casualty a small Memorial Cross, colloquially referred to as a "Silver Cross" because of its colour.
25 Davidson, "Social Adjustment," 23.
26 *Verdun Directory 1929-1930*, 11, located in box A-80, VBA.
27 1941 Census, vol. 2, 210.
28 By 1941 this ratio had climbed to 26,940 per square mile. See *Annuaire statistique du Québec, 1940* (Quebec: Bureau des Statistiques, 1941), 63; and 1941 Census, vol. 2, 9-10.
29 John H. Thompson with Allen Seager, *Canada 1922-1939: Decades of Discord* (Toronto: McClelland and Stewart, 1985), 99-100; Linteau, *Histoire de Montréal*, 355-8.
30 See for example Michiel Horn, ed., *The Depression in Canada* (Toronto: Copp Clark Pitman, 1988). For this decade as it affected Verdun, see Suzanne Clavette, "Des bons aux chèques: Aide aux chômeurs et crise des années 1930 à Verdun" (MA thesis, Université du Québec à Montréal, 1986). This work helped in preparing this section.
31 Thompson with Seager, *Decades of Discord*, 215.
32 Denyse Baillargeon, *Ménagères au temps de la crise* (Montreal: Éditions du remue-ménage, 1991), 20-1.
33 P.H. Lane, "Unemployment Relief 1929-1936," typewritten report of the Verdun Unemployment Relief Commission, 1936, 3, box A-237, file 24, VBA," 1.
34 Clavette, "Des bons aux chèques," 113-14; *Guardian* (Verdun), 11 July 1941; Lane, "Unemployment Relief 1929-1936," 3. At the peak of the crisis in Verdun in March 1933, 14,823 Verdunites depended on direct relief payments totalling $100,000 monthly. Others depended on public works assignments.
35 Clavette, "Des bons aux chèques," 111-16, 324, and 337.
36 Lane, "Unemployment Relief," 2.
37 Baillargeon, *Ménagères*, 200-1. See also Lane, "Unemployment Relief," 3. Verdun was proportionately far more generous in its relief allocations than was Montreal, and Linteau calls Verdun one of the most generous municipalities in the country (*Histoire de Montréal*, 379). Even in 1944, the city held a picnic for 1,500 local children whose families could not afford a vacation. *Montreal Daily Star*, 24 August 1944.
38 *Guardian* (Verdun), 21 February 1941.
39 The *Montreal Daily Star*, 4 May 1940, quotes several Montreal aldermen as wishing that their city had followed Verdun's lead.
40 *Guardian* (Verdun), 11 July 1941.
41 None of the people interviewed for this study who grew up during the Depression were willing to characterize these years as worse than difficult, and, even at that, they had wonderful memories of the 1930s. Tellingly, perhaps, none of them was older than eleven in 1929.

42 Three 1933 master's theses by researchers from McGill University's innovative Social Research Group, headed by Carl Dawson and Leonard Marsh, explored different aspects of the British immigrant experience in Montreal in the first decades of the twentieth century. These studies, Davidson, "Social Adjustment"; Mary E. Ramsden, "Dependency among British Immigrants in Montreal"; and Lloyd G. Reynolds, "Occupational Adjustment of the British Immigrant," formed the basis for Reynolds's 1935 volume, *The British Immigrant: His Social and Economic Adjustment in Canada* (Toronto: Oxford University Press, 1935). This last work, and Davidson's, describe Verdun as a city with a strong British character and identity in the years before the Second World War. Parts of this section have been published in Serge Marc Durflinger, "Owing Allegiance: The British Community in Verdun, Quebec during the Second World War," *Canadian Ethnic Studies* 36, 1 (2004): 3-23.

43 Reynolds, *British Immigrant*, 77-80; Davidson, "Social Adjustment," 48.

44 Reynolds estimates the proportion at one-third, although information in the 1941 Census makes this seem unlikely. Reynolds, *British Immigrant*, 123; 1941 Census, vol. 2, 734.

45 1931 Census, vol. 2, 758. In 1931, only 8.4 percent of Montrealers were born in the British Isles, and in 1941, 5.38 percent. *Annuaire du Canada, 1943-44* (Ottawa: Bureau des Statistics, 1945), 123; Reynolds, *British Immigrant*, 116. Reynolds employs the category "British-born" as opposed to the census's "British Isles" and thus includes 977 Newfoundlanders and 217 people born in other British dominions and possessions. As a result, his interpretation of the census data shows Verdun's population as being 25.9 percent British born (p. 128).

46 1941 Census, vol. 3, 398. The addition to the total of 1,051 Verdunites born in other British possessions (including 879 Newfoundlanders) brings the proportion to 18.3 percent.

47 *Annuaire du Canada, 1943-44*, 123. Only Victoria (31.37 percent), Vancouver (26.33 percent), Calgary (21.94 percent), Hamilton (21.13 percent), and Toronto (20.72 percent) are listed as having higher proportions of British-born residents than Verdun. The figure for Westmount was 15.55 percent based on a population of 26,047.

48 Reynolds, *British Immigrant*, 138-9.

49 Ibid., 207-8 and 212 n 2; Davidson, "Social Adjustment," 55ff.

50 Hervé Ferland, *Sensationnel assassinat au Natatorium de Verdun* (Montreal: Privately printed, [1946?]), Canadiana Room, Verdun Cultural Centre, 4.

51 Wilson Dornan, interview by author, 21 September 1993. Another Verdunite, Joseph Way, mentioned the Verdun "accent," which was common in the 1940s. He claimed that, while in the navy during the war, he could tell immediately if a speaker was from Verdun, and he was rarely wrong. Interview by author, 15 November 1992.

52 Gabrielle Roy makes this clear in *Bonheur d'occasion* when describing her main character's flirtation with the idea of moving to Verdun: "Giddy with pride and envy, she thought of a house for rent on the Boulevard LaSalle ... Why not? she said to herself. We have the money now. We're not obliged to live in Saint Henri anymore." Roy, *Bonheur d'occasion* (Montreal: Société des Éditions Pascale, 1945; translated by Hanna Josephson as *The Tin Flute* (1947; republished Toronto: McClelland and Stewart, 1969), 274.

53 O.J. Firestone, "Measurement of Housing Needs, Supply and Post War Requirements," in *Housing and Community Planning: A Series of Lectures Delivered at McGill University, November 2, 1943-March 21, 1944*, ed. School of Architecture (Montreal: McGill University, 1944), 113 and 116-17.

54 *Gazette* (Montreal), 9 August 1941; *Montreal Daily Star*, 16 August 1941.

55 Aileen Ross, "The French and English Social Elites of Montreal" (MA thesis, University of Chicago, 1941), 52-3.

56 Davidson also noted a form of old-world class-consciousness transferred to Verdun by its British immigrant population. "Social Adjustment," 50 and 209.

57   The language map that Davidson provides shows very clearly that, overall, no neat division between the languages existed in Verdun. Ibid., 25.

58   For a contemporary discussion, see Leo Zakuta, "The Natural Areas of the Montreal Metropolitan Community with Special Reference to the Central Area" (MA thesis, McGill University, 1948), 10-13. When away from the Montreal area, for example, Verdunites usually identified themselves as Montrealers and were normally considered as such.

59   Ibid., 46-8.

60   *Guardian* (Verdun), 12 October 1944.

61   *Messenger/Le Messager* (Verdun), 13 April 1944, author's translation.

62   See Tom MacDonnell, *Daylight upon Magic: The Royal Tour of Canada 1939* (Toronto: Macmillan, 1989).

63   *Guardian* (Verdun), 19 May 1939. See also Durflinger, "Owing Allegiance," 9-10.

64   *Guardian* (Verdun), 4 August 1939. A year earlier, during the Czech crisis that resulted in the Munich Agreement, the paper had noted that "the spirit that caused Verdun to send more men overseas during the war, proportionately speaking, than any other Canadian town, is still very much alive today." 30 September 1938.

65   Verdun High School, *Annual*, 1939, 20, 25-6, and 32. The *Annuals* of Verdun High School covering the years 1939-45 are located in the Canadiana Room, Verdun Cultural Centre. Ottawa high school students expressed similar reactions. See Christine Hamelin, "A Sense of Purpose: Ottawa Students and the Second World War," *Canadian Military History* 6, 1 (1997): 34-41.

66   Verdun High School, *Annual*, 1939, 19-39, Canadiana Room, Verdun Cultural Centre.

67   Verdun High School, *Annual*, 1940 and 1945, Canadiana Room, Verdun Cultural Centre.

Chapter 2: Once More into the Breach

1   *Guardian* (Verdun), 1 September 1939.

2   *Montreal Daily Star*, 14 September 1939; *Guardian* (Verdun), 22 September 1939. The *Montreal Daily Star*, 16 August 1941, repeated this claim more or less as a fact and in a postwar accounting, the *Guardian* (Verdun), 31 October 1946, stated that "according to available information," Verdun again led the country in the percentage of enlistments. Certain English-speaking Montreal-area cities and neighbourhoods, such as Westmount, Point St Charles, and Notre-Dame-de-Grâce also produced large numbers of enlistments, but none achieved the status that Verdun claimed.

3   See Jean-Yves Gravel, "Le Québec militaire, 1939-1945," in *Le Québec et la Guerre*, ed. Jean-Yves Gravel (Montreal: Boréal Express, 1974), 78ff.

4   Joseph Way, interview by author, 21 September 1993.

5   *Gazette* (Montreal), 6 November 2005; index cards of the Mayor's Cigarette Fund (hereafter MCF), box A-536, Verdun Borough Archives (hereafter VBA).

6   Information obtained from mainly undated wartime press clippings provided by Verdunite Stuart Carson, who collected them during the war. See also Pierre Vennat, *Les héros oubliés: L'histoire inédite des militaires canadiens-français de la Deuxième Guerre mondiale*, 3 vols. (Montreal: Méridien, 1997-98).

7   Violet Hartley to MCF, 2 November 1942, box A-340, VBA.

8   Sheila Graham to author, 27 January 1993.

9   Gordon Galbraith, interview by author, 13 November 1993.

10   This point is also made by Douglas How, *One Village, One War 1914-1945* (Hantsport, NS: Lancelot Press, 1995), 160.

11   *Globe and Mail*, 5 September 1940; Emo to MCF, 30 November 1941, box A-615, VBA.

12   General Advisory Committee on Demobilization and Rehabilitation, "Statistical Analysis of Discharges from Armed Forces of Canada 3-9-39 to 31-3-42," MG 27, vol. 61, file 527-62 (3), Library and Archives Canada (hereafter LAC).

13 W.A.B. Douglas and Brereton Greenhous, *Out of the Shadows* (Toronto: Oxford University Press, 1977), 36.
14 Suzanne Clavette, "Des bons aux chèques: Aide aux chômeurs et crise des années 1930 à Verdun" (MA thesis, Université du Québec à Montréal, 1986), 117; R.B. Joan Adams, interview by author, 6 October 1993.
15 Joseph Way, interviews by author, 15 November 1992 and 21 September 1993.
16 There were a dozen or more examples of Verdun fathers and sons or daughters serving during the war. Wartime press clippings courtesy of Stuart Carson.
17 Douglas Whyte, interview by author, 21 January 1994.
18 Sydney Ashford, interview by author, 12 January 1993.
19 Joseph Way, interviews by author, 15 November 1992 and 21 September 1993.
20 These cards are located in box A-536, VBA. See Chapter 3 for a discussion of the Mayor's Cigarette Fund. See also Serge Marc Durflinger, "Owing Allegiance: The British Community in Verdun, Quebec during the Second World War," *Canadian Ethnic Studies* 36, 1 (2004): 3-23.
21 The *Guardian* (Verdun), 31 October 1946, citing the 1945 municipal census as its source, claimed that more than 6,500 Verdunites had been in uniform. After 1943, local censuses specifically questioned residents on military service. (The manuscript censuses no longer exist.) If this estimate is reasonably accurate, then the figure of 6,316 used to determine a social profile of Verdunites in uniform represents some 97 percent of the contemporary accounting of Verdunites known to have been on active service. This is sufficient to elaborate accurate trends from the statistics. A "Summary of Enlistments" to 31 March 1945 prepared in June 1945 by the Department of Veterans' Affairs tabulated voluntary enlistments by service according to municipality, county, or census districts. Because in many cases enlistment figures for outlying districts were consolidated into a regional or municipal total, it is difficult to obtain a reliable or exact statistic for each Canadian municipality. The figure cited for Verdun is 6,465 not including NRMA men, the Canadian Women's Army Corps and the Women's Division of the Royal Canadian Air Force, which according to the Mayor's Cigarette Fund totalled at least another 388 service people, making a total of 6,853. The "Summary" was provided by Professor Terry Copp of the Laurier Centre for Military Strategic and Disarmament Studies, Wilfrid Laurier University. See the document online at http://info.wlu.ca/~wwwmsds.
22 In November 1944, fully 43 percent of the nearly 450,000 men on strength of the Canadian Army were stationed in Canada or "Adjacent Territories," and nearly one-third of those men were on NRMA service. Some were undoubtedly Verdunites. E.L.M. Burns, *Manpower in the Canadian Army 1939-1945* (Toronto: Clarke, Irwin, 1956), 13.
23 The 1941 census lists 11,506,655 Canadians, of whom 1,029,510 males and more than 49,000 females served during the war, for a ratio of roughly 1 in 10.67. See C.P. Stacey, *Arms, Men and Governments: The War Policies of Canada, 1939-1945* (Ottawa: Queen's Printer, 1970), 590.
24 Less than 1 percent of the 6,316 names on the MCF's mailing list could not be comfortably assigned to one of the two main language groups. Additional information, such as given names of parents and siblings, school attended, place of employment, street address, and birthplace facilitated the task. Very few names were of neither British nor French ancestry.
25 David Zimmerman has concluded that only 9 percent of Canada's non-officer naval personnel were born in Quebec and that only 10.5 percent were Quebec residents when they enlisted. Zimmerman's data indicate even lower percentages for officers. These figures, based on a random sample of 1,179 cases, suggest that perhaps 10 percent of Quebec's sailors were Verdunites. See Zimmerman, "The Social Background of the Wartime Navy: Some Statistical Data," in *A Nation's Navy: In Quest of Canadian Naval Identity*, ed. Michael Hadley, Rob Huebert, and Fred Crickard (Montreal and Kingston: McGill-Queen's University Press, 1996), 261-3.

26 Burns, *Manpower,* 123-5.
27 René Bisson, interview by author, 21 July 1994. This veteran noted the difficulty experienced by many French-speaking Canadian soldiers in a clearly English-speaking environment. For NRMA data, see Burns, *Manpower,* 121. See also Daniel Byers, "Mobilising Canada: The National Mobilization Act, the Department of National Defence and Compulsory Military Service in Canada, 1940-1945," *Journal of the Canadian Historical Association* 7 (1996): 175-203.
28 The oft-quoted figure of 19 percent French speakers in the military includes those from outside Quebec. Gravel, "Le Québec militaire," 84; for more detail on enlistments by French speakers, see Serge Bernier and Jean Pariseau, *Les Canadiens français et le bilinguisme dans les Forces armées canadiennes.* Vol. 1, *1763-1969: Le spectre d'une armée bicéphale* (Ottawa: Service historique de la Défense nationale, 1987), 129-40; Stacey, *Arms, Men and Governments,* 420-4 and 590.
29 This rough figure is obtained by dividing the number of English-speaking Canadian enlistees during the Second World War (no less than 850,000) by the number of English speakers in the general population (slightly more than 8 million). These figures include non-British ethnics.
30 Taylor to MCF, 14 January 1945, box A-348, VBA.
31 A sampling of *Canada's Weekly* finds Verdunites pictured in its issues of 5 November 1943, 10 December 1943, 31 December 1943, 18 February 1944, 18 August 1944, 5 January 1945, 26 January 1945, and 9 March 1945. See also D.F. Griffin, *First Steps to Tokyo: The Royal Canadian Air Force in the Aleutians* (Toronto: J.M. Dent and Sons, 1944), photo between pages 10 and 11 of Aircraftsman Alphonso Tanguay of Verdun who "keeps the morale of fighter pilots high through the hot meals, cleanliness, and repartee he serves up as maitre d'hotel of their mess"; and Hugh Garner, *Storm Below* (Toronto: Ryerson Press, 1968, originally published 1949). See also for example Charles Chauveau, *Soixante-cinq ans d'histoire: Notes historiques sur le Royal 22e Régiment,* Vol. 3 (Quebec: Le Régiment, 1983); and Betty Warrilow, *Nabob: The First Canadian Manned Aircraft Carrier* (Owen Sound, ON: Escort Carrier Association, 1989).
32 *Guardian* (Verdun), 15 September 1939 and 20 December 1940.
33 Terry Copp, *The Brigade* (Stoney Creek, ON: Fortress Publications, 1992), 9 and 12.
34 *Montreal Daily Star,* 8 September 1939.
35 "List of Units Mobilized in Montreal that Served Overseas During the Second World War," 140.045 (D3), Directorate of History and Heritage, National Defence Headquarters. I am indebted to Dr Ken Reynolds for this information. See also *Montreal Daily Star,* 4, 18, and 21 September 1939.
36 Joseph Way, a naval veteran, expressed surprise when reminded that nearly 1,000 Verdunites served in the air force. Interview by author, 15 November 1992.
37 1941 Census, vol. 3, 198. With an average age of forty-five among residents, Verdun was tied with Sherbrooke for second-youngest city in Canada, behind Sudbury. 1941 Census, vol. 9, 46. Burns, *Manpower,* 145-7, notes that 17.5 percent of Canadian males aged fourteen to sixty-four up to May 1945 served in the armed forces. This age range is that of the standard working-age population. Available evidence does not determine the date of enlistment and marital status of Verdunites on active service.
38 1941 Census, vol. 5, 478-9. See also Clavette, "Des bons aux chèques," 323.
39 Box A-333, VBA, contains nominal roll material for 1940-41.
40 *Guardian* (Verdun), 15 November 1940.
41 *Guardian* (Verdun), 19 December 1941. Of 871 men on active service listed by this newspaper a year earlier, on 20 December 1940, only 22 were French speakers – a mere 2.5 percent.

42 A. Davidson Dunton, in his introduction to Elizabeth Armstrong's *French Canadian Opinion on the War, January 1940-June 1941* (Toronto: Ryerson Press, 1942), v, believed that US entry into the war "broadened the thinking of many French Canadians about the world-wide issues involving Canada." In other words, once the war was no longer viewed as defending Britain's interests, support widened and enlistments increased among French speakers.

43 *Guardian* (Verdun), 20 December 1940 and 17 February 1944; Clavette, "Des bons au chèques," 117.

44 *Guardian* (Verdun), 24 November 1939 and 27 April 1944.

45 More than 1,200 parishioners were on active service. *Guardian* (Verdun), 2 July 1943; *Messenger/Le Messager* (Verdun), 8 November 1945.

46 St Willibrord Parish Honour Rolls, provided by Stewart Carson, Verdun; *Guardian* (Verdun), 29 October 1943 and 9 November 1944.

47 Minutes of the 41st-47th Annual Congregational Meetings 1940-1946, Minutes of Congregational Meetings, Book 2, Chalmers United Church, Verdun.

48 *Proceedings* of the 86th Annual Synod of the Diocese of Montreal, 24-27 April 1945, 128-30, archives of the Church of St John the Divine, Verdun.

49 St Clement's Anglican Church Honour Roll, located in St Clement's, Verdun; Honour Roll in the archives of St John the Divine Anglican Church, Verdun.

50 *Album Souvenir Jubilé d'or, Paroisse Notre-Dame-de-la Garde, 1944-1994* (Verdun, 1994), 23.

51 For a review of French-speaking sentiment during the war, see André Laurendeau, *La crise de la conscription 1942* (Montreal: Les éditions du jour, 1962); and Paul-André Comeau, *Le Bloc populaire 1942-1948* (Montreal: Éditions Québec/Amérique, 1982). Gravel, *Le Québec et la Guerre,* provides a concise indictment of the military's language policy, especially early in the war. See also Douglas and Greenhous, *Out of the Shadows,* 239-41; Bernier and Pariseau, *Les Canadiens français et le bilinguisme;* and K.H.B. Gallant, "The Development of the Canadian Army as a Unilingual Institution in a Bilingual State" (MA thesis, McGill University, 1969). Also useful is Vennat, *Héros oubliés,* a history of French Canada at war as seen through the pages of Montreal's *La Presse.*

52 Gravel, *Le Québec et la Guerre,* 86-92 and 97; Gallant, "Development of the Canadian Army," 78-9 and 133. Stacey, *Arms, Men and Governments,* 420-4, provides a cursory and uncritical treatment of the Department of National Defence's attempts at accommodating French speakers.

53 Gravel, *Le Québec et la Guerre,* 93-4.

54 Douglas and Greenhous, *Out of the Shadows,* 240-1.

55 *Montreal Daily Star,* 5 January 1940. In 1944, only 7.8 percent of air force personnel were French speakers, while the figure was only 2.9 percent for officers. Gravel, *Le Québec et la Guerre,* 95 and 98-9.

56 Gabrielle Roy, *Bonheur d'occasion* (Montreal: Société des Éditions Pascale, 1945); Roger Lemelin, *Les Plouffes* (Quebec: Beauchemin, 1948).

57 *Guardian* (Verdun), 18 April 1941.

58 Gravel, *Le Québec et la Guerre,* 85.

59 1941 Census, vol. 3, 550. Thirty-two percent of French speakers in Verdun defined themselves as unilingual. Many were under fourteen (not yet having any significant exposure to English), and many were female.

60 Léopold Lefort, telephone interview by author, 23 November 1995. Clavette, "Des bons aux chèques," 144-8 and 169, has shown that before 1939 a lower proportion of French speakers than English speakers applied for unemployment relief in Verdun. Although it does not automatically follow that a smaller proportion of French-speaking employable men were in fact unemployed, especially given the Catholic charities to which many did apply for

assistance, her findings suggest that in the first years of the war fewer French speakers than English speakers in Verdun might have felt an economic need to enlist.

61 *Guardian* (Verdun), 16 July 1943

62 Population growth in 1944 and 1945 was probably minimal in congested Ward 3. The municipal census of 31 December 1945 shows the population of Verdun as 74,087, an increase of only 516 since 1943. Most newcomers settled in Ward 4. According to the city clerk, Arthur Burgess, the ward population figures for December 1943 *included* those men and women in the armed forces. Burgess to J.C. Gray, Wartime Housing Limited, 2 February 1945, box A-331, file 3, VBA. A close on-site inspection of the housing on the streets of Ward 3, which has barely changed since the war, is revealing. Taking into account the number of flats and the 1941 average family sizes (between 3.6 and 4.2 members), one cannot escape the conclusion that the population of the ward was somewhat greater than indicated in the municipal census. But in the absence of firmer evidence, this must remain the basic comparative source.

63 1941 Census, vol. 9, 85 and 98.

64 Whyte believed that the twelfth member was rejected as medically unfit. Peer pressure may have influenced these young men's decisions, and those of hundreds of others.

65 Douglas Whyte, interview by author, 21 January 1994.

66 Burns, *Manpower*, 26.

67 1941 Census, vol. 2, 800. The data provided by Zimmerman, "Social Background of the Wartime Navy," 272, indicate that 71 percent of RCNVR officers had attended university. The highest-ranking Verdunite was Col. Percy John Philpott, born in England in 1897 and much decorated during the First World War. But, as he settled in Verdun only in 1940, in which year he rejoined the army, he barely qualifies as a Verdunite. *Guardian* (Verdun), 28 February 1946. Verdun also produced an air force wing commander and a squadron leader, a naval commander, and several army majors.

68 Zimmerman's preliminary analysis suggests that very few French Canadian officers were on naval service. While about 15 percent of RCNVR officers resided in Quebec on enlistment, 40 percent of these were born outside Canada, usually in the British Isles. He also notes that few of the Catholic officers born in Quebec were "unquestionably French Canadian." Zimmerman, "Social Background of the Wartime Navy," 262-6.

69 Gravel, *Le Québec et la Guerre*, 90.

70 Jean Bruce, *Back the Attack!* (Toronto: Macmillan, 1995), vii, 38, 75, and 94. A few women listed by the MCF never served overseas.

71 Maj Walter H. Scott, District Recruiting Officer, to Wilson, 4 November 1942, box A-331, file 6, VBA.

72 *Guardian* (Verdun), 20 August 1943.

73 R.B. Joan Adams, interviews by author, 6 October and 8 November 1993; *Guardian* (Verdun), 20 March 1942; Geneviève Auger and Raymonde Lamothe, *De la poêle à frire à la ligne de feu: La vie quotidienne des québécoises pendant la guerre '39-'45* (Montreal: Boréal Express, 1981), 171-4. See also Ruth R. Pierson, *"They're Still Women after All": The Second World War and Canadian Womanhood* (Toronto: McClelland and Stewart, 1986); Barbara Dundas, *A History of Women in the Canadian Military* (Montreal: Art Global, 2000); Bruce, *Back the Attack!*; and Carolyn Gossage, *Greatcoats and Glamour Boots* (Toronto: Dundurn Press, 1991).

74 *Guardian* (Verdun), 18 April 1941.

75 A. Fortescue Duguid, *History of the Canadian Grenadier Guards 1760-1964* (Montreal: Gazette Printing Company, 1965), 359-60; *Guardian* (Verdun), 3 October 1941.

76 *Guardian* (Verdun), 18 and 26 June 1942, 17 February 1944, and 1 March 1945; City of Verdun, Council Minutes (hereafter cited as "Council Minutes"), 23 June 1942. Poor recruitment

was part of a national trend, and the value of the reserve army was questioned following the war. Burns, *Manpower*, 136-40.

77 Council Minutes, 8 June 1943. Throughout the war, dozens of Verdunites served in the Veterans' Guard, a military organization made up of First and some Second World War veterans employed in various guard and training duties as well as auxiliary services.

78 *Guardian* (Verdun), 11, 18, and 25 June 1943. Paul P. Hutchison, *Canada's Black Watch: The First Hundred Years* (Montreal: Black Watch [Royal Highland Regiment of Canada], 1962), 216. During the Second World War many Verdunites were killed, wounded, or taken prisoner in the course of their service with the Black Watch, which suffered the heaviest casualty toll of any Canadian infantry regiment during the war. Of the over 850 men of the 1st Battalion who left Canadian shores in 1940, only nine returned with the unit in late 1945 (other survivors having returned in earlier drafts). The senior man was Company Sgt-Maj W.F.L. Frost, of Sixth Avenue in Verdun. *Messenger/Le Messager* (Verdun), 22 November 1945; *Guardian* (Verdun), 1 November 1945. The historical links between Verdun and the Black Watch were further cemented in 1999 when the city bestowed on the regiment the Freedom of the City.

79 Burgess, "Verdun: La plus grande banlieue résidentielle de Montréal," box A-237, file 12, VBA. Stewart Carson maintained a scrapbook of press clippings dealing with Verdunites' activities overseas. The scrapbook, made available by Mr Carson, strongly endorses Burgess's views. Even a random reading of the metropolitan press yields numerous announcements of Verdunites' promotions, gallantry awards, and becoming casualties.

80 Taylor to MCF, 14 January 1945, box A-348, VBA.

81 *Spectator* (Hamilton), 19 September 1942, in the Canadian War Museum's searchable database of wartime news clippings. See "Democracy at War: Canadian Newspapers and the Second World War," http://warmuseum.ca/cwm/newspapers/intro_e.html. All *Spectator* and *Globe and Mail* references are from this source.

82 *Guardian* (Verdun), 25 September and 9 October 1942.

83 See George F. Beurling and Leslie Roberts, *Malta Spitfire: The Story of a Fighter Pilot* (Toronto: Oxford University Press, 1943); Brian Nolan, *Hero: The Buzz Beurling Story* (Toronto: Lester and Orpen Dennys, 1981).

84 Beurling was variously nicknamed "Buzz" or "Screwball." He undertook a cross-Canada tour in the winter of 1943 to promote the sale of war bonds, and transferred to the RCAF in September 1943. He shot down two more German aircraft before the end of 1943, bringing his final wartime score to 31⅓ enemy aircraft destroyed. By the time of his discharge in 1944, he had attained the rank of flight lieutenant. Beurling was killed in an airplane crash in Rome in 1948.

85 Shapiro's article appeared in the *Gazette* (Montreal), 9 November 1942; *Montreal Daily Star*, 4 November 1942. Beurling's roots in Verdun were frequently mentioned in the articles about him appearing in the metropolitan press.

86 *Guardian* (Verdun), 23 October 1942; Douglas Whyte, interview by author, 21 January 1994; Nolan, *Hero*, 73. Montrealer Mary Peate wrote in a draft manuscript of her excellent book, *Girl in a Sloppy Joe Sweater: Life on the Canadian Home Front during World War Two* (Montreal: Optimum Publishing, 1988), that some Verdun boys she met as a teenager during the war bragged about Beurling for the duration of a long streetcar ride. Information courtesy of Mary Peate. Beurling's investiture at Buckingham Palace in May 1943 reportedly drew such a large crowd that traffic around the palace was snarled for hours. *Guardian* (Verdun), 28 May 1943; *Messenger/Le Messager* (Verdun), 27 May 1943.

87 *Guardian* (Verdun), 30 October 1942.

88 *Montreal Daily Star*, 10 November 1942.

89 If King was excited to meet Beurling it is not reflected in his unremarkable diary entry of the event on 9 November 1942: "Around 6:30, Pilot Officer Beurling arrived at the East Block, and I welcomed him on behalf of the government and thanked him on behalf of the people as well." See King's diaries on the website of the Library and Archives Canada, http://king.collectionscanada.ca.

90 Mayor Wilson became heavily involved in organizing this event, and the city's share of its cost was more than $800. Executive Committee Minutes, 9 November 1942.

91 *Guardian* (Verdun), 13 November 1942.

92 Whyte was very proud of Verdun's RAF war hero, especially since a good deal of intercity and interservice rivalry existed among the cadet corps in the Montreal area. Douglas Whyte, interview by author, 21 January 1994. Beurling's exploits stimulated RCAF enlistments from Verdun and encouraged recruitment in Verdun High School's air cadet squadron.

93 Douglas Whyte, interview by author, 21 January 1994; *Guardian* (Verdun), 13 November 1942.

94 Council Minutes, 23 November 1942. I resided on Beurling Avenue in Verdun for eleven years and played sports at Beurling Park.

95 *Montreal Daily Star*, 11 November 1942.

96 *La Presse* (Montreal), 11 November 1942, author's translation.

97 *Guardian* (Verdun), 9 and 16 April 1943; *Gazette* (Montreal), 3 April 1943; Verdun High School, *Annual*, 1943, 45 and 51, Canadiana Room, Verdun Cultural Centre; John Buck, interview by author, 19 March 1996; Laurel S. Buck to author, 22 August 1995.

98 Weeks to MCF, 24 June 1943; Cruick to MCF, no date [1943], box A-340, VBA. When another Verdunite, Halifax bomber pilot Henry Malkin, Distinguished Flying Cross and Bar, gained prominence later in the war, the *Guardian* contented itself with referring to him as "a second Beurling." The British-born Malkin, who enlisted as an aircraftsman, was promoted to wing commander in March 1944 and served as one of Verdun's top-ranking officers during the war. *Guardian* (Verdun), 7 May 1943 and 9 March 1944; *Gazette* (Montreal), 5 April 1943. Pilot Officer J.A.L. Lymburner, a French-speaking Verdunite, was another double-DFC recipient who served in 425 (Alouette) Squadron, RCAF. Vennat, *Héros oubliés*, vol. 3, *Du Jour-J à la mobilisation*, 470.

99 *Guardian* (Verdun), 30 December 1942.

100 Flood to MCF, 30 November 1941, box A-333, VBA.

101 Staff Sgt R.M. Thomas, RCASC, to MCF, no date [April 1941], box A-333, VBA.

102 Sgt J. Dunster, RCE, to MCF, 17 December 1941; Taylor to MCF, 4 April 1941, box A-333; Adams to MCF, no date [1942], box A-339, VBA.

103 Kenneth Slade, interview by author, 8 October 1993; Joseph Way, interview by author, 21 September 1993.

104 Gibbons to MCF, 14 December 1941, box A-333; Elder to MCF, 1 August 1944, box A-348, VBA.

105 White to MCF, 25 January 1942; Horsely to MCF, no date [1941], box A-333, VBA. A "sapper" is the generic term for a member of the Royal Canadian Engineers and is also the rank designation equivalent to a "private" soldier in much of the rest of the army.

106 In Second World War veteran Earle Birney's satirical novel, *Turvey, A Military Picaresque* (Toronto: McClelland and Stewart, 1949; reprinted 1963), about the misadventures of a private soldier in the Canadian army during the Second World War, two soldiers ignore Turvey because they were "in deep reminiscences; they had discovered they were from the same home town" (p. 229).

107 Pyndus to MCF, no date [late 1944], box A-348, VBA.

108 *Guardian* (Verdun), 15 June 1944. In late 1942, individuals could no longer ship newspapers overseas, although publishers could do so on a subscription basis. *Guardian* (Verdun), 20 November 1942.

109 Smith to MCF, 19 June 1943, box A-340, VBA.
110 Palmquist to MCF, 13 September 1942, box A-339, VBA.
111 Kitching to MCF, no date [1942], box A-339, VBA.
112 *Guardian* (Verdun), 2 May 1941.
113 Brunet to MCF, 2 April 1941, box A-333, VBA, author's translation.
114 Burns, *Manpower,* 4.

Chapter 3: City Hall Goes to War
1 *Guardian* (Verdun), 27 January 1960 and 24 May 1945.
2 Box A-198, file 32, "Mayor Edward Wilson," Verdun Borough Archives (hereafter VBA). Some mayors in other Canadian cities did as much, for example the mayor of Ottawa, Stanley Lewis. See Jeffrey A. Keshen, *Saints, Sinners, and Soldiers: Canada's Second World War* (Vancouver: UBC Press, 2004), 34.
3 *Messenger/Le Messager* (Verdun), 10 February 1949; *Guardian* (Verdun), 27 September 1945. Most of the short municipal histories in the city archives bear Burgess's signature. He was particularly conscientious about detailing Verdun's military and civil contributions to the war effort.
4 Box A-198, file 32, VBA. Despite his position, French's role in the community was discreet. Neither the *Guardian* nor historical files in municipal archives divulge much about his personal life. The city manager system coordinated and centralized municipal services and expenditures and provided a strong sense of administrative continuity. See Thomas J. Plunkett, *Municipal Organization in Canada* (Montreal: Canadian Federation of Mayors and Municipalities, 1955), 26-33.
5 Wilson did engage in a running war of words with the Ligue des Propriétaires de Verdun, typically over budget matters and the exercise of municipal power, and their exchanges occasionally reflected divisions between French and English speakers.
6 *Guardian* (Verdun), 12 January 1940. On the eve of women in Quebec gaining the right to vote in provincial elections in April 1940, city council voted 5-1 to refuse women the municipal vote. Later that month, Aldermen Brown and Scurrah presented a motion to increase the number of women allowed to vote. This was defeated 5-2, indicating a linguistic divide on the matter. *Montreal Daily Star,* 2 and 16 April 1940.
7 *Guardian* (Verdun), 24 March 1939.
8 *Guardian* (Verdun), 31 March 1939.
9 *Guardian* (Verdun), 7 April 1939. Curiously, this newspaper provides no voting breakdown, although it notes that about 65 percent of eligible residents cast their votes.
10 *Guardian* (Verdun), 14 March 1941.
11 *Guardian* (Verdun), 2 February 1940.
12 Frederick Bruce Horn, letter in *Guardian* (Verdun), 24 January 1941.
13 Letter signed "A Proprietor of Ward 4," *Guardian* (Verdun), 2 April 1943. The executive committee was abolished in a citywide referendum in August 1945. *Guardian* (Verdun), 30 August 1945; City of Verdun, Council Minutes (hereafter cited as "Council Minutes"), 28 August and 11 September 1945.
14 Charles E. Fayle, letter in *Guardian* (Verdun), 2 April 1943.
15 *Guardian* (Verdun), 11 April 1941; André St. Denis, "Pourcentage du vote donné le 7 avril 1941," box A-57, file 5, "Municipal Elections 1941," VBA. Wilson received dozens of congratulatory letters and telegrams from all over the Montreal area and further afield. One came from J.A. Gagnon, perhaps Verdun's leading merchant, and another from Yves Leduc, a local lawyer, Liberal, and strong supporter of the war effort.
16 Noëlla Bisson, interview by author, 21 July 1994, author's translation. She especially meant that part of Verdun east of Willibrord Avenue.

17 Regimental Sgt Maj C.S. Bacon to MCF, 9 April 1941, box A-333, VBA.
18 *Guardian* (Verdun), 16 July 1943.
19 *Guardian* (Verdun), 19 March 1943.
20 From text of Wilson's address over CFCF Radio, 1 April 1943, in box A-57, file 12, "Municipal Election 1943," VBA. Wilson's patriotic pronouncements were published in the *Montreal Daily Star*, 2 and 3 April 1943.
21 *Guardian* (Verdun), 9 April 1943.
22 Letter signed "Fifth Avenue," *Guardian* (Verdun), 16 April 1943; Swain to MCF, no date [winter 1941-42], box A-333, VBA; Mrs Edythe Senior to Wilson, 18 October 1942, box A-339, VBA.
23 *Guardian* (Verdun), 29 March 1945; *Messenger/Le Messager* (Verdun), 22 and 29 March 1945.
24 *Guardian* (Verdun), 5 April 1945; *Messenger/Le Messager* (Verdun), 12 April 1945.
25 Council Minutes, 7 September 1939.
26 The cities of Westmount and Outremont acted similarly. *Montreal Daily Star*, 5 September 1939.
27 Box A-331, file 6, "Guerre 1939-43," VBA.
28 The city of Montreal cut off aid as soon as a man was mobilized for internal security duties. *Guardian* (Verdun), 1 September 1939; Council Minutes, 31 August and 7 September 1939.
29 Executive Committee Minutes, 31 August 1939; Council Minutes, 7 and 18 September 1939; *Montreal Daily Star*, 1 September 1939.
30 "Rapport re assistance aux familles d'énnemis internés," 12 November 1940, box A-361, file "Enemy Aliens 1940-1942," VBA.
31 Not every Quebec municipality was so patriotic. Drummondville's municipal council passed a resolution firmly denouncing Canadian participation in the war. Jean Thibault, *Drummondville à l'heure de la guerre 1939-1945* (Drummondville: La Société d'histoire de Drummondville, 1994), 8.
32 Norman Rogers to Arthur Burgess, 6 June 1940, box A-331, file 6, VBA; *Guardian* (Verdun), 31 May 1940.
33 *Guardian* (Verdun), 14 and 28 June 1940; Executive Committee Minutes, 25 June 1940.
34 Executive Committee Minutes, 12 and 18 August 1941.
35 *Guardian* (Verdun), 14 June 1940.
36 Council Minutes, 25 June 1940; see correspondence in box A-331, file 6, VBA.
37 For the particulars of the NRMA, see Daniel Byers, "Mobilising Canada: The National Resources Mobilization Act, the Department of National Defence, and Compulsory Military Service in Canada, 1940-1945," *Journal of the Canadian Historical Association* 7 (1996): 175-203; J.L. Granatstein and J.M. Hitsman, *Broken Promises: A History of Conscription in Canada* (Toronto: Oxford University Press, 1977); and E.L.M. Burns, *Manpower in the Canadian Army 1939-1945* (Toronto: Clarke, Irwin, 1956).
38 *Guardian* (Verdun), 9 and 23 August 1940.
39 *Guardian* (Verdun), 23 August 1940; Burns, *Manpower*, 126. Barr had a son serving in the RCAF at the time, who was killed in action in 1942.
40 *Guardian* (Verdun), 11 September 1942.
41 Council Minutes, 8 September 1942; Arthur Burgess to the commanding officer of the Canadian army training base at Petawawa, 10 May 1943; Burgess to Pte Paul Perrault, Petawawa, 11 May 1943, and reply 16 May 1943; Sgt Roger Dulude to Burgess, 17 May 1943, box A-331, file 1, VBA. City officials were alarmed to learn that three policemen were found medically unfit for military duty and released. Executive Committee Minutes, 22 February and 14 April 1943.

42 "Employees on Military Service," 29 December 1942, "Exemptions du service militaire des policiers et pompiers de Verdun," October 1944, and miscellaneous correspondence, box A-331, file 1, VBA. All whose deferral was sought by the city were French speakers. See miscellaneous exchange of correspondence from September 1942 to January 1944 between the city, the Department of National Defence, and the Department of National War Services, box A-331, file 1, VBA. The police and fire services employed 100 men. Once hostilities ended, city council unanimously requested the earliest possible discharge of all Verdun policemen and firemen on NRMA or general service. Council Minutes, 14 May 1945; Burgess to A. MacNamara, Deputy Minister of Labour, National Selective Service, 8 June 1945, box A-331, file 1, VBA.

43 These statistics are from Keshen, *Saints, Sinners, and Soldiers*, 25. See also MG 30 E 133, McNaughton Papers, vol. 259, file 932-52, "Cigarette Funds and Cigarette Distribution Overseas," Library and Archives Canada (hereafter LAC).

44 Canada formed women's divisions to the three armed services only in 1941 and 1942.

45 Council Minutes, 25 April and 8 May 1916.

46 RG 44, vol. 70, Register of War Charities Organizations, LAC.

47 *Guardian* (Verdun), 24 August 1944.

48 *Montreal Daily Star*, 4 March 1940.

49 According to Paul Fussell, himself an American Second World War veteran, "anyone in the services who did not smoke cigarettes was looked on as a freak." Fussell, *Wartime: Understanding and Behaviour in the Second World War* (New York: Oxford University Press, 1989), 144-5. See also MG 30 E 133, McNaughton Papers, vol. 259, file 932-52, "Cigarette Funds and Cigarette Distribution Overseas," LAC.

50 *Guardian* (Verdun), 30 December 1941.

51 An example can be found in box A-348, file "1944-45," VBA. Chapter 7 examines the substantial electoral dividends of the MCF for Wilson.

52 See listings in RG 44, Vol. 70, Register of War Charities Organizations; and box A-322, file 1, VBA.

53 *Guardian* (Verdun), 10 and 24 October 1941. Chapter 5 discusses the Red Cross and other social groups.

54 *Guardian* (Verdun), 5 October 1944.

55 *Guardian* (Verdun), 12 October 1944.

56 *Guardian* (Verdun), 30 December 1941.

57 *Guardian* (Verdun), 13 August and 10 September 1943.

58 Executive Committee Minutes, 24 February 1941. Information on group and individual donations is found in box A-348, general correspondence file, and box A-322, file 1, VBA.

59 Lapointe to Wilson, 25 September 1943, box A-348, correspondence file, VBA.

60 B.A. Garson, Wellington Theatre Ltd., to Wilson, 28 December 1943, box A-348, file "1944-45," VBA.

61 Box A-322, file 1; box A-348, correspondence file, VBA.

62 Wilson to Maureen Flannery, 27 May 1942, box A-348, correspondence file, VBA.

63 Tarr to Wilson, October [no date] 1943 and 10 November 1943, and Wilson to Tarr, 9 October 1943, box A-348, correspondence file, VBA.

64 *Guardian* (Verdun), 19 and 30 December 1941.

65 Mayor's Cigarette Fund, press release 10 January 1945, box A-322, file 1; *Guardian* (Verdun), 24 August 1944, 18 January 1945, and 31 October 1946. Wilson's son-in-law, Warrant Officer Alex Stevenson, RCAF, a Verdunite, was posted missing and presumed dead for some time until word was received that he had been taken prisoner by the Germans. He also received cigarettes, nominally from his father-in-law. *Messenger/Le Messager* (Verdun), 19 July 1945.

66 J. Herbert Hodgins et al., *Women at War* (Toronto: Maclean's Publishing, 1943), 50.

67 Trooper W. Gibson to MCF, 25 August 1944, box A-348, file "1944-45," VBA. John Ellis, *The Sharp End of War: The Fighting Man in World War II* (Newton Abbot, UK: David and Charles, 1980), 294-5, shows the link between smoking and morale in the Allied armies.
68 Company Sgt Maj H.P. Charters, MM, RCE, to MCF, postmarked 15 January 1944, box A-348, VBA.
69 Pte W.D. MacDonald to MCF, 6 July 1941, box A-333, VBA. The cigarettes did not please all recipients. Trooper Lorne Barnewall, a scout leader in Verdun, wrote that he disliked "the Army habits one gets into ... I don't like drinking, smoking and carousing around." Box A-348, file "Fonds cigarettes du maire," VBA.
70 Signalman W.E. Payne, Royal Canadian Corps of Signals, to MCF, 13 September 1942, box A-339; Petty Officer Frank D. Harris to MCF, no date [1942], box A-333, VBA.
71 Lance-Cpl J. Flood, RCASC, attached 10th Field Ambulance, to MCF, 20 August 1942, box A-339, VBA.
72 Cobb to MCF, 20 February 1942; Holt to MCF, no date [1942], box A-339, VBA.
73 Guardsman A. Stoddart, 21st Canadian Armoured Regiment (The Governor General's Foot Guards), to MCF, 24 October 1944, box A-348, file "1944-45," VBA.
74 Leading Aircraftsman J.R. Blain, RCAF, to MCF, 18 February 1945, box A-348, VBA.
75 Colligan to MCF, April [no date] 1941, box A-333, VBA.
76 Gélinas to MCF, 17 December 1941, box A-615, VBA.
77 Tremblay to MCF, 2 April 1941, box A-615, VBA.
78 Cpl J. Aldridge, RCAF, to MCF, no date [early 1942], box A-333, VBA.
79 Blampied to MCF, no date [1941], box A-333, file "A," VBA.
80 *Guardian* (Verdun), 16 October 1942. The letter, dated 22 August 1942, was from Cpl J.W. Brazill, Royal Montreal Regiment, to MCF, box A-339, VBA.
81 Lance-Cpl George Shutter, Canadian Provost Corps, to MCF, 29 September 1942, box A-339, VBA.
82 Pte Marcel Sarrasin, RCASC, to MCF, 25 October 1944, file "1944-45," box A-348, VBA.
83 Mrs L.R. Brown to MCF, 24 October 1942, box A-339, file "Requests for 4th Shipment of Cigarettes Overseas," VBA.
84 Frost to MCF, 6 April 1941, box A-333, VBA.
85 Cape to MCF, no date [1942], box A-339, VBA.
86 Brodeur to MCF, 3 March 1941, box A-333, VBA, author's translation. Although 20 percent of the cigarette recipients were French speaking, city hall received very few letters written in French. Some French speakers wrote in English.
87 Meilleur to MCF, 5 March 1942, box A-333, VBA, author's translation.
88 Gunner Richard H. Smith, RCA, to MCF, 19 June 1943, box A-340, VBA.
89 J.A. Callahan, Supervisor, Canadian YMCA Overseas, to MCF, 21 July 1943, box A-340, VBA.
90 René Patenaude, Secretary, MCF, to George Pifher, Director of Voluntary and Auxiliary Services, Department of National War Services, 19 October 1945, box A-348, VBA; *Guardian* (Verdun), 3 October 1946.
91 Leon Trebert, Registrar, War Charities Act, War Charities Division, Department of National Health and Welfare, to Burgess, 7 February 1947, box A-322, file 1, VBA.
92 Council Minutes, 13 December 1949; and M.T. Chisholm, Receptionist (for Medical Superintendent), to Burgess, 12 January 1950, box A-322, file 1, VBA.
93 Quoted in David J. Freeman, *Canadian Warship Names* (St Catharines, ON: Vanwell, 2000), 89. Much of the material here related to *Dunver* was previously published in Serge Durflinger, "'Nothing Would be Too Much Trouble': Hometown Support for H.M.C.S. *Dunver*, 1943-1945," *Northern Mariner* 12, 4 (2002): 1-12. A photo essay of the vessel can be found in Cliff Quince and Serge Durflinger, "Through the Eye of the Lens: Photographs from Aboard the Frigate HMCS *Dunver*, 1943-45," *Canadian Military History* 10, 2 (2001): 60-8.

94 Freeman, *Canadian Warship Names*, 90 and 137.

95 Reference to Côté's letter of 13 November 1941 is made in a press release from the Director-ate of Naval Information published in *Le Devoir* (Montreal), 11 May 1943. The destroyer HMS *Verdun* was named for the First World War battle.

96 In August 1943 Mayor Wilson, using data obtained from the files of the Mayor's Cigarette Fund, estimated that 800 Verdunites, nearly 20 percent of residents in uniform, were in the navy – a higher-than-average proportion of one city's enlistees in that service. Wilson to Capt J.E. Oland, Naval-Officer-in-Charge, Montreal, 24 August 1943, box A-331, file 7, VBA.

97 Paymaster Lt-Cdr Robert Pennington, Secretary, Naval Board, to Wilson, 10 September 1942, box A-331, file 7, "Guerre 1939-1948 et HMCS *Dunver*," VBA. A similar situation oc-curred at almost exactly the same time in Edmonton because of the similarity with "Edmundston," the name of a ship already in service with the RCN. See Bruce Ibsen, "A Name If Necessary, But Not Necessarily a Name: Why There Was No H.M.C.S. Edmonton," in *For King and Country: Alberta in the Second World War*, ed. Kenneth W. Tingley (Edmonton: Provincial Museum of Alberta, 1995), 139-41. During the war several hundred Canadian warships were named for Canadian communities, large and small.

98 Freeman, *Canadian Warship Names*, 90 and 292.

99 *Guardian* (Verdun), 25 September 1942.

100 "Competition to name a Canadian Warship in Honor of Verdun" (list of contest results); Wilson to Pennington, 3 November 1942, box A-331, file 7, VBA. All correspondence is lo-cated in this file. Loss through fire of the *Messenger* for this period has made it impossible to determine whether the contest was advertised in French. No evidence in the city ar-chives suggests that it was.

101 Macdonald to Wilson, 10 April 1943, box A-331, file 7, VBA.

102 J.B.O. Saint-Laurent, Secrétaire, La Ligue des Propriétaires de Verdun, to Burgess; 7 May 1943, box A-331, file 7, VBA, author's translation.

103 Georges Boivin, Secrétaire, Société Saint-Jean-Baptiste, Section Notre-Dame-de-la-Paix, to Burgess, 31 May 1943, box A-331, file 7, VBA, author's translation. The Société's sugges-tion was itself a unilingual name.

104 Macdonald, devoting considerable attention to this potentially embarrassing situation, wrote Côté on 21 July suggesting the name "Ville de Verdun," as had been done with "Ville de Québec." Côté wisely replied that the unilingualism of this name might make it unac-ceptable to a large number of his English-speaking constituents. Côté to Macdonald, 24 July 1943, box A-331, file 7, VBA.

105 Photograph of the event with caption, box A-242, file 35, VBA; "Livre d'Or des Visiteurs, Ville de Verdun," City Hall, Verdun. In addition to *Dunver*, the minesweeper *Westmount* and the frigate *Beacon Hill* (named for Victoria) also had commanders from their name-sake communities. This was not necessarily the design of NSHQ, however. See Rick James, "The West Coast's Very Own Frigate," *Argonauta* (Canadian Nautical Research Society) 11, 1 (1994): 18.

106 J.D. Prentice, Acting Captain, Captain (D) Halifax, to Rear-Admiral Leonard Murray, Com-mander-in-Chief, Canadian Northwest Atlantic, 7 October 1943, RG 24, vol. 11,555, file N.S. D. 4-29-0, LAC; NSHQ to Naval-Officer-in-Charge Quebec, 09/2017; NOIC Quebec to NSHQ 10/1623; NSHQ to NOIC Quebec 11/1717, RG 24, vol. 5836, file NS8000 – 381/12, LAC. *Dunver* was the only Canadian warship to be named through the transposition of letters or syllables.

107 Robert Bruce to author, March 1994.

108 A. Keith Givens to author, June 1994; Clifford Biggar to author, June 1994.

109 Macdonald to Wilson, 10 April 1943, box A-331, file 7, VBA.

110 Capt Helen Curwood, Acting Commandant, WVRC, to Burgess, 21 June 1943, box A-331, file 7, VBA.

111 Lt André Marcil, for Lt-Cdr Woods, to Wilson, 13 September 1943, box A-331, file 7, VBA.

112 "Re: Verdun Frigate Reception at Wood Hall Friday 24th September 1943," box A-331, file 7, VBA; *Guardian* (Verdun), 17 September and 1 October 1943; Executive Committee Minutes, 14 September 1943.

113 Quoted in *Guardian* (Verdun), 1 October 1943. Born into a seafaring family in Liverpool in 1899, Woods was a First World War veteran and master of merchant vessels between the wars. He had moved to Verdun in 1930. *Guardian* (Verdun), 15 June 1944. Woods was named an OBE (Officer of the Order of the British Empire) in the King's New Year's Honour List in January 1944 – an award that brought great pride to Verdun. *Guardian* (Verdun), 6 and 13 January 1944; Burgess to Woods, 19 January 1944, box A-242, file 35, VBA.

114 Lt Gordon K. Daley, Directorate of Special Services, NSHQ, to Mrs H.S. Angus, Imperial Order Daughters of the Empire, 19 May 1943, MG 28, I 17, vol. 23, file 1, "Adoption of Ships," LAC.

115 "List of articles sent to the crew of H.M.C.S. *Dunver* since the adoption of this ship by the citizens of the City of Verdun," 17 March 1945, box A-331, file 7, VBA; Wilson to Woods, 24 September 1943, and René Patenaude, Secretary, MCF, to Woods, 21 December 1943, box A-348, VBA.

116 Capt L.J.M. Gauvreau, RCN, Naval-Officer-in-Charge Quebec, to Burgess, 8 October 1943; Burgess to Woods, 18 April 1944, box A-331, file 7, VBA. Wartime restrictions on the production of non-essential consumer goods drastically curtailed the manufacturing of irons and washing machines. For example, the production of washing machines fell from 117,512 in 1940 to a mere 13,200 a year later. Statistics from Keshen, *Saints, Sinners, and Soldiers*, 94.

117 Wilson to Lt William Davenport, commanding officer, *Dunver*, 6 September 1944, and reply, 29 November 1944, box A-331, file 7, VBA. Victoria also provided *Beacon Hill* with two washing machines and a piano, and was even able to procure for its ship some toasters and irons. James, "West Coast's Very Own Frigate," 18. North Bay, Ontario, organized a Comfort Fund Committee for sailors serving aboard the corvette *North Bay*. Residents contributed enough money to purchase a washing machine for the vessel and also sent a phonograph and many other small items. See Cuthbert Gunning, *H.M.C.S. "North Bay": One Ship's Role in War and Peace 1943-1992* (North Bay, ON: privately printed, 1995), 8-9 and 39.

118 In 1945 the city established a "Special Fund" for *Dunver*. When the ship was decommissioned, the remaining $211 was turned over to the MCF. Council Minutes, 21 October 1946.

119 The money for the projector was provided by such groups as the Imperial Corps of Frontiersmen, the Legion, the Lion's Club, the Verdun Community Club, St Willibrord's Social Club, and the Verdun Voters' League. The projector was not actually received aboard ship until 5 April, with the first movie shown two days later. Acting Cdr St. Clair Balfour, RCNVR, to Wilson, 7 April 1945, box A-331, file 7, VBA; *Messenger/Le Messager* (Verdun), 21 December 1944; *Guardian* (Verdun), 21 December 1944; *Gazette* (Montreal), 23 January 1945; Burgess to J.R. French, 6 February 1945, box A-331, file 7, VBA.

120 Council Minutes, 13 November 1944.

121 Walter Finlay to author, April 1994.

122 Fifteen former crewmen, none of whom was from Verdun, answered the author's questionnaire regarding their service in *Dunver*: St. Clair Balfour, Clifford Biggar, Robert Bruce, C.C. Chapman, John Croal, Frank Dion, Walter Finlay, A. Keith Givens, Albert Jackson, D.P. Keller, Walter Mitham, Clifford Quince, John Seale, Harry Speed, and D.C. Walsh. Three other men sent photos only: Douglas Earish, Gordon Hill, and E.L. Taylor.

123 Jean Nugent to Mrs Bella Nugent, no date cited, quoted in *Guardian* (Verdun), 27 July 1944.

124 Lt-Cdr Scott Fyfe, for Director of Naval Information, to Burgess, 10 February 1945, box A-331, file 7, VBA.
125 *Guardian* (Verdun), 26 October 1944.
126 Royal Canadian Navy Press Release, 12 February 1945, box A-331, file 7, VBA; *Montreal Daily Star*, 13 February 1945; *Guardian* (Verdun), 15 February 1945. A postwar reassessment of U-boat kills has credited two British warships with the destruction of *U-484*. *Dunver, Hespeler,* and the British aircraft are now considered to have attacked a non-U-boat contact. Axel Niestlé, *German U-Boat Losses During World War II: Details of Destruction* (London: Greenhill Books, 1998), 69 and 229. The press and population of Red Deer, Alberta, also keenly followed the service of their namesake ship, a Bangor-class minesweeper, even though no residents served aboard. See Michael Dawe, "Community in Transition: Red Deer in the Second World War," in Tingley, *For King and Country*, 126.
127 Clifford Biggar to author, July 1994.
128 *Gazette* (Montreal), 25 October 1943; *Guardian* (Verdun), 6 January 1944; *Montreal Daily Star*, 13 February 1945; *Messenger/Le Messager* (Verdun), 7 March 1946. Nine of fifteen former crewmen were nevertheless able to recall and name shipmates originally from Verdun.
129 One crewman recalled that life aboard *Dunver* was so pleasant because of the "diversity of backgrounds and hometowns in Canada and Newfoundland" of the crew. Walter Mitham to author, May 1994.
130 *Messenger/Le Messager* (Verdun), 12 December 1946; *Gazette* (Montreal), 12 December 1946. As of 2006, the bell was hanging in the Verdun branch of the Royal Canadian Legion. Sections of *Dunver's* rusted hull still exist as part of a breakwater in Royston, British Columbia.
131 *Guardian* (Verdun), 22 September 1939.
132 Executive Committee Minutes, 18 and 25 September 1939.
133 *Guardian* (Verdun), 24 November 1939; *Messenger/Le Messager* (Verdun), 19 June 1990, special supplement, "50ᵉ anniversaire de l'Auditorium de Verdun."
134 Quoted in *Guardian* (Verdun), 28 June 1940. City council had made the same offer on 27 May.
135 Council Minutes, 25 June, 2, 9, and 23 July 1940.
136 Council Minutes, 21 October 1940. The irate Verdun Red Devils Hockey Club sought $6,750 for losses actual and anticipated.
137 Council Minutes, 27 January 1941.
138 J.R. French, "Statement Showing Revenue at Auditorium from Hockey Leagues, November 14, 1939 to April 4, 1940," 10 April 1940, box A-330, file 4, and "Statement of Revenue and Expenditures for the Municipal Auditorium, for Year Ended December 31, 1940," 24 March 1941, box A-330, file 8, VBA.
139 Council Minutes, 29 April and 2 and 22 July 1941. The auditorium was still occasionally used for various public war-related events, such as Victory Loan rallies and other patriotic causes.
140 *Le Canada*, 14 August 1941. Other RCASC and RCE units and detachments also made use of the auditorium before war's end.
141 *Guardian* (Verdun), 14 November 1941.
142 Ibid.
143 *Guardian* (Verdun), 28 November 1941; letter from 3rd (Reserve) Division, RCASC, to city hall, 27 October 1941, box A-330, file 8, VBA.
144 *Guardian* (Verdun), 1 May 1942.
145 Quoted in *Guardian* (Verdun), 30 October 1942.
146 Problems in Halifax are well documented in Jay White, "Conscripted City: Halifax and the Second World War" (PhD diss., McMaster University, 1994). Cuthbert Gunning, *North*

224 Notes to pages 75-81

Bay's Fort Chippewa 1939-1945 (North Bay, ON: privately printed, 1991), 72-3, and Thibault, *Drummondville,* 119-26, also describe similar problems.
147 *Guardian* (Verdun), 25 July 1941.
148 Council Minutes, 22 November 1943 and 24 January 1944; box A-330, file 4, "Hockey," VBA.
149 Municipal statistics published in the *Guardian* (Verdun), 18 May 1944, showed that the city had recorded a budget surplus of over $16,000 in the previous fiscal year while reducing its bonded debt by $350,000.
150 *Guardian* (Verdun), 21 June 1945; box A-258, file 1-3, VBA.
151 "Roving Reporter," *Guardian* (Verdun), 13 September 1945; Council Minutes, 24 September 1945. Fears of juvenile crime may have influenced municipal authorities' desire to have the building returned as soon as possible. City hall believed that the availability of recreational facilities would lessen the likelihood of local delinquency.
152 Council Minutes, 11 and 18 February, 11 March, and 1 April 1946.

Chapter 4: The People's Response

1 Verdun War Savings Committee, Minutes, 28 November 1940, box A-331, file 6, Verdun Borough Archives (hereafter cited as VBA).
2 A Red Cross booklet published in 1942 included a chapter on air-raid precautions stating that the distance from German-occupied Norway to Canada was less than some missions then flown by the Royal Air Force. *Emergencies in War*, p. 68, box A-331, file 5, "Canadian Red Cross – General," VBA.
3 *Montreal Daily Star*, 5 and 11 September, 13 October, and 30 November 1939. See also Jay White, "Conscripted City: Halifax and the Second World War" (PhD diss., McMaster University, 1994), 131. White notes that, including all who assisted in any capacity, 6,000 Haligonians performed Civilian Protection Committee duties during the war.
4 *Montreal Daily Star*, 6 September and 21 October 1939; *Guardian* (Verdun), 3 October 1941. On 5 September 1939 Sherbrooke city council discussed imposing a partial blackout.
5 *Spectator* (Hamilton), 20 December 1940.
6 CPC Minutes, 19 June 1940, box A-258, file 4, VBA.
7 CPC Minutes, 25 October 1940, box A-258, file 4, VBA; *Guardian* (Verdun), 16 January 1942.
8 CPC Minutes, 25 June 1940, box A-258, file 4, VBA.
9 Press release issued following the CPC meeting of 25 June 1940, box A-322, file 3-A, "C.P.C. – General," VBA.
10 Circular letter from Wilson to Verdun clergy, 28 June 1940, box A-276, file 2, "Comité Protection Civile Verdun – Correspondence." Wilson's words were borrowed from Charles Barnes.
11 1941 Census, vol. 3, 76, 198, and 398; Charles Moyce, Secretary, Canadian Corps Association, Section No. 1, Verdun, to Burgess, 10 September 1942. Although the minimum age for joining the CPC was set at forty, Verdunites aged thirty-five to thirty-nine in 1941 attained this age before the CPC disbanded in 1945.
12 CPC registration form, box A-322, file 3, VBA.
13 CPC Minutes, 5 July 1940, box A-258, file 4, VBA. For the February 1941 statistics, see box A-276, file 2, VBA. The number of French-speaking district wardens fluctuated by one or two in 1942 and 1943. Verdun CPC list of officers, 30 December 1942, box A-322, file 3-A, VBA; *Guardian* (Verdun), 25 June 1943.
14 CPC Minutes, 31 July 1940, box A-258, file 4, VBA. The growing Verdun contingent of the CPC was part of a larger Quebec-wide network of 28,000 people enrolled in ARP activities by November 1940. Geneviève Auger and Raymonde Lamothe, *De la poêle à frire à la ligne*

de feu: La vie quotidienne des québécoises pendant la guerre '39-'45 (Montreal: Boréal Express, 1981), 107.

15 *Guardian* (Verdun), 30 August 1940.

16 CPC Minutes, 25 October 1940, box A-258, file 4, VBA. Some of the volunteer firemen might be also included in the number enrolled in the first-aid course. The city agreed to loan seventy-five rubber coats and 100 pairs of rubber boots for use by the CPC volunteer firemen.

17 CPC Minutes, 31 July and 25 October 1940, box A-258, file 4, VBA; *Guardian* (Verdun), 3 October 1941; *Centre Hospitalier de Verdun 1932-1982* (booklet), box A-242, file 12, VBA.

18 CPC, report on "Organization and Activities," 17 June 1941, box A-276, file 2, VBA.

19 Barr to Wilson, 9 January 1942, box A-276, file 2, VBA.

20 The guest list is in box A-276, file 2, VBA.

21 Wilson noted this in a letter to the Verdun Catholic School Commission reminding it of the need for individual schools to make arrangements to safeguard the lives of pupils. Wilson to R.E. Mackay, Secretary, VCSC, 10 January 1942, box A-322, file 3-A, VBA.

22 CPC Minutes, 20 November 1940, box A-258, file 4, VBA.

23 Executive Committee Minutes, 15 October 1940.

24 Barr to Cornwall (Ontario) Volunteer Guard, 31 October 1940, box A-276, file 2, VBA.

25 *Guardian* (Verdun), 3 October 1941.

26 By March 1942, the federal government had placed the Montreal area in category C (slight risk). Only that part of Quebec east of Sorel remained in category B. *Montreal Daily Star*, 3 March 1942. As late as November 1943, however, the federal government still categorized Montreal as at risk. *Guardian* (Verdun), 11 November 1943.

27 Wilson to Barnes, 12 December 1941, box A-322, file 3-A, VBA. The mayor sent three letters on this date to various authorities demanding action on matters related to the Verdun CPC.

28 *Canada at War*, no. 23, April 1943, 33-4.

29 Ross to Burgess, 26 January 1942, box A-322, file 3, VBA.

30 Ross to local CPC organizations, 14 January 1942, box A-322, file 3-A, VBA.

31 *Guardian* (Verdun), 16 January 1942.

32 *Guardian* (Verdun), 30 August 1940; Executive Committee Minutes, 12 August 1941.

33 Wilson to Barr, 30 May 1942, box A-276, file 2.

34 *Messenger/Le Messager* (Verdun), 14 January 1943; box A-331, file 6, VBA. The government distributed an impressive amount of equipment to provincial ARP organizations including two million gas respirators, 150,000 steel helmets, 80,000 stirrup pumps, 1,000 sirens, 12,000 firemen's coats, 30,000 flashlights, and 40,000 overalls. *Canada at War*, no. 25, June 1943, 31.

35 CPC, report on "Organization and Activities," 17 June 1941, box A-276, file 2, VBA.

36 Ibid. See also *Guardian* (Verdun), 16 May 1941.

37 Barr to R.B. Joan Adams, 8 May 1941, box A-322, file 3, VBA. In June 1942, Montreal's ARP auxiliary fire service organized a women's division – the first of its kind in North America. Auger and Lamothe, *De la poêle à frire*, 109.

38 In the summer of 1943 Verdun received permission from provincial CPC headquarters to organize blackouts covering only its territory. *Guardian* (Verdun), 25 June 1943.

39 CPC, "Trial Blackout, Instructions to Wardens" and "Organization and Activities," in box A-276, file 2, VBA; *Guardian* (Verdun), 13 June 1941. The CPC wardens were also on the lookout for any "criminal acts" occurring in these brief moments of total darkness.

40 Wilson to Ross, 12 December 1941; Ross to Francis Fauteux, City Solicitor, no date [late June 1941], box A-322, file 3-A, VBA.

41 Burgess to Gaboury, 2 March 1942, and reply, 5 March 1942, box A-322, file 3-B, VBA.

42 CPC, report on "Organization and Activities," 17 June 1941, box A-276, file 2, VBA.
43 Verdun CPC press release, no date [February 1942], box A-322, file 3-B, VBA.
44 *Guardian* (Verdun), 23 October 1942.
45 *Guardian* (Verdun), 29 October 1943.
46 *Guardian* (Verdun), 7 September 1944.
47 *Guardian* (Verdun), 31 October 1941.
48 Ross to Burgess, 26 January 1942, box A-322, file 3, VBA.
49 *Messenger/Le Messager* (Verdun), 29 July 1943.
50 C. Meehan, Secretary-Adjutant, Verdun CPC, to Burgess, 22 October 1943, box A-322, file 3-A, VBA.
51 Barr to Gaboury, 17 December 1943, box A-276, file 2, VBA. Similar problems afflicted ARP organizations elsewhere. Nationally, 775 communities had set up CPC units. The peak year was 1942 with 280,000 Canadians nominally engaged in ARP duties. Many units had begun winding down before the end of 1943. Steven Lee, "Power, Politics and the Cold War: The Canadian Civil Defence Program and the North Atlantic Alliance, 1945-1959" (MA thesis, McGill University, 1987), 12. As of July 1943, 226,800 Canadians, including 45,000 women, in 622 communities still volunteered for ARP duties. In the areas of primary importance along both coasts and including certain industrial areas of Quebec and Ontario, ARP organizations could count on the services of more than 14,500 firemen, 26,000 first-aid workers and stretcher bearers, 6,500 nurses, and 1,600 physicians. *Canada at War*, no. 21, February 1943, 21; and no. 24, May 1943, 26.
52 *Guardian* (Verdun), 22 June 1944. Gordon Galbraith recalled that he was never the least bit worried about an air raid or any other enemy action in wartime Verdun. Interview by author, 13 November 1993.
53 *Guardian* (Verdun), 22 June 1944.
54 Provincial CDC Circular Letter No. 26, 13 October 1944, box A-322, file 3-A, VBA; *Guardian* (Verdun), 5 October 1944 and 22 February 1945.
55 "Campagne Nationale de Récupération," pamphlet published by the Ministère des Services nationaux de guerre, April 1941, box A-331, file 2, "Salvage," VBA.
56 Miss E. Heywood to Edward Wilson, 11 June 1941, box A-452, file "Salvage Campaign, 1941-44," VBA. The patriotic Miss Heywood also informed Wilson, "I was more than pleased to think we had a decent Englishman to represent the City when our beloved King and Queen came to Montreal ... I come from Lancashire also."
57 *Le Canada*, 1 August 1941, author's translation; *Gazette* (Montreal), 1 August 1941; *La Patrie* (Montreal), 31 July 1941. "Aluminum Scrap is wanted to help in Scrapping Hitler," ran one headline in the *Messenger*, 31 July 1941. Salvaging aluminum was problematic because many pots and pans had too little aluminum content to be useful. In Britain, according to one author, "throughout the country, there were strategic piles of unwanted cooking pans." Richard Connaughton, *Celebration of Victory: V-E Day 1945* (London: Brassey's, 1995), 79.
58 *Guardian*, 8 August 1941.
59 *Messenger* (Verdun), 31 July 1941. Ottawa estimated in 1942 that one ton of waste paper yielded sufficient reusable material to produce 1,500 shell containers, while twenty-five old automobiles would yield enough metal to produce a tank. *Canada at War*, no. 11, 1 February 1942, 14.
60 *Guardian* (Verdun), 15 August 1941; C.T. Russell to Wilson, 30 Aug 1941, box A-452, file "Salvage Campaign 1941-44," VBA. The Verdun and Montreal press frequently overestimated, sometimes wildly, the tonnage of salvaged goods.
61 *Gazette* (Montreal), 9 August 1941.
62 *Canada at War*, no. 11, 1 February 1942, 14-15.

63 From the autumn of 1940 to the end of 1941, Verdun's Woodland Boy Scout troop had made 10,000 house calls across the Island of Montreal and collected 43 tons of newsprint. They donated their money to a Boy Scout Spitfire Drive and to the Mayor's Cigarette Fund. *Guardian* (Verdun), 23 January 1942.

64 Jean Cool to City of Verdun, 19 January 1942, box A-331, file 2, VBA, author's translation.

65 Executive Committee Minutes, 22 December 1941; City of Verdun, Council Minutes (hereafter "Council Minutes"), 19 January 1942; RG 44, vol. 72, War Charities Organizations, LAC; Arthur Burgess to E.W. Stapleford, Director of Voluntary Services, Department of National War Services (DNWS), 1 April 1942, box A-331, file 2, VBA. Similar efforts were made by the civic administrations of nearby Westmount, Lachine, and Outremont. In November 1941, two Verdun aldermen met with Westmount officials to review Westmount's recently established salvage organization. Council Minutes, 24 November 1941. One very successful salvage operation was set up in Winnipeg a full year before the creation of the national campaign. Gertrude Laing, *A Community Organizes for War* (Winnipeg, 1948), 22-9.

66 Verdun Salvage Committee, "Report of Salvage Collections for February 1942," 5 March 1942, box A-331, file 2, VBA; *Messenger/Le Messager* (Verdun), 5 March 1942.

67 Detailed monthly reports prepared by the VSC showing the number of pickups, the tonnage of kinds of material salvaged, and the value obtained through resale are located in box A-331, file 2, VBA.

68 DNWS, National Salvage Division, Statement of Salvage Operations, to 30 November 1942, dated 10 December 1942; and to 13 December 1943, dated 14 January 1944, box A-331, file 2, VBA.

69 Arthur Burgess to Roger Charbonneau, Provincial Organizer, National Salvage Campaign, 4 February 1942; Burgess to Steinberg's Wholesale Groceterias, 23 February 1942; Burgess to William Knightley, Supervisor, National Salvage Campaign, 16 April 1942 and reply, 21 April 1942, box A-331, file 2, VBA.

70 Transportation continued to be the greatest problem and expense in salvage operations. "Noms des propriétaires des camions prêtés re: cueillette de la Récupération 22 avril 1942," box A-331, file 2, VBA; *Gazette* (Montreal), 23 April 1942, claimed that this salvage drive yielded 600 tons of material, which is unlikely.

71 "Gigantic Salvage Collection – 22 April," City of Verdun press release, 14 April [?] 1942, box A-331, file 2, VBA.

72 Wilson to Barr, 5 October 1944, box A-331, file 2, VBA. By 1943 there was little else of practical value for the CPC to do in Verdun.

73 Verdun Salvage Committee, "Statements of Receipts and Expenditures," 1942 to 1945, and VSC reply to questionnaire sent by Roger Charbonneau, Provincial Organizer, National Salvage Campaign, June 1942, box A-331, file 2, VBA.

74 By the spring of 1943, the prices for many commodities, especially rubber, had actually fallen. "List of prices re: salvage materials," prepared by the city of Verdun's purchasing agent, G.E. Noël, 20 May 1943.

75 Technically, this was a contravention of the War Charities Act of 1939, which in 1941 had been amended to disallow any fundraising necessitating expenditures of 25 percent or more of gross receipts. This problem had become common nationwide but was clearly difficult to monitor.

76 Box A-452, file "Salvage Campaign 1941-1944"; and material in box A-331, file 2, VBA.

77 Alfred Dubeau died in 1943.

78 Quoted in *Guardian* (Verdun), 11 May 1944; see also *Guardian* (Verdun), 1 May 1942.

79 Auger and Lamothe, *De la poêle à frire*, 61.

80 *Messenger/Le Messager* (Verdun), 28 January 1943. In wartime Verdun, more paper was amassed by weight than steel, which corresponded with the central and eastern Canadian trend. The reverse occurred in the west. Nationally, the most profit came from the sale of rags and old clothes.

81 *Guardian* (Verdun), 11 May 1944.

82 *Canada at War*, no. 36, May 1944, 40.

83 *Guardian* (Verdun), 12 April 1945; DNWS Bulletin No. 96, 15 May 1945, box A-331, file 2, VBA.

84 *Guardian* (Verdun), 12 April and 3 May 1945; example of flyer and photo-description of event, box A-331, file 2, VBA. Boy Scouts contributed valuable war work in Verdun.

85 Verdun Salvage Committee, "Report of Salvage Collections," 1942-45; DNWS, National Salvage Division, Statement of Salvage Operations to 31 December 1943, dated 14 January 1944, box A-331, file 2, VBA. In its 1945 annual report, the city of Westmount claimed that from 1941 until September 1945 the staggering total of 1,882 tons of salvage was collected in that city, which had less than half the population of Verdun.

86 Circular letters from DNWS, 15 and 26 September 1945; Council Minutes, 9 October 1945; DNWS to Burgess, 5 March 1946 and 12 April 1946, and reply 29 May 1946, box A-331, file 2, VBA.

87 J. Douglas Gibson, "Financing the War," in *Canadian War Economics*, ed. J.F. Parkinson (Toronto: University of Toronto Press, 1941), 38-9.

88 Norman Hillmer, "Victory Loans," in *The New Canadian Encyclopedia* (Edmonton: Hurtig, 1988), vol. 4, 2262. Desmond Morton and J.L. Granatstein note that $10.2 billion was raised. *Victory 1945: Canadians from War to Peace* (Toronto: HarperCollins, 1995), 86.

89 Verdun War Savings Committee, Minutes, 28 November and 5 December 1940, box A-331, file 6, VBA.

90 J.R. French to city council, 13 January 1941, box A-331, file 1, "War: Salaries, Military Training, Bonus, etc.," VBA. While purchasers could cash them in at any time, 75 percent of Victory Loan sales remained in government coffers at the end of 1944. *Canada's Weekly*, 7 September 1945.

91 E.J. Quinn, Associate Director, Payroll Savings Division, National War Savings Committee, to City of Verdun, no date [probably April 1941], box A-331, file 1, VBA; *Montreal Daily Star*, 16 April 1941.

92 It was easier for the employees to agree to the scheme because the city simultaneously increased weekly salaries $3.75 as a cost of living allowance. J.R. French to Executive Committee, 7 and 19 January 1942; Council Minutes, 7 January 1942 and 11 September 1945. In the twelve months ending January 1942, $28,000 had been raised from municipal employees, a figure that well satisfied the city council. Burgess memo, 28 January 1942, box A-331, file 1, VBA.

93 "War Certificates Campaign – November 1941," box A-331, file 6, VBA.

94 Material in box A-331, file 6, VBA.

95 Verdun War Savings Committee, Minutes, 5 December 1940, box A-331, file 6, VBA.

96 *Guardian* (Verdun), 12 and 19 July 1940; Serge Marc Durflinger, "Owing Allegiance: The British Community in Verdun, Quebec during the Second World War," *Canadian Ethnic Studies* 36, 1 (2004): 14.

97 *Guardian* (Verdun), 25 April 1941; *Canada's Weekly*, 14 April 1944 (published in London for Canadians overseas). War Savings Certificates were sold at 80 percent of their face value and matured to 100 percent seven and a half years later. Morton and Granatstein, *Victory 1945*, 86. By March 1943, the number of students enrolled in Verdun's Protestant schools had dropped to 4,700. The fundraising efforts of Verdun students compare favourably with those of Edmonton, whose high school students purchased $1,145 in War Savings

Stamps in November 1941. See Jeffrey Keshen, "Morale and Morality on the Alberta Home Front," in *For King and Country: Alberta in the Second World War*, ed. Kenneth W. Tingley (Edmonton: Provincial Museum of Alberta, 1995), 155.

 98 *Guardian* (Verdun), 2 July 1943.

 99 Gibson, "Financing the War," 38 and 41.

100 *Guardian* (Verdun), 30 May 1941.

101 *Guardian* (Verdun), 6 June 1941.

102 *Montreal Daily Star*, 12 June 1941.

103 *Guardian* (Verdun), 13 June 1941.

104 *Messenger/Le Messager* (Verdun), 26 April 1945. Other cities, too, engaged in rivalries over the amounts of money raised. See Jeffrey A. Keshen, *Saints, Sinners, and Soldiers: Canada's Second World War* (Vancouver: UBC Press, 2004), 33-4.

105 French to Executive Committee, 10 June 1941, box A-331, file 1, VBA.

106 *Guardian* (Verdun), 12 November 1943; Council Minutes, 8 November 1943.

107 J.R. French to city council, 9 March 1942, and his reports following each Victory Loan campaign, box A-331, file 1, VBA; *Guardian* (Verdun), 24 April 1942.

108 *Guardian* (Verdun), 12 November 1943; Council Minutes, 8 November 1943.

109 Council Minutes, 13 November 1944.

110 *Guardian* (Verdun), 7 May 1943.

111 *Guardian* (Verdun), 16 November 1944; see also material in box A-331, file 1, VBA.

112 *Guardian* (Verdun), 17 May 1945; Executive Committee Minutes, 28 May 1945; box A-331, file 1, VBA. Exhorting Verdunites to invest in the war against Japan, the *Messenger* reminded readers unequivocally that "Canadians were at Hong Kong! Our Australian brothers are menaced! ... Japan must be levelled to a couple of barren rocks." 26 April 1945. Despite its 125 percent subscription, Verdun did not place in the top ten Canadian oversubscribed cities in May 1945. Glace Bay, Nova Scotia, led the country with 151 percent. *Montreal Daily Star*, 18 June 1945.

113 French to Executive Committee, 3 November 1945, box A-331, file 1, VBA; *Guardian* (Verdun), 1 and 15 November 1945.

114 For the contributions of Canadian women during the Second World War, see Ruth R. Pierson, *"They're Still Women after All": The Second World War and Canadian Womanhood* (Toronto: McClelland and Stewart, 1986); Ruth R. Pierson, *Canadian Women and the Second World War*, historical booklet 37 (Ottawa: Canadian Historical Association, 1983); Carolyn Gossage, *Greatcoats and Glamour Boots* (Toronto: Dundurn Press, 1991); Auger and Lamothe, *De la poêle à frire*; and Jeffrey A. Keshen, "Revisiting Canada's Civilian Women during World War II," *Histoire sociale/Social History* 30, 60 (1997): 239-66.

115 For a good discussion of Canadian women's paramilitary groups, see Jean Bruce, *Back the Attack!* (Toronto: Macmillan, 1995), 21-35.

116 *Guardian* (Verdun), 26 July 1940; *Gazette* (Montreal), 26 April 1941; other information in box A-331, file 7, "Guerre 1939-48," VBA.

117 Her candidacy is discussed in Chapter 7.

118 R.B. Joan Adams, interview by author, 8 November 1993; Paul P. Hutchison, *Canada's Black Watch: The First Hundred Years* (Montreal: Black Watch [Royal Highland Regiment of Canada], 1962), 196.

119 Unidentified Montreal newspaper article, probably April 1941, copied from the personal files of R.B. Joan Adams.

120 *Montreal Daily Star*, 10 April 1941.

121 *Guardian* (Verdun), 23 August 1940 and 22 August 1941.

122 *Gazette* (Montreal), 26 April 1941.

123 R.B. Joan Adams, interview by author, 8 November 1993.

124 That the Verdun unit was merely a branch of the Westmount parent organization did not sit well with some of the Verdun women. Events reached a climax in March 1941, when Mrs Pauline McKibbon, at the helm of the Verdun WVRC, sought to sever ties with the Westmount group and create an independent Verdun organization. She failed and relinquished her command. WVRC, Minutes of Meeting, 17 March 1941; McKibbon to City of Verdun, 19 March 1941; and Arthur Burgess's marginal notation of 21 March 1941, box A-330, file 5, VBA; *Guardian* (Verdun), 21 March 1941.

125 Pierson, "*They're Still Women*," 265 n 41, has estimated that by March 1943, nearly two years after the creation of the Canadian Women's Army Corps, approximately ninety women's military auxiliary groups totalling over 7,100 members existed in Canada. Most petitioned Ottawa for some sort of formal recognition as participants in the war effort. Gossage, *Greatcoats and Glamour Boots*, 24-5. WVRC units were also established in Ontario, New Brunswick, and Nova Scotia. *Gazette* (Montreal), 26 April 1941; *Montreal Daily Star*, 1 June 1941.

126 *Guardian* (Verdun), 20 March 1942; R.B. Joan Adams, interview by author, 8 November 1993. Nevertheless, Pierson, in "*They're Still Women*," has shown that much of the work assigned these women in uniform fell within the traditional female occupational sphere. A good deal of WVRC work remained gender-based, perhaps no activity more so than the ongoing clothing collection for British victims of war. Women of the WVRC gathered, cleaned, mended, and packed clothing, often late into the night. Adams, interview, 8 November 1993.

127 *Guardian* (Verdun), 10 July 1942; R.B. Joan Adams, interview by author, 8 November 1993.

128 *Guardian* (Verdun), 3 October 1941.

129 Unidentified Montreal newspaper clipping, October 1942, copied from the personal files of R.B. Joan Adams. In an earlier speech to the women of Verdun's Chalmers United Church, she insisted that women engaged in war work or patriotic causes were "Canada's shock force." On this occasion, Adams emphasized gender differences as opposed to gender equality. In a May 1942 speech to the Verdun Sisterhood, she repeated the male-inspired view that women made excellent industrial labourers because they were more dexterous than men, more docile, and less prone to monotony. Moreover, she insisted that any family dislocation linked to increased female wage work be attributed to the war itself and not to women's abdication of their social responsibilities. To avoid any such difficulties, she offered the government the following advice: "give our women homes, destroy the slums, and they will seek employment within the home and never desire to leave it." *Guardian* (Verdun), 15 May 1942.

130 *Messenger/Le Messager* (Verdun), no date [January 1942], from the personal files of R.B. Joan Adams.

131 Mary Davidson, "The Social Adjustment of British Immigrant Families in Verdun and Point St. Charles" (MA thesis, McGill University, 1933), 53-4.

132 *Guardian* (Verdun), 16 and 23 October 1942, 11 October 1945.

133 Charles Graves, *Women in Green: The Story of the W.V.S.* (London: Heinemann, 1948), 45-6. R.B. Joan Adams, interviews by author, 6 October and 8 November 1993.

134 *Guardian* (Verdun), 23 May 1941. See also Durflinger, "Owing Allegiance," 14.

135 Wilson to Panet, 10 July 1941, box A-331, file 6, VBA; *Messenger/Le Messager* (Verdun), 10 July 1941, estimated the crowd at 18,000.

136 *Montreal Daily Star*, 15 August 1941.

137 *Montreal Daily Star*, 16 August 1941.

138 Maurice Hébert, publiciste du gouvernement et directeur général de l'Office du Tourisme, to Wilson, 18 August 1941, and reply, 26 August 1941, box A-331, file 7, VBA, author's translations;

La Presse (Montreal), 4 September 1941; *Le Canada*, 2 September 1941; Burgess to Recruiting Centre, MD 4, 29 June 1944, box A-331, file 7, VBA.
139 Council Minutes, 9 September 1941; *Guardian* (Verdun), 12 September 1941.
140 *Guardian* (Verdun), 11 September 1942; City of Verdun press release, 3 September 1942, box A-331, file 6, VBA; Durflinger, "Owing Allegiance," 15.
141 As of 2004 the Verdun Branch of the Royal Canadian Legion continued to organize the only known Ypres Day Parade in Canada, though it was a shadow of former celebrations.
142 *Guardian* (Verdun), 28 April 1939.
143 *Guardian* (Verdun), 26 April 1940.
144 *Guardian* (Verdun), 1 May 1942.
145 Peter G. Goheen, "Symbols in the Streets," *Urban History Review* 18, 3 (1990): 237-40.

Chapter 5: Institutions and Industry
1 Perhaps no one was more active in this manner than Mayor Edward Wilson, who was a member (sometimes honorary) of a dozen or more community-based associations and boards with social, ethnic, religious, business, civic, and educational affiliations.
2 Lloyd G. Reynolds, *The British Immigrant: His Social and Economic Adjustment in Canada* (Toronto: Oxford University Press, 1935), 138-9; Mary Davidson, "The Social Adjustment of British Immigrant Families in Verdun and Point St. Charles" (MA thesis, McGill University, 1933), 211.
3 Suzanne Clavette, "Des bons aux chèques: Aide aux chômeurs et crise des années 1930 à Verdun" (MA thesis, Université du Québec à Montréal, 1986), 43-4. Mgr Richard almost single-handedly built up his huge parish (as well as others in Verdun), controlled the Verdun Catholic School Commission, and in 1932 had erected l'Hôpital Christ-roi, a Catholic institution.
4 Gertrude Laing, *A Community Organizes for War* (Winnipeg, 1948), 1.
5 In 1939 Ottawa passed the War Charities Act, which defined and regulated the activities of the tens of thousands of non-profit war charities that eventually registered with the government. A bewildering array of patriotic charities of all sizes were registered in this fashion. The war charities were administered by the Department of National War Services. See RG 44, vols. 66 and 67, Registers of War Charities Organizations, Library and Archives Canada (hereafter LAC).
6 Laing, *A Community Organizes for War*, 16.
7 Jay White, "Conscripted City: Halifax and the Second World War" (PhD diss., McMaster University, 1994), 253.
8 While both Canadian linguistic groups contributed to Canada's war effort, they only occasionally did so jointly, with French-language participation normally subordinated to the English. This might explain in part the lack of recognition accorded French-speaking groups generally in both English- and French-language historiographies of Canada's Second World War home front.
9 Arthur Burgess, "Cité de Verdun: La plus grande banlieue residentielle de Montréal," typewritten manuscript, March 1962, box A-237, file 12, Verdun Borough Archives (hereafter VBA).
10 City of Verdun, Council Minutes (hereafter "Council Minutes"), 7 September 1939; *Guardian* (Verdun), 8 September 1939.
11 Executive Committee Minutes, 18 September 1939.
12 *Guardian* (Verdun), 22 September 1939; Minutes of the Fifth Annual Meeting of the Canadian Red Cross Society, Verdun Branch, 11 February 1944, box A-331, file 5, VBA. Mrs Wermenlinger, wife of Verdun's MP at the start of the war, and Mrs Lafleur, wife of Verdun's MLA, were also early Red Cross organizers.

13 *Guardian* (Verdun), 3 November 1939.
14 For example, the claim is somewhat misleading that in 1943 over 2.6 million Canadians of all ages worked for the Red Cross. Only between 700,000 and 800,000 of these were women workers producing items for overseas distribution, a proportion at any given time of 26 to 30 percent. The remainder were volunteers engaged in other essential, though often occasional, work, such as staffing offices, hospitals, and clinics. The figure also includes hundreds of thousands of schoolchildren working for the Red Cross from time to time as a regular school activity. *Facts on Red Cross Activities* (Toronto: Canadian Red Cross Society, 1944), p. 31, box A-331, file 5, VBA. See also the Canadian Red Cross Society's *Annual Report*, 1939, RG 44, vol. 39, LAC.
15 *Guardian* (Verdun), 27 February 1941; 1941 Census, vol. 2, 256-7. In 1944, the city estimated that at its peak the Red Cross comprised 1,300 women organized in thirty-three subgroups. Arthur Burgess, "Verdun's War Effort," *Canada's Weekly*, 14 April 1944, p. 41, box A-242, file 50, "Période de Guerre," VBA. The *Montreal Daily Star*, 16 August 1941, using municipally supplied statistics, stated 1,800 Verdun women were engaged in Red Cross work. In any case, over 1,400 Verdun women seem to have worked for the Red Cross at one time or another during the war.
16 Geneviève Auger and Raymonde Lamothe, *De la poêle à frire à la ligne de feu: La vie quotidienne des québécoises pendant la guerre '39-'45* (Montreal: Boréal Express, 1981), 109-11.
17 *Guardian* (Verdun), 22 September 1939.
18 *Guardian* (Verdun), 29 September 1939.
19 *Guardian* (Verdun), 16 February 1940.
20 Canadian Red Cross Society, Verdun Branch (list of officers and executive committee), 7 July 1944, box A-331, file 5, VBA.
21 By comparison, the local branch of the Imperial Order Daughters of the Empire had only eleven active members in February 1940, and this after nineteen years of existence. The IODE was a middle- or upper-class organization that attracted few Verdunites. In May 1940 the Verdun IODE registered as a war charity and pledged to provide comforts and clothing, especially knitted goods, to Canadian troops slated to go overseas. *Montreal Daily Star*, 20 February 1940; *Guardian* (Verdun), 6 October 1939 and 23 February 1940.
22 "Liste des organisations de charité dans les paroisses canadiennes-françaises de la Cité de Verdun," 30 October 1941, box A-331, file 6, VBA.
23 *Guardian* (Verdun), 28 February 1941; *Montreal Daily Star*, 13 March 1940; Minutes of the Fifth Annual Meeting of the Canadian Red Cross Society, Verdun Branch, 11 February 1944, box A-331, file 5, VBA.
24 Noted in Auger and Lamothe, *De la poêle à frire*, 111.
25 *Guardian* (Verdun), 24 November 1939 and 15 March 1940; *Montreal Daily Star*, 15 November 1939.
26 *Montreal Daily Star*, 15 November 1939. This system of Red Cross canvassing was employed in Verdun throughout the war.
27 *Montreal Daily Star*, 23 November 1939.
28 *Guardian* (Verdun), 24 January 1941; box A-331, file 5, VBA.
29 *Guardian* (Verdun), 19 March 1943 and 24 February 1944.
30 In March 1944, a Red Cross appeal netted $350 from Verdun's Catholic students, with a disproportionately high $100 contributed by the city's only English-language parish, St Willibrord's. Procès-verbaux du Conseil des Commissaires, Commission des Écoles Catholiques de Verdun, 14 March 1944, Archives de la CECV.
31 *Guardian* (Verdun), 9, 16, and 23 August 1940.
32 *Guardian* (Verdun), 3 November 1939.
33 *Chalmers United Church: Fifty Years 1899-1949* (Verdun, 1949), 18 and 21; Minutes of the

42nd to the 47th Annual Congregational Meetings 1941-46, Minutes of Congregational Meetings, Book 2, Chalmers United Church, Verdun.

34 *Guardian* (Verdun), 5 April 1940.

35 Auger and Lamothe, *De la poêle à frire*, 109.

36 Minutes of the Fifth Annual Meeting of the Canadian Red Cross Society, Verdun Branch, 11 February 1944, box A-331, file 5, VBA. Similar talks given by repatriated prisoners of war across Canada all mentioned the essential work of the Red Cross.

37 *Facts on Red Cross Activities*, p. 11, box A-331, file 5, VBA.

38 Quoted in *Guardian* (Verdun), 3 February 1944.

39 *Guardian* (Verdun), 3 February 1944.

40 *Guardian* (Verdun), 2 and 23 November 1944.

41 Minutes of the Fourth Annual Meeting of the Canadian Red Cross Society, Verdun Branch, 9 February 1943, box A-331, file 5, VBA.

42 Minutes of the Fifth Annual Meeting of the Canadian Red Cross Society, Verdun Branch, 11 February 1944, box A-331, file 5, VBA. There is no surviving evidence to determine whether there was a language element to this decline in membership.

43 Minutes of the 42nd to the 47th Annual Congregational Meetings 1941-46, Chalmers United Church, Verdun. Jay White, in his study of Halifax during the war, notes in a general discussion of female voluntarism that "enthusiasm waned in the latter stages of the war when the novelty of the experience wore off and the long hours and meagre rewards began to take their toll." "Conscripted City," 254.

44 Minutes of the Fourth Annual Meeting of the Canadian Red Cross Society, Verdun Branch, 9 February 1943, box A-331, file 5, VBA.

45 1941 Census, vol. 2, 718-19.

46 Unfortunately, postwar fires destroyed the wartime records at both the Verdun Legion and the Legion's Quebec Command headquarters.

47 *The 1939 Anniversary Programme of the Verdun (No. 4) Branch of the Canadian Legion, British Empire Service League, Verdun*, 31 October 1939, 6, provided courtesy of Sydney Ashford.

48 *Montreal Daily Star*, 31 May 1940; *1939 Anniversary Programme*, 11 and 31.

49 *1939 Anniversary Programme*, 18-19 and inside back cover.

50 Ibid., 31.

51 Desmond Morton and Glenn Wright, *Winning the Second Battle: Canadian Veterans and the Return to Civilian Life, 1915-1930* (Toronto: University of Toronto Press, 1987), 215 and 218.

52 *Guardian* (Verdun), 14 December 1944.

53 Clifford H. Bowering, *Service: The Story of the Canadian Legion 1925-1960* (Ottawa: Canadian Legion, 1960), 103-21; *Montreal Daily Star*, 28 May 1940.

54 See Chapter 7 for a full discussion of the 1942 plebiscite in Verdun.

55 Harold C. Cross, *One Hundred Years of Service with Youth: The Story of the Montreal Y.M.C.A.* (Montreal: Southam Press, 1951), 288, 317, and 331. The Verdun YMCA did not operate a hostel.

56 Davidson, "Social Adjustment," 213.

57 "Report of Member Associations for the Calendar Year 1941," and letter from Walter Kemball, Executive Secretary of the Southwestern Branch, to R.E.G. Davis of the National Council of the YMCA, 16 May 1941, MG 28, I 95, vol. 291, file 17, LAC.

58 See list in MG 28, I 95, vol. 291, file 18, LAC. Davidson, "Social Adjustment," 97, noted that Verdun's "Y" was "an institution ... not much used by the poorer classes." East of Church Avenue, there were fewer people as well as a lower percentage of English speakers than elsewhere in Verdun.

59   Annual report of the Southwestern YMCA 1939-1940, MG 28, I 95, vol. 291, file 18, LAC.
60   Ibid.
61   Ibid.; Cross, *One Hundred Years of Service*, 325.
62   Annual report of the Southwestern YMCA 1939-1940, MG 28, I 95, vol. 291, file 18, LAC; *Guardian* (Verdun), 8 September 1939. Mrs Gladys MacFarlane and Miss Hannah Baird, who were lost in the sinking, were Verdun's first fatal casualties of the Second World War. *Montreal Daily Star*, 10 October 1939.
63   Annual report of the Southwestern YMCA 1939-1940, MG 28, I 95, vol. 291, file 18, LAC.
64   "Model Aeroplane Building By Y.M.C.A. Boys in Co-operation with the R.C.A.F., Department of Armaments," no date [1941?], MG 28, I 95, vol. 291, file 18, LAC; *Guardian* (Verdun), 3 October 1941.
65   R.S. Hosking, note to file of 4 February 1941, MG 28, I 95, vol. 108, file 20, LAC.
66   Walter Kemball, Executive Secretary of the Southwestern Branch of the YMCA, to Richard S. Hosking, National Council of the YMCA, 7 June 1941, and additional material in MG 28, I 95, vol. 108, file 20, "Defence Industries Limited, Brownsburg, Quebec, Correspondence and Miscellaneous 1940-1944," LAC.
67   "List of Public Buildings in Verdun at January 20th/40," box A-237, file 40, VBA; City of Verdun Annual Report, 1944, box A-99, VBA.
68   *Chalmers United Church 1899-1974* (Verdun, 1974), 13, Archives of Chalmers United Church, Verdun.
69   "Roll of Honor," St Williborod's Parish, Verdun, September 1939-June 1944, mimeograph provided courtesy of Mr Stewart Carson, former warden.
70   *Chalmers United Church: Fifty Years 1899-1949* (Verdun: 1949), 13, commemorative booklet found in box A-242, file 16, VBA.
71   Ibid., 14; Minutes of the 44th to 48th Annual Congregational Meetings 1943-1947, Minutes of Congregational Meetings, Book 2, Chalmers United Church, Verdun.
72   *Messenger/Le Messager* (Verdun), 8 November 1945; "Roll of Honor," St Williborod's Parish, Verdun. The comforts included woollen socks, mitts, toothpaste, gum, and razor blades. *Guardian* (Verdun), 29 October 1943.
73   *Guardian* (Verdun), 3 and 17 October 1941.
74   *Messenger/Le Messager* (Verdun), 8 November 1945.
75   1941 Census, vol. 4, 158-61.
76   *Album Souvenir de la Bénédiction solenelle de l'église Notre-Dame Auxiliatrice* (Verdun, May 1942); *Album souvenir 75e Anniversaire de la Paroisse Notre-Dame-Des-Sept-Douleurs Verdun 1899-1974* (Verdun, 1974); *25ième Anniversaire de la fondation de la paroisse Notre-Dame-de-Lourdes* (Verdun, October 1953); and *Les 50 ans de Notre-Dame-de-Lourdes Verdun 1928-1978* (Verdun, 1978). All located in the Canadiana Room, Verdun Cultural Centre.
77   Annual report of the Protestant Board of School Commissioners (Montreal), 1939-40, p. 4, Archives of the Protestant School Board of Greater Montreal (hereafter PSBGM Archives).
78   Annual report of the Protestant Board of School Commissioners (Montreal), 1940-41, pp. 6 and 8, PSBGM Archives. On the other hand, John Parker, who taught at Woodland School from 1940 to 1942, has not recalled that the war significantly affected his teaching habits. There were occasional discussions about the war in his elementary class, but he organized no special war-related events with his pupils. Interview by author, 14 January 1994.
79   Verdun High School, *Annual*, 1941, 7, Canadiana Room, Verdun Cultural Centre. Like young Protestant Verdunites, high school students in Dorchester, New Brunswick, were convinced that the war was just and based their "loyalty" in "a revealing trinity: the British Empire, Canada, and the local community." Douglas How, *One Village, One War 1914-1945* (Hantsport, NS: Lancelot Press, 1995), 259. One study of two Ottawa high schools notes that students there "took on serious responsibilities and acquired a remarkable sense of

purpose." Christine Hamelin, "A Sense of Purpose: Ottawa Students and the Second World War," *Canadian Military History* 6, 1 (1997): 35.

80 Verdun High School, *Annual*, 1941, 6, Canadiana Room, Verdun Cultural Centre.

81 Montreal Protestant Central School Board, Board Meeting Agenda, 22 December 1942 (M261a), PSBGM Archives; *Guardian* (Verdun), 25 June 1944.

82 St Willibrord High School, *Green and White Annual*, 1944, provided by Paul Moreau, Lasalle, Quebec. See also *Revue Souvenir: Jubilé d'or de la Commission des Écoles Catholiques de Verdun 1898-1948* (Verdun: Commission des Écoles Catholiques de Verdun, 1948), 26-7, Archives de la CECV, in which some of the over 600 former students on active service are remembered for having rendered "the supreme sacrifice for God and Country."

83 Louise Matthews, "Diary of a Sodalist," 25 October 1943, in St Willibrord High School, *Green and White Annual*, 1944, 15.

84 St Willibrord High School, *Green and White Annual*, 1944, 21 and 27.

85 Verdun High School, *Annual*, 1941, 5, Canadiana Room, Verdun Cultural Centre.

86 Ibid., 9-10; *Guardian* (Verdun), 6 September 1940.

87 Annual reports of the Protestant Board of School Commissioners (Montreal), 1942-43, p. 7, and 1943-44, p. 4, PSBGM Archives; *Annuals*, 1941-46. In comparison, it has been estimated that between 1941 and 1944 attendance at Edmonton high schools decreased as much as 50 percent. Many of the dropouts seem to have found full-time employment to assist their mothers, who were struggling to make ends meet on meagre Dependants' Allowances. See Jeffrey A. Keshen, "Morale and Morality on the Alberta Home Front," in *For King and Country: Alberta in the Second World War*, ed. Kenneth W. Tingley (Edmonton: Provincial Museum of Alberta, 1995), 156.

88 Verdun High School, *Annual*, 1943, 42, Canadiana Room, Verdun Cultural Centre. Weintraub went on to produce films for the National Film Board and write books, articles, and plays on the theme of language relations in Montreal, as well as on other topics.

89 Verdun High School, *Annual*, 1941, 57, Canadiana Room, Verdun Cultural Centre; Annual reports of the Protestant Board of School Commissioners (Montreal), 1940-41, p. 9, and 1941-42, pp. 11-12, PSBGM Archives; *Guardian* (Verdun), 28 November 1941.

90 Verdun High School, *Annual*, 1942, 8, Canadiana Room, Verdun Cultural Centre; *Guardian* (Verdun), 23 January 1942.

91 Annual reports of the Protestant Board of School Commissioners (Montreal), 1942-43, p. 13, and 1943-44, p. 26, PSBGM Archives; Verdun High School, *Annual*, 1944, 35, and 1945, 30, Canadiana Room, Verdun Cultural Centre. The Verdun High School Air Cadet Squadron was not disbanded until 1966. Charles Elliott, *A Short History of Verdun High School 1912-1984* (Montreal: PSBGM, 1990), 14. In January 1943 all Edmonton high schools combined mustered about 750 cadets aged twelve to seventeen, an unimpressive figure for a city of over 90,000. Keshen, "Morale and Morality," 155.

92 See for example the Procès-verbeaux du Conseil de Commissaires, CECV, 9 December 1941 and frequently thereafter, Archives de la CECV. The Parents Association of St Willibrord Parish noted in 1945 that "grave friction is arising between the French- and English-speaking Catholics because several hundred English-speaking Catholic children have had to be accommodated in classes in French-speaking schools because of lack of accommodation in their own schools." *Guardian* (Verdun), 15 March 1945.

93 Procès-verbeaux, CECV, 14 November 1939, 9 February, 27 May, and 30 July 1940, 4 February and 24 March 1941, 7 April and 5 May 1942, and 9 November 1943, Archives de la CECV.

94 Annual report of the Protestant Board of School Commissioners (Montreal), 1941-42, pp. 9-10, PSBGM Archives.

95 Annual report of the Protestant Board of School Commissioners (Montreal), 1943-44, p. 11, PSBGM Archives.

96   Author's translation, Canadiana Room, Verdun Cultural Centre.

97   Robert Rumilly, *Histoire de la Société Saint-Jean-Baptiste de Montréal: Des patriotes au fleurdelisé 1934-1948* (Montreal: L'Aurore, 1975), 452-4.

98   Ibid., 485. On page 486 of Rumilly's skewed and anti-Semitic work, he claims without providing any evidence that 90 percent of French Canadians agreed with this sentiment.

99   Ibid., 488-9; Alphonse de la Rochelle, chef du secrétariat, La Société Saint-Jean-Baptiste to Lt-Col Eugène Nantel, Director of Auxiliary Services, MD 4, 1 December 1939 and reply 2 December 1939, microfilm 8003, pp. 001958-59, Archives nationales du Québec (hereafter ANQ), Montreal.

100   See the exchange of correspondence between Alphonse de la Rochelle, chef du secrétariat, La Société Saint-Jean-Baptiste, Lt-Col Eugène Nantel, Director of Auxiliary Services, MD 4, and W. Gordon Gunn, Registrar, National War Charities, Department of the Secretary of State, Ottawa, 4-22 June 1940, microfilm 8003, pp. 002011-23, and also the extract from the Société's Executive Council Meeting of 2 July 1940, microfilm 8003, p. 002047, ANQ.

101   See microfilm 8003, pp. 002136-53, ANQ; and Rumilly, *Histoire de la Société Saint-Jean-Baptiste,* 488-9 and 497. Rumilly frankly documents the Société's antiwar views and especially its vehement opposition to conscription and Jewish immigration to Canada (pp. 448-541). The Société Saint-Jean-Baptiste de Montréal claimed 8,000 members in 1942, 8,500 in 1943, and 9,100 in 1944 (p. 537). Still, Red Cross working units organized by the many chapters of the Société Saint-Jean-Baptiste across Quebec provided over 23,000 knitted items during the war. Auger and Lamothe, *De la poêle à frire,* 111. The wartime attitudes expressed by the elitist Société Saint-Jean-Baptiste in Montreal or Quebec City did not apply to all French-speaking Quebecers.

102   The Chevaliers de Colomb, for example, was perhaps a more popular group, since it was seen as class inclusive. Some French-speaking traditional elites therefore considered it a vulgar association, with an "Irish taint." Everett C. Hughes, *French Canada in Transition* (Chicago: University of Chicago Press, 1943), 123, 127-8.

103   Auger and Lamothe, *De la poêle à frire,* 55.

104   See box A-348, correspondence file, VBA.

105   C.P. Stacey, *Arms, Men and Governments: The War Policies of Canada, 1939-1945* (Ottawa: Queen's Printer, 1970), 504.

106   J. de N. Kennedy, *History of the Department of Munitions and Supply* (Ottawa: King's Printer, 1950), vol. 1, 8.

107   For further details on Canadian war production and its importance to the Canadian economy and to the Allied war effort, see ibid.; H. Duncan Hall and C.C. Wrigley, *Studies of Overseas Supply* (London: HMSO, 1956); and H. Duncan Hall, *North American Supply* (London: HMSO, 1955).

108   A good summary of Montreal's military-industrial expansion can be found in Economics and Statistics Branch, Department of Munitions and Supply (DMS), "War Employment in Canada – Geographical Report," 5th ed., 15 January 1944, RG 28 A, vol. 187, LAC.

109   Economics and Statistics Branch, DMS, "Report on Government-Financed Expansion and Industrial Capacity in Canada as at December 31, 1943," 29 February 1944, RG 28 A, vol. 188, LAC.

110   Kennedy, *Department of Munitions and Supply,* vol. 1, 77. Some of this material on Defence Industries Limited was published in Serge Durflinger, "Making Wartime Continue: War Industry and Economic Recovery in Verdun, Quebec 1941-1946," in *Canada 1900-1950: A Country Comes of Age,* ed. Serge Bernier and John Macfarlane, 77-86 (Montreal: Organization for the History of Canada, 2003).

111 Council Minutes, 11 March and 27 August 1940.
112 Burgess to the War Supply Board, 4 April 1940, box A-331, file 6, VBA. Municipalities across Canada lobbied Ottawa for defence contracts or military installations. For a description of the origins and responsibilities of this department, see Kennedy, *Department of Munitions and Supply*, vol. 1, 3-9.
113 G.K. Sheils, Director of Administration, War Supply Board, to Burgess, 9 April 1940, box A-331, file 6, VBA; "Capital Requirements of Defence Industries Limited 1941," RG 95, vol. 591, file "Defence Industries Limited," LAC.
114 Economics and Statistics Branch, DMS, "Report on Government-Financed Expansion and Industrial Capacity in Canada as at December 31, 1943," 29 February 1944, RG 28 A, vol. 188, LAC; "Capital Requirements of Defence Industries Limited 1941," RG 95, vol. 591, file "Defence Industries Limited," LAC; Ken Smith, *Ajax: The War Years 1939/45* (Toronto: Ken Smith and Alger Press, 1989), 129; *Messenger/Le Messager* (Verdun), 1 June 1944.
115 DMS, "Report of the Arsenals and Small Arms Ammunition Branch," 1943, pp. 18-19, RG 28 A, vol. 26, file 1, LAC; Kennedy, *Department of Munitions and Supply*, vol. 1, 77-85; *Guardian* (Verdun), 20 December 1940.
116 Kennedy, *Department of Munitions and Supply*, vol. 1, 110-34 and 301.
117 Economics and Statistics Branch, DMS, "Report on Government-Financed Expansion and Industrial Capacity in Canada as at December 31, 1943," 29 February 1944, RG 28 A, vol. 188, LAC. The small businesses evicted by government expropriation of the site were displeased, and at least some at first "refused to move." Hugh H. Turnbull, Acting Secretary, DMS, to W.J. Neville, DMS, 18 October 1940, RG 28, vol. 383, file 4-L-42, "Expropriation of Dominion Textile Co. Ltd., Verdun, P.Q.," LAC.
118 *Guardian* (Verdun), special supplement, 23 May 1946. By comparison, the enormous plant of Sorel Industries Limited, which produced the 25-pounder gun – the standard artillery piece of Commonwealth field regiments – contained approximately 600,000 square feet of factory space and employed 3,000 workers. At its peak, DIL-Verdun employed 6,800. See Kennedy, *Department of Munitions and Supply*, vol. 1, 193.
119 Kennedy, *Department of Munitions and Supply*, vol. 1, 77.
120 DMS, "Report of the Arsenals and Small Arms Ammunition Branch," 1943, pp. 19-20, RG 28 A, vol. 26, file 1, LAC. This report noted that "it has been extremely difficult to establish a stabilized picture at [the Verdun] plant due to the frequently changing requirements" (p. 20). See also Kennedy, *Department of Munitions and Supply*, vol. 1, 77-9 and 83.
121 *Guardian* (Verdun), 23 May 1946 and special supplement, 23 May 1946.
122 DMS, "Report of the Arsenals and Small Arms Ammunition Branch," 1943, p. 22, RG 28 A, vol. 26, file 1, LAC; Kennedy, *Department of Munitions and Supply*, vol. 1, 83-4.
123 Kennedy, *Department of Munitions and Supply*, vol. 1, 88. During the war British industry produced approximately 10 billion rounds of small-arms ammunition and the rest of the Commonwealth, nearly 4 billion. The United States manufactured the enormous total of 42 billion. Hall and Wrigley, *Studies of Overseas Supply*, 51 and 477; Hall, *North American Supply*, 427.
124 Kennedy, *Department of Munitions and Supply*, vol. 1, 76.
125 Economics and Statistics Branch, DMS, "Estimated Production of Firms Engaged in War Production," 20 February 1941, RG 28 A, vol. 188, LAC.
126 Economics and Statistics Branch, DMS, "Estimated Employment on War Production," 18 October 1943, RG 28 A, vol. 188, LAC. The proportion in Verdun rises to 18 percent if the figure of 4,949 employed in Verdun in July 1943 is used, as stated in Economics and Statistics Branch, DMS, "War Employment in Canada – Geographical Report," 5th ed., 15 January 1944, RG 28 A, vol. 187, LAC.

127 Council Minutes, 7 May 1941; Côté to city council, 15 May 1941, box A-331, file 6, VBA, author's translation.
128 *Guardian* (Verdun), 20 December 1940.
129 Executive Committee Minutes, 13 January 1941.
130 *Guardian* (Verdun), special supplement, 23 May 1946.
131 Executive Committee Minutes, 2 February 1942. The DIL-Verdun site apparently offered employees the best available conveniences and comforts. *Guardian* (Verdun), special supplement, 23 May 1946.
132 *Spectator* (Hamilton), 9 November 1942.
133 Council Minutes, 7 January 1942. See Chapter 6 on the housing crisis in Verdun.
134 Executive Committee Minutes, 23 June, 30 and 31 July 1942.
135 Howe to Wilson, 12 August 1942, text reproduced in Executive Committee Minutes, 12 August 1942.
136 R.R. Buchanan, Personnel Superintendent, Verdun Works, DIL, to Wilson, 13 October 1942, box A-322, file 1, VBA.
137 L.R. Wood, Secretary, Silver Bullet Club, to Norman Dawe, Municipal Playgrounds Commissioner, no date [May 1942], and reply, 1 June 1942, box A-258, VBA; Executive Committee Minutes, 9 November 1942.
138 *Guardian* (Verdun), 23 December 1943; *Messenger/Le Messager* (Verdun), 23 December 1943.
139 *Guardian* (Verdun), 12 March 1943.
140 *Guardian* (Verdun), 2 April 1943.
141 Kennedy, *Department of Munitions and Supply*, vol. 1, 83 and 86.
142 *Guardian* (Verdun), special supplement, 23 May 1946. War Assets, a Crown corporation created by order-in-council in November 1943, served as a clearing house for all surplus government wares.
143 *Guardian* (Verdun), 24 May 1945 and 13 September 1945.
144 *Guardian* (Verdun), special supplement, 23 May 1946.
145 *Guardian* (Verdun), 1 November 1945 and special supplement, 23 May 1946.
146 *Guardian* (Verdun), 2 May 1946 and special supplement, 23 May 1946.
147 Because of Côté's rather muted stance on the war, discussed in Chapter 7, he heard little praise in Verdun. Howe had added the reconstruction portfolio to that of munitions and supply in October 1944; they were merged in December 1945.
148 *Guardian* (Verdun), 23 May 1946.
149 See also *Globe and Mail*, 1 June 1946.

Chapter 6: Family and Social Dislocation

1 For example, in June 1944 one women living in Edmonton wrote her husband overseas: "I am far from as helpless as I once thought I was. I depended on you for everything but have made the pleasant discovery I can handle almost anything on my own ... I have been able to take care of everything ... With a given sum, I can budget my expenses and do really well." Lynn Fish, ed., "Kathlyn's Letters," *Beaver* 81, 5 (2001): 18.
2 John Parker, an elementary school teacher at Woodland School, recalled that the war was not a particularly noteworthy period for him. His most vivid memories focus on his personal life and work experience, both, he recalled, only indirectly affected by wartime conditions. Interview by author, 14 January 1994.
3 For a detailed overview of Canadian wartime housing policy and problems, see Humphrey Carver, *Houses for Canadians* (Toronto: University of Toronto Press, 1948); and John C. Bacher, "Keeping to the Private Market: The Evolution of Canadian Housing Policy 1900-1949" (PhD diss., McMaster University, 1985), published as *Keeping to the Marketplace: The*

Evolution of Canadian Housing Policy (Montreal and Kingston: McGill-Queen's University Press, 1993).

4 *Montreal Daily Star*, 25 November and 16 December 1939. Virtually every week in the first year of the war, this newspaper's real estate section detailed housing construction in Verdun.

5 Statistic from Jeffrey A. Keshen, *Saints, Sinners, and Soldiers: Canada's Second World War* (Vancouver: UBC Press, 2004), 78.

6 Quoted in Bacher, "Private Market," 276.

7 Bacher, "Private Market," 287.

8 WPTB Rentals Administration to Wilson, 7 February 1941, box A-331, file 7, Verdun Borough Archives (hereafter VBA); Bacher, "Private Market," 288-92.

9 Harry Shaver, Canadian Corps Association, to city council, no date [spring 1941], box A-331, file 7, VBA; Executive Committee Minutes, 3 February 1941.

10 Burgess, marginal notation to City of Verdun, Council Minutes extract of 29 April 1941; Legion to city council, 23 September 1941, box A-331, VBA.

11 *Guardian* (Verdun), 25 October 1940, 4 July 1941, 20 March 1942, and 21 May 1943; *Montreal Daily Star*, 11 May 1940.

12 1941 Census, vol. 9, 166. By the winter of 1944, municipal census figures showed Verdun's population had increased a whopping 5,947 over the previous year. Even if the figures are exaggerated, overcrowding must have been severely exacerbated. *Guardian* (Verdun), 17 February 1944.

13 *Guardian* (Verdun), 3 February 1943; Suzanne Clavette, "Des bons aux chèques: Aide aux chômeurs et crise des années 1930 à Verdun" (MA thesis, Université du Québec à Montréal, 1986), 89 n 59. Jay White offers the view that in Halifax illegal rent increases were not as rife as the common perception has held. Moreover, in many cases the problem was not the cost of housing but its quality. "Conscripted City: Halifax and the Second World War" (PhD diss., McMaster University, 1994), 161-8 and 185-93.

14 Canadian Corps Association to Quebec Attorney General, 10 March 1940, and Théo. de la Madeleine, Secretary, La Ligue des Propriétaires de Verdun, to Arthur Burgess, 4 April 1940, box A-331, file 3, "National Housing Act," VBA.

15 Eve Tremain and Marguerite Panet, Montreal Soldiers' Wives' League, to Mrs E.B. Savage, President, MSWL, 20 April 1942, MG 28, I 311, MSWL, vol. 5, file 3, "Housing Correspondence 1942-43," Library and Archives Canada (hereafter LAC).

16 "Report on Housing Problems, May 1942," MG 28, I 311, MSWL, vol. 5, file 4, "Housing Report 1942-45," LAC.

17 "Report on Housing Problems," 29 January 1943, submitted by Eve Tremain, and "List of Families Living in Undesirable Quarters," 10 April 1943, MG 28, I 311, MSWL, vol. 5, file 3, "Housing Correspondence 1942-43," LAC.

18 Shaver to city council, no date [spring 1941], box A-331, file 7, VBA.

19 *Guardian* (Verdun), 7 May 1943.

20 City of Verdun, Council Minutes (hereafter "Council Minutes"), 14 February 1944; *Guardian* (Verdun), 2 March 1944. The situation in Montreal seemed far worse. Hundreds of families squatted in empty warehouses or lived in garages or flimsy shacks that they had built themselves. In December 1943, 966 Montreal commercial properties were occupied by 1,110 families totalling 5,922 people, of whom 3,206 were children. Wilson to Paul-Émile Côté, MP, 29 July 1943, box A-331, file 7, "Guerre 1939-1948," VBA; Bacher, "Private Market," 335; Bacher, *Keeping to the Marketplace*, 149-52; Geneviève Auger and Raymonde Lamothe, *De la poêle à frire à la ligne de feu: La vie quotidienne des québécoises pendant la guerre '39-'45* (Montreal: Boréal Express, 1981), 84-5. See also Chris Lyons, "Battles on the Homes Front: Montreal's Response to Federal Housing Initiatives, 1941-1947," MA graduate essay, Concordia University, 2002, 22-3.

21 *Guardian* (Verdun), 9 March 1944; Lillas V. Ferguson, Secretary, Verdun Women's Club, to city council, 5 February 1945, box A-331, file 3, "National Housing Act," VBA; Council Minutes, 12 February 1945.

22 Auger and Lamothe, *De la poêle à frire,* 85.

23 Bacher, "Private Market," 350-1.

24 See for example *Guardian* (Verdun), 2 March and 20 April 1944.

25 *Guardian* (Verdun), 8 June 1944. The Glasgows' loss is detailed in Chapter 8.

26 Gold to Gordon, 30 October 1945, RG 56, vol. 17, file 105-10, LAC.

27 *Guardian* (Verdun), 20 April 1944.

28 *Guardian* (Verdun), 27 April 1944.

29 *Guardian* (Verdun), 14 September 1944.

30 Council Minutes, 14 February 1944; *Guardian* (Verdun), 20 and 27 April 1944; Verdun's response to the Quebec Economic Advisory Board, Survey on Housing Situation, 14 December 1944, box A-331, file 3, VBA. Whether or not Wilson was aware of the national situation, Ottawa knew that other Canadian cities were more desperate than Verdun. Conditions were considered worse in Halifax, Ottawa, Hull, Toronto, Hamilton, Vancouver, and Victoria.

31 Carver, *Houses for Canadians,* 121-2; Bacher, "Private Market," 386.

32 R.H. Wygant to *Messenger/Le Messager* (Verdun), 20 April 1944.

33 *Guardian* (Verdun), 1 February 1945.

34 *Guardian* (Verdun), 15 February 1945. "Zombie" was pejorative slang for men conscripted for home defence under the terms of the National Resources Mobilization Act.

35 *Guardian* (Verdun), 8 March 1945. The Society of Verdun Servicemen's Families, formed in late 1944 or early 1945, sought to improve the living conditions of families such as those described in these letters. Despite obtaining the public support of many of Verdun's political, business, religious and community leaders, the group met with limited success. None of its records seems to have survived. See box A-331, file 3, VBA.

36 Lyons, "Homes Front," 40.

37 Hébert to Wilson, 10 June 1945, box A-348, VBA.

38 Desmond Morton and J.L. Granatstein, *Victory 1945: Canadians from War to Peace* (Toronto: HarperCollins, 1995), 133; *Guardian* (Verdun), 31 May 1945. Bacher, however, demonstrates that Ottawa was hesitant and sometimes grudging in its assistance schemes for wartime housing. *Keeping to the Marketplace,* passim.

39 *Messenger/Le Messager* (Verdun), 21 February 1946; *Guardian* (Verdun), 4 April 1946.

40 Lyons, "Homes Front," 41.

41 *Guardian* (Verdun), 8 March 1945; Council Minutes, 22 January and 5 February 1945.

42 Alfred Bonin, Secrétaire, La Ligue des Propriétaires de Verdun, to WPTB, 25 January 1945, box A-331, file 3, VBA. In July 1945, the WPTB Rentals Administration decreed that no landlord (save a discharged service person) could force a tenant to vacate a flat on the grounds that the landlord or one of the landlord's relatives sought to occupy the dwelling. This decision was poorly received by landlords. *Gazette* (Montreal), 25 July 1945. Montreal's landlord class at city hall proved equally obstructionist to tenants' and federal efforts to take advantage of Ottawa's policies. See Lyons, "Homes Front," 2-6 and passim.

43 "Canadian Rental and Eviction Controls: World War II and the Post War Years," prepared by E.E. Booth under the direction of Owen Lobley, Rentals Administrator, 1 December 1947, pp. 54-5, RG 64, vol. 29, LAC.

44 Morton and Granatstein, *Victory 1945,* 168.

45 *Guardian* (Verdun), 8 March and 9 August 1945. Bacher, *Keeping to the Marketplace,* 174-5, notes the potential for similar violence elsewhere in Canada.

46 Quoted in *Gazette* (Montreal), 26 April 1945.

47 Ibid.
48 *Guardian* (Verdun), 16 May 1946. Veterans and citizens' groups in other Canadian cities, especially Vancouver, took similar action. Bacher, *Keeping to the Marketplace*, 174-5.
49 Executive Committee Minutes, 10 June 1941.
50 Quoted in *Guardian* (Verdun), 7 May 1943. The view of Morton and Granatstein, *Victory 1945*, 167, that since 1929 in Canada "almost nothing had been done to build or renew housing" does not apply to Verdun, where housing construction was always a civic priority.
51 Quoted from Verdun's response to the Quebec Economic Advisory Board, Survey on Housing Situation, 14 December 1944, box A-331, file 3, VBA. In contrast, Calgary could build only 300 homes in the first three years of the war. Jeffrey A. Keshen, "Morale and Morality on the Alberta Home Front," in *For King and Country: Alberta in the Second World War*, ed. Kenneth W. Tingley (Edmonton: Provincial Museum of Alberta, 1995), 148.
52 Quebec Economic Advisory Board, Survey on Housing Situation, 14 December 1944, box A-331, file 3, VBA.
53 Ibid.; *Messenger/Le Messager* (Verdun), 21 February 1946. Verdun was well ahead of the national average. For example, in 1943, only 15,000 housing units were built across Canada. Keshen, *Saints, Sinners, and Soldiers*, 76.
54 *Guardian* (Verdun), 12 and 26 July 1945.
55 This statistic is taken from the text of a pre-election speech that Wilson delivered over CFCF Radio, probably on 31 March 1945. Box A-57, file 6, "Municipal Elections 1945," VBA.
56 Council Minutes, 12 March 1945
57 Burgess to James C. Bruce, Wartime Housing Limited, 2 February 1945, box A-331, VBA.
58 Council Minutes, 26 March and 23 and 30 April 1945; box A-331, file 3, VBA.
59 Thomas Gray, General Manager, Wartime Housing Limited, to Wilson, 14 April 1945; Council Minutes, 16 and 30 April 1945; "Project for the Construction of One Hundred Dwellings on Egan Avenue," 3 May 1945, box A-331, file 3, VBA; *Messenger/Le Messager* (Verdun), 26 July 1945.
60 Robert England, *Discharged: A Commentary on Civil Re-establishment of Veterans in Canada* (Toronto: Macmillan, 1943), 149-52.
61 J.L. Granatstein and Desmond Morton, *A Nation Forged in Fire* (Toronto: Lester and Orpen Dennys, 1989), 166-7.
62 England, *Discharged*, 152.
63 *Guardian* (Verdun), 4 September 1942 and 17 September 1943.
64 R.B. Joan Adams, interview by author, 6 October 1993.
65 *Guardian* (Verdun), 17 and 24 September 1943.
66 Ibid.
67 *Guardian* (Verdun), 2 March 1944. Catholics in Verdun were cared for by their parish Société Saint-Vincent-de-Paul or by one of over thirty groups that made up the Federation of Catholic Charities and the Federation of French Charities. *Montreal Daily Star*, 3 October 1944; *Guardian* (Verdun), 8 February 1945.
68 See also Nick Mika and Helma Mika, *Belleville: Portrait of a City* (Belleville, ON: Mika Publishing, 1983), 47-55.
69 *Guardian* (Verdun), 14 September and 5 October 1944; *Montreal Daily Star*, 4 October 1944.
70 *Guardian* (Verdun), 2 March 1944 and 15 March 1945.
71 Denyse Baillargeon, *Ménagères au temps de la crise* (Montreal: Éditions du remue-ménage, 1991), 139.
72 Verdun Protestant Hospital, *Annual Report*, 1940, 33; and 1941, 33. The annual reports are located in the library of the Douglas Hospital, Verdun.
73 Verdun Protestant Hospital, *Annual Report*, 1942, 27-8.

74 Verdun Protestant Hospital, *Annual Report*, 1943, 30.
75 *Messenger/Le Messager* (Verdun), 15 June 1944.
76 Verdun Protestant Hospital, *Annual Report*, 1944, 28; and 1945, 26; *Guardian* (Verdun), 26 April 1945. In the United States, wives and families of military personnel serving overseas sometimes suffered considerable stress-related disorders, including depression, alcoholism, frequent diarrhoea, and headaches. Richard R. Lingeman, *Don't You Know There's a War On? The American Home Front 1941-45* (New York: G.P. Putnam's Sons, 1970), 97.
77 Verdun Protestant Hospital, *Annual Report*, 1946, 27. The Depression had also caused much personal anxiety. But since psychiatric-hospital admissions consistently increased during the war, it is possible that personal problems occasioned by the war, perhaps more clearly defined emotionally and psychologically than had been the case during the Depression, elicited a more sympathetic response from medical authorities.
78 Esther M. Beith, Child Welfare Association of Montreal, report for Mrs Guy Robinson, Chairman Welfare Committee MSWL, 4 October 1943, MG 28, I 311, MSWL, vol. 2, file 53, "Well Baby Clinics, 1943-44," LAC. French-speaking families could obtain the services of privately financed local Catholic charities and a network of "Gouttes de lait" baby clinics.
79 Ibid.
80 Edna Somerville, Welfare Convenor, Black Watch (RHR) of Canada Women's Division, to MSWL, 30 September 1943, MG 28, I 311, MSWL, vol. 2, file 53, "Well Baby Clinics, 1943-44," LAC.
81 Circular letter to welfare convenors of women's auxiliaries, 15 October 1943, MG 28, I 311, MSWL, vol. 2, file 53, "Well Baby Clinics, 1943-44," LAC.
82 Mrs G.D. Robinson, Chairman Welfare Committee MSWL, to Esther Beith, CWA, 29 January 1944, MG 28, I 311, MSWL, vol. 2, file 53, "Well Baby Clinics, 1943-44," LAC. According to the responses of their respective women's auxiliaries, the Royal Montreal Regiment had 150 Verdunites serving in its ranks at that time whereas the Black Watch counted 109.
83 Auger and Lamothe, *De la poêle à frire*, 124-8.
84 E. Lalande, MD, Director, Department of Day Nurseries, Ministry of Health and Social Welfare, to Miss Margaret Grier, National Selective Service Women's Division, 9 July 1943, and exchange of correspondence 21 July and 9 August 1943, RG 27, Department of Labour, vol. 611, "Quebec Ministry of Health. Dominion-Provincial Wartime Day Nurseries," file 6-52-5-2, vol. 1, LAC.
85 Dominion-Provincial Wartime Day Nursery, Record of Approval, National Selective Service, no date, RG 27, vol. 611, "Quebec Ministry of Health. Dominion-Provincial Wartime Day Nurseries," LAC. The parish hall was fully renovated and equipped, and the children were served two meals daily. The cost to mothers was between 20 and 35 cents a day.
86 Reports for May and August 1943, Dominion-Provincial Wartime Day Nurseries, RG 27, vol. 611, "Quebec Ministry of Health. Dominion-Provincial Wartime Day Nurseries," files 6-52-5-1 and 6-52-5-2, vol. 1, LAC. Twenty-eight day nurseries operated in Ontario. Auger and Lamothe, *De la poêle à frire*, 121-6.
87 RG 27, vol. 611, "Quebec Ministry of Health. Dominion-Provincial Wartime Day Nurseries," file 6-52-5-2, vol. 2, LAC; *Guardian* (Verdun), 11 October 1945; Ruth R. Pierson, *"They're Still Women after All": The Second World War and Canadian Womanhood* (Toronto: McClelland and Stewart, 1986), 53. Timothy Findley's novella *You Went Away* (Toronto: HarperCollins, 1996), which is set in Ontario during the Second World War, details the hardships encountered by a woman raising children alone following the enlistment of her husband. Gunda Lambton's *Sun in Winter: A Toronto Wartime Journal 1942-1945* (Montreal and Kingston: McGill-Queen's University Press, 2003) vividly highlights the difficulties of being a single mother in wartime Toronto.
88 Mary Peate, *Girl in a Sloppy Joe Sweater: Life on the Canadian Home Front during World War Two* (Montreal: Optimum Publishing, 1988), 93-6.

89 Mary Jane Lennon, *On the Home Front* (Erin, ON: Boston Mills Press, 1981), 91-3. Keshen, *Saints, Sinners, and Soldiers*, 194-227, offers an overview of Canadian children's wartime experiences.
90 *Montreal Daily Star*, 29 April 1940; *Guardian* (Verdun), 10 January 1941 and 1 May 1942.
91 Wilson Dornan, interview by author, 21 September 1993.
92 *Guardian* (Verdun), 19 January 1940, 24 January 1941, 13 February 1942, and 5 February 1943. Cases brought before a local magistrate do not represent all instances of crime in the community, since not all crime is reported and not all that is reported results in court appearances.
93 *Guardian* (Verdun), 4 June 1943.
94 *Guardian* (Verdun), 18 September 1942.
95 *Guardian* (Verdun), 30 October 1942.
96 *Guardian* (Verdun), 16 April 1943.
97 *Guardian* (Verdun), 14 May 1943 and 3 February 1944. There was only one recorded murder in Verdun in the years 1939-46; see *Montreal Daily Star*, 12 September 1939 and 14 March 1940.
98 Executive Committee Minutes, 24 April 1944.
99 Morton and Granatstein, *Victory 1945*, 171 and 207.
100 *Guardian* (Verdun), 12 July 1945 and 11 April 1946.
101 The Canadian literature is sparse. The best source is Keshen, *Saints, Sinners, and Soldiers*, ch. 8. On page 213, he notes that the incidence of wartime juvenile crime nationwide was exaggerated, then and since. See also Jeffrey Keshen, "Wartime Jitters over Juveniles: Canada's Delinquency Scare and Its Consequences, 1939-1945," in *Age of Contention: Readings in Canadian Social History, 1900-1945,* ed. Jeffrey Keshen, 364-86 (Toronto: Harcourt Brace Canada, 1997); White, "Conscripted City," passim; Auger and Lamothe, *De la poêle à frire,* passim. For the United States, see Richard Polenberg, *War and Society: The United States 1941-1945* (Westport, CT: Greenwood Press, 1980); Jack Goodman, ed., *While You Were Gone* (New York: Simon and Schuster, 1946); Francis E. Merrill, *Social Problems on the Home Front* (New York: Harper and Brothers, 1948).
102 Jean Bruce, *Back the Attack!* (Toronto: Macmillan, 1995), 67; see also *Guardian* (Verdun), 11 May 1944. White, "Conscripted City," 339, also cites overcrowding and reduced recreational opportunities as encouraging juvenile crime in Halifax.
103 Until 3 November 1942 a juvenile delinquent was an offender aged sixteen or younger. At that time the Juvenile Delinquency Act was amended to define juvenile offenders as eighteen or younger. Executive Committee Minutes, 14 December 1942.
104 *Guardian* (Verdun), 12 April 1940. In the 1920s and early 1930s, juvenile crime rates had been very low in Verdun compared to other districts in the Montreal area. Herman R. Ross, "Juvenile Delinquency in Montreal" (MA thesis, McGill University, 1932), 108.
105 Keshen, "Morale and Morality," 154-5; Morton and Granatstein, *Victory 1945*, 207.
106 *Guardian* (Verdun), 18 and 25 June 1943.
107 *Guardian* (Verdun), 20 August 1943; Béatrice Ste-Marie, interview by author, 19 October 1994. Much more serious outbursts of wartime youth violence occurred in Prince Rupert, Vancouver, and Toronto, for example. Morton and Granatstein, *Victory 1945*, 208.
108 *Guardian* (Verdun), 24 February and 20 July 1944.
109 *Guardian* (Verdun), 18 December 1942.
110 Wilson municipal pre-election speech, probably 31 March 1945, box A-57, file 6, VBA.
111 *Guardian* (Verdun), 29 June 1944.
112 Council Minutes, 10 October 1944. Other Canadian municipalities noticed the importance of increasing recreational facilities to minimize delinquency. See Keshen, *Saints, Sinners, and Soldiers*, 213.
113 The precise origin of the zoot-suit fad is unclear, although it almost certainly began in New York City. For background, see Mauricio Mazon, *The Zoot-Suit Riots: The Psychology*

of Symbolic Annihilation (Austin: University of Texas Press, 1984), 6-7. Parts of this section were published in Serge Durflinger, "Bagarres entre militaires et 'zoot-suiters' survenues à Montréal et à Verdun, juin 1944," in *L'impact de la Deuxième Guerre mondiale sur les sociétés canadienne et québécoise,* ed. Serge Bernier, 7-21 (Montreal: Université du Québec à Montréal et la direction histoire et patrimoine de la Défense nationale, Ottawa, 1998).

114 Mazon, *The Zoot-Suit Riots,* passim. For a brief discussion of postwar zooter criminality in Toronto, see Mariana Valverde, "Building Anti-Delinquent Communities: Morality, Gender and Generation in the City," in *A Diversity of Women: Ontario, 1945-1980,* ed. Joy Parr (Toronto: University of Toronto Press, 1995), 26-9.

115 Norman Bowen, a sailor, recalled that in Montreal, "When we went ashore we'd go in a bunch," or else there was a chance "you could wind up in the gutter." Quoted in Keshen, *Saints, Sinners, and Soldiers,* 20.

116 *La Presse* (Montreal), 29 May 1944; *Montreal Daily Star,* 1 June 1944.

117 *Guardian* (Verdun), 1 June 1944. Information available in the Verdun and Montreal press does not pinpoint the date of these disturbances, although 29 or 30 May is most likely. These incidents followed separate gang fights along the boardwalk the previous month, although nothing suggests that these outbreaks of youth violence were linked.

118 *Guardian* (Verdun), 8 June 1944.

119 *La Presse* (Montreal), 5 June 1944.

120 *Montreal Daily Star,* 5 June 1944; *La Presse* (Montreal), 5 June 1944. Author's translation.

121 *Guardian* (Verdun), 8 June 1944; *Messenger/Le Messager* (Verdun), 8 June 1944.

122 *Guardian* (Verdun), 8 June 1944.

123 *Messenger/Le Messager* (Verdun), 8 June 1944.

124 Ruth Wolstein, "L'habit zoot," in Verdun High School, *Annual,* 1943, 33, Canadiana Room, Verdun Cultural Centre; Wilson Dornan, interview by author, 21 September 1993.

125 "Board of Inquiry," HMCS *Hochelaga,* Montreal, 5 June 1944, RG 24, vol. 11,110, file 55-2-1/423, "Disturbances in Montreal," LAC.

126 *Guardian* (Verdun), 22 June 1944. The naval inquiry into the matter, which heard testimony from sailors, shore patrolmen, onlookers, zooters, and the owner of the pavilion, attempted to exonerate the sailors. These self-serving findings were rejected by the naval secretary in Ottawa and by other high-ranking officers in the Canadian Northwest Atlantic Command. Nothing came of the inquiry, and the report was simply filed away. "Board of Inquiry," HMCS *Hochelaga,* Montreal, 5 June 1944, RG 24, vol. 11,110, file 55-2-1/423, "Disturbances in Montreal," LAC.

127 *Messenger/Le Messager* (Verdun), 8 June 1944; "Board of Inquiry," HMCS *Hochelaga,* Montreal, 5 June 1944, RG 24, vol. 11,110, file 55-2-1/423, "Disturbances in Montreal," LAC.

128 *Messenger/Le Messager* (Verdun), 8 June 1944.

129 *Guardian* (Verdun), 15 June 1944. Reed was not the only Verdunite who supported the sailors. One of the few French-speaking sailors involved in the melee remarked that some of the many Verdunites who had gathered to watch the brawl openly offered the sailors drinks, indicating local sympathy for the men in uniform. "Board of Inquiry," HMCS *Hochelaga,* Montreal, 5 June 1944, RG 24, vol. 11,110, file 55-2-1/423, "Disturbances in Montreal," LAC.

130 William Weintraub, *City Unique: Montreal Days and Nights in the 1940s and 50s* (Toronto: McClelland and Stewart, 1996), 51-2; Keshen, *Saints, Sinners, and Soldiers,* 207, makes this point as well about a 1943 disturbance in Toronto.

131 "Board of Inquiry," HMCS *Hochelaga,* Montreal, 5 June 1944, RG 24, vol. 11,110, file 55-2-1/423, "Disturbances in Montreal," LAC. David forgot that Verdun was something of a navy town: over 1,000 Verdunites were on naval service during the war. It is far from certain that local sailors and their families would have had much to fear from Verdun zooters.

132 Gunner R.I. Rowe to MCF, 14 September 1944, box A-348, VBA.
133 Council Minutes, 7 and 11 September 1939; *Montreal Daily Star,* 12 September 1939.
134 Upton to Wilson, 8 October 1939, and Burgess to Upton, 23 October 1939, box A-331, file 6; Council Minutes, 10 October 1939.
135 *Canada at War,* no. 13, April 1942, 47.
136 Joseph Schull, *The Great Scot: A Biography of Donald Gordon* (Montreal and Kingston: McGill-Queen's University Press, 1979), 54ff.; Morton and Granatstein, *Victory 1945,* 76; Peter S. McInnes, *Harnessing Labour Confrontation: Shaping the Postwar Settlement in Canada, 1943-1950* (Toronto: University of Toronto Press, 2002), 32-3.
137 Auger and Lamothe, *De la poêle à frire,* 53-9; Pierson, *They're Still Women,* 40; Schull, *Great Scot,* 61-7; Magda Fahrni, "Under Reconstruction: The Family and the Public in Postwar Montréal, 1944-1949" (PhD diss., York University, 2001), 42. Schull refers to Canadian women as the "field force" of the WPTB (p. 63).
138 Wilson Dornan, interview by author, 21 September 1993.
139 Executive Committee Minutes, 26 October 1942; press release, City of Verdun, February 1943, box A-331, file 7, VBA; Verdun Catholic School Commission, Minutes of the Board of School Commissioners, 6 April and 19 July 1943, and 7 and 21 March 1944.
140 Duncan McDowell, *Quick to the Frontier: Canada's Royal Bank* (Toronto: McClelland and Stewart, 1993), 293; *Royal Bank Magazine,* June and July 1943, Archives of the Royal Bank of Canada, Montreal.
141 *Messenger/Le Messager* (Verdun), 27 May 1943; *Montreal Daily Star,* 9 April 1942; *Guardian* (Verdun), 10 April 1942 and 30 July 1943. For a review of black market activity, see Jeffrey Keshen, "One for All or All for One: Government Controls, Black Marketing and the Limits of Patriotism, 1939-47," *Journal of Canadian Studies* 29, 4 (1994-95): 111-43.
142 *Guardian* (Verdun), 19 April and 3 May 1945.
143 Executive Committee Minutes, 13 October and 23 November 1942.
144 See Chapter 8 for information on Verdun's manpower losses during the war.

Chapter 7: The Political War
1 *Guardian* (Verdun), 6 and 13 October 1939. For a review of the 1939 Quebec election, see Conrad Black, *Duplessis* (Toronto: McClelland and Stewart, 1977), 193-222; and Jean-Guy Genest, *Godbout* (Sillery, QC: Septentrion, 1996).
2 The newly formed Federation of Liberal Clubs ran a united campaign for the party for the first time "in many elections." Charles Barr, a well-known Liberal, mediated the reconciliation and served as Comeau's campaign manager. *Guardian* (Verdun), 7 July and 6 October 1939.
3 *Guardian* (Verdun), 13 October 1939.
4 Ibid. There were numerous other Liberal calls for the Conservative English-language community to "set aside party ties." A greater proportion of English speakers than French speakers was over the age of twenty-one, adding to the existing electoral strength of the 58 percent of Verdunites who were English speaking.
5 *Guardian* (Verdun), 20 October 1939.
6 *Guardian* (Verdun), 20 and 24 October 1939.
7 *Guardian* (Verdun), 27 October and 24 November 1939.
8 *Montreal Daily Star,* 9 November 1939.
9 *Montreal Daily Star,* 24 February 1940. For a review of the 1940 federal election, see J.L. Granatstein, *Canada's War: The Politics of the Mackenzie King Government 1939-1945* (Toronto: Oxford University Press, 1975), 72-113.
10 *Montreal Daily Star,* 5 September 1939 and 21 February 1940.
11 *Guardian* (Verdun), 2 and 16 February 1940.

12   *Guardian* (Verdun), 9 February and 1 March 1940.
13   *Montreal Daily Star*, 8 March 1940.
14   *Montreal Daily Star*, 9 and 14 March 1940.
15   David Lewis, *The Good Fight: Political Memoirs 1909-1958* (Toronto: Macmillan, 1981), 457-8.
16   *Guardian* (Verdun), 1 March 1940.
17   *Gazette* (Montreal), 21 March 1940.
18   *Guardian* (Verdun), 8 March 1940.
19   *Montreal Daily Star*, 14 March 1940; *Guardian* (Verdun), 15 March 1940.
20   R.B. Joan Adams, interview by author, 8 November 1993.
21   *Guardian* (Verdun), 29 March 1940.
22   Ferland's link to a brutal crime the previous year, in which a night watchman at the Verdun Auditorium was savagely beaten by thugs allegedly acting on Ferland's orders, was either forgotten or forgiven by a large number of electors. Ferland was acquitted of charges brought against him in connection with this crime. *Montreal Daily Star*, 1, 19, 22, 23, and 28 December 1939.
23   Michiel Horn, "Lost Causes: The League for Social Reconstruction and the Co-operative Commonwealth Federation in Quebec in the 1930s and 1940s," *Journal of Canadian Studies* 19, 2 (1984): 144.
24   J.L. Granatstein, "The Armed Forces' Vote in Canadian General Elections 1940-1968," *Journal of Canadian Studies* 4, 1 (1969): 7.
25   Ibid., 13; *Montreal Daily Star*, 6 April 1940.
26   The *Guardian* (Verdun), 23 January 1942, referred to Verdun as "truly united, working together, a stiff warning to Hitler and little Mussolini." This newspaper consistently reported Verdunites of both language groups as coexisting happily, even though it sometimes reported issues that had linguistic disputes at their core. In fact, close reading of wartime editions of the *Guardian* indicates that it was hardly sympathetic to French speakers.
27   House of Commons, *Debates*, 12 February 1942.
28   *Guardian* (Verdun), 13 March 1942.
29   House of Commons, *Debates*, 22 June 1942.
30   *La Presse* (Montreal), 24 April 1942; *Guardian* (Verdun), 24 April 1942; *Montreal Daily Star*, 22 April 1942.
31   Perhaps Côté realized he was not a great fit for his constituency. Prime Minister King's diary entry for 5 October 1942 notes that the MP appeared willing to resign his seat in order to make way for Maj-Gen L.R. LaFlèche, newly appointed minister of national war services. Diaries of William Lyon Mackenzie King, http://king.collectionscanada.ca.
32   *Guardian* (Verdun), 24 April 1942; *Montreal Daily Star*, 25 April 1942. An editorial in the *Guardian* of 29 May 1942 strongly endorsed Comeau for being one of only seven MLAs to vote against a provincial measure calling on the federal government not to amend the NRMA or impose conscription.
33   *Guardian* (Verdun), 24 April 1942.
34   City of Verdun, Council Minutes, 20 April 1942; *Guardian* (Verdun), 24 April 1942; the Ligue's petition is in box A-331, file 6, Verdun Borough Archives (hereafter VBA).
35   *Guardian* (Verdun), 1 May 1942; *Montreal Daily Star*, 27 April 1942.
36   *Guardian* (Verdun), 1 May 1942.
37   Unfortunately, copies of Verdun's bilingual newspaper, *Messenger/Le Messager*, for the period up to January 1943 were lost in a fire. One brief synopsis in a collection of oral testimony from long-time Verdun residents observed that many respondents recalled anxiety that their male relatives would be conscripted. Hélène Laprise, ed., *Les aînés de Verdun vous racontent* (Verdun: Conseil pour les aînés de Verdun, 2000), 18.

38 The only Quebec ridings with larger proportions of "yes" votes than Verdun were the overwhelmingly English-speaking ones of Mont-Royal (82 percent), St Lawrence-St George (81 percent), and Cartier (71 percent). Others voting "yes" were Outremont (61 percent), St Anne (59 percent), St Antoine-Westmount (59 percent), Laurier (57 percent), and Jacques Cartier (55 percent). André Laurendeau, *La Crise de la conscription 1942* (Montreal: Les éditions du jour, 1962), 120; Philip Stratford, ed., *André Laurendeau: Witness for Québec* (Toronto: Macmillan, 1973), 92; *La Presse* (Montreal), 28 April 1942; *Guardian* (Verdun), 1 May 1942; *Montreal Daily Star*, 28 April 1942.

39 *Guardian* (Verdun), 1 May 1942.

40 House of Commons, *Debates*, 22 June 1942.

41 *Guardian* (Verdun), 17 July 1942.

42 Wilfrid Sanders, *Jack and Jacques: A Scientific Approach to the Study of French and Non-French Thought in Canada* (Toronto: Ryerson Press, 1943), 22. Even if much of French Canadian opinion, especially the nationalist leadership, publicly appeared indifferent towards the war, obviously extremely few French Canadians hoped for other than a complete Allied victory. See Richard Jones, "Politics and Culture: The French Canadians and the Second World War," in *The Second World War as a National Experience*, ed. Sidney Aster, 82-91 (Ottawa: Canadian Committee for the History of the Second World War, 1981).

43 On the 1944 provincial election see Black, *Duplessis*, 277-8; and Genest, *Godbout*, 280-8.

44 *Montreal Daily Star*, 28 and 31 July 1944; *Guardian* (Verdun), 3 August 1944. Saskatchewan had gone to extraordinary lengths to enable soldiers to vote in 1944; Morton and Granatstein, *Victory 1945*, 134. Whenever feasible, Quebecers on active service stationed in Quebec were given forty-eight hours' leave to vote in their constituencies and return to their bases.

45 *Guardian* (Verdun), 20 July and 3 August 1944; *Montreal Daily Star*, 5 August 1944. Although it is not known what percentage of Verdunites who voted were women, the *Guardian*, on 10 August 1944, firmly believed that a larger proportion of English-speaking women had voted than of French-speaking. The *Montreal Daily Star*, 8 August 1944, was of the same opinion for the Montreal area generally.

46 *Guardian* (Verdun), 20 and 27 July 1944; *Messenger/Le Messager* (Verdun), 15 June 1944.

47 *Guardian* (Verdun), 27 July and 3 August 1944; Herbert F. Quinn, "The Quebec Provincial Election of 1944: An Analysis of the Election in the Democratic Process" (MA thesis, McGill University, 1946), 36.

48 *Guardian* (Verdun), 3 August 1944. In this election, twenty of twenty-four CCF candidates were French speakers – a hopeful sign for a party that had been repeatedly rejected *en masse* by the French-speaking electorate everywhere it had fielded candidates. Horn, "Lost Causes," 150-1. In 1943 the Catholic church in Quebec had lifted its moral ban on voting for the "socialist" CCF.

49 Next to the editorial appeared a large ad from the Quebec Liquor Commission stating in a bold headline: "Quebec Province Enjoys the Highest Rations in Canada – A Result of Foresight and Good Administration." *Guardian* (Verdun), 3 August 1944.

50 *Messenger/Le Messager* (Verdun) published ward and poll breakdowns on 10 August 1944; Quinn, "Quebec Provincial Election," Tables 3 and 4, unnumbered pages at the back; *Guardian* (Verdun), 10 August 1944.

51 *Messenger/Le Messager* (Verdun), 10 August 1944; Quinn, "Quebec Provincial Election," 19, 37-8, 44, 59, and Tables 3 and 4.

52 David Lewis, *Good Fight*, 210; Duarte Nuno Lopes, "The Co-operative Commonwealth Federation in Québec, 1932-1950" (MA thesis, McGill University, 1986), 162, makes the same inaccurate assessment.

53 *Guardian* (Verdun), 8 March 1945; Legislative Assembly of the Province of Quebec, *Journals*, vol. 80, 1 March 1945, 97. Comeau had always voted against motions rebuking Ottawa's conduct of the war, even mild ones supported by his own party. See, for example, Legislative Assembly of the Province of Quebec, *Journals*, vol. 79, 26 April 1944, 339.
54 For a review of the 1945 election, see Granatstein, *Canada's War*, 382-418.
55 As early as September 1943, 71 percent of Canadians polled stated that they wanted social reforms following the war. Sanders, *Jack and Jacques*, 37.
56 *Guardian* (Verdun), 19 April and 3 May 1945.
57 *Guardian* (Verdun), 24 and 31 May 1945; *Montreal Daily Star*, 9 June 1945.
58 *Messenger/Le Messager* (Verdun), 15 February 1945.
59 *Guardian* (Verdun), 26 April 1945.
60 *Guardian* (Verdun), 10 May 1945. The Tories had written off the votes of most French speakers, and this was made plain when Pagé, a French speaker, proclaimed his view that Canadians, like Americans, should have no "hyphenated" citizens. *Guardian* (Verdun), 7 June 1945.
61 *Guardian* (Verdun), 24 May 1945.
62 *Guardian* (Verdun), 17 May 1945.
63 The *Guardian* reported that Côté recognized that the Liberal vote in Verdun represented a vote of confidence in the King government and the Liberals' social agenda more than a vote for him personally. *Guardian* (Verdun), 14 June 1945; *Montreal Daily Star*, 1 and 12 June 1945.
64 *Montreal Daily Star*, 19 June 1945; Granatstein, "Armed Forces' Vote," 9.
65 MacWilliams to Wilson, 15 May 1945, and Lemieux to Wilson, 16 May 1945, box A-348, VBA. Seeking to shore up support among the ranks, the Conservatives also sent gifts of cigarettes to the troops. Granatstein, *Canada's War*, 412.

Chapter 8: Peace and Reconstruction

1 For an overview see Jeffrey A. Keshen, *Saints, Sinners, and Soldiers: Canada's Second World War* (Vancouver: UBC Press, 2004); J.L. Granatstein and Desmond Morton, *Victory 1945: Canadians from War to Peace* (Toronto: HarperCollins, 1995).
2 Leonard Marsh, *Report on Social Security for Canada* (Ottawa: King's Printer, 1943).
3 For preceding paragraphs see *Guardian* (Verdun), 10 May 1945; *Messenger/Le Messager* (Verdun), 10 May 1945.
4 *Guardian* (Verdun), 10 May 1945; *Messenger/Le Messager* (Verdun), 10 May 1945, author's translation; Ted Barris and Alex Barris, *Days of Victory: Canadians Remember 1939-1945* (Toronto: Macmillan, 1995), 210-11; Wilson Dornan, interview by author, 21 September 1993.
5 *Guardian* (Verdun), 2 August 1945. VJ Day found many of them home on leave awaiting training for service against the Japanese.
6 *Guardian* (Verdun), 16 August 1945; *Messenger/Le Messager* (Verdun), 23 August 1945; City of Verdun, Council Minutes, 14 August 1945.
7 Still the best books on this subject are Robert England, *Discharged: A Commentary on Civil Re-establishment of Veterans in Canada* (Toronto: Macmillan, 1943); and Walter S. Woods, *Rehabilitation: A Combined Operation* (Ottawa: Queen's Printer, 1953). See also the excellent collection of essays in Peter Neary and J.L. Granatstein, eds., *The Veterans Charter and Post-War Canada* (Montreal and Kingston: McGill-Queen's University Press, 1998).
8 Douglas Whyte, interview by author, 21 January 1994; René Bisson, interview by author, 21 July 1994.
9 *Globe and Mail*, 22 September 1945.
10 *Guardian* (Verdun), 27 June 1946.
11 *Spectator* (Hamilton), 15 April 1944.

12 One man, who as a youngster during the war delivered newspapers in Courtenay, BC, has recalled the hidden grief he felt when he knew a bereaved family would read their loved one's obituary in the newspaper he brought. He always acted as if nothing had happened. After joining the air force and witnessing the death of a young man from his hometown, he never discussed it with the boy's parents: "I was still pretending, just as I had pretended about the others from our town who died in the war. But deep down inside we never forget." Lewis Parke, letter to *Legion* magazine, November-December 2003.

13 Sgt J.B. Fulham to MCF, 22 September 1944, box A-601, Verdun Borough Archives. It made sad reading to follow several series of grateful letters to the Mayor's Cigarette Fund from young men who were later killed in action. The details in the letters and the manner of their expression often allowed their personalities to show through.

14 *Guardian* (Verdun), 31 October 1946.

15 Nick Mika and Helma Mika, *Belleville: Portrait of a City* (Belleville, ON: Mika Publishing, 1983), 283. A powerful account of an American city's bereavement can be found in Alex Kershaw, *The Bedford Boys: One American Town's Ultimate D-Day Sacrifice* (Cambridge, MA: Da Capo Press, 2003).

16 *Guardian* (Verdun), 25 September and 23 October 1942.

17 Charles Elliott, *A Short History of Verdun High School 1912-1984* (Montreal: PSBGM, 1990), 14.

18 Quoted in Barry Broadfoot, *Six Years of War 1939-1945* (Toronto: Doubleday, 1974), 169.

19 England, *Discharged,* ix, has remarked that "demobilization begins ... when war begins" and that by 1943 Canadian military discharges averaged over 2,000 a month. Morton and Granatstein, *Victory 1945,* 151, note that about one-third of Canadian service people were discharged before VE day.

20 *Messenger/Le Messager* (Verdun), 1 March 1945.

21 *Guardian* (Verdun), 16 August 1945. See also Terry Copp and Bill McAndrew, *Battle Exhaustion: Soldiers and Psychiatrists in the Canadian Army, 1939-1945* (Montreal and Kingston: McGill-Queen's University Press, 1990).

22 Quoted in *Guardian* (Verdun), 12 April 1945.

23 John Neal, "Life in Lower Slobovia," *McGill News,* summer 1990, 10.

24 Morton and Granatstein, *Victory 1945,* 160-2. Between 1939 and 1945 divorces rose 150 percent in Canada.

25 *Guardian* (Verdun), 25 October 1945.

26 Canadian National Institute for the Blind client questionnaire, Norman Daniel, 24 October 1945. Verdunite Charlemagne Dion was also blinded and lost an arm from the premature detonation of a grenade while training in Britain in March 1943. "Employment Prospect Questionnaire," 25 February 1944. Both documents located in Sir Arthur Pearson Association of War Blinded Archives, Ottawa

27 *Guardian* (Verdun), 25 April, 6, 20, and 27 June 1946. In 1948, Daniel left St Dunstan's a qualified physiotherapist and returned to the Montreal area to establish a practice.

28 In 1941, fewer than one in five Verdun households (17.9 percent) had the use of an automobile. Of Canadian cities with a population of 30,000 or more, only Montreal had a lower average (15.7 percent). 1941 Census, vol. 9, 83 and 142-4.

29 *Guardian* (Verdun), 6 June 1946. Joan Adams was also a driver for the Voluntary Transport League, one of only a handful of women engaged in that capacity. R.B. Joan Adams, interview by author, 6 October 1993.

30 Quoted in Morton and Granatstein, *Victory 1945,* 155.

31 *Gazette* (Montreal), 1 October 1945.

32 *Guardian* (Verdun), 27 September 1945.

33 *Guardian* (Verdun), 5 October 1945; *Gazette* (Montreal), 2 October 1945. Six weeks later, the seventy-three men of No. 1 Road Construction Unit, RCE, had a similar, though smaller,

ceremony at the auditorium. Although some Verdunites had served in this unit as well, few remained by November 1945. On 2 February 1946, another small unit of engineers paraded in Verdun. *Guardian* (Verdun), 22 November 1945 and 7 February 1946; *Messenger/ Le Messager* (Verdun), 22 November 1945.

34 See MG 28, I 311, MSWL, Vol. 3, file 54, "British Wives 1944-46." The Scottish widow of Pte. Donald Malcolm MacKillop made her way to Verdun to stay with his parents. MacKillop had been killed in action in Normandy in 1944 while serving with the Black Watch. *Guardian* (Verdun), 19 April 1945.

35 *Guardian* (Verdun), 21 February 1946. By 31 December 1946 nearly 48,000 wives (94 percent of them British) and 22,000 children (97 percent of them British) of Canadian servicemen had arrived in Canada. Perhaps 7 or 8 percent of Canadians serving overseas married, a rate that would translate into approximately 450 marriages by Verdunites serving overseas. But it does not appear that this many Verdunites took overseas brides. See Joyce Hibbert, ed., *The War Brides* (Toronto: PMA Books, 1978), 156.

36 Pierre Vennat, *Les héros oubliés: L'histoire inédite des militaires canadiens-français de la Deuxième Guerre mondiale,* vol. 3, *Du Jour-J à la mobilisation* (Montreal: Méridien, 1998), 324-6.

37 Mrs J.W. Verdon to Mrs Wright, MSWL, no date [September 1945], MG 28, I 311, MSWL, vol. 3, file 54, "British Wives 1944-46," LAC.

38 *Messenger/Le Messager* (Verdun), 13 and 20 September 1945. The city's muted response did not seem to rankle the local veteran community. In recognition of their ceaseless wartime efforts on behalf of Verdunites on active service, Wilson and Arthur Burgess were granted honorary memberships in the local branch of the Canadian Legion. *Guardian* (Verdun), 13 September 1945.

39 *Guardian* (Verdun), 15 November 1945 and 4 July 1946.

40 In the working-class Rosemount district of Montreal, the Labour Progressive Party held block parties to raise funds to provide returned wounded men with $50 gifts. Most Verdun members of this party appeared to be English speakers living in the east end. *Guardian* (Verdun), 15 February 1945.

41 *Guardian* (Verdun), 13 September 1945.

42 City of Verdun, Council Minutes, 26 February and 2 December 1946. England, *Discharged,* 331, believed in 1943 that the "most effective" memorial would be the willingness of a community to assure the successful re-establishment of all its veterans.

43 Morton and Granatstein, *Victory 1945,* 250. The only other testimonial commissioned in the city was an impressive stained-glass window installed in St Clement's Anglican Church on Wellington Street in 1950. A 1945 Gallup poll indicated that 90 percent of Canadians preferred a "living" memorial, such as a library, community hall, or sporting facility. *Municipal Review of Canada,* April 1945, 22.

44 "Verdun Meets the Reconstruction Challenge," 3 December 1945, box A-198, file 2, Verdun Borough Archives. The article was probably written by Arthur Burgess. *Guardian* (Verdun), 12 July 1945.

45 Woods, *Rehabilitation,* xiii and 17-30. See also Morton and Granatstein, *Victory 1945,* 133, 144-50. England, *Discharged,* 332, notes that already in 1943 a vast amount of information was available on re-establishment programs and that rehabilitation was a very popular topic among veterans.

46 *Guardian* (Verdun), 27 September 1945; Woods, *Rehabilitation,* 299. One Verdun veteran kept his copy of *The Common-Sense of Re-establishment* for half a century. Kenneth Slade, interview by author, 8 October 1993.

47 Quoted in *Guardian* (Verdun), 18 January 1945.

48 England, *Discharged,* 224ff.; Woods, *Rehabilitation,* 72ff. See also Desmond Morton and Glenn Wright, *Winning the Second Battle: Canadian Veterans and the Return to Civilian Life, 1915-1930* (Toronto: University of Toronto Press, 1987).

49 Neal, "Lower Slobovia," 10. Research for this work found only one other Verdun veteran who attended university immediately after the war, Peter Sinclair, who also served in the RCAF. Surely there were others.

50 Verdun High School, *Annual,* 1946, 5, Canadiana Room, Verdun Cultural Centre.

Conclusion

1 "Verdun Meets the Reconstruction Challenge," box A-198, file 2, Verdun Borough Archives (hereafter VBA).

2 *Canada's Weekly,* 14 April 1944, copy located in box A-242, file 50, VBA. Some of the other cities featured in this occasional series were Brantford (5 November 1943), Medicine Hat (10 December 1943), and Moncton (31 December 1943).

3 *Municipal Review of Canada,* April 1943, 3; *Guardian* (Verdun) 7 May 1943.

4 "Verdun, Fastest Growing City in Quebec, Blazes Civic Efficiency Trail for Others," *Financial Post* (Toronto), 12 January 1946. This article was based on a draft prepared by the city of Verdun, probably written by Arthur Burgess, and submitted for use by the *Financial Post.*

5 Jean Barrière, "Cité de Verdun: Aperçu historique, administration, commerce et industrie" (MA research paper, École des hautes études commerciales, Montreal, 1947), 40.

6 *Messenger/Le Messager* (Verdun), 25 March 1943.

7 "Verdun, Fastest Growing City in Quebec," *Financial Post* (Toronto), 12 January 1946.

8 Ibid. Verdun's population peaked at more than 80,000 in the 1960s.

9 Wilson Dornan, who grew up in east-end Verdun during the war, has recalled that several neighbouring families were French speaking, and, although communication with them was difficult at times, there was no sense of animosity. He felt that neighbourhood identification meant that he could depend on them if ever he needed their help. Dornan believed that language was an occasional barrier but not a permanent impediment to harmonious relations between neighbours in Verdun. Wilson Dornan, interview by author, 21 September 1993. All English speakers formally or informally interviewed for this study made similar points. But Suzanne Clavette, "Des bons aux chèques: aide aux chômeurs et crise des années 1930 à Verdun" (MA thesis, Université du Québec à Montréal, 1986), 81 n 25, writes, "Conflicts between English speakers and French speakers are part of daily life in Verdun. Fights between schoolboys from each language group ... are well-known facts" (author's translation). Clavette's sources were French speakers, which implies the existence of two different sets of oral histories about Verdun during the 1930s and 1940s – one English and one French.

10 Sidney Aster, ed., *The Second World War as a National Experience* (Ottawa: Canadian Committee for the History of the Second World War, 1981).

11 *Guardian* (Verdun), 30 October 1942. The bilingual *Messenger/Le Messager* covered the French-language community's social organizations, religious life, and politics and provided a distinctly French Canadian outlook on local issues. But the *Messenger* was less strident than the larger, more overtly patriotic *Guardian* (Verdun) in reporting war-related events on the local scene.

12 Quoted from Wilson's handwritten editorial changes to the text of his address delivered on CFCF Radio, probably 31 March 1945, box A-57, file 6, VBA.

13 Aster, *National Experience,* 2.

Select Bibliography

Archival Sources

Numerous archives were consulted in the course of writing this history. In the City of Verdun, the Verdun Borough Archives were essential. At city hall one can find the City of Verdun Council Meeting Minutes and City of Verdun Executive Committee Meeting Minutes. Also consulted were a selection of local church, school, and hospital archives. The following manuscript and record groups were consulted at Library and Archives Canada:

MG 28, I 17 Imperial Order Daughters of the Empire
MG 28, I 311 Montreal Soldiers' Wives' League
MG 28, I 95 Young Men's Christian Association
MG 30, A 118 Robert H. Haddow
MG 30, E 133 A.G.L. McNaughton
RG 24 National Defence
RG 27 Labour
RG 28 Munitions and Supply
RG 38 Veterans' Affairs
RG 44 National War Services
RG 46 Canadian Transport Commission
RG 56 Central Mortgage and Housing
RG 95 Corporations Branch

Selected Interviews

R.B. Joan Adams. 6 October and 8 November 1993. Williamsburg, Ontario.
Sydney Ashford. 12 January 1993. Verdun, Quebec.
René Bisson and Noëlla Bisson. 21 July 1994. Verdun, Quebec.
John Buck. 19 March 1996. Verdun, Quebec.
Wilson Dornan. 21 September 1993. Mascouche, Quebec.
Gordon Galbraith. 13 November 1993. Brockville, Ontario.
Léopold Lefort. 23 November 1995. Montreal, Quebec.
John Parker. 14 January 1994. Montreal, Quebec.
Béatrice Ste-Marie. 19 October 1994. Verdun, Quebec.
Kenneth Slade. 8 October 1993. Mascouche, Quebec.
Joseph Way. 15 November 1992 and 21 September 1993. Mascouche, Quebec.
Douglas Whyte. 21 January 1994. Verdun, Quebec.

Other Sources

Allison, Les. *Canadians in the Royal Air Force.* Roland, MB: privately printed, 1978.
Armstrong, Elizabeth. *French Canadian Opinion on the War, January 1940-June 1941.* Toronto: Ryerson Press, 1942.
Artibise, A.F.J., and Gilbert A. Stelter, eds. *The Canadian City: Essays in Urban History.* Carleton Library no. 109. Toronto: Macmillan, 1979.

–. *The Usable Urban Past.* Carleton Library no. 119. Toronto: Macmillan, 1979.

Aster, Sidney, ed. *The Second World War as a National Experience.* Ottawa: Canadian Committee for the History of the Second World War, 1981.

Auger, Geneviève, and Raymonde Lamothe. *De la poêle à frire à la ligne de feu: La vie quotidienne des québécoises pendant la guerre '39-'45.* Montreal: Boréal Express, 1981.

Bacher, John C. *Keeping to the Marketplace: The Evolution of Canadian Housing Policy.* Montreal and Kingston: McGill-Queen's University Press, 1993.

–. "Keeping to the Private Market: The Evolution of Canadian Housing Policy 1900-1949." PhD diss., McMaster University, 1985.

Baillargeon, Denyse. *Ménagères au temps de la crise.* Montreal: Éditions du remue-ménage, 1991.

Barrière, Jean. "Cité de Verdun: Aperçu historique, administration, commerce et industrie." MA research paper, École des hautes études commerciales, Montreal. 1947.

Barris, Ted, and Alex Barris. *Days of Victory: Canadians Remember 1939-1945.* Toronto: Macmillan, 1995.

Bernier, Serge. "French-Canadians in the Canadian Armed Forces in 1944." In *The Second Quebec Conference Revisited. Waging War, Formulating Peace: Canada, Great Britain, and the United States in 1944-45,* ed. David B. Woolner, 194-202. New York: St Martin's Press, 1998.

Bernier, Serge, and Jean Pariseau. *Les canadiens français et le bilinguisme dans les Forces armées canadiennes.* Vol. 1: *1763-1969: Le spectre d'une armée bicéphale.* Ottawa: Service historique de la Défense nationale, 1987.

Beurling, G.F., and Leslie Roberts. *Malta Spitfire: The Story of a Fighter Pilot.* Toronto: Oxford University Press, 1943.

Black, Conrad. *Duplessis.* Toronto: McClelland and Stewart, 1977.

Bothwell, Robert, and William Kilbourn. *C.D. Howe: A Biography.* Toronto: McClelland and Stewart, 1979.

Bowering, Clifford H. *Service: The Story of the Canadian Legion.* Ottawa: Canadian Legion, 1960.

Broadfoot, Barry. *Six Years of War 1939-1945.* Toronto: Doubleday, 1974.

–. *The Veterans' Years.* Vancouver: Douglas and McIntyre, 1985.

Bruce, Jean. *Back the Attack!* Toronto: Macmillan, 1985.

Buck, M. Laurel. *Stream of Memory.* Ste-Anne-de-Bellevue, QC: Shoreline, 1994.

Burns, E.L.M. *Manpower in the Canadian Army 1939-1945.* Toronto: Clarke, Irwin, 1956.

Byers, Daniel. "Mobilising Canada: The National Mobilization Act, the Department of National Defence and Compulsory Military Service in Canada, 1940-1945." *Journal of the Canadian Historical Association* 7 (1996): 175-203.

Calder, Angus. *The People's War: Britain 1939-1945.* London: Jonathan Cape, 1969.

Canada. *Fifth Census of Canada, 1911.* Ottawa: Dominion Bureau of Statistics, 1912.

–. *Sixth Census of Canada, 1921.* Ottawa: Dominion Bureau of Statistics, 1924.

–. *Seventh Census of Canada, 1931.* Ottawa: Dominion Bureau of Statistics, 1933.

–. *Eighth Census of Canada, 1941.* Ottawa: Dominion Bureau of Statistics, 1950.

–. House of Commons. *Debates.* 1936-1945.

Carnegie, David. *The History of Munitions Supply in Canada 1914-1918.* London: Longmans, Green, 1925.

Carver, Humphrey. *Compassionate Landscape.* Toronto: University of Toronto Press, 1975.

–. *Houses for Canadians.* Toronto: University of Toronto Press, 1948.

Clavette, Suzanne. "Des bons aux chèques: Aide aux chômeurs et crise des années 1930 à Verdun." MA thesis, Université du Québec à Montréal, 1986.

Comeau, Paul-André. *Le Bloc populaire 1942-1948*. Montreal: Éditions Québec/Amérique, 1982.

Copp, Terry. *The Brigade*. Stoney Creek, ON: Fortress Publications, 1992.

Copp, Terry, and Bill McAndrew. *Battle Exhaustion: Soldiers and Psychiatrists in the Canadian Army, 1939-1945*. Montreal and Kingston: McGill-Queen's University Press, 1990.

Coyne, Kevin. *Marching Home: To War and Back with the Men of One American Town*. New York: Penguin Books, 2004.

Crooks, Sylvia. *Homefront and Battlefront: Nelson BC in World War II*. Vancouver: Granville Island Publisher, 2005.

Cross, Harold C. *One Hundred Years of Service with Youth: The Story of the Montreal Y.M.C.A.* Montreal: Southam Press, 1951.

Curtis, C.A. "War-time Problems of Local Government." *Canadian Journal of Economics and Political Science* 9, 3 (1943): 394-404.

Cuthbertson, Wendy. "Pocketbooks and Patriotism: The 'Financial Miracle' of Canada's World War II Victory Bond Program." In *Canadian Military History since the 17th Century*, ed. Yves Tremblay, 177-85. Proceedings of the Canadian Military History Conference, Ottawa, 5-9 May 2000. Ottawa: Department of National Defence, 2001.

Davidson, Mary. "The Social Adjustment of British Immigrant Families in Verdun and Point St. Charles." MA thesis, McGill University, 1933.

Dawe, Michael. "Community in Transition: Red Deer in the Second World War." In *For King and Country: Alberta in the Second World War*, ed. Kenneth W. Tingley, 119-38. Edmonton: Provincial Museum of Alberta, 1995.

Déziel, Julien. *History of Verdun 1665, 1876-1976*. Verdun, QC: Centennial Committee, 1976. Revised 1978.

Douglas, W.A.B., and Brereton Greenhous. *Out of the Shadows: Canada in the Second World War*, Toronto: Oxford University Press, 1977.

Durflinger, Serge. "Bagarres entre militaires et 'zoot-suiters' survenues à Montréal et à Verdun, juin 1944." In *L'impact de la Deuxième Guerre mondiale sur les sociétés canadienne et québécoise*, ed. Serge Bernier, 7-21. Montreal: Université du Québec à Montréal; Ottawa: La direction histoire et patrimoine de la Défense nationale, 1998.

–. "Making Wartime Continue: War Industry and Economic Recovery in Verdun, Quebec 1941-1946." In *Canada 1900-1950: A Country Comes of Age*, ed. Serge Bernier and John Macfarlane, 77-86. Montreal: Organization for the History of Canada, 2003.

–. "'Nothing Would Be Too Much Trouble': Hometown Support for H.M.C.S. *Dunver*, 1943-1945." *Northern Mariner* 12, 4 (2002): 1-12.

–. "Owing Allegiance: The British Community in Verdun, Quebec during the Second World War." *Canadian Ethnic Studies* 36, 1 (2004): 4-23.

Elliott, Charles E. *A Short History of Verdun High School 1912-1984*. Montreal: Protestant School Board of Greater Montreal, 1990.

England, Robert. *Discharged: A Commentary on Civil Re-establishment of Veterans in Canada*. Toronto: Macmillan, 1943.

Fahrni, Magda. "Counting the Costs of Living: Gender, Citizenship, and Politics of Prices in 1940s Montreal." *Canadian Historical Review* 83, 4 (2002): 483-504.

–. "The Romance of Reunion: Montreal Veterans Return to Family Life, 1944-1949." *Journal of the Canadian Historical Association* 9 (1998): 187-208.

–. "Under Reconstruction: The Family and the Public in Postwar Montréal, 1944-1949." PhD diss., York University, 2001.

Findley, Timothy. *You Went Away*. Toronto: HarperCollins, 1996.

Firestone, O.J. "Measurement of Housing Needs, Supply and Post War Requirements." In *Housing and Community Planning: A Series of Lectures Delivered at McGill University,*

November 2, 1943-March 21, 1944, ed. School of Architecture. Montreal: McGill University, 1944.

Fish, Lynn, ed. "Kathlyn's Letters." *Beaver* 81, 5 (2001): 13-23.

Freeman, David J. *Canadian Warship Names*. St Catharines, ON: Vanwell, 2000.

Gallant, K.H.B. "The Development of the Canadian Army as a Unilingual Institution in a Bilingual State." MA thesis, McGill University, 1969.

Gallant, Mavis. *Home Truths*. Toronto: Macmillan, 1981.

Garner, Hugh. *Storm Below*. 1949. Reprint, Toronto: Ryerson Press, 1968.

Genest, Jean-Guy. *Godbout*. Sillery, QC: Septentrion, 1996.

Gibson, J. Douglas. "Financing the War." In *Canadian War Economics*, ed. J.F. Parkinson, 33-46. Toronto: University of Toronto Press, 1941.

Glashan, Keith. *Montreal's Navy*. Montreal: privately printed, 1985.

Goheen, Peter G. "Symbols in the Streets." *Urban History Review* 18, 3 (1990): 237-40.

Goodman, Jack, ed. *While You Were Gone*. New York: Simon and Schuster, 1946.

Gossage, Carolyn. *Greatcoats and Glamour Boots*. Toronto: Dundurn Press, 1991.

Gouin, Jacques. *Lettres de guerre d'un Québécois, 1942-1945*. Montreal: Éditions du jour, 1975.

Graham, Gwethalyn. *Earth and High Heaven*. Philadelphia: J.B. Lippincott, 1944.

Granatstein, J.L. "The Armed Forces' Vote in Canadian General Elections 1940-1968." *Journal of Canadian Studies* 4, 1 (1969): 6-16.

–. *Canada's War: The Politics of the Mackenzie King Government, 1939-1945*. Toronto: Oxford University Press, 1975.

–. *The Politics of Survival: The Conservative Party of Canada, 1939-1945*. Toronto: University of Toronto Press, 1970.

Granatstein, J.L., and J.M. Hitsman. *Broken Promises: A History of Conscription in Canada*. Toronto: Oxford University Press, 1977.

Granatstein, J.L., and Desmond Morton. *A Nation Forged in Fire*. Toronto: Lester and Orpen Dennys, 1989.

Gravel, Denis, and Hélène Lafortune. *Verdun: 125 ans d'histoire 1875-2000*. Montreal: Archiv-Histo, 2000.

Gravel, Jean-Yves, ed. *Le Québec et la Guerre*. Montreal: Boréal Express, 1974.

Gunning, Cuthbert. *H.M.C.S. "North Bay": One Ship's Role in War and Peace 1943-1992*. North Bay, ON: privately printed, 1995.

–. *North Bay: The War Years*. North Bay, ON: privately printed, 1990.

Hale, James. *Branching Out: The Story of the Royal Canadian Legion*. Ottawa: Royal Canadian Legion, 1995.

Hall, H. Duncan. *North American Supply*. London: HMSO, 1955.

Hall, H. Duncan, and C.C. Wrigley. *Studies of Overseas Supply*. London: HMSO, 1956.

Hamelin, Christine. "A Sense of Purpose: Ottawa Students and the Second World War." *Canadian Military History* 6, 1 (1997): 34-41.

Hart, Scott. *Washington at War: 1941-1945*. Englewood Cliffs, NJ: Prentice Hall, 1970.

Hibbert, Joyce, ed. *The War Brides*. Toronto: PMA Books, 1978.

Hillmer, Norman, Bohdan Kordan, and Lubomyr Luciuk, eds. *On Guard for Thee: War, Ethnicity and the Canadian State, 1939-1945*. Ottawa: Canadian Committee for the History of the Second World War and Ministry of Supply and Services, 1988.

Horn, Michiel. "Lost Causes: The League for Social Reconstruction and the Co-operative Commonwealth Federation in Quebec in the 1930s and 1940s." *Journal of Canadian Studies* 19, 2 (1984): 132-156.

–, ed. *The Depression in Canada*. Toronto: Copp Clark Pitman, 1988.

How, Douglas. *One Village, One War 1914-1945*. Hantsport, NS: Lancelot Press, 1995.

Hughes, Everett C. *French Canada in Transition*. Chicago: University of Chicago Press, 1943.

Hurst, Alan M. *The Canadian Y.M.C.A. in World War II*. N.p.: National War Services Committee of the National Council of the Y.M.C.A. of Canada, [1949?].

Ibsen, Bruce. "A Name If Necessary, But Not Necessarily a Name: Why There Was No H.M.C.S. Edmonton." In *For King and Country: Alberta in the Second World War,* ed. Kenneth W. Tingley, 139-44. Edmonton: Provincial Museum of Alberta, 1995.

Irving, Allan. "Leonard Marsh and the McGill Social Science Research Project." *Journal of Canadian Studies* 21, 2 (1986): 6-25.

James, Rick. "The West Coast's Very Own Frigate." *Argonauta* 11, 1 (1994): 17-19.

Jamieson, Stuart M. "French and English in the Institutional Structure of Montreal: A Study of the Social and Economic Division of Labour." MA thesis, McGill University, 1938.

Jones, Richard. "Politics and Culture: The French Canadians and the Second World War." In *The Second World War as a National Experience*, ed. Sidney Aster, 82-91. Ottawa: Canadian Committee for the History of the Second World War, 1981.

Kennedy, J. de N. *History of the Department of Munitions and Supply*. 2 vols. Ottawa: King's Printer, 1950.

Kershaw, Alex. *The Bedford Boys: One American Town's Ultimate D-Day Sacrifice*. Cambridge, MA: Da Capo Press, 2003.

Keshen, Jeffrey A. "Morale and Morality on the Alberta Home Front." In *For King and Country: Alberta in the Second World War,* ed. Kenneth W. Tingley, 145-62. Edmonton: Provincial Museum of Alberta, 1995.

–. "One for All or All for One: Government Controls, Black Marketing and the Limits of Patriotism, 1939-47." *Journal of Canadian Studies* 29, 4 (1994-95): 111-43.

–. "Revisiting Canada's Civilian Women during World War II." *Histoire sociale/Social History* 30, 60 (1997): 239-66.

–. *Saints, Sinners, and Soldiers: Canada's Second World War*. Vancouver: UBC Press, 2004.

–. "Wartime Jitters over Juveniles: Canada's Delinquency Scare and Its Consequences, 1939-1945." In *Age of Contention: Readings in Canadian Social History, 1900-1945,* ed. Jeffrey Keshen, 364-86. Toronto: Harcourt Brace Canada, 1997.

Kimber, Stephen. *Sailors, Slackers, and Blind Pigs: Halifax at War*. Toronto: Doubleday, 2002.

Laing, Gertrude. *A Community Organizes for War*. Winnipeg, 1948.

Lambton, Gunda. *Sun in Winter: A Toronto Wartime Journal 1942-1945*. Montreal and Kingston: McGill-Queen's University Press, 2003.

Laprise, Hélène. *Les aînés de Verdun vous racontent.* Verdun: Conseil pour les aînés de Verdun, 2000.

Laurendeau, André. *La crise de la conscription 1942*. Montreal: Les éditions du jour, 1962.

Lefebvre, Florent. *The French-Canadian Press and the War*. Toronto: Ryerson Press, 1940.

Lemelin, Roger. *Les Plouffes*. Quebec: Beauchemin, 1948.

Lennon, Mary Jane. *On the Homefront*. Erin, ON: Boston Mills, 1981.

Lewis, David. *The Good Fight: Political Memoirs 1909-1958*. Toronto: Macmillan, 1981.

Lingeman, Richard R. *Don't You Know There's a War On? The American Home Front 1941-45*. New York: G.P. Putnam's Sons, 1970.

Linteau, Paul-André. *Histoire de Montréal depuis la Confédération*. Montreal: Boréal, 1992.

Lopes, Duarte Nuno. "The Co-operative Commonwealth Federation in Quebec, 1932-1950." MA thesis, McGill University, 1986.

Lyons, Christopher M. "Battles on the Homes Front: Montreal's Response to Federal Housing Initiatives, 1941-1947." MA research paper, Concordia University, 2002.

McInnes, Peter S. *Harnessing Labour Confrontation: Shaping the Postwar Settlement in Canada, 1943-1950*. Toronto: University of Toronto Press, 2002.

MacLennan, Hugh. *Two Solitudes*. Toronto: Bryant Press, 1945.

McNeil, Bill. *Voices of a War Remembered*. Toronto: Doubleday, 1991.

Marsh, Leonard. *Employment Research*. McGill Social Research Series. Toronto: Oxford University Press, 1935.

−. *Report on Social Security for Canada*. Ottawa: King's Printer, 1943.

Mazon, Mauricio. *The Zoot-Suit Riots: The Psychology of Symbolic Annihilation*. Austin: University of Texas Press, 1984.

Merrill, Francis E. *Social Problems on the Home Front*. New York: Harper and Brothers, 1948.

Metson, Graham. *An East Coast Port: Halifax at War, 1939-1945*. Toronto: McGraw-Hill Ryerson, 1981.

Mika, Nick, and Helma Mika. *Belleville: Portrait of a City*. Belleville, ON: Mika Publishing, 1983.

Miller, Ian. "Toronto's Response to the Outbreak of War, 1939." *Canadian Military History* 11, 1 (2002): 5-23.

Morton, Desmond. *1945: When Canada Won the War*. Historical booklet 54. Ottawa: Canadian Historical Association, 1995.

Morton, Desmond, and J.L. Granatstein. *Victory 1945: Canadians from War to Peace*. Toronto: HarperCollins, 1995.

Morton, Desmond, and Glenn Wright. *Winning the Second Battle: Canadian Veterans and the Return to Civilian Life, 1915-1930*. Toronto: University of Toronto Press, 1987.

Murphy, Tony, and Paul Kenny. *The War at Our Doorstep: St. John's during World War Two – An Album*. St John's, NL: Harry Cuff Publications, 1989.

Nadeau, Jean Marie. *Horizons d'après-guerre*. Montreal: Lucien Parizeau et Compagnie, 1944.

Neary, Peter, and J.L. Granatstein, eds. *The Veterans Charter and Post-War Canada*. Montreal and Kingston: McGill-Queen's University Press, 1998.

Nolan, Brian. *Hero: The Buzz Beurling Story*. Toronto: Lester and Orpen Dennys, 1981.

Novak, Dagmar. *Dubious Glory: The Two World Wars and the Canadian Novel*. New York: Peter Lang, 2000.

O'Brien, Kenneth Paul, and Lynn Hudson Parsons, eds. *The Home Front War: World War II and American Society*. Westport, CT: Greenwood Press, 1995.

Oliver, Dean F. "'My Darlin' Clementine'? Wooing Zombies for $6.50 a Night: General Service-NRMA Relations in Wartime Calgary." *Canadian Military History* 7, 3 (1998): 46-54.

−. "When the Battle's Won: Military Demobilization in Canada 1939-1946." PhD diss., York University, 1996.

Oppenheimer, Melanie. "Controlling Civilian Volunteering: Canada and Australia during the Second World War." *War and Society* 22, 2 (2004): 27-50.

Peate, Mary. *Girl in a Sloppy Joe Sweater: Life on the Canadian Home Front During World War Two*. Montreal: Optimum Publishing, 1988.

Perrett, Geoffrey. *Days of Sadness, Years of Triumph: The American People 1939-45*. New York: Coward McCann and Geoghegan, 1973.

Pierson, Ruth R. *Canadian Women and the Second World War*. Historical booklet 37. Ottawa: Canadian Historical Association, 1983.

−. *"They're Still Women after All": The Second World War and Canadian Womanhood*. Toronto: McClelland and Stewart, 1986.

Plunkett, Thomas J. *Municipal Organization in Canada*. Montreal: Canadian Federation of Mayors and Municipalities, 1955.

Polenberg, Richard. *War and Society: The United States 1941-1945*. Westport, CT: Greenwood Press, 1980.

Quince, Cliff, and Serge Durflinger. "Through the Eye of the Lens: Photographs from Aboard the Frigate HMCS *Dunver*, 1943-45." *Canadian Military History* 10, 2 (2001): 60-8.

Quinn, Herbert F. "The Quebec Provincial Election of 1944: An Analysis of the Election in the Democratic Process." MA thesis, McGill University, 1946.

Ramsden, Mary E. "Dependency among British Immigrants in Montreal." MA thesis, McGill University, 1933.

Reynolds, Lloyd G. *The British Immigrant: His Social and Economic Adjustment in Canada*. Toronto: Oxford University Press, 1935.

–. "Occupational Adjustment of the British Immigrant." MA thesis, McGill University, 1933.

Ripley, Donald F. *The Home Front: Wartime Life in Camp Aldershot and Kentville, Nova Scotia*. Hantsport, NS: Lancelot Press, 1991.

Robinson, Daniel. *The Measure of Democracy: Polling, Market Research and Public Life, 1930-1945*. Toronto: University of Toronto Press, 1999.

Rogers, Donald I. *Since You Went Away*. New Rochelle, NY: Arlington House, 1973.

Ross, Aileen. "The French and English Social Elites of Montreal." MA thesis, University of Chicago, 1941.

Ross, Herman R. "Juvenile Delinquency in Montreal." MA thesis, McGill University, 1932.

Roy, Gabrielle. *Bonheur d'occasion*. Montreal: Société des Éditions Pascale, 1945. Translated by Hanna Josephson as *The Tin Flute*, 1947. Republished Toronto: McClelland and Stewart, 1969.

Rutherdale, Robert. *Hometown Horizons: Local Responses to Canada's Great War*. Vancouver: UBC Press, 2004.

Sanders, Wilfrid. *Jack and Jacques: A Scientific Approach to the Study of French and Non-French Thought in Canada*. Toronto: Ryerson Press, 1943.

Schlegel, Marvin. *Conscripted City: Norfolk in World War II*. 1951. Reprinted Norfolk, VA: *The Virginian-Pilot* and *The Ledger Star*, 1991.

–. "Writing Your Community's War History." Special issue, *American Association for State and Local History Bulletin* (Raleigh, NC) 1, 11 (1946).

Schull, Joseph. *The Great Scot: A Biography of Donald Gordon*. Montreal and Kingston: McGill-Queen's University Press, 1979.

Scott, David. *The Home Front in the Second World War*. Ottawa: Supply and Services, 1995.

Seabrook, Thomas G. "The Nature of Attachments of Residents to Their Neighbourhoods." MA thesis, McGill University, 1964.

Sethna, Christabelle. "Wait Till Your Father Gets Home: Absent Fathers, Working Mothers and Delinquent Daughters in Ontario during World War II." In *Family Matters: Papers in Post-Confederation Canadian Family History*, ed. Lori Chambers and Edgar-André Montigny, 19-37. Toronto: Canadian Scholars' Press, 1998.

Shipley, Robert. *To Mark Our Place: A History of Canadian War Memorials*. Toronto: NC Press, 1987.

Smith, Ken. *Ajax: The War Years 1939/45*. Toronto: Ken Smith and Alger Press, 1989.

Stacey, C.P. *Arms, Men and Governments: The War Policies of Canada, 1939-1945*. Ottawa: Queen's Printer, 1970.

–. *Six Years of War: The Official History of the Canadian Army in the Second World War*. Vol. 1 (4th corrected printing). Ottawa: Queen's Printer, 1966.

Stacey, C.P., and Barbara Wilson. *The Half-Million: The Canadians in Britain, 1939-1946*. Toronto: University of Toronto Press, 1987.

Stelter, Gilbert A. "A Sense of Time and Place: The Historian's Approach to Canada's Urban Past." In *The Canadian City: Essays in Urban History*, ed. A.F.J. Artibise and Gilbert A. Stelter, 420-41. Carleton Library no. 109. Toronto: Macmillan, 1977.

Stevenson, Michael. *Canada's Greatest Wartime Muddle: National Selective Service and the Mobilization of Human Resources during World War II*. Montreal and Kingston: McGill-Queen's University Press, 2001.

Struthers, James. *No Fault of Their Own: Unemployment and the Canadian Welfare State, 1914-1941*. Toronto: University of Toronto Press, 1983.

Thibault, Jean. *Drummondville à l'heure de la guerre 1939-1945*. Drummondville, QC: Société d'histoire de Drummondville, 1994.

Tingley, Kenneth W., ed. *For King and Country: Alberta in the Second World War*. Edmonton: Provincial Museum of Alberta, 1995.

Tomas, Diane. "Strathroy, Ontario 1939-1945: A Small Canadian Town Goes to War." Seminar paper, Wilfrid Laurier University, April 1997.

Vennat, Pierre. *Les héros oubliés: L'histoire inédite des militaires canadiens-français de la Deuxième Guerre mondiale*. 3 vols. Montreal: Méridien, 1997-98.

Weintraub, William. *City Unique: Montreal Days and Nights in the 1940s and 1950s*. Toronto: McClelland and Stewart, 1996.

White, James F.E. "The Ajax Affair: Citizens and Sailors in Wartime Halifax, 1939-1945." MA thesis, Dalhousie University, 1984.

White, Jay. "Conscripted City: Halifax and the Second World War." PhD diss., McMaster University, 1994.

Woods, Walter S. *Rehabilitation: A Combined Operation*. Ottawa: Queen's Printer, 1953.

Zakuta, Leo. "The Natural Areas of the Montreal Metropolitan Community with Special Reference to the Central Area." MA thesis, McGill University, 1948.

Zimmerman, David. "The Social Background of the Wartime Navy: Some Statistical Data." In *A Nation's Navy: In Quest of Canadian Naval Identity*, ed. Michael Hadley, Rob Huebert, and Fred Crickard, 256-79. Montreal and Kingston: McGill-Queen's University Press, 1996.

Index

Voluntary Transport League, 196, 197
volunteers, 108, 135
    competition for, 115
    diffusion of, 116
    in home defence, 27
    patriotism of, 108
    women, 108, 233n43
voting, 52, 189-90
    ethnicity and, 189
    language and, 173, 190
    overseas service and, 54, 55, 181-2
    by servicemen, 175, 176, 188-9
    by women, 174, 182

wage and price controls, 165
Wales, Edward, prince of, 11
Wallis, Lt-Col, 197
War Assets Corporation, 87, 134
war brides, 197-8
war charities, 108, 115, 135, 152, 231n5
War Charities Act, 227n75, 231n5
war industries. *See* defence industries
War Loan campaigns, 94
war memorial, 199
War Savings, 78
    Certificates, 94, 96, 122
    Committee (VWSC), 94, 95
    Stamps, 95, 96, 122, 127
War Supply Board, 128-9
Ward 1, 34, 36, 39t
    aldermen from, 53
    and conscription plebiscite, 179
    enlistment from, 37
    French speakers in armed forces from, 38
    in municipal elections, 54, 55
    officers from, 40
Ward 2, 36, 39t
    aldermen from, 53
    and conscription plebiscite, 179
    enlistment from, 37
    French speakers in armed forces from, 38
    in municipal elections, 55
    officers from, 40
Ward 3, 36
    aldermen from, 53
    in conscription plebiscite, 179-80
    educational level of, 38
    enlistment from, 37, 38, 40, 49
    in municipal elections, 54, 55, 56
    officers from, 40

in provincial elections, 171, 184
    unemployment in, 38
Ward 4, 36, 39t
    in 1939 provincial election, 171
    in 1944 provincial election, 184
    aldermen from, 50, 52-3
    in conscription plebiscite, 180
    English speakers in, 52
    as English speaking, Protestant, 32
    enlistment from, 37-8
    housing construction in, 136, 148
    in municipal elections, 50, 52-3, 54, 55, 56
    officers from, 40
    unemployment in, 38
warships, 67
    goods sent to, 70, 222n116-19
Wartime Housing Limited, 149
Wartime Prices and Trade Board (WPTB), 137, 138, 141, 142, 145, 150, 160, 165, 166, 240n42
Wartime Salvage Limited, 91
Way, Joseph, 22, 23, 24, 47, 209n51, 212n36
Weatherbee, J.A., 124
Weeks, George J., 46
Weintraub, William, 124
Well Baby Clinic, 153-4
Wermenlinger, Jules, 172, 174
Westmount, 180
    educational levels in, 28-9, 40
    enlistment from, 210n2
    officers from, 29, 40
    population, 13
    Red Cross in, 111
    Royal Montreal Regiment's return to, 197
    social circumstances of, 28-9
    Verdun compared to, 28-9
    WVRC in, 99, 100
Weyburn (HMCS), 97
White, H.H., 47
White, Jay, 5, 108, 233n43, 239n13
Whyte, Douglas, 24, 40, 44, 45, 193
widows, 208n24
Willingdon, Viscount, 116
Wilson, Edward, 3, 16, 41, 42, 45, 50-1, 76, 106, 202
    aldermen and, 53
    and armoury at Verdun Auditorium, 73, 74, 75, 76
    on blackouts, 85

and Call to Arms, 104
and Canadian Legion, 117, 250n38
and Canadian War Services Fund, 125
and CCF, 55, 182, 184, 186, 187, 188, 189
and child welfare, 154
and conscription, 178, 179
and CPC, 79, 80, 82, 83
on DIL as industrial park, 135
and *Dunver*, 67-8, 71
and enemy aliens, 57
on enlistment in navy, 221n96
and executive committee, 53
and exemptions from service, 58, 59
and Ferland, 52-3
and French speakers, 52, 54
as head of VSC, 89
housing shortage, 138, 139, 142, 143, 146,
  148-9
on inter-community relations, 204
and Ligue des Propriétaires de Verdun,
  217n5
and MCF, 59, 60, 66, 189
and mobilization for home defence, 58
in municipal elections, 52-6, 198
on naming of *Dunver*, 67-8
on overseas votes, 181
in patriotic causes, 54-5
photographs, *following p. 112*
positions held by, 51
as president of Red Cross, 110, 112
on price gouging, 165
on ration board, 166
and RCA Victor, 132
and Reconsecration Week, 105
and Red Cross, 62
and rental prices, 137
and repatriation of troops, 197
and reserve army, 75
Ross's praise of, 86
on St Willibrord's, 122
and salvage collections, 88, 91, 92
and Société Saint-Jean-Baptiste, 127
son-in-law as casualty, 194
and Universal carrier, 104
and V for Victory emblem, 104
on Victory Bonds, 97
on VWSC, 94
on war as everyone's war, 78
and war savings, 94-5
and zoot-suit disturbances, 163

Wilson, Elizabeth, 50, 96, 110, 116, 152, 154
"Wings for Britain" Fund, 99
women
  as agricultural labourers, 99
  in air force, 99
  in armed forces, 21
  in auxiliary units, 116
  of Chalmers United Church, 113
  child care for, 155
  as community leaders, 102
  consciousness raising, 102
  contributions by, 98-9
  in defence industries, 99, 127, 130-1, 155
  election platform for, 174
  employment of, 127, 152, 155, 158
  gender defamation, 102
  influence of war on, 136
  and juvenile delinquency, 158
  and Liberal party, 182
  in navy, 99
  numbers of enlistees, 41
  organizations, 98-9, 101, 103
  in overseas service, 41
  and prices of goods, 165-6
  recruitment centre for, 41
  in Red Cross, 109, 110, 111, 113, 116, 135,
    232n14
  rights of, 102
  role of, 41, 102, 150
  of St Willibrord parish, 113
  sale of War Savings Certificates, 94
  salvage collection by, 92-3
  separation from husbands, 151
  and street lighting, 167
  and Victory Loans, 96
  in Voluntary Transport League, 249n29
  as volunteers, 108, 233n43
  voting by, 52, 174, 182
  in YMCA, 119-20
women's auxiliaries, 82, 84, 94, 96, 101, 116,
  139-40
  and housing, 139-40
Women's Regional Advisory Committees,
  165
Women's Royal Canadian Naval Service,
  71, 98-9
Women's Volunteer Reserve Corps
  (WVRC), 41, 78, 98-103, 108
  Adams as head of, 23, 41, 173
  on conscription, 178

and CPC, 82, 84-5
and DIL, 133
and *Dunver,* 70
photograph, *following p. 112*
in Reconsecration Week parade, 105
and salvage collections, 88, 91
tag days for MCF, 60
and Victory Loans, 96
and War Savings, 94
Woodland Park, 105
   Black Watch celebratory concert in, 192
   CCF rally in, 186
   reading of Call to Arms in, 104
   recruitment tent in, 42
   sing-songs in, 159
   Victory Loan rally in, 96
   and zoot-suiters, 161
Woodland School, 234n78
Woods, William, 48, 69, 70, 71, 72
   photograph, *following p. 112*
woodworking plant, 132-3
working classes, 3, 7, 15, 17, 204
   and Canadian Legion, 116
   and closure of war industries, 134
   and demobilization, 134
   and educational vs training for
      returned service people, 200
   English speakers in, 53
   French-speaking, 127
   housing shortage, 137
   living conditions, 144
   patriotism of, 98
   salvage collection from, 89
   as tenants, 53
   and Victory Loans, 98

and war savings, 95
and WVRC, 100
working-class families
   housing for, 139
   living conditions, 150
   need for two incomes, 141
Wray, Fred, 48
Wrens. *See* Women's Royal Canadian
   Naval Service

Young Men's Christian Association
   (YMCA), 108, 118-20, 135
   as auxiliary service, 117
   and casualties, 193
   DIL and, 120
   as English speaking, Protestant, 126
   English-speaking community and, 107
   and juvenile delinquency, 159
   and Red Cross, 109
   Southwestern Branch, 119
   Summer Vacation Club, 119
   women's volunteer committee, 119-20
Young Women's Christian Association
   (YWCA), 94
youths
   and approach of war, 19-20
   arrests of, 159
   employment in war industries, 156
   enlistment of, 157
   and VE Day, 191
Ypres, Second Battle of, 105
Ypres Day, 21, 105-6, 118, 179

Zakuta, Leo, 18
zoot-suit disturbances, 160-4, 168